The Book of Mormon:
Fourth Nephi
Through Moroni,
From Zion to Destruction

RELIGIOUS STUDIES CENTER PUBLICATIONS

BOOK OF MORMON SYMPOSIUM SERIES

The Book of Mormon: The
Keystone Scripture
The Book of Mormon: First
Nephi, the Doctrinal
Foundation
The Book of Mormon: Second
Nephi, the Doctrinal Structure
The Book of Mormon: Jacob
Through Words of Mormon,
To Learn with Joy
The Book of Mormon: Mosiah,
Salvation Only Through Christ

The Book of Mormon: Alma,
The Testimony of the Word
The Book of Mormon: Helaman
Through 3 Nephi 8, According
to Thy Word
The Book of Mormon:
3 Nephi 9–30, This Is My Gospel
The Book of Mormon:
Fourth Nephi Through Moroni,
From Zion to Destruction

MONOGRAPH SERIES

Nibley on the Timely and the
Timeless
Deity and Death
The Glory of God Is
Intelligence
Reflections on Mormonism
Literature of Belief
The Words of Joseph Smith
Book of Mormon Authorship
Mormons and Muslims
The Temple in Antiquity
Isaiah and the Prophets
Scriptures for the Modern World

The Joseph Smith Translation:
The Restoration of Plain and
Precious Things
Apocryphal Writings and the
Latter-day Saints
The Pearl of Great Price:
Revelations From God
The Lectures on Faith in
Historical Perspective
Mormon Redress Petitions:
Documents of the 1833–1838
Missouri Conflict
Joseph Smith: The Prophet, the Man

SPECIALIZED MONOGRAPH SERIES

Supporting Saints: Life Stories
of Nineteenth-Century
Mormons
The Call of Zion: The Story of
the First Welsh Mormon
Emigration
The Religion and Family
Connection: Social Science
Perspectives

Welsh Mormon Writings
from 1844 to 1862: A
Historical Bibliography
Peter and the Popes
John Lyon: The Life of a
Pioneer Poet
Latter-day Prophets
and the United States
Constitution

OCCASIONAL PAPERS SERIES

Excavations at Seila, Egypt

The Book of Mormon:
Fourth Nephi Through Moroni,
From Zion to Destruction

Papers from the Ninth Annual
Book of Mormon Symposium, 1994

Edited by Monte S. Nyman and Charles D. Tate, Jr.

Religious Studies Center
Brigham Young University
Provo, Utah

Library of Congress Catalog Card Number: 94–74981
ISBN 0–88494–974–5

First Printing, 1995

Distributed by BOOKCRAFT, INC.
Salt Lake City, Utah

Printed in the United States of America

Contents

Introduction

This ninth volume is the final volume in the Book of Mormon Symposia Series. In October 1985, under the direction of the late Professor Paul R. Cheesman, a general symposium on the Book of Mormon was held on the Brigham Young University campus. Selected papers from that symposium were published in *The Book of Mormon: The Keystone Scripture*, the first one of this series. It contained the following papers in order of appearance:

The Challenge of the Book of Mormon, Daniel H. Ludlow

What the Book of Mormon Tells Us About Jesus Christ, Robert J. Matthews

The Ministry of the Father and the Son, Robert L. Millet

A Comparison of Book of Mormon, Bible, and Traditional Teachings on the Doctrines of Salvation, Joseph F. McConkie

The Beginnings of Christianity in the Book Of Mormon, Kent P. Jackson

The Three Nephite Churches of Christ, Rodney Turner

Fasting in the Book of Mormon and the Bible, Stephen D. Ricks

Faith, Hope, Charity, Larry E. Dahl

Love in the Book of Mormon, Gayle O. Brown

Before Columbus, George F. Carter

Categories of Evidence for Old World Contacts with Ancient America, Norman Totten

Cultural Parallels Between the Old World and the New World, Paul R. Cheesman

The Bering Strait and American Indian Origins, James R. Christianson

Book of Mormon—Transmission from Translator to Printed Text, George A. Horton, Jr.

"Lest Ye Become As the Nephites of Old," Susan Black

Professor Cheesman retired after that first symposium and Professor Monte S. Nyman was made director of the Book of Mormon area of the Religious Studies Center, and he proposed continuing the symposia by going through the Book of Mormon in sections. Consequently, the second symposium was held in October 1986 and the subject was the book of 1 Nephi. The following selected papers were published in the second volume of the series, in *The Book of Mormon: First Nephi, The Doctrinal Foundation*:

The Book of Mormon: A Great Answer to "The Great Question," Elder Neal A. Maxwell

The Title Page, Daniel H. Ludlow

The Calling of a Prophet, John W. Welch

Father Lehi, H. Donl Peterson

Lehi and Nephi: Faith unto Salvation, Monte S. Nyman

The Prophet Nephi, Rodney Turner

The Book of Mormon Plates, Rex C. Reeve, Jr.

"Behold, I Have Dreamed a Dream," Susan Easton Black

Stela 5, Izapa: A Layman's Consideration of the Tree of Life Stone, Alan K. Parrish

The Mysteries of God Revealed by the Power of the Holy Ghost, Gerald N. Lund

Another Testament of Jesus Christ, Robert L. Millet

Early Christianity and 1 Nephi 13-14, Stephen E. Robinson

Establishing the Truth of the Bible, Robert J. Matthews

A Land of Promise, Choice Above All Other Lands, Philip M. Flammer

From Small Means the Lord Brings About Great Things, Clark V. Johnson

Lehi's Journeys, Paul R. Cheesman

Transoceanic Crossings, John L. Sorenson

The Prophecies of the Prophets, Robert E. Parsons

Textual Evidences for the Book of Mormon, Paul Y. Hoskisson

B. H. Roberts: The Book of Mormon and the Atonement, Truman G. Madsen

Conclusion and Charge, Jeffrey R. Holland

The third symposium was held in October 1987 and the papers in volume 3, *The Book of Mormon: Second Nephi, The Doctrinal Structure*, were as follows:

In 1988 the fourth symposium covered Jacob through the Words of Mormon in the following papers:

"The Law and the Light," Elder Boyd K. Packer

Jacob: Prophet, Theologian, Historian, Robert J. Matthews

"I Speak Somewhat Concerning That Which I Have Written," Cheryl Brown

"We Did Magnify Our Office unto the Lord," Richard O. Cowan

Botanical Comparisons in the Allegory of the Olive Tree, Wilford M. Hess

The Religion of Moses and the Book of Mormon, Lauri Hlavaty

Prophetic Decree and Ancient Histories Tell the Story of America, Clark V. Johnson

Enos: His Mission and His Message, Dennis L. Largey

The Testimony of Christ Through the Ages, Joseph Fielding McConkie

Sherem the Anti-Christ, Robert L. Millet

To Learn with Joy: Sacred Preaching, Great Revelation, Prophesying, Monte S. Nyman

The Small Plates of Nephi and the Words of Mormon, Eldin Ricks

Pride and Riches, Chauncey C. Riddle

Enos and the Words Concerning Eternal Life, David R. Seely

Literary Reflections on Jacob and His Descendants, John S. Tanner

Morality and Marriage in the Book of Mormon, Rodney Turner

The Testimony of Amaleki, Gary R. Whiting

Volume 5. Since the Annual Sidney B. Sperry Symposium covers the scripture to be studied in the Gospel Doctrine Sunday School classes in the Church, their director asked the Book of Mormon Symposium Committee to allow that his symposium be held in October and that ours be held in February.

Consequently our fifth symposium, on the subject of the book of Mosiah, was held in February 1990. The following papers from that symposium were published:

"The Children of Christ," Elder Neal A. Maxwell

Volume 6, *Alma, The Testimony of the Word*, contains the following papers:

The State of the Soul Between Death and the Resurrection, Monte S. Nyman

A New Meaning of "Restoration": The Book of Mormon on Life After Death, Richard O. Cowan

The Law of Justice and the Law of Mercy, H. Donl Peterson

The Captain and the Covenant, Thomas R. Valletta

Hagoth and the Polynesians, Robert E. Parsons

The Book of Alma as a Prototype for Teaching the Word of God, Gerald Hansen, Jr.

Teaching in Black and White: Antithetic Parallel Structure in the Book of Alma, Its Form and Function, Donald W. Parry

Nephi's Freedom Thesis and the Sons of Helaman, K. Douglas Bassett

The Record of Alma: A Prophetic Pattern of the Principles Governing Testimony, Fred E. Woods

The next volume covered Helaman through 3 Nephi 8 with the following papers:

Jesus the Christ—Our Master and More, Elder Russell M. Nelson

The Only Sure Foundation: Building on the Rock of Our Redeemer, Robert L. Millet

The Promised Land and Its Covenant Peoples, Douglas Brinley

Patterns of Apostasy in the Book of Helaman, Robert J. Matthews

The Decline of the Nephites: Rejection of the Covenant and Word of God, John L. Fowles

They Did Remember His Words, Brett P. Thomas

Nephi's Ultimate Encounter with Deity: Some Thoughts on Helaman 10, Andrew C. Skinner

Mormon's Philosophy of History: Helaman 12 in the Perspective of Mormon's Editing Procedure, Thomas W. Mackay

The Restoration of Plain and Precious Parts: The Book of Helaman, Monte S. Nyman

The Terrifying Book of Helaman, Gerald Hansen, Jr.

Prophets and Perplexity: The Book of Helaman as a Case Study, R. Wayne Shute and Wayne E. Brickey

Days of Wickedness and Vengeance: Analysis of 3 Nephi 6 and 7, Chauncey C. Riddle

"Yield Your Heart to God"—the Process of Sanctification, W. Ralph Pew

Nephite Trade Networks and the Dangers of a Class Society, Allen J. Christenson

Leitworter in Helaman and 3 Nephi, Ronald D. Anderson

The Lamanites—A More Accurate Image, Richard O. Cowan

Secret Covenant Teachings of Men and the Devil in Helaman Through 3 Nephi 8, Victor L. Ludlow

The eighth volume covered the rest of 3 Nephi Chapters 9–30:

"This Is My Gospel," Robert L. Millet

Jesus the Savior in 3 Nephi, Robert J. Matthews

The Designations Jesus Gives Himself in 3 Nephi, Monte S. Nyman

Geological Upheaval and Darkness in 3 Nephi 8-10, Alvin K. Benson

Repentance: The Gift of Love, Mae Blanch

Moses and Jesus: The Old Adorns the New, S. Kent Brown

The Commandment to Be Perfect, Gary R. Whiting

The Savior's Missionary Training Sermon in 3 Nephi, Robert A. Cloward

"Pray Always": Learning to Pray as Jesus Prayed, Donald W. Parry

The Twelve: A Light unto This People, Kenneth W. Anderson

The Doctrine of a Covenant People, Joseph Fielding McConkie

One by One: The Fifth Gospel's Model of Service, Richard Neitzel Holzapfel

The Symbolic Unity of Christ's Ministry in 3 Nephi, Neal E. Lambert

Gathering to the Temple: Teachings of the Second Day, Gerald Hansen, Jr.

The Church Shall Bear My Name and Be Built upon My Gospel, Richard O. Cowan

The Three Nephites and the Doctrine of Translation, Clyde J. Williams

This final volume covers 4 Nephi through Moroni 10. There were 36 papers presented and the referees selected the following papers: (See Table of Contents)

As the general editors of the last eight volumes of the Book of Mormon Symposium series, we thank our many participants for their willingness to study the text, and write the papers, and come to the BYU campus, and present them at our annual symposia. We also thank those who participated, but whose papers were not selected by our referees for inclusion in a volume. We appreciate the various referees who have carefully read and evaluated the manuscripts. A special thanks to Lillian Wilbur, Barbara Crawley, Charlotte Pollard, and many part-time editorial assistants for their untiring efforts to bring about the publication of these volumes.

The great lesson we have observed from these symposia is that there is much more in the Book of Mormon than can be gleaned from a casual reading. The Book of Mormon opens its treasures to those who diligently study it in thoughtfulness and with the Spirit. It remains our testimony that it is a true book of scripture for all humankind to learn God's plan from.

Monte S. Nyman
Charles D. Tate, Jr.

Alive in Christ: The Salvation of Little Children

1

Robert L. Millet

*T*he eighth chapter of Moroni contains an epistle Mormon wrote to his son, Moroni, soon after his call to the ministry. It begins with Mormon's encouragement and his expression of confidence in his son, as well as a statement of his daily petition to the heavens in behalf of Moroni. "I am mindful of you always in my prayers," Mormon declares, "continually praying unto God the Father in the name of his Holy Child, Jesus, that he, through his infinite goodness and grace, will keep you through the endurance of faith on his name to the end" (Moroni 8:3). But this epistle was not written solely as an expression of a father's satisfaction on behalf of a faithful son. Rather, Mormon had learned of disputations among the Nephites concerning the baptism of little children. His letter was a powerful appeal to root out and remove such heresy from among the Saints, as well as an explanation as to why that doctrine was abominable and abhorrent to that Lord who loves little children perfectly.

Original Sin

After his vision of the celestial kingdom, the Prophet Joseph Smith recorded, "I also beheld that all children who die before they arrive at the years of accountability are saved in the celestial kingdom of heaven" (D&C 137:10). This idea was not entirely new to the Prophet in 1836, for he had learned from the Book of Mormon and previous revelations of the Lord's disposition in regard to the status of children. An angel explained to king Benjamin that "the infant

Robert L. Millet is dean of Religious Education and professor of Ancient Scripture at Brigham Young University.

perisheth not that dieth in his infancy" (Mosiah 3:18). After having described the nature of those who come forth in the first resurrection, Abinadi says simply, "And little children also have eternal life" (Mosiah 15:25). A revelation given in September 1830 specifies that "little children are redeemed from the foundation of the world through mine Only Begotten" (D&C 29:46). What happened, then? Why did the pernicious belief that little children should ever require baptism become an issue amongst the Christian religions of the world?

Nephi beheld in vision that "an exceedingly great many" people would stumble and fall because plain and precious truths would be taken away or kept back from the earliest biblical records and many thereby would wander in doctrinal darkness, eventually becoming subject to the snares of Satan (1 Nephi 13:20–42). Some of the most critical verities of salvation to be lifted or twisted from their pristine purity are the truths dealing with the Creation, the Fall, and the Atonement. I assume such matters were taught more plainly in the early ages of this world by virtue of the clarity and power in which they are proclaimed and stressed in the Book of Mormon and the Joseph Smith Translation of the Bible. A misunderstanding of the nature of the fall of Adam, for example, has led to some of the most serious heresies and perversions in religious history. Without the exalting knowledge of such matters as the Fall as a foreordained act, a God-inspired and predesigned plan for the perpetuation and preservation of the human family—parent to the atonement of Christ—people struggle to find meaning in the involvement of our first parents in Eden. Others allegorize or spiritualize away the plain meanings of the scriptures regarding the Fall and thus cloud in mystery the true purposes behind the Atonement. When revelation is wanting, when unillumined people seek for understanding of heavenly and eternal matters, they are left to their own resources—to the powers of reason and the limitations of the human intellect.

One of the most influential philosopher-theologians in Christian history was St. Augustine (AD 350–430), a man whose writings and teachings have had a marked impact on the formulation of both Catholic and Protestant beliefs. S. E. Frost, a historian, describes Augustine's thought on the doctrine of "original sin" thus:

> The first man, Adam, set the pattern for all future life of men. Adam, he taught, committed sin and thus handed on to all men the effects of this sin. He corrupted the entire human race, so that all men are condemned to sin for all times. Adam's

sin, therefore, is hereditary. But God can reform corrupted man by his grace. . . . Thus man, a creation of the all-ruling power of the universe, created out of nothing, inherits the weaknesses and sins of the first man. He must pay the price for this sin. But the all-ruling can and does select some men for forgiveness and leaves others to the natural results of Adam's sin. Man is lost forever unless the Creator of the universe chooses to save him. (63)

The false doctrine of original sin is based upon the notion that Adam and Eve's disobedience was an act of overt rebellion against the Almighty, an attempt to usurp the knowledge available only to the gods. How much more ennobling and soul-satisfying is the true doctrine of the Fall, the assurance that Adam—also known as Michael, the prince and archangel—"fell that men might be; and men are, that they might have joy" (2 Nephi 2:25). How much more gratifying it is to know that through the atonement of Christ, the act of redemption on the part of the "Lamb slain from the foundation of the world" (Rev 13:8), *"men will be punished for their own sins, and not for Adam's transgression"* (AF 2; emphasis added).[1] One wonders what a difference it would make in the Christian world if the following simple yet profound truths from Joseph Smith's translation of Genesis had not been lost from the Bible:

And he called upon our father Adam by his own voice, saying: I am God; I made the world, and men before they were in the flesh. And he also said unto him: If thou wilt turn unto me, and hearken unto my voice, and believe, and repent of all thy transgressions, and be baptized, even in water, in the name of mine Only Begotten Son, who is full of grace and truth, which is Jesus Christ, the only name which shall be given under heaven, whereby salvation shall come unto the children of men, ye shall receive the gift of the Holy Ghost, asking all things in his name, and whatsoever ye shall ask, it shall be given you. And our father Adam spake unto the Lord, and said: Why is it that men must repent and be baptized in water? And the Lord said unto Adam: Behold, I have forgiven thee thy transgression in the Garden of Eden. Hence came the saying abroad among the people, that the Son of God hath atoned for original guilt, wherein the sins of the parents cannot be answered upon the heads of the children, for they are whole from the foundation of the world. (Moses 6:51–54; also JST Gen 6:52–56; emphasis added)

An equally vicious falsehood which follows on the heels of original sin is the moral depravity of man and his complete inability

---

[1]   For a discussion of the fact that Adam and Eve's act was transgression and not sin, see Joseph Fielding Smith, *Doctrines of Salvation* 1:114. An excellent treatment of the view of the Fall is in LaMar Garrard's, "The Fall of Man."

to choose good over evil. As an illustration, S. E. Frost describes the notions of Augustine thus:

> The conception of individual freedom was denied by Saint Augustine. According to him, mankind was free in Adam, but since Adam chose to sin, he lost freedom not only for himself, but for all men and for all time. Now no one is free, but all are bound to sin, are slaves of evil. But God makes a choice among men of those whom he will save and those whom he will permit to be destroyed because of sin. This choice is not influenced by an act of an individual man, but is determined only by what God wants.
>
> In Augustine we find both fatalism and predestination as far as the individual man is concerned. With Adam there was no fatalism. He was free. But God knew even then how Adam would act, knew he would sin. Thus, from the beginning God made up his mind whom he would save. These were predestined from the first to salvation, and all the rest were predestined to eternal punishment. (150–51)[2]

Reasoning of this sort surely came from reading such passages as Romans 7 without the understanding provided by the Prophet Joseph Smith. This particular chapter in the New Testament, for example, suggests that the Apostle Paul (and thus all humans by extension) is a depraved and helpless creature who muddles in sin as a result of a carnal nature, an evildoer with little or no hope of deliverance. The Joseph Smith Translation of Romans 7 presents a significantly different picture of Paul and of all humankind; it might well be called "Paul: Before and After the Atonement," or "The Power of Christ to Change Men's Souls." In the King James Version Paul introspects as follows: "I am carnal, sold under sin. For that which I do I allow not: for what I would, that do I not; but what I hate, that do I. . . . For I know that in me (that is, in my flesh,) dwelleth no good thing: for to will is present with me; but how to perform that which is good I find not" (Rom 7:14–15, 18). The Joseph Smith Translation lays stress where Paul surely intended it: upon the fact that through the atonement of Christ man is made free from the pull and stain of sin. "When I was under the law [of Moses], I was yet carnal, sold under sin. *But now I am spiritual; for that which I am commanded to do, I do; and that which I am commanded not to allow, I allow not. For what I know is not right I would not do; for that which*

---

2   See also Martin Luther's debate with Erasmus the humanist on the nature of free will in Martin Luther, *The Bondage of the Will*, trans. Henry Cole, Grand Rapids, MI: Baker Book House, 1976.

is sin, I hate." Finally, "For I know that in me, that is, in my flesh, dwelleth no good thing; for to will is present with me, but to perform that which is good I find not, *only in Christ*" (JST Rom 7:14–16, 19; emphasis added). The testimony of Lehi confirms this truth: "Adam fell that men might be; and men are, that they might have joy. And the Messiah cometh in the fulness of time, that he may redeem the children of men from the fall. And *because that they are redeemed from the fall they have become free forever, knowing good from evil; to act for themselves and not be acted upon*" (2 Nephi 2:25–26; emphasis added; compare Hel 14:30).

The Practice of Infant Baptism

Infant baptism is the result of a major doctrinal misunderstanding, a lack of appreciation for the full impact of Christ's atonement upon humankind. A form of the heretical practice seems to predate the Christian era by many centuries. The Lord Jehovah spoke to his servant Abraham of a number of the theological errors of that day, some of which appear to be tied to ignorance of the true nature and scope of the Atonement.

> And it came to pass, that Abram fell on his face, and called upon the name of the Lord. And God talked with him, saying, My people have gone astray from my precepts, and have not kept mine ordinances, which I gave unto their fathers; and they have not observed mine anointing, and the burial, or baptism wherewith I commanded them; But have turned from the commandment, and taken unto themselves the washing of children, and the blood of sprinkling; and have said that the blood of the righteous Abel was shed for sins;[3] and have not known wherein they are accountable before me. (JST Gen 17:3–7; emphasis added)

This passage clearly demonstrates the inseparable relationship between atonement and accountability. Simply stated, the atonement of Jesus Christ—the greatest act of love and intercession in all eternity—defines the bounds and limits of accountability. One of the unconditional benefits of the Atonement is the fact that no man or woman will be held responsible for or denied blessings related to a law whose adoption and application were beyond their power. This

---

[3] This is a particularly interesting heresy. It may well be that the Apostle Paul had reference to this problem in Hebrews 12:24.

principle underlies the doctrine concerning the salvation of little children who die. Children are not accountable for their deeds and therefore are not required to participate in gospel ordinances prepared for accountable persons.

The level of innocence in children was also a matter which arose in discussions between the Christians and the Jews in the meridian of time. Paul emphasizes that the law of circumcision and "the tradition [should] be done away, which saith that little children are unholy; for it was had among the Jews" (D&C 74:6). Joseph Smith's translation of the Bible is a witness that Jesus taught concerning the innocent status of children: "Take heed that ye despise not one of these little ones; for I say unto you, that in heaven their angels [spirits] do always behold the face of my Father which is in heaven. For the Son of man is come to save that which was lost, and to call sinners to repentance; but these little ones have no need of repentance, and I will save them" (JST Matt 18:10–11; emphasis added; see also 19:13–14).

During the Great Apostasy (after the first century of the Christian era) the doctrine of infant baptism again reared its ugly head. Elder James E. Talmage writes, "There is no authentic record of infant baptism having been practiced during the first two centuries after Christ, and the custom probably did not become general before the fifth century; from the time last named until the Reformation, however, it was accepted by the dominant church organization" (The Articles of Faith 126). Elsewhere Elder Talmage observes:

> Not only was the form of the baptismal rite radically changed [during the time of the apostasy], but the application of the ordinance was perverted. The practice of administering baptism of infants was recognized as orthodox in the third century and was doubtless of earlier origin. In a prolonged disputation as to whether it was safe to postpone the baptism of infants until the eighth day after birth—in deference to the Jewish custom of performing circumcision on that day—it was generally decided that such delay would be dangerous, as jeopardizing the future well-being of the child should it die before attaining the age of eight days, and that baptism ought to be administered as soon after birth as possible. (The Great Apostasy 119)

The false doctrine of infant baptism was introduced in the Americas during approximately the same period. Quoting and expounding upon the Lord's words to him, Mormon instructed Moroni as follows (from Moroni 8):

1. The Lord came into the world not to call the righteous but sinners to repentance (Moroni 8:8). The immediate application of this principle is, of course, in regard to little children, the only ones, save Jesus only, who live without sin. To say that the whole need no physician is to say that redemption from sin is only requisite for those who are under the bondage of sin (compare Mark 2:17). All others, especially those who suppose they have no sin (see John 9:41; Rom 3:23; 1 John 1:8), are in dire need of that safety and security that come only in and through the atoning blood of Christ.

2. Little children are whole, for they are not capable of committing sin (Moroni 8:8). Modern revelation affirms that "little children are redeemed from the foundation of the world through mine Only Begotten," meaning that the Atonement has been in effect as an integral part of the plan of salvation from the time of our premortal existence. "Wherefore, they cannot sin, for power is not given unto Satan to tempt little children, until they begin to become accountable before me" (D&C 29:46–47). It is not to say that children cannot do things that are evil, that they cannot perform deeds that under other circumstances would be called sinful. They certainly can do such things. The revelations teach that their actions are covered by the merciful ministry of our Master. In this sense they cannot sin. Thus, "little children are holy, being sanctified through the atonement of Jesus Christ" (74:7).

3. The "curse of Adam" is taken from children in Christ, that it has no power over them (Moroni 8:8). The "curse of Adam" is presumably the effects of the Fall. In one sense, the curse of Adam, meaning an original sin or "original guilt" (Moses 6:54), is taken away from all men and women. Adam and Eve's transgression in Eden was forgiven them (Moses 6:53), and no person is held responsible for something our first parents did (AF 2). In another sense, the curse of Adam, meaning the fallen nature that comes as a direct result of the Fall (1 Nephi 10:6; 2 Nephi 2:21; Alma 42:6–12; Ether 3:2), is taken away from children as an unconditional benefit of the atonement of Christ (Mosiah 3:16).

4. The law of circumcision is done away in Christ (Moroni 8:8). Circumcision was instituted in the days of Abraham as a token of the covenant God made with the Father of the Faithful and his posterity. Male children were circumcised at *eight days* as a token and reminder that children are not accountable until they are *eight years*

of age (JST Gen 17:11; compare D&C 68:25). In Moroni 8:8, Mormon teaches that with the atoning sacrifice accomplished, circumcision is no longer required as a part of the Abrahamic covenant.

5.   Baptizing infants is solemn mockery before God; to do so is to deny the mercies and atoning power of Christ, as well as the power of the Holy Spirit (Moroni 8:9, 20, 23). To baptize children is to ignore, to shun, to deny outright what has been taught from the beginning of time by prophets and seers—"that the Son of God hath atoned for original guilt" (Moses 6:54).

6.   Leaders of the Church should teach parents that they must repent and be baptized and humble themselves as their little children (Moroni 8:10). The Savior's command for us to "become as little children" (Matt 18:3) is not alone a call to humility and submission (see Mosiah 3:19); it is a call to become clean, innocent, and justified by virtue of the blood of Christ, through the sanctifying powers of the Holy Ghost. Children are not innocent because they are good by nature. Benjamin taught that "In Adam, or by nature, they fall," but, thankfully, "the blood of Christ atoneth for their sins" (Mosiah 3:16). Children are innocent because the Lord decreed that they be so.

In modern revelation the Lord declares: "Every spirit of man was innocent in the beginning; and God having redeemed man from the fall, men became again, in their infant state, innocent before God" (D&C 93:38). How do persons become again, in "their infant state, innocent before God"? Does this not have reference to the fact that men and women left the premortal existence clean and free from sin through the powers of the Atonement and that they become innocent in regard to law and sin as infants through that same Atonement? Elder Orson Pratt asked:

> Why was the Lamb, considered as 'slain from the foundation of the world'? . . . The very fact, that the atonement which was to be made in a future world, was considered as already having been made, seems to show that there were those who had sinned, and who stood in need of the atonement. The nature of the sufferings of Christ was such that it could redeem the spirits of men as well as their bodies. . . . All the spirits when they come here are innocent, that is, if they have ever committed sins, they have repented and obtained forgiveness through faith in the future sacrifice of the Lamb. (54, 56)

7.   The ordinance of baptism appropriately follows the principle of repentance. Since little children, through Christ, are in no need of repentance, they are in no need of baptism (Moroni 8:11, 19, 25).

It makes little sense to symbolize a child's rise from spiritual death to life. Little children are alive in Christ—free from the sins of the sinful world (vv 12, 22). Elder Bruce R. McConkie taught: "Spiritual death passes upon all men when they become accountable for their sins. Being thus subject to sin they die spiritually; they die as pertaining to the things of the Spirit; they die as pertaining to the things of righteousness; they are cast out of the presence of God" (*The Promised Messiah* 349–50).

8. Any who suppose that children need baptism are devoid of faith (Moroni 8:14). They do not believe what Christ has done or what he can do for little children, or, for that matter, for all others. It is impossible to exercise saving faith in that which is untrue (Alma 32:21) or in that of which we are completely ignorant. Faith is based upon evidence or assurance (JST Heb 11:1).

9. Because a belief in infant baptism demonstrates a significant departure from the faith of Jesus Christ, any who continue in this belief shall perish eventually as pertaining to the things of righteousness (Moroni 8:16). Truly, salvation comes only in and through our Lord and Savior (Mosiah 3:17; see also Acts 4:12; Moses 6:52).

10. All children are alike in regard to the atonement of Christ (Moroni 8:17, 19, 22). To borrow Nephi's words, all children, "black and white, bond and free, male and female . . . all are alike unto God" (2 Nephi 26:33; see also Smith, *Doctrines of Salvation* 2:53, 55).

11. All little children are alive in Christ, as are those "that are without the law. For the power of redemption cometh on all them that have no law" (Moroni 8:22). Two groups of people in scripture are referred to as dying "without law." The first group consists of the heathen nations, those who will not receive the fulness of gospel light and understanding and who thereby qualify for a terrestrial inheritance (see D&C 45:54; 76:72). The other group consists of those who never have an opportunity to receive the gospel in this life but who would have done so had the opportunity presented itself (D&C 137:7–8). As Jacob explains:

> Where there is no law given there is no punishment; and where there is no punishment there is no condemnation; and where there is no condemnation the mercies of the Holy One of Israel have claim upon them, because of the atonement; for they are delivered by the power of him. For the atonement satisfieth the demands of [God's] justice upon all those who have not the law given to them. (2 Nephi 9:25–26)

Truly, as Benjamin declares, Christ's blood "atoneth for the sins of those who have fallen by the transgression of Adam, who have died not knowing the will of God concerning them, or who have ignorantly sinned" (Mosiah 3:11). Or, as Abinadi testifies, those who "died before Christ came, in their ignorance, not having salvation declared unto them" are those who "have part in the first resurrection" (Mosiah 15:24).

12.   To baptize children is to deny the mercies of Christ and the power of his Holy Spirit, and to put "trust in dead works" (Moroni 8:23). Dead works are not animated or motivated by the power of the Spirit and are neither God-ordained nor God-approved. In short, to baptize children is to perform ordinances which not only do not channel power from the heavens to the earth and manifest the powers of godliness (D&C 84:20), but instead tend to block that divine power through trifling with sacred things. In this sense, infant baptism is worse than false; it is perverse. Joseph Smith summarizes the issue concisely: "The doctrine of baptizing children, or sprinkling them, or they must welter in hell, is a doctrine not true, not supported in Holy Writ, and is not consistent with the character of God" (*Teachings of the Prophet Joseph Smith* 197; hereafter *TPJS*).

Related Questions

A number of questions arise about the salvation of little children. For some of these questions we have adequate answers in scripture or through the teachings of latter-day prophets and apostles. For others, we are left to wait patiently upon the Lord for further light and knowledge. Such questions might be as follows:

• *Why do some children die and others live?* We do not know. "We must assume that the Lord knows and arranges beforehand who shall be taken in infancy and who shall remain on earth to undergo whatever tests are needed in their cases" (McConkie, "The Salvation of Little Children" 6). Lacking a memory of what went before and in some cases having only a general outline of what will come hereafter, Latter-day Saints are not in a position to provide all of the answers to all of the questions that might arise. We rest secure in the knowledge that God is our Father, that he is intimately acquainted with each of us, that he knows the end from the beginning and that he will arrange premortal, mortal, and postmortal conditions for our eternal best interest. We rest secure in the knowledge that God knows what is best for each of us, and that he will bring to pass those conditions which will maximize our growth and further our opportunities for exaltation.

An eye of faith provides us with a heavenly perspective, a divinely discriminating view of things as God sees them. The Prophet Joseph Smith asks, "Why is it that infants, innocent children, are taken away from us, especially those that seem to be the most intelligent and interesting?" He reflects upon the waywardness of the world and provides at least a partial answer to this most difficult question: "The strongest reasons that present themselves to my mind are these: This world is a very wicked world; and it is a proverb that the 'world grows weaker and wiser'; if that is the case, the world grows more wicked and corrupt. In the earlier ages of the world a righteous man, and a man of God and of intelligence, had a better chance to do good, to be believed and received than at the present day; but in these days such a man is opposed and persecuted by most of the inhabitants of the earth, and he has much sorrow to pass through here." Then, evidencing the perspective of those who see with the eye of faith, the Prophet adds, *"The Lord takes many away even in infancy, that they may escape the envy of man, and the sorrows and evils of this present world; they were too pure, too lovely, to live on earth; therefore, if rightly considered, instead of mourning we have reason to rejoice as they are delivered from evil, and we shall soon have them again."* Finally, Joseph concludes: "The only difference between the old and young dying is, one lives longer in heaven and eternal light and glory than the other, and is freed a little sooner from this miserable wicked world. Notwithstanding all this glory, we for a moment lose sight of it, and mourn the loss, but we do not mourn as those without hope" (*TPJS* 196–97; emphasis added).

In commenting upon the Prophet's remarks, Elder Bruce R. McConkie said:

> There are certain spirits who come into this life only to receive bodies; for reasons that we do not know, but which are known in the infinite wisdom of the Eternal Father, they do not need the testing, probationary experiences of mortality. We come here for two great reasons—the first, to get a body; the second, to be tried, examined, schooled, and tested under mortal circumstances, to take a different type of probationary test than we underwent in the pre-mortal life. There are some of the children of our Father, however, who come to earth

to get a body—for that reason solely. They do not need the testings of this mortality. (Funeral address)

- *What of the mentally deficient?* What is to become of those not capable of distinguishing completely between good and evil, those who never come to comprehend sin and grasp the miracle of forgiveness through the atoning blood of Christ? What is the disposition of the Lord with regard to those who never arrive mentally at the age of accountability, those who are in some way deficient in understanding of these vital matters? The revelations of the Restoration are not silent here. To six elders of the Church in September 1830 the Lord explained: "Little children are redeemed from the foundation of the world through mine Only Begotten; wherefore, they cannot sin, for power is not given unto Satan to tempt little children, until they begin to become accountable before me; for it is given unto them even as I will, according to mine own pleasure, that great things may be required at the hand of their fathers." All who have knowledge have been commanded to repent. Of them who have "no understanding" the Lord has said: "And he that hath no understanding, it remaineth in me to do according as it is written" (D&C 29:46–50; see also D&C 68:25–28). This may also be one group described by Mormon as those who "are without the law" (Moroni 8:22).

Elder Bruce R. McConkie has written the following concerning the status of the mentally deficient:

> It is with them as it is with little children. They never arrive at the years of accountability and are considered as though they were little children. If because of some physical deficiency, or for some other reason unknown to us, they never mature in the spiritual or moral sense, then they never become account-able for sins. They need no baptism; they are alive in Christ; and they will receive, inherit, and possess in eternity on the same basis as do all children. ("The Salvation of Little Children" 6; see also Smith, *Doctrines of Salvation* 2:55–56)

- *Joseph Smith's vision of the celestial kingdom indicates that "all children who die before they arrive at the years of accountability are saved in the celestial kingdom of heaven" (D&C 137:10). The word used is saved. Will they be exalted?* With but few exceptions, the word *salvation* as used in scripture means exaltation or eternal life. Abinadi declares in his sermon to the priests of Noah that "little children also have eternal life" (Mosiah 15:25). Joseph Smith states that "children will be enthroned in the presence of God and the Lamb; ... they will there enjoy the fullness of that light, glory, and intelligence, which is prepared in the Celestial Kingdom" (*TPJS* 200).[4]

• *Will children who die ever be tested?* A righteous man or woman cannot take a backward step spiritually after death; in short, the righteous have completed their days of probation in mortality. Amulek informs us that our disposition here will be our disposition hereafter (see Alma 34:32–35). Such is the case with regard to little children. They were pure in this existence, will be pure in the world of spirits, and will come forth in the resurrection of the pure in heart at the appropriate time. At the time of the second coming of Christ, wickedness will be cleansed from the face of the earth. The great Millennium will be ushered in with power, and then Satan and his hosts will be bound by the righteousness of the people (see 1 Nephi 22:26). During this glorious era of enlightenment, the earth shall be given to the righteous "for an inheritance; and they shall multiply and wax strong, and *their children shall grow up without sin unto salvation*" (D&C 45:58; emphasis added). The devil will be loosed at the end of the Millennium. Could not those who left mortality without trial be tested during that "little season"? Certainly not. These children will already have come forth from the graves as resurrected and immortal beings. How could such persons—whose salvation is already assured—possibly be tested? To reason otherwise is to place God and all exalted beings in peril of apostasy. In the words of President Joseph Fielding Smith:

> Satan will be loosed to gather his forces after the millennium. The people who will be tempted, will be people living on this earth, and they will have every opportunity to accept the gospel or reject it. Satan will have nothing to do whatever with little children, or grown people who have received their resurrection and entered into the celestial kingdom. *Satan cannot tempt little children in this life, nor in the spirit world, nor after the resurrection. Little children who die before reaching the years of accountability will not be tempted.* (Smith, *Doctrines of Salvation* 2:56–57; emphasis added; compare McConkie, "The Salvation of Little Children" 6)

---

[4] Some have suggested that the doctrinal context for the Prophet Joseph Smith's statement about the salvation of little children is D&C 137:7–9, that is, that those children who would have received the gospel had they been afforded the opportunity in this life, shall receive all of the blessings of exaltation. Surely much more remains to be revealed in regard to this glorious concept.

At this point it is helpful to consider the tender words of Mormon: "Behold, I speak with boldness, having authority from God; and I fear not what man can do; for perfect love casteth out all fear. And I am filled with charity, which is everlasting love; wherefore, all children are alike unto me; wherefore, I love little children with a perfect love; and they are all alike and partakers of salvation" (Moroni 8:16–17). We would suppose that God will eventually reveal more of the particulars of this doctrine to the Church through his appointed servants in days to come. In the meantime, however, we are under obligation to believe and teach that which we have received from an omniscient and all-loving God.

• *What is the status of children in and after the Resurrection?* The Prophet Joseph Smith has brought comfort and consolation and comprehension to man in this day regarding death and the world beyond the grave. In speaking in 1842 of the status of children in the resurrection, the Prophet taught:

> As concerning the resurrection, I will merely say that all men will come from the grave as they lie down, whether old or young; there will not be 'added unto their stature one cubit,' neither taken from it; all will be raised by the power of God, having spirit in their bodies, and not blood. (*TPJS* 199–200; emphasis added)

Some two years later, in the King Follett discourse, Joseph repeated the same doctrine. He delivered the comforting assurance to grieving parents who had lost little ones that they would again enjoy the companionship of their children and that these tiny ones would not grow in the grave, but they would come forth as they had been laid to rest—as children (*History of the Church* 6:316).

Some confusion arose over the years after the Prophet Joseph Smith's death concerning his teachings on the status of children in the resurrection. Some erroneously claimed the Prophet taught that children would be resurrected as children and never grow, but would remain in that state through all eternity. President Joseph F. Smith collected testimonies and affidavits from a number of persons who had heard the King Follett Sermon, and it was his powerful witness that the Prophet had taught the truth but had been misunderstood by some. President Smith spoke the following in 1895 at the funeral of Daniel W. Grant, the child of Heber J. Grant:

Under these circumstances, our beloved friends who are now deprived of their little one, have great cause for joy and rejoicing, even in the midst of the deep sorrow that they feel at the loss of their little one for a time. They know he is all right; they have the assurance that their little one has passed away without sin. Such children are in the bosom of the Father. They will inherit their glory and their exaltation, and they will not be deprived of the blessings that belong to them. . . . All that could have been obtained and enjoyed by them if they had been permitted to live in the flesh will be provided for them hereafter. They will lose nothing by being taken away from us in this way.

This is a consolation to me. Joseph Smith, the Prophet, was the promulgator under God of these principles. He was in touch with the heavens. God revealed himself unto him, and made known unto him the principles that lie before us, and which are comprised in the everlasting gospel. Joseph Smith declared that the mother who laid down her little child, being deprived of the privilege, the joy, and the satisfaction of bringing it up to manhood or womanhood in this world, would after the resurrection, have all the joy, satisfaction and pleasure, and even more than it would have been possible to have had in mortality, in seeing her child grow to the full measure of the stature of its spirit. If this be true, and I believe it, what a consolation it is. . . . It matters not whether these tabernacles mature in this world, or have to wait and mature in the world to come, according to the word of the Prophet Joseph Smith, the body will develop, either in time or in eternity, to the full stature of the spirit, and when the mother is deprived of the pleasure and joy of rearing her babe to manhood or womanhood in this life, through the hand of death, that privilege will be renewed to her hereafter, and she will enjoy it to a fuller fruition than it would be possible for her to do here. When she does it there, it will be with certain knowledge that the results will be without failure; whereas here, the results are unknown until after we have passed the test. (*Gospel Doctrine* 152–54; see also Smith, "Status of Children in the Resurrection" 567–74)[5]

Children will come forth from the grave as children, be raised to maturity by worthy parents, and be entitled to receive all of the ordinances of salvation that eventuate in the everlasting continuation of the family unit (Smith, *Doctrines of Salvation* 2:54; see also McConkie, "The Salvation of Little Children" 5). There are no joys of more transcendent beauty than family joys and surely no sorrows more poignant than family sorrows. God lives in the family unit and knows family feelings. He provides a means—through the mediation of his Only Begotten—whereby families may be reunited and affections renewed. "All your losses will be made up to you in the resurrection," the Prophet Joseph Smith declared, "provided you

---

[5] For President Smith's discussion of the misunderstanding of Joseph's original teachings, see "Status of Children in the Resurrection."

continue faithful. By the vision of the Almighty I have seen it" (*TPJS* 296).

Conclusion

Seeing our day and recognizing full well that because of a great apostasy many plain and precious truths concerning agency, accountability, and atonement would be lost, Mormon and Moroni drew upon their own dealings with a doctrinal difficulty in the Church in order to leave us a confirming witness of the truth concerning the mortal status and eternal salvation of little children. Little children shall live! What more perfect evidence of an omniscient and all-loving God than the doctrine which proclaims that little children who die are heirs of celestial glory! They will have no blessings withheld or opportunities denied. The testimony of the Book of Mormon and the latter-day oracles is certain and clear: children who die before the time of accountability shall come forth in the resurrection of the just and go on to enjoy all of the privileges associated with eternal life and the family unit. In speaking of the fruits of this everlasting principle, Elder Bruce R. McConkie, a modern apostle, wrote:

> Truly it is one of the sweetest and most soul-satisfying doctrines of the gospel! It is also one of the greatest evidences of the divine mission of the Prophet Joseph Smith. In his day the fiery evangelists of Christendom were thundering from their pulpits that the road to hell is paved with the skulls of infants not a span long because careless parents had neglected to have their offspring baptized. Joseph Smith's statements, as recorded in the Book of Mormon and latter-day revelation, came as a refreshing breeze of pure truth: *little children shall be saved*. Thanks be to God for the revelations of his mind where these innocent and pure souls are concerned! ("The Salvation of Little Children" 7)

BIBLIOGRAPHY

Frost, S. E. *The Basic Teachings of the Great Philosophers*. New York: New Home Library, 1942.

Garrard, LaMar. "The Fall of Man." *Principles of the Gospel in Practice*. Salt Lake City: Randall Book, 1985. 39–70.

History of the Church. 7 vols. Salt Lake City: Deseret Book, 1980.

McConkie, Bruce R. Funeral Address for Rebecca Adams (28 Oct 1967). Copy in possession of author.

———. *The Promised Messiah*. Salt Lake City: Deseret Book, 1978.

———. "The Salvation of Little Children." *Ensign* (Apr 1977) 7:3–7.

Pratt, Orson. *The Seer*. Orem, UT: Grandin Book, 1990.

Smith, Joseph F. *Gospel Doctrine: Sermons and Writings of President Joseph F. Smith*. Salt Lake City: Deseret Book, 1986.

———. "Status of Children in the Resurrection." *Improvement Era* (May 1918) 21:567–74; also in *Messages of the First Presidency*. Comp. James R. Clark. 6 vols. Salt Lake City: Bookcraft, 1965–75. 5:91–98.

Smith, Joseph Fielding. *Doctrines of Salvation*. 3 vols. Comp. Bruce R. McConkie. Salt Lake City: Bookcraft, 1956.

Talmage, James E. *The Articles of Faith*. Salt Lake City: The Church of Jesus Christ of Latter-day Saints, 1975.

———. *The Great Apostasy*. Salt Lake City: Deseret Book, 1973.

Teachings of the Prophet Joseph Smith. Comp. Joseph Fielding Smith. Salt Lake City: Deseret Book, 1976.

The Mission of Jesus Christ— Ether 3 and 4

2

Robert J. Matthews

*T*he nature and purpose of all true scripture is to testify of Jesus Christ, and the Book of Mormon does that most generously and effectively. My topic will center primarily on Ether, chapter 3, which contains an account of a personal visit of the Lord Jesus Christ to the brother of Jared about 2,200 years before he (Christ) was born in the flesh. This event is entirely unknown outside of the Book of Mormon and thus no other people besides the Latter-day Saints have this information in their literature. The record not only tells of a magnificent manifestation, but interwoven in the story are several fundamental doctrines of the gospel of Jesus Christ.

The Tower of Babel

Christ visits the brother of Jared somewhere in the Near East about 2200 BC, a few years after the scattering and confusion that followed the destruction of the tower of Babel. The Bible gives an account of this tower in Genesis, chapter 11. The book of Ether is a record of one group, consisting of a few families, whose language was not confounded by God. This group, under the leadership of Jared and his brother, was led by the Lord away from the land of the tower and eventually brought to the Western Hemisphere. The brother of Jared was one of the greatest prophets of all time. The Book of Mormon does not disclose his name, but it was made known through a revelation to the Prophet Joseph Smith as Mahonri Moriancumer

Robert J. Matthews is professor emeritus of Ancient Scripture at Brigham Young University.

("Questions and Answers" 704–05). The visit of the Lord to the brother of Jared occurs about four years after the tower's destruction, and before his group embarks on the ocean trip to America. I feel that the best approach to discussing the Lord's visit to the brother of Jared is to read each verse and then comment upon it.

Revelation on the Top of the Mountain

I'll begin with Ether 3:1:

> And it came to pass that the brother of Jared . . . went forth unto the mount, which they called the mount Shelem, because of its exceeding height, and did molten out of a rock sixteen small stones; and they were white and clear, even as transparent glass; and he did carry them in his hands upon the top of the mount, and cried again unto the Lord.

Interestingly the sixteen stones are described as being "clear, even as transparent glass." Although we do not know the exact date of the tower of Babel, it is commonly placed at about 2200 BC. We may wonder how early the art of glassworking was known. William S. Ellis, in the *National Geographic Magazine* for December 1993, reports that "the most reliable research places the invention of glass sometime in the third millennium before the birth of Christ, in Mesopotamia, or present-day Iraq and Syria" (43–44) and further "the earliest known glassmakers worked in Mesopotamia as far back as 2500 BC, crafting beads and other small objects to imitate precious stones" (44). Mesopotamia is the general area, and the date of 2500 BC indicates that glass may have been made as much as 300 years before the tower of Babel and, thus, substantiates the story of the brother of Jared. We do not need historical proof to confirm the record, yet it is interesting to see a bit of secular confirmation that it could have happened as the record said it did.

That the brother of Jared went to talk with the Lord at the top of mount Shelem, which was of exceeding height, is likewise interesting. High mountain peaks have often been the places where God has communed with his prophets. We have only to think of Mt. Sinai with Moses (Ex 19–20); the Mount of Transfiguration with Peter, James, and John (Matt 17); Enoch upon mount Simeon (Moses 7:2–4); Nephi receiving revelation on a high mountain (1 Nephi 11:1; 18:3); and still another mount known only to Moses (Moses 1:1, 42) to sense there is a pattern in this thing. Each of these events occured on separate mountains, but all were sites of unusual spiritual experiences in which the Lord was present. A dedicated temple is the usual house of the Lord—often called the mountain of the Lord's house—and is the place where he communes with his servants, but in the absence of a temple, mountain peaks have been used. Perhaps God chooses such peaks because they have not been polluted by sinful man. (For a discussion of mountain tops as places where the Lord has appeared to his prophets see Joseph Fielding Smith, *Doctrines of Salvation* 2:232–33.)

The Fall and the Atonement

It was upon the top of mount Shelem that the brother of Jared prayed to the Lord. We shall read from Ether 3:2:

> Now behold, O Lord, and do not be angry with thy servant because of his weakness before thee; for we know that thou art holy and dwellest in the heavens, and that we are unworthy before thee; because of the fall our natures have become evil continually; nevertheless, O Lord, thou hast given us a commandment that we must call upon thee, that from thee we may receive according to our desires.

Several important theological concepts are involved in this verse: First is a statement regarding the character of the Lord, that he is holy and dwells in heaven. Second is a declaration that mankind is unworthy before the Lord, and the explanation that "because of the fall our natures have become evil continually." The brother of Jared plainly declares that the fall of Adam has an effect on all mankind, making all of us mortal. This is the "natural man" concept taught elsewhere in the Book of Mormon, in the Bible, and in the Doctrine and Covenants. It is very evident that this great prophet had a knowledge of the Fall and of its effect on human nature. This concept is projected in Mosiah 3:19, saying that "the natural man is an enemy to God, and has been from the fall of Adam"; and in 1 Nephi 10:6, declaring that "all mankind were in a lost and in a fallen state, and ever would be save they should rely upon this Redeemer"; and Alma 22:13, 14, saying that because of the fall of man "he could not merit anything of himself" (see also Hel 14:14–16; Alma 42:2–14; D&C 1:18–20). Through Isaiah the Lord spoke of unregenerated man, saying: "For my thoughts are not your thoughts, neither are your ways my ways, saith the LORD. For as the heavens are higher than the earth, so are my ways higher than your ways, and my thoughts than your thoughts" (Isa 55:8–9). Because of the Fall which has come upon every man, woman, and child, a Redeemer is absolutely necessary, and that Redeemer is Jesus Christ. No one can be saved without him.

A third theological tenet found in Ether 3:2 explains that the Lord is approachable through prayer, that he has commanded mankind to pray to him so that we may "receive according to our desires." That we receive what we desire should be both a joy and a caution. This idea is frequently stated in the Book of Mormon, as in Alma 29:4; 41:5; and Jacob 4:15 wherein men have received both good and bad, "because they desired it."

In the next two verses the brother of Jared pleads with the Lord to be merciful and have pity on the people:

> And I know, O Lord, that thou hast all power, and can do whatsoever thou wilt for the benefit of man; therefore touch these stones, O lord, with thy finger, and prepare them that they may shine forth in darkness; and they shall shine forth unto us in the vessels which we have prepared, that we may have light while we shall cross the sea. Behold, O Lord, thou canst do this. We know that thou art able to show forth great power, which looks small unto the understanding of men. (Ether 3:4–5)

Note the further declaration regarding God's character and potential, having "all power," even "great power," and being able to do whatsoever he wanted to benefit man. However, natural, fallen man is so far beneath the level of God, and understands so infinitesimally little about the works of the Lord, that even when the Lord shows forth great power they often fail to see the significance, and it "looks small" to them. I think Nephi had the same thing in mind when he wrote that what some esteem to be of great worth, both to the soul and body, others trample under their feet (1 Nephi 19:7). He also said:

> I am left to mourn because of the unbelief, and the wickedness, and the ignorance, and the stiffneckedness of men; for they will not search knowledge, nor understand great knowledge, when it is given unto them in plainness, even as plain as word can be. (2 Nephi 32:7)

And Jacob said it like this:

> O the vainness, and the frailties, and the foolishness of men! When they are learned they think they are wise, and they hearken not unto the counsel of God,

> for they set it aside, supposing they know of themselves, wherefore, their wisdom is foolishness and it profiteth them not. And they shall perish. (2 Nephi 9:28)

Paul likewise was acquainted with this condition that is so prevalent among mankind, and he correctly stated that the natural man does not receive the things of the Spirit of God, neither *can* he know them, for they are discerned only by the Spirit. And being without the Spirit, the natural man sees the wisdom of God as foolishness (1 Cor 2:14). I think these passages convey precisely what the brother of Jared meant when he said that the work of God looks small to the understanding of men.

Absolute Reality of Spirit Matter

The record continues in Ether 3:6–10:

> And it came to pass that when the brother of Jared had said these words, behold, the Lord stretched forth his hand and touched the stones one by one with his finger. And the veil was taken from off the eyes of the brother of Jared, and he saw the finger of the Lord; and it was as the finger of a man, like unto flesh and blood; and the brother of Jared fell down before the Lord, for he was struck with fear.
>
> And the Lord saw that the brother of Jared had fallen to the earth; and the Lord said unto him: Arise, why hast thou fallen?
>
> And he saith unto the Lord: I saw the finger of the Lord, and I feared lest he should smite me; for I knew not that the Lord had flesh and blood.
>
> And the Lord said unto him: Because of thy faith thou hast seen that I shall take upon me flesh and blood; and never has man come before me with such exceeding faith as thou hast; for were it not so ye could not have seen my finger. Sawest thou more than this?
>
> And he answered: Nay; Lord, show thyself unto me.

Among the fundamental doctrinal truths contained in the foregoing passage, we find that a spirit has the appearance of flesh and blood even though it is spirit material. We know from Doctrine and Covenants 129 that if the brother of Jared had tried to touch the finger of the Lord he could not have felt it, since mortals cannot physically feel a spirit body. The very fact that section 129 poses the physical handshake as a means of detecting the difference of a spirit from a resurrected body is evidence that a spirit has the appearance, if not the texture of a body, and cannot be differentiated by the eye alone. Secondly, because the brother of Jared had such great faith (exceeding that of earlier prophets), he was able to see the Lord. Thirdly, this event demonstrates that a person must personally ask and seek to obtain spiritual blessings. At first the brother of Jared saw only the finger of the Lord. The Lord asked him if he saw more than this. Then the brother of Jared asked to see more. There is a principle at work here: the Lord was nurturing and nudging him along to the point where he would ask to see more—priming the pump, so to speak, until he finally says, "Lord, show thyself unto me" (v 10).

The Necessity of Commitment

The account continues in Ether 3:11–14:

> And the Lord said unto him: Believest thou the words which I shall speak?
>
> And he answered: Yea, Lord, I know that thou speakest the truth, for thou art a God of truth, and canst not lie.
>
> And when he had said these words, behold, the Lord showed himself unto him, and said: Because thou knowest these things ye are redeemed from the fall; therefore, ye are brought back into my presence; therefore I show myself unto you.
>
> Behold, I am he who was prepared from the foundation of the world to redeem my people. Behold, I am Jesus Christ. I am the Father and the Son. In me shall all mankind have life, and that eternally, even they who shall believe on my name; and they shall become my sons and my daughters.

We notice that the Lord tested the brother of Jared and got a commitment from him *before* he showed him more. This is seen in the words: "Believest thou the words which I shall speak?" This called forth the additional verbal affirmation that God is a God of truth who cannot lie. Having obtained the necessary commitment, the Lord then showed himself to the brother of Jared and told him he was redeemed from the Fall and brought back into the presence of the Lord. The Lord also identified himself as Jesus Christ, who had been prepared and appointed from the very beginning as the Redeemer.

Jesus Gives Eternal Life to Those Who Believe

A significant statement occurs at this juncture which deserves further comment because it has been reworded in our current edition from the way it read in previous editions. The Lord touched the sixteen stones, causing them to shine with visible light. In all editions of the Book of Mormon from 1830, the Lord said in Ether 3:14, "In me shall all mankind have *light* and that eternally, even they who shall believe on my name; and they shall become my sons and my daughters." This makes a marvelous metaphor since the topic of light started this whole episode, and having illuminated the stones, the Lord says that he is also the source of light to mankind. However, since 1981 the word *light* has been replaced with the word *life*. The statement now reads: "In me shall all mankind have *life*, and that eternally, even they who shall believe on my name; and they shall become my sons and my daughters."

The change of wording from *light* to *life* was brought about in the following manner. During the preparation of the 1981 edition, it was brought to the attention of the Brethren that even though all printed editions of the Book of Mormon to this time had read *light*, the printer's manuscript, from which the type was set for the first edition of the Book of Mormon, clearly said *life*. The Scriptures Publications Committee, consisting of three members of the Twelve, unanimously agreed that *life* was a stronger word than *light*, and since the manuscript read *life*, the correction should be made. An examination of the context also justifies this correction, for they who believe will become the sons and daughters of Christ. They are thus spiritually begotten by him and are given eternal life, which includes having eternal light, but is far, far greater.[1]

Many Prophets Have Seen the Premortal Jesus

The narrative continues through Ether 3:15–16:

> And never have I showed myself unto man whom I have created, for never has man believed in me as thou hast. Seest thou that ye are created after mine own image? Yea, even all men were created in the beginning after mine own image.
> Behold, this body, which ye now behold, is the body of my spirit; and man have I created after the body of my spirit; and even as I appear unto thee to be in the spirit will I appear unto my people in the flesh.

---

[1] Some editions of the Book of Mormon published by the RLDS Church have used "life" for this passage.

Perhaps verse 15 should be noted with some explanation, since it seems to imply that the Lord had never appeared to man on this earth before that time, when in fact the scriptures record that he had appeared to Adam (D&C 107:54) and to Enoch (Moses 7:2–4, 28, 29) and to many other patriarchs (D&C 107:54), all of whom date earlier than the brother of Jared. This is not as much of a contradiction as may first appear, but it is a statement of degree. In an earlier appearance of the Lord to the brother of Jared recorded in Ether 2:14, the text precisely says that the Lord "stood in a cloud and talked with him." The *cloud* was undoubtedly a necessary barrier to the clarity of the vision. Evidently what is meant in the statement we are discussing is that the brother of Jared on mount Shelem saw the body of the Lord in greater clarity and fuller detail than in the earlier vision and also more clearly than the earlier patriarchs had. This was apparently because of the greater faith which he possessed (see vv 9 and 15). (For a longer discussion of this subject see Smith, *Answers to Gospel Questions* 2:123–26.)

Brother of Jared Sees All Things

We continue our reading with Ether 3:25–27:

> And when the Lord had said these words, he showed unto the brother of Jared all the inhabitants of the earth which had been, and also all that would be; and he withheld them not from his sight, even unto the ends of the earth.
>
> For he had said unto him in times before, that if he would believe in him that he could show unto him all things—it should be shown unto him; therefore the Lord could not withhold anything from him, for he knew that the Lord could show him all things.
>
> And the Lord said unto him: Write these things and seal them up; and I will show them in mine own due time unto the children of men.

The striking contribution of these verses is that not only did the Lord manifest himself to the brother of Jared, but he also showed him all things pertaining to this earth: past, present, and future. A record of this was written by the brother of Jared, and was later translated by Mosiah (Mosiah 28:11–19). Moroni also engraved this record on the plates that we now call the *sealed portion* of the gold plates that the Prophet Joseph obtained from the Hill Cumorah. These sealed plates contain a record of the "very things that the brother of Jared saw" (Ether 4:4) and are identified as a revelation of all things from the "beginning of the world to the ending thereof" (2 Nephi 27:7, 10). Several of the Lord's prophets have seen similar visions of things from the beginning of the world to the end. This, no doubt, was the case with Adam, and Enoch, and Lehi, Nephi, Isaiah, John the Revelator, and Joseph Smith. Such was also the experience of the brother of Jared. The prophet Moroni said that "there never were greater things made manifest than those which were made manifest to the brother of Jared" (Ether 4:4). Moroni has given us only a very small part of the account in the book of Ether.

The Sealed Record Yet to be Available

The Lord was emphatic that the brother of Jared was to seal up his record of the visions he had received and not tell the people of his day, but he promised that they would be shown to future generations who had faith. In Ether 4:1–7, the prophet Moroni gives us some information on the subject:

> And the Lord commanded the brother of Jared to go down out of the mount from the presence of the Lord, and write the things which he had seen; and they were forbidden to come unto the children of men until after that he should be lifted up upon the cross; and for this cause did king Mosiah keep them, that they should not come unto the world until after Christ should show himself unto his people.
>
> And after Christ truly had showed himself unto his people he commanded that they should be made manifest.
>
> And now, after that, they have all dwindled in unbelief; and there is none save it be the Lamanites, and they have rejected the gospel of Christ; therefore I [Moroni] am commanded that I should hide them up again in the earth.
>
> Behold, I have written upon these plates the very things which the brother of Jared saw; and there never were greater things made manifest than those which were made manifest unto the brother of Jared.
>
> Wherefore the Lord hath commanded me to write them; and I have written them. And he commanded me that I should seal them up; and he also hath commanded that I should seal up the interpretation thereof; wherefore I have sealed up the interpreters, according to the commandment of the Lord.
>
> For the Lord said unto me: They shall not go forth unto the Gentiles until the day that they shall repent of their iniquity, and become clean before the Lord.
>
> And in that day that they shall exercise faith in me, saith the Lord, even as the brother of Jared did, that they may become sanctified in me, then will I manifest unto them the things which the brother of Jared saw, even to the

> unfolding unto them all my revelations, saith Jesus Christ, the Son of God, the Father of the heavens and of the earth, and all things that in them are.

We see from the foregoing that the record of the brother of Jared was made known to the Nephites during that righteous period after the Savior ministered to them (see Ether 4:2). But when they fell into wickedness after some 200 years, the information was taken away from them and will only be made known again, through the sealed plates, when we are ready, which I suppose will be during the Millennium.

Summary

These few verses from Ether chapter 3 contain significant utterances about the reality of God, his character and power, and his benevolence. They also discuss the nature of man, his fallen status, and his weakness in comparison with God. That the Lord hears and answers prayer and responds to the desires and needs of his children is also illustrated in these passages. Furthermore, these verses put in unmistakable language the mission of the Lord Jesus Christ as the Redeemer of the world, and that mankind, in the beginning, was created in the same image and shape and likeness as Christ. These verses do not simply tell about Christ, but they contain the words of Jesus himself declaring his own identity and saving power. An additional and very important aspect of this chapter is the clear demonstration that a spirit body looks like a flesh and blood body. Finally we learn that the brother of Jared was redeemed from the Fall and granted a personal and very detailed vision of the Lord himself, with whom he conversed, and also he was shown all things pertaining to the past, present, and future of this earth and its inhabitants. We will have this complete record someday if and when we are worthy.

What is the value to us in knowing of these things that happened so long ago? I cannot speak for others, but when I read of the experiences of the brother of Jared there wells up within me a desire to have faith like he had and my testimony and love for the Lord increases. My soul "hungers" and wants to feast upon the same kind of spiritual food that the brother of Jared ate. Reading the brief account of the experiences of the brother of Jared is an appetizer which arouses a desire to someday have such an experience myself.

That promise is given to everyone when the time and conditions are right.

Surely, chapters 3 and 4 of Ether are two of the outstanding chapters of all sacred literature and are true to the scriptural purpose of testifying of Jesus Christ.

BIBLIOGRAPHY

Ellis, William S. "Glass: Capturing the Dance of Light." *National Geographic Magazine* (Dec 1993) 184:37–69.

"Questions and Answers." *Improvement Era* (June 1905) 8:704–05.

Smith, Joseph Fielding. *Answers to Gospel Questions.* 5 vols. Salt Lake City: Deseret Book, 1963.

———. *Doctrines of Salvation.* 3 vols. Salt Lake City: Bookcraft, 1954–1956.

"The Knowledge Hid Up Because of Unbelief"   3

Kenneth W. Anderson

*T*oday, the word of the Lord to the modern world through the prophet Moroni is: "Come unto me, O ye Gentiles, and I will show unto you the greater things, the knowledge which is hid up because of unbelief. Come unto me, O ye house of Israel, and it shall be made manifest unto you how great things the Father hath laid up for you, from the foundation of the world; and it hath not come unto you, because of unbelief" (Ether 4:13–14). The purpose of this chapter is to identify the knowledge of God which is hid up from men and women because of unbelief and then to show the pattern of performance required for believers to find the great things laid up for them. Ultimately, the message of the Book of Mormon is that the Lord can show all things to each individual believer.

While there are many meanings of belief, we shall speak of *casual belief* and *causal belief. Casual belief* is a passive kind of belief that never stirs the soul to do anything more than think with the mind. It is the belief Jesus referred to when he said to those who professed faith or belief but did not want to do any works: "Therefore wilt thou know, O vain man, that faith without works is dead and cannot save you? Thou believest there is one God; thou doest well; the devils also believe, and tremble; thou hast made thyself like unto them, not being justified" (JST James 2:18–19).

Causal belief is the belief that leads to action. The scriptures equate it with faith. It is the substance of hope, the mental assurance of things hoped for but not seen (JST Heb 11:1). Faith and causal belief are a gift of God given to men and women who live the laws

Kenneth W. Anderson is associate dean of Continuing Education at Brigham Young University.

which entitle them to this endowment of power, for it is a power (D&C 130:20–21). There is an uncommon dimension of faith in a few men and women that, when exercised in a true belief of Jesus Christ, causes the elements to react both physically and spiritually. This uncommon faith has a catalytic power to direct all matter and make earthly energy sources submissive. In the gospel sense this causal belief or faith generates salvation and eternal life. The promise is absolute that the correct faith in Jesus Christ is the power base that leads to salvation and exaltation.

Another term we need to define is *mystery*. In this chapter, mystery denotes a spiritual truth that was once hidden but now is revealed. It would have remained unknown were it not for special revelation that brought it to light. For example, *God* is a spiritual mystery to most of the world, but he has revealed himself to his prophets throughout the history of the world including those today, and we can exercise our faith in those revelations.

King Limhi correctly said of the record of Ether: "Doubtless a great mystery is contained within these plates" (Mosiah 8:19). The plates required a seer to unlock that mystery because the brother of Jared wrote in a language which could not be read (Ether 3:24). Moroni said the words on the record were "mighty even . . . unto the overpowering of man to read them" (12:24), but they were to be hidden from the people until after Christ had "glorif[ied his] name in the flesh" (3:21). Moroni was commanded to "write them" and to "seal up the interpretation thereof" (Ether 4:5). Moroni said:

> For the Lord said unto me: They shall not go forth unto the Gentiles until the day that they shall repent of their iniquity, and become clean before the Lord. And in that day that they shall exercise faith in me, saith the Lord, even as the brother of Jared did, that they may become sanctified in me, then I will manifest unto them the things which the brother of Jared saw, even to the unfolding unto them all my revelations, saith Jesus Christ. (Ether 4:6–7)

What specific knowledge did the brother of Jared possess which was hidden up because of unbelief? First, he understood the character of the Godhead—God our Father, his Son, Jesus Christ, and the Holy Ghost. The Prophet Joseph Smith taught: "There are but a very few beings in the world who understand rightly the character of God. . . . The great majority of mankind do not comprehend anything, either that which is past, or that which is to come, as it respects their relationship to God. If men do not comprehend the character of God, they do not comprehend themselves" (*Teachings of the Prophet Joseph Smith* 343; hereafter *TPJS*). He also said: "God himself was once as we are now, and is an exalted man, and sits enthroned in yonder heavens! That is the great secret. . . . I say, if you were to see him today, you would see him like a man in form—like yourselves in all the person, image, and very form as a man" (*TPJS* 345).

Elder Bruce R. McConkie has noted the following:

> The profound truth concerning God is that he is a Holy Man, a personage of tabernacle, a being in whose image and likeness mortal man was made. His work and his glory are to bring to pass the immortality and eternal life of man. Eternal life is the name of the kind of life he lives, and until men know that he is a Holy Man, they will never have the desire and the incentive to become like him and to be inheritors of eternal life. . . . To Enoch the Lord identified himself by saying: "Behold, I am God; Man of Holiness is my name; Man of Counsel is my name; and Endless and Eternal is my name, also" (Moses 7:35). (*A New Witness* 59–60)

The brother of Jared knew Jesus Christ. The LDS Bible Dictionary notes that Jesus

> is the firstborn of the Father in the spirit and the Only Begotten of the Father in the flesh. He is Jehovah, and was foreordained to his great calling in the Grand Councils before the world was. He was born of Mary at Bethlehem, lived a sinless life, and wrought out a perfect atonement for all mankind by the shedding of his blood and his death on the cross. He rose from the grave and brought to pass the bodily resurrection of every living thing and the salvation and exaltation of the faithful. He is the greatest Being to be born on this earth—the perfect example—and all religious things should be done in his name. . . . [For] his name is above every name, and is the only name under heaven by which we can be saved. He will come again in power and glory to dwell on the earth, and will stand as Judge of all mankind at the last day. (633)

The brother of Jared also knew the nature of the Holy Ghost, the third member of the Godhead. As the name implies, the Holy Ghost is a personage of Spirit, not possessing a body of flesh and bones (D&C 130:22). He is manifested to us on the earth both as the *power* of the Holy Ghost and as the *gift* of the Holy Ghost. The power can come upon any of us before baptism and is the convincing witness that the gospel is true. It gives us a testimony of Jesus Christ and of his work and the work of his servants upon the earth. The gift can come only after proper and authorized baptism, and it is conferred by the laying on of hands (Moroni 2:1–3). The gift of the Holy Ghost is the right to have the companionship of the Holy Ghost. More powerful than that which is available before baptism, it acts as a cleansing agent to purify and sanctify members from all sin. Thus receiving it is often spoken of as a baptism of "fire." The Holy Ghost knows all things (D&C 35:19) and can lead us to know of future events (2 Peter 1:21). "Other names that sometimes refer to the Holy Ghost are Holy Spirit, Spirit of God, Spirit of the Lord, Comforter, and Spirit" (LDS Bible Dictionary 704). Even though we have the right to receive the companionship of the Holy Ghost, actually gaining it requires personal obedience and worthiness.

How did the human race come to a knowledge of God? When God created Adam and Eve and placed them on this earth, he endowed them with knowledge of his existence. They enjoyed communion with him, and there was no veil to separate them. God conversed with Adam face to face; Adam stood in his presence, received his instruction, and beheld his glory. When Adam and Eve were driven out of the garden, they retained their knowledge of God. They knew the real facts: God had created them and they were accountable to him for their conduct. It was by manifestation of himself to man, even after the Fall, that the knowledge of God continued to be known by Adam and his posterity. Though they were separated from God's presence and did not see his face, they heard his voice. This laid the foundation for the mental exercise of their faith, through which they could obtain a knowledge of God's character and also of his glory. The whole human family in the early age of their existence had this knowledge disseminated among them. Thus the existence of God became an object of faith. Their evidence of God was the testimony from their fathers, the testimony of man. This shared knowledge and testimony of the reality of God as their Father stirred up the faith of multitudes to seek after him—to search after a knowledge of his character, attributes, and perfections, until they became extensively acquainted with him, and not only to commune with him and behold his glory, but to be partakers of his power and stand in his presence (*Lectures on Faith* 2:12–35; hereafter *LF*).

What is the pattern of performance required for believers to find the great things laid up for them? The general invitation from the Lord to "come unto me, O ye Gentiles, and I will show unto you . . . knowledge . . . hid up because of unbelief" is unto all people, Latter-day Saint and non-member alike (Ether 4:13). Who could not benefit from a knowledge of the Godhead, their character and attributes? However, the more specific invitation to "Come unto me, O ye House of Israel, and it shall be made manifest unto you . . . [the] great things the Father hath laid up for you" indentifies the favorites of heaven, even Covenant Israel (4:14). They are to be the receptors not only of the knowledge of the Godhead, but also of manifestations that reveal great things "from the foundation of the world" (Ether 4:14). The greatest thing to be revealed was the pattern of performance required of men and women to be saved and exalted. This pattern of perform-ance laid up by the Father is called the "great plan of our God"—"the plan of salvation"—the "plan of happiness" (2 Nephi 9:13; Moses 6:62; and Alma 42:8).

The plan of salvation is a divinely established system of laws and ordinances which empower God's spirit children to develop faith sufficient to be saved. The plan was activated by the creation of man and woman on this earth; their fall from God's presence; and the great atoning sacrifice of the Son of God, Jesus Christ. The plan of salva-tion, also called the Gospel of Jesus Christ (3 Nephi 27:13–21), is an established order of God that requires obedience to laws and ordi-nances, and which order, when entered into by covenant, guarantees eternal life, which is the quality of life God lives.

The exercise of true faith in Jesus Christ, plus repentance from sin leads to the watery grave of baptism by immersion in the hope of having sin remitted. Legal administrators then bestow the Gift of the Holy Ghost upon that soul. This is the gift above gifts, for the Holy Ghost is the Revelator and the Sanctifier within the established order of the great plan of our God. The Holy Ghost will, with edifying, instructive and corrective revelations to the heart and mind of man and woman, lead them because of their personal faith through a cleansing process until their sins are remitted. This process of sanc-tification in Jesus Christ, when completed, becomes a key to obtaining great knowledge, for "in that day that they shall exercise faith in me, saith the Lord . . . that they may become sanctified in me, then I will manifest unto them the things which the brother of Jared saw, even to the unfolding unto them all my revelations" (Ether 4:7).

How did the brother of Jared develop the belief—the faith—to cause his soul to leap from faith to perfect knowledge? And, second, how did he become sanctified? We will consider these two questions for they are central to finding hidden knowledge and the manifesting of great things promised to Israel.

The Prophet Joseph Smith taught

> three things are necessary for any rational and intelligent being to exercise faith in God unto life and salvation.

> First, the idea that he actually exists; Secondly, a *correct* idea of his character, perfections, and attributes; Thirdly, an actual knowledge that the course of life which one is pursuing is according to His will. For without an acquaintance with these three important facts, the faith of every rational being must be imperfect and unproductive. But with this understanding, it can become perfect and fruitful (*LF* 3:2–5).

The "great mystery" of the Godhead was revealed and made known to the brother of Jared. It was a central factor in his faith in approaching and receiving instruction from God. The brother of Jared not only knew God existed, but was acquainted with his character, perfections, and attributes. He knew God was "holy and dwellest in the heavens" (Ether 3:2); that he was "merciful" (v 3); has all power (v 4); was "a God of truth, and canst not lie" (v 12); that he was compassionate (1:35); slow to anger (vv 36–37); God was abundant in goodness (vv 42–43); he was a God of justice and judgment (2:14–15); he was no respecter of persons (1:36–37); and he was a God of love (vv 40–43; 2:14; and Hel 15:3).

A correct understanding of the attributes of God is and always has been essential to gaining of faith and salvation! In the *Lectures on Faith* we read: "Let us here observe that the real design which the God of heaven had in view in making the human family acquainted with his attributes was that they might be enabled to exercise faith in him . . . and through the exercising [of] faith in him, might obtain eternal life. For without the idea of the existence of the attributes which belong to God, the minds of men could not have power to exercise faith in him so as to lay hold upon eternal life" (*LF* 4:2). Faith is a mental and spiritual exercise.

The brother of Jared was told "never has man come before me with such exceeding faith as thou hast" (Ether 3:9). "The God of heaven, understanding most perfectly the constitution of human nature and the weakness of man, knew what was necessary to be revealed and what ideas needed to be planted in their minds to enable them to exercise faith in him unto eternal life" (*LF* 4:2). How would you like to have "the mind of Christ" implanted in you? That blessing is for Israel, the favorite of heaven.

The brother of Jared knew he was a favorite of heaven; he knew he had embraced the order of things which God had established for the redemption of man. This knowledge empowered him with a mental and spiritual confidence not only to draw near to the Lord, but also to lay hold of answers to the problems which vexed his life.

The knowledge the brother of Jared had that his course of life was according to the will of God is marvelously recorded in the scriptures. He was "highly favored of the Lord" (Ether 1:34); the Lord always heard and responded to his inquiries and petitions with personal instruction "because this long time ye have cried unto me" (v 43). The Lord brought the brother of Jared and his family and friends forth "where there never had man been" and "even to that great sea which divideth the lands . . . being directed continually" by his hand (Ether 2:5, 6, 13). The brother of Jared was chastened by the Lord and repented of his evil. He learned the "Spirit will not always strive" with anyone who is disobedient (v 15). Twice he declared to the Lord, "I have performed the work which thou hast commanded me" (vv 18, 22). The truth is that the brother of Jared had so many personal revelations from the Lord that he knew his own course in life was according to the will of God. Instead of rejecting divine correction, he absorbed it, repented of all evil, and, by this process, increased his personal faith in the Lord. His faith was productive and fruitful and led to a perfect knowledge of God.

The second question was, how did the brother of Jared become sanctified? His sanctification came, as it comes to all to whom it comes, as a direct result of "yielding [his] heart unto God" (Hel 3:35). He constantly created a wholesome environment where the Holy Ghost could edify, instruct, and correct him with the word of truth. Our Lord and Savior, Jesus Christ, in his great intercessory prayer for his apostles in the Holy Land spoke of sanctification coming through reception of the word. He plead with the Father for the Twelve saying, "Sanctify them through thy truth: thy word is truth" (John 17:17). The brother of Jared constantly heard and felt the word of truth come through him. The word of truth came because of his experience with God, who will be as compassionate with us as he was with him. More of the word of God came to the brother of Jared in the valley of Nimrod when "the Lord came down and talked with [him]; and [the Lord] was in a cloud, and the brother of Jared saw him not" (Ether 2:4). Just as Moses led the children of Israel in the wilderness with the word of God, so the brother of Jared led his people with the word giving "directions whither they should travel" (v 5). After four years of living in tents on the seashore, the brother of Jared was visited of the Lord, who "stood in a cloud and talked with him for the space of three hours" and "chastened him because he remembered not to call upon the name of the Lord" (v 14). The brother of Jared received the sanctifying word of truth and repented of this evil and "did call upon the name of the Lord for his brethren who were with him" (v 15). It was evil for a man "highly favored of the Lord" not to call upon God for and in behalf of "his brethren." He had a priesthood assignment and duty to receive the word and go at the head of these people (1:42). His prophetic duty as a seer was both to receive the word and to be the clear channel of truth for his family, Jared's family and their friends (vv 40–43; Mosiah 8:15–18). These sanctifying experiences with the word came as an unfolding and cleansing process which included chastening. The Lord has said: "For all those who will not endure chastening . . . cannot be sanctified" (D&C 101:5). Later, when the sanctification process was complete and the brother of Jared's faith had matured, the Lord "could show unto him all things" and "not withhold anything from him" (Ether 3:26). He had become sanctified and perfect in Christ Jesus.

Now, since the brother of Jared and "many" others obtained sanctification, which was their key to great knowledge, eternal life and the presence of God, how can we obtain the same today? The use of the word "unfolding" (Ether 4:7) verifies an orderly gaining of faith and gradual sanctification process. Learning to live the principles of the gospel and receive instructive revelation from the Holy Ghost does not happen all at once. It is a growing and maturing process just as it was for the brother of Jared. However, the same sanctifying and revelatory process is available to the Saints today. For "he that believeth these things which I have spoken, him will I visit with the manifestations of my Spirit, and he shall know and bear record. For because of my Spirit he shall know that these things are true" (v 11).

President Ezra Taft Benson has counseled:

> We must be careful, as we seek to become more and more godlike, that we do not become discouraged and lose hope. Becoming Christlike is a lifetime pursuit and very often involves growth and change that is slow, almost imperceptible. The scriptures record remarkable accounts of men whose lives

changed dramatically, in an instant, as it were. Though they are real and powerful, they are the exception more than the rule. For every Paul, for every Enos, and for every King Lamoni, there are hundreds of thousands of people who find the process of repentance much more subtle, much more imperceptible. Day by day they move closer to the Lord, little realizing they are building a godlike life. They live quiet lives of goodness, service, and commitment. They are like the Lamanites, who the Lord said "were baptized with fire and with the Holy Ghost, and they knew it not (3 Nephi 9:20). (5)

Some members of the Church may suppose this marvelous manifestation of truth to the worthy soul is only for the General Authorities, but President Joseph Fielding Smith gave a great insight to the general membership when he said,

> The question frequently arises: "Is it necessary for a member of the Council of the Twelve to see the Savior in order to be an apostle?" It is their privilege to see him if occasion requires, but the Lord has taught that there is a stronger witness than seeing a personage, even of seeing the Son of God in a vision. . . . When Spirit speaks to spirit, the imprint on the soul is far more difficult to erase. Every member of the Church should have impressions that Jesus is the Son of God indelibly pictured on his soul through the witness of the Holy Ghost (979).

While we are growing in this gospel pattern, prayer is a basic but vital element. President Harold B. Lee said,

> The most important thing you can do is to learn to talk to God. Talk to Him as you would talk to your father, for He is your Father, and He wants you to talk to Him. He wants you to cultivate ears to listen, when He gives you the impressions of the Spirit to tell you what to do. If you learn to give heed to the sudden ideas which come to your minds, you will find those things coming through in the very hour of your need. If you will cultivate an ear to hear these promptings, you will have learned to walk by the Spirit of revelation. (3–4)

Revelation that leads to sanctification seems to begin with those small impressions to the heart and mind. When we act upon them, they tend to generate both an increased belief in being led by the Spirit and by an increased confidence that God knows and cares about us. With our continued responding to spiritual impressions, the flow of instruction from the Holy Ghost increases. Other channels of revelation begin to open, such as dreams and waking visions. Most instruction is personal and family centered. It is always stewardship bound, which means no one would ever receive instruction for someone in higher authority and responsibility. And while all members are authorized to receive this instruction within their stewardships, that which comes, if correct, will always be in agreement with instruction from the Council of the First Presidency and Quorum of the Twelve.

In the revelation designated as the "olive leaf," the Lord gives additional instruction to bring about this sanctification process in the members:

> Draw near unto me and I will draw near unto you; seek me diligently and ye shall find me; ask, and ye shall receive; knock, and it shall be opened unto you. . . . Behold, that which you hear is as the voice of one crying in the wilderness—in the wilderness, because you cannot see him—my voice, because my voice is Spirit; my Spirit is truth; truth abideth and hath no end; and if it be in you it shall abound. . . . Therefore, sanctify yourselves that your minds become single to God, and the days will come that you shall see him; for he will unveil his face unto you, and it shall be in his own due time, and in his own way, and according to his own will. (D&C 88:63–68)

Sanctification is a central destination which all believers must reach if they are to receive the "great things laid up" for them. However, some members of the Church perceive difficulty in obtaining faith great enough to lead to being sanctified. It is not a quick process. The mental exertion of exercising faith and performing acts of obedience required for progressing toward sanctification has always appeared to be more difficult than relying on humans or things. As a result, some individuals may be distracted, grow negative and cynical, disbelieving that these truths pertain to them. They sometimes begin to contend, either verbally or quietly in their hearts, with the word of God, supposing he doesn't hear their prayers. The Lord spoke of those individuals to Moroni, saying: "And he that will contend against the word of the Lord, let him be accursed; and he that shall deny these things, let him be accursed; for unto them will I show no greater things, saith Jesus Christ" (Ether 4:8). The Lord also noted that "all those who will . . . deny me, cannot be sanctified" (D&C 101:5).

Today, we see dissidents raising their voices in opposition to Church leaders. Elder Boyd K. Packer commented on this, saying: "Not too many days ago in a moment of great concern over a rapid series of events that demonstrated the challenge of those within the Church who have that feeling of criticism and challenge and apostasy, I had an impression, as revelations are. It was strong and it was clear, because lingering in my mind was 'why? why? when we need so much to be united.' And there came the answer: 'It is permitted to be so now that the sifting might take place, and it will have negligible effect upon the Church'" (CES).

In The Church of Jesus Christ of Latter-day Saints there is an intimate relationship between sustaining the Brethren and sanctification. The quality and quantity of our sanctification is, in large measure, a product of the quality and quantity of our sustaining the living prophets and apostles in our words and our deeds. They are mouthpieces of the Lord, the clear voice of truth. The following words came to Heber C. Kimball at Far West, Missouri, on 6 April 1839:

> Verily I say unto my servant Heber, thou art my son, in whom I am well pleased; for thou art careful to hearken to my words, and not transgress my law, nor rebel against my servant Joseph Smith, for thou hast a respect to the words of mine anointed, even from the least to the greatest of them; therefore thy name is written in heaven, no more to be blotted out forever, because of these things; and this Spirit and blessing shall rest down upon thy posterity for ever and ever. (Whitney 242)

The Prophet Joseph taught:

> God hath not revealed anything to Joseph, but what He will make known unto the Twelve, and even the least Saint may know all things as fast as he is able to bear them, for the day must come when no man need say to his neighbor, Know ye the Lord; for all shall know Him (who remain) from the least to the greatest. How is this to be done? It is to be done by . . . the other Comforter spoken of, which will be manifest by revelation. (*TPJS* 149)

Then he asked,

> Now what is this other Comforter? It is no more nor less than the Lord Jesus Christ Himself; and this is the sum and substance of the whole matter; that when any man obtains this last Comforter, he will have the personage of Jesus Christ to attend him, or appear unto him from time to time, and even He will manifest the Father unto him, and they will take up their abode with him, and the visions of the heavens will be opened unto him, and the Lord will teach him face to face, and he may have a perfect knowledge of the mysteries of the Kingdom of God. (*TPJS* 150–51)

The word of the Lord to Moroni for all Israel is: "Behold, when ye shall rend that veil of unbelief which doth cause you to remain in your awful state of wickedness, and hardness of heart, and blindness of mind, then shall the great and marvelous things which have been hid up from the foundation of the world from you—yea, when ye shall call upon the Father in my name, with a broken heart and a contrite spirit, then shall ye know that the Father hath remembered the covenant which he made unto your fathers, O house of Israel" (Ether 4:15). This covenant was a promised restoration of all blessings from God, including the faith and power and order of the ancient Saints to administer the fulness of the gospel of Jesus Christ, the plan of salvation with all its attendant and revealed blessings. And it comes to every soul, male and female, who believes the word of God spoken by authorized, legal administrators, assigned by God himself to perform the life-giving ordinances for the believing soul. Obedience to this covenant is an absolute guarantee of sanctification and eternal life.

The Lord instructs: "Therefore, repent all ye ends of the earth, and come unto me, and believe in my gospel, and be baptized in my name; for he that believeth and is baptized shall be saved; but he that believeth not shall be damned; and signs shall follow them that believe in my name" (Ether 4:18).

Is it proper to seek for spiritual gifts, not signs, but spiritual gifts? Is it correct and not asking amiss to pray for the soul-sanctifying privilege of seeing the face of the Lord Jesus while we yet dwell as mortals on this earth?

Elder Bruce R. McConkie stated, "If we are to see his face in that eternal realm, where the same sociality that exists among us here, then coupled with eternal glory, shall endure everlastingly, can we go amiss by seeking to establish that sociality here and now? Are we not commanded: Ask and ye shall receive; seek and ye shall find; knock and it shall be opened?" (369).

Finally, Moroni says:

> And now I . . . bid farewell unto the Gentiles, yea, and also unto my brethren whom I love, until we shall meet before the judgment-seat of Christ, where all men and women shall know that my garments are not spotted with your blood. And then shall ye know that I have seen Jesus, and that he hath talked with me face to face, and that he told me in plain humility, even as a man telleth another in mine own language, concerning these things. . . . And now, I would commend you to seek this Jesus of whom the prophets and apostles have written, that the grace of God the Father, and also the Lord Jesus Christ, and the Holy Ghost, which beareth record of them, may be and abide in you forever. (Ether 12:38–41)

There are people on the earth today who have seen the Lord. Many ask the Brethren if they have seen him. Elder Boyd K. Packer taught: "I said there was a question that could not be taken lightly nor answered at all without the prompting of the Spirit. I have not asked that question of others, but I have heard them answer it—but not when they were asked. They have answered it under the prompting of the Spirit, on sacred occasions, when 'the Spirit beareth record'" (D&C 1:39). He continued: "I have heard one of my brethren declare: 'I know from experiences, too sacred to relate, that Jesus is the Christ.' I have heard another testify: 'I know that God lives; I know that the Lord lives. And more than that, I know the Lord.' It was not their words that held the meaning or the power. It was the Spirit. 'For when a man speaketh by the power of the Holy Ghost the power of the Holy Ghost carrieth it unto the hearts of the children of men'" (2 Nephi 33:1). Elder Packer then said: "I have come to know that the witness does not come by seeking after signs. It comes through fasting and prayer, through activity and testing and obedience. It comes through sustaining the servants of the Lord and following them" ("The Spirit Beareth Record" 88).

The title page to the Book of Mormon prophetically tells that Jesus Christ manifests "himself unto all nations," which ultimately means individual men and women of all nations (see also 3 Nephi 11:15). May the Lord bless us to know of his existence, his character and attributes, and to know that the course we are pursuing is according to his will. May the Lord increase our faith and lead us to sanctification so we will be fruitful in the knowledge of him. May we avoid contending with the word of God, and, more particularly, may we be free from contending against the words of his apostles, for these legal administrators are the very channel of light and truth through which salvation and eternal life will come to any of us. The Council of the First Presidency and the Quorum of the Twelve hold the keys to obtaining the lesser and higher ordinances in which the power of Godliness is manifest unto men and women in the flesh—the very covenant-making opportunities that lead by our obedience to the sacred sanctification process and to the perfections of Jesus Christ. Having these endowments of power, we will then be able to allow the Lord to reveal his will to us in any manner he chooses, even to the unfolding of all his revelations as we have need.

BIBLIOGRAPHY

Benson, Ezra Taft. "A Mighty Change of Heart." *Ensign* (Oct 1989) 19:2–5.

The Lectures on Faith in Historical Perspective. Eds. Larry E. Dahl and Charles D. Tate, Jr. Provo, UT: Religious Studies Center, Brigham Young Univ, 1990.

Lee, Harold B. "President Lee Gives Solemn Witness." *Church News* (3 Mar 1973) 3–4.

McConkie, Bruce R. *A New Witness for the Articles of Faith.* Salt Lake City: Deseret Book, 1985.

Packer, Boyd K. CES Religious Educators Symposium, Brigham Young Univ (10 Aug 1993).

———. "Spirit Beareth Record." *Ensign* (June 1971) 1:87–88; also in *Conference Report* (Apr 1971) 122–28.

Smith, Joseph Fielding. "The First Presidency and the Council of the Twelve." *Improvement Era* (Nov 1966) 69:977–79.

Teachings of the Prophet Joseph Smith. Comp. Joseph Fielding Smith. Salt Lake City: Deseret Book, 1976.

Whitney, Orson F. *Life of Heber C. Kimball.* Salt Lake City: Bookcraft, 1945.

The Jaredites—A Case Study in Following the Brethren

4

Douglas E. Brinley

A distinguishing feature of The Church of Jesus Christ of Latter-day Saints is the principle of continuous revelation: God speaks to his children through prophet-servants today as well as in former times (see Amos 3:7). The principle of revelation separates Latter-day Saints from all other religions, for our claim of administering the true gospel is based on this premise: In 1820, God called a young man to the prophetic office and subsequently sent eight angels to restore the gospel and priesthood keys that enable men and women to qualify for exaltation. Moroni restored the gospel in the form of a set of plates which contain the everlasting gospel. John the Baptist; Peter, James, and John; Moses; Elias; and Elijah restored priesthood keys for the salvation and exaltation of God's children. John Taylor explained that true religion has a heavenly connection:

> A good many people, and those professing Christians, will sneer at the idea of present revelation. *Whoever heard of true religion without communication with God?* To me the thing is the most absurd thing that the human mind could conceive of. I do not wonder, when the people generally reject the principle of present revelation, that skepticism and infidelity prevail to such an alarming extent. I do not wonder that so many men treat religion with contempt, and regard it as something not worth the attention of intelligent beings, *for without revelation religion is a mockery and a farce.* If I can not have a religion that will lead me to God, and place me *en rapport* with him, and unfold to my mind the principles of immortality and eternal life, I want nothing to do with it. (*Journal of Discourses* 16:371; emphasis added; hereafter *JD*)

Douglas E. Brinley is associate professor of Church History and Doctrine at Brigham Young University.

A Book of Mormon Message

A prominent theme of the Book of Mormon is, however, that people seldom follow the Lord's servants when they are sent among the people, especially when living conditions are soft, comfortable, easy, and prosperity abounds. During these periods, people ignore God, reject his prophets, and become distracted from their goal to obtain "immortality and eternal life."

From the rebellion of Laman and Lemuel against Lehi and against Nephi to the fall of Moroni's people, the Book of Mormon is replete with examples of people who ignored the counsel of their living prophets. The result was a "ripening in iniquity" until the inhabitants were destroyed by civil war or natural disasters (see 2 Nephi 28:16; Alma 10:19; Hel 5:2; 6:40; 8:26; 11:37; 13:14; 3 Nephi 8; Ether 2:9; and 9:20).

The People of Jared

One of the most poignant examples of the destruction of an entire civilization is found in the book of Ether. The fall of the people of Jared was especially tragic in light of the numerous times God sent prophets to warn them that they were bringing a curse upon the land that would end in their "utter destruction" if they did not repent. Eventually the entire nation was engulfed in a civil war that brought about their extinction as a people—leaving only Coriantumr and the prophet-recorder, Ether, as the lone survivors. Moroni warned the latter-day inhabitants of the land to avoid the pattern that destroyed the former occupants of the land:

> And this cometh unto you, O ye Gentiles, that ye may know the decrees of God—that ye may repent, and not continue in your iniquities until the fulness come, that ye may not bring down the fulness of the wrath of God upon you as the inhabitants of the land have hitherto done. (Ether 2:11)

The Pattern of Destruction

One way to view the fall of the Jaredites is to observe the four points of sequence that led to their downfall:

1. God sent prophets to call the people to repentance.
2. They warned them of destruction if they didn't repent.
3. The people choose to repent or reject the prophetic message.
4. The consequences of their decision.

This pattern is repeated at least six times in the Jaredite record until the people are destroyed under the reign of Coriantumr, who ignored the counsel of Ether until repentance was not possible (see Ether 15:1–2). Moroni explained that it was the Lord who brought about the destruction of this people (6:16, 21). "And now," wrote the abridger, "I proceed to give an account of those ancient inhabitants who were destroyed *by the hand of the Lord* upon the face of this north country" (1:1; emphasis added). Let us now examine these six episodes that ended in the destruction of an entire nation.

Jaredites in the Land

The Jaredites were led to the land of promise by the Lord at the time of the "great tower" and the confusion of tongues (see Gen 11; Ether 1:33).[1] As they multiplied and spread throughout the land, they became a large and prosperous people. They began as a righteous colony, having been "taught to walk humbly before the Lord; and they were also taught from on high" (Ether 6:17).

As they grew in number, the people desired a king, in spite of the objections of the brother of Jared, who cautioned them that having a king would not be wise in the long run (see Ether 6:23; 7:5). At a much later date, Mosiah, the Nephite seer who first translated the record of this fallen people from twenty-four gold plates, also warned the Nephites of the dangers of a kingship. His counsel came from the antics of king Noah, son of Zeniff, and also from translating the record of the people of Jared:

> How much iniquity doth one wicked king cause to be committed, yea, and what great destruction! . . .

---

[1]   The tower of Babel incident is thought to have occurred approximately 2200 BC (see LDS Bible Dictionary 635). Later editions of the dictionary delete the years of specific events from Adam to King Saul. Also, the term "tower of Babel" is not used in the Book of Mormon record.

> Now I say unto you, ye cannot dethrone an iniquitous king save it be through much contention, and the shedding of much blood.
>
> For behold, he has his friends in iniquity, and he keepeth his guards about him; and he teareth up the laws of those who have reigned in righteousness before him; and he trampleth under his feet the commandments of God;
>
> And he enacteth laws, and sendeth them forth among his people, yea, laws after the manner of his own wickedness; and whosoever doth not obey his laws he causeth to be destroyed; and whosoever doth rebel against him he will send his armies against them to war, and if he can he will destroy them; and thus an unrighteous king doth pervert the ways of all righteousness.
>
> And now behold I say unto you, it is not expedient that such abominations should come upon you. (Mosiah 29:17, 21–24)

Under Mosiah's wise counsel, and after he had translated the account of the Jaredites, the Nephites changed their form of government to judges rather than kings when his sons refused to lead the people (see Mosiah 29:1–3, 38–39).

Episode 1 — The Reign of Kings

Like their later Israelite counterparts, the people of Jared wanted a king. After the brother of Jared warned against this form of government, he relented but no one wanted the office. Finally, one of the sons of Jared, Orihah, consented and was anointed ruler (Ether 6:22–27). Orihah and his successor-son, Kib, were righteous kings, but Kib's son, Corihor, rebelled against his father, overthrowing him and taking him captive. While in prison—more likely a house arrest—Kib bore a son, Shule, who "became mighty as to the strength of a man" (7:8). This son was sympathetic to his father and succeeded in repelling Corihor and restoring Kib to his throne. Kib passed his office on to Shule. However, one of Corihor's sons, Noah, in attempting to overthrow Shule, took him captive and would have executed him except the sons of Shule "crept into the house of Noah by night and slew him, and broke down the door of the prison and brought out their father, and placed him upon his throne in his own kingdom" (v 18). Thus men began to covet the throne, and rebellion and mischief continued. The son of Noah, Cohor, succeeded in dividing the people into two groups: "And there were two kingdoms, the kingdom of Shule, and the kingdom of Cohor" (v 20). In a subsequent battle, Shule killed Cohor and united the kingdom.

It was in this setting that prophets came forth to warn the people that their wickedness violated their covenant with God and that judgments were imminent without swift repentance. This was the first of six episodes where prophets were sent to warn the Jaredites that their wickedness was offensive to the Lord (see Ether 2:7–12). This first episode follows four steps in the sequence to destruction: (1) prophets are sent, (2) a message of warning is given, (3) the people respond, and (4) this time the outcome is favorable.

Sequence to Destruction

PROPHET(S): Unnamed, but "sent from the Lord" (Ether 7:23).

MESSAGE: "The wickedness and idolatry of the people was bringing a curse upon the land, and they should be destroyed if they did not repent" (v 23)

RESPONSE OF THE PEOPLE: "The people did revile against the prophets, and did mock them" (v 24).

OUTCOME: Before any judgments began, king Shule "did execute a law throughout all the land, which gave power unto the prophets" to "go whithersoever they would; and by this cause the people were brought unto repentance" (v 25), and "there were no more wars in the days of Shule" (v 27). Unfortunately, this principle of religious freedom, protected by kingly edict under Shule, was withdrawn by later rulers.

Episode 2 — The Days of Jared

Two men, Jared, the son of Omer, and Akish conspired to the throne and organized a secret combination to kill Omer. But the Lord warned Omer "in a dream that he should depart out of the land," leaving the throne to Jared (Ether 9:3). Having tasted power, however, Akish decided to kill Jared so that he himself could become king. Internal dissent among his sons led to Akish's death, restoring Omer to the kingship. His son, Emer, followed him as ruler, and governed in peace for the next 62 years. The people multiplied and prospered, insomuch that the Lord "began again to take the curse from off the land" (Ether 9:16). Emer's son, Coriantum, and his son, Com, also became kings and ruled in righteousness and the people were blessed.

However, after several generations of peace, wickedness returned. "The people had spread again over all the face of the land, and there began again to be an exceedingly great wickedness upon the face of the land, and Heth began to embrace the secret plans again of old, to destroy his father" (Ether 9:26). Heth became king by murdering his father, Com, and prophets were sent forth to warn the people of impending judgments.

Sequence to Destruction

PROPHETS: Unnamed, but from the Lord (Ether 9:28).

MESSAGE: "That [the people] must prepare the way of the Lord or there should come a curse upon the face of the land; yea, even there should be a great famine, in which they should be destroyed if they did not repent" (v 28)

RESPONSE OF THE PEOPLE: "But the people believed not the words of the prophets, but they cast them out; and some of them they cast into pits and left them to perish" (v 29).

OUTCOME: This time the government did not protect the prophets in freedom to teach repentance in the land, but threatened the lives of the prophets. "And it came to pass that they did all these things according to the commandment of the king, Heth" (v 29) Consequently, judgments: "And it came to pass that there began to be a great dearth upon the land, and the inhabitants began to be destroyed exceedingly fast" (v 30). Upon threat of destruction by poisonous serpents and drought, the people "began to repent of their iniquities and cry unto the Lord. And it came to pass that when they had humbled themselves sufficiently before the Lord he did send rain upon the face of the earth; and the people began to revive again" (vv 34–35).

Episode 3 — The Days of Com$_2$

Peace and prosperity reigned in the land for another generation before Heth's grandson, Riplakish, came to power. Unfortunately, he introduced polygamy, whoredoms, and high taxes, and built prisons to house those who would not pay taxes, putting to death those who would not labor. The people rebelled against his policies and killed him. His son Morianton restored a measure of peace again among the people for several generations until the reign of Com$_2$.

Sequence to Destruction

PROPHETS: "Many prophets" (Ether 11:1-8).

MESSAGE: "Prophesied of the destruction of that great people except they should repent, and turn unto the Lord, and forsake their murders and wickedness" (vv 1–8)

RESPONSE OF THE PEOPLE: "The prophets were rejected by the people, and they fled unto [Com$_2$] for protection, for the people sought to destroy them" (v 2).

OUTCOME: Com$_2$ protected the prophets, and there was a delay in the judgments of the Lord. Com$_2$ "was blessed in all the remainder of his days" (v 3).

Com$_2$ was a righteous ruler as was his son Shiblom. One of Shiblom's brothers, however, rebelled against Shiblom and caused that "all the prophets who prophesied of the destruction of the people should be put to death" (Ether 11:5). Thus, "there began to be an exceedingly great war in all the land" (v 4). Moroni describes the situation:

> There was great calamity in all the land, for [these prophets] had testified that a great curse should come upon the land, and also upon the people, and that there should be a great destruction among them, such an one as never had been upon the face of the earth, and their bones should become as heaps of earth upon the face of the land except they should repent of their wickedness.
>
> And they hearkened not unto the voice of the Lord, because of their wicked combinations; wherefore, there began to be wars and contentions in all the land, and also many famines and pestilences, inasmuch that there was a great destruction, *such an one as never had been known upon the face of the earth;* and all this came to pass in the days of Shiblom. (Ether 11:6–7; emphasis added)

This great destruction resulted in "heaps" of bodies upon the earth which eventually caused the people to repent, and "inasmuch as they did [repent] the Lord did have mercy on them" (Ether 11:8).

Episode 4 — The Days of Ethem

Three generations later, Ethem ascended to the throne and did "execute judgment in wickedness all his days" (Ether 11:14). Prophets renewed their cry for repentance.

Sequence to Destruction

PROPHETS: "In the days of Ethem there came many prophets, and prophesied again unto the people" (Ether 11:12).

MESSAGE: "They did prophesy that the Lord would utterly destroy them from off the face of the earth except they repented of their iniquities" (v 12)

RESPONSE OF THE PEOPLE: "The people hardened their hearts, and would not hearken unto their words; and the prophets mourned and withdrew from among the people" (v 13).

OUTCOME: The prophets were silenced and the Lord withdrew his spirit from the people. A series of wars began to decimate the people. The Lord provided numerous opportunities for the people to repent and change their ways, but they would not.

Episode 5 — The Days of Coriantor

A series of political power struggles resulted in further war, and the Lord sent prophets to warn the people to repent (Ether 11:20). Moron was taken captive and bore a son named Coriantor who spent his days in captivity also. Coriantor became the father of the prophet Ether (v 23).

Sequence to Destruction

PROPHETS: "In the days of Coriantor there also came many prophets" (Ether 11:20).

MESSAGE: "[These prophets] prophesied of great and marvelous things, and cried repentance unto the people, and [said] that except they should repent the Lord God would execute judgment against them *to their utter destruction;* And that the Lord God would send or bring forth another people to possess the land, by his power, after the manner by which he brought their fathers" (Ether 11:20–21; emphasis added).

RESPONSE OF THE PEOPLE: "And they did reject all the words of the prophets, because of their secret society and wicked abominations" (v 22).

OUTCOME: Civil war began to destroy the inhabitants of the land.

Though Coriantor fathered Ether in captivity, it appears that the prophet-writer of the Jaredite record should rightfully have been the king. But his grandfather, Moron, had been deposed by an unnamed "descendant of the brother of Jared" (Ether 11:17). We do not know who this man was. The record is not clear if this person is Coriantumr's father, or even his grandfather. If it was, it makes the relationship between Ether and Coriantumr more delicate and may account for Coriantumr's rejection of Ether's message to him. He may have seen Ether as trying to bring his kingdom down so that he could assume the mantle of leadership.

Ether cried "from the morning, even until the going down of the sun, exhorting the people to believe in God unto repentance lest they should be destroyed" (Ether 12:3):

> He truly told them of all things, from the beginning of man; and that after the waters [of the flood] had receded from off the face of this land it became a choice land above all other lands, a chosen land of the Lord; wherefore the Lord would have that all men should serve him who dwell upon the face thereof;
>
> And that it was the place of the New Jerusalem, which should come down out of heaven, and the holy sanctuary of the Lord.
>
> Behold, Ether saw the days of Christ, and he spake concerning a New Jerusalem upon this land. (Ether 13:2–4)

But the people rejected Ether's message and "esteemed him as naught, and cast him out; and he hid himself in the cavity of a rock by day, and by night he went forth viewing the things which should come upon the people" (Ether 13:13).

Episode 6 — The Reign of Coriantumr

Many sought to wrest the kingdom from Coriantumr. And although there was constant warfare, the people refused to be humble, even when Ether told Coriantumr how he could save his life and the lives of his family and subjects as well.

Sequence to Destruction

PROPHET: Ether, son of Coriantor.

MESSAGE: "Prophesy unto Coriantumr that, if he would repent, and all his household, the Lord would give unto him his kingdom and spare the people—otherwise they should be destroyed, and all his household save it were himself. And he should only live to see the fulfilling of the prophecies which had been spoken concerning another people receiving the land for their inheritance; and Coriantumr should receive a burial by them; and every soul should be destroyed save it were Coriantumr" (Ether 13:20–21).

RESPONSE OF CORIANTUMR: "Coriantumr repented not, neither his household, neither the people; and the wars ceased not; and they sought to kill Ether, but he fled from before them and hid again in the cavity of the rock" (13:22).

OUTCOME: The destruction of the Jaredite civilization—Coriantumr and Ether the only survivors.

Ether's Prophecy

Ether's prophecy becomes a remarkable example of how prophets are able to see the end from the beginning and give inspired and detailed utterances long before such particulars could be known rationally. The extent of this prophecy by Ether becomes evident as we follow Coriantumr to the end of his reign and view how improbable Ether's prediction was at the time he confronted the king.

To illustrate how implausible Ether's prophecy must have seemed to Coriantumr, the record shows that he should have died several times from wounds and loss of blood, if not infection. But Ether had told him that he alone of all of his subjects would survive and be buried by another people who would inhabit the land (Ether 13:20–21; see also Omni 1:14–22).

The magnitude of Ether's prediction deepened as Coriantumr confronted his antagonist, Shiz. After an especially fierce battle, Moroni wrote:

> When Coriantumr had recovered of his wounds, he began to remember the words which Ether had spoken unto him.
>
> He saw that there had been slain by the sword already nearly two millions of his people, and he began to sorrow in his heart; yea, there had been slain two millions of mighty men, and also their wives and their children.
>
> He began to repent of the evil which he had done; he began to remember the words which had been spoken by the mouth of all the prophets, and he saw them that they were fulfilled thus far, every whit; and his soul mourned and refused to be comforted. (Ether 15:1–3)

Battle Casualties

Millions of people died before Coriantumr admitted that Ether had spoken the truth to him, but by then it was too late. To provide some perspective of the magnitude of the slaughter among Coriantumr's people, we note that at the time Ether approached him with a solution to save people, Coriantumr presided over a kingdom numbering millions of inhabitants. The record says that "there had been slain two millions of mighty men, and also their wives and their children" (Ether 15:2). If even half of these men were married and the average family size included a wife and only two to three children, there would have been six to eight million people in his kingdom. From the American Revolutionary War through the Vietnam conflict (including the Civil War)—wars that introduced weapons of mass destruction—"only" 652,769 Americans died on the battlefield[2] compared to the millions killed in these final Jaredite struggles where the people died in hand-to-hand combat.

The Fulfillment of Ether's Prophecy

The magnitude of Ether's prophecy deepens. At the time he approached Coriantumr and delivered his inspired ultimatum, Cori-

---

[2] When other war-related deaths are included—sickness and infections from wounds—a total of 1,178,066 deaths are attributable to all wars that the United States has fought as a nation (see *The World Almanac* 698).

antumr could have reasonably scoffed at Ether's prediction because of the vast numbers of inhabitants comprising his kingdom. To believe that all of his subjects could be killed before he was—given the fact that he apparently *led* his troops into battle and would be one of the first to engage the enemy—would no doubt seem preposterous. Surely Ether's prophecy could not be fulfilled. For example, the record states: "Shared . . . also gave battle unto Coriantumr; and he did bring him into captivity" (Ether 13:23); yet Coriantumr was not killed. Coriantumr's sons retook the kingdom by beating Shared and restoring the kingdom to their father. He and Shared later fought again, and before Coriantumr finally killed Shared, "Shared wounded Coriantumr in his thigh, that he did not go to battle again for the space of two years" (v 31).

On another occasion Coriantumr fought against Lib, who wounded him. When he recovered from that wound, he killed Lib. However, Lib's brother Shiz swore that he would avenge his brother's blood, and "pursued after Coriantumr, and he did overthrow many cities, and he did slay both women and children, and he did burn the cities. And there went up a fear of Shiz throughout all the land" (Ether 14:12, 17–18). He was so barbaric that many people fled to his camp, thinking that he surely would conquer Coriantumr—for Shiz had "sworn to avenge himself upon Coriantumr of the blood of [Lib]," determined that Ether's prophecy that Coriantumr would not fall by the sword would never be fulfilled. "Shiz smote upon Coriantumr that he gave him many deep wounds; and Coriantumr, having lost much blood, fainted, and was carried away [by his people] as though he were dead" (Ether 14:30). Shiz must have thought he had killed Coriantumr at that time, but Coriantumr recovered to fight another day.

The ensuing battles became so fierce that Coriantumr offered to give up the kingdom if they would only spare his people (Ether 15:4-5, 7). But Shiz's condition that Coriantumr "give himself up, that [Shiz] might slay him with his own sword," was not acceptable, and more battles ensued (Ether 15:5, 7).

The Final Battle

As Coriantumr saw his people being decimated, he again offered Shiz the kingdom if he would simply cease fighting, but Shiz would not relent. They fought again "and when the night came they had all fallen by the sword save it were fifty and two of the people of Coriantumr, and sixty and nine of the people of Shiz" (Ether 15:23). The next day's battle reduced those numbers to 27 and 32 (v 25), and the last battle left only Shiz and Coriantumr facing each other.

> When they had all fallen by the sword, save it were Coriantumr and Shiz, behold Shiz had fainted with the loss of blood.
> And it came to pass that when Coriantumr had leaned upon his sword, that he rested a little, he smote off the head of Shiz.
> And it came to pass that after he had smitten off the head of Shiz, that Shiz raised upon his hands and fell; and after that he had struggled for breath, he died.
> And it came to pass that Coriantumr fell to the earth, and became as if he had no life. (Ether 15:29–33)

Ether "went forth, and beheld that the words of the Lord had all been fulfilled" (Ether 15:33). Now his remarkable prophecy, uttered in detail many years earlier, was almost complete. "Coriantumr was discovered by the people of Zarahemla; and he dwelt with them for the space of nine moons" before he died (Omni 1:21).

The Jaredites had had many opportunities to turn their civilization around and avoid the judgments that eventually destroyed them. From the beginning they had been warned that "this is a land which is choice above all other lands; wherefore he that doth possess it shall serve God or shall be swept off; for it is the everlasting decree of God. And it is not until the fulness of iniquity among the children of the land, that they are swept off" (Ether 2:10). Many prophets had warned that their doom would come when they refused to repent and "serve the God of the land, who is Jesus Christ" (v 12). Thus a great people destroyed themselves because they refused to follow the counsel of the Lord's prophets.

A Message for our Day

Moroni saw our day in vision when his people, much like Ether's, were gone (see Mormon 8:34–35). He felt impressed to point out parallels between his own people, the Jaredites, and us latter-day inhabitants of the promised land. He pleaded for us to "repent, and not continue in your iniquities until the fulness come, that ye may not bring down the fulness of the wrath of God upon you as the *inhabi-*

tants of the land have hitherto done" (Ether 2:11; emphasis added). Will we follow the counsel of God's prophets any better than the former inhabitants did? If we are not wiser than they were, we will suffer their same fate.

We must heed the prophets of our day. The Lord has organized his Church and kingdom on the earth with a First Presidency and a Quorum of Twelve Apostles, each member sustained as a prophet, seer, and revelator. Every six months we have the opportunity to listen to their counsel and warnings on how we should improve our lives so we can avoid the tragedies that destroyed this land's former inhabitants.

Conclusion

The principle of following God's prophets has always been a test for the children of God. It continues to be the principle that will determine whether or not Zion will be established on the earth in the latter-days. Zion can be built up only as pure-in-heart individuals accept counsel and direction from living prophets. In a day of relative ease and prosperity, that is not an easy challenge. The Prophet Joseph Smith acknowledged that we wrestle with this principle:

> There are those who profess to be Saints who are too apt to murmur and find fault, when any advice is given, which comes in opposition to their feelings, even when they, themselves, ask for counsel; much more so when counsel is given unasked for, which does not agree with their notion of things; but brethren, we hope for better things from the most of you; we trust that you desire counsel, from time to time, and that you will cheerfully conform to it, whenever you receive it from a proper source. (*History of the Church* 4:45)

Our destiny in this dispensation, as it was for the Nephites and Jaredites, will be determined by our willingness to heed the counsel of the living prophets. Wilford Woodruff warned the Latter-day Saints of going against prophetic counsel:

> We, as a people, should not treat lightly this counsel, for I will tell you in the name of the Lord—and I have watched it from the time I became a member of this Church—there is no man who undertakes to run counter to the counsel of the legally authorized leader of this people that ever prospers, and no such man ever will prosper. . . . You will find that all persons who take a stand against this counsel will never prosper. . . . When counsel comes we should not treat

it lightly, no matter to what subject it pertains, for if we do it will work evil unto us. (JD 14:33; emphasis added)

Only when people are willing to follow God's prophets can Zion be established. They must be pure in heart and willing and anxious to receive and implement inspired counsel, and thereby carry out the will of God.

BIBLIOGRAPHY

History of the Church. 7 vols. Salt Lake City: Deseret Book, 1962.

Journal of Discourses. 26 vols. 1854-86.

The World Almanac and Book of Facts. Ed. Mark S. Hoffman. New York: Pharos Books, 1993.

The "Author" and the "Finisher" of the Book of Mormon

5

John M. Butler

Joseph Smith, the Mormon Prophet, is a name that has been "had for good and evil among all nations, kindreds, and tongues," as foretold by the angel Moroni in 1823 (JS-H 1:33). With more than 20,000 books and pamphlets referring to the Prophet Joseph Smith in the library of the Church (Benson, *Teachings* 103), Moroni's prophecy has undeniably come to pass. Many people outside The Church of Jesus Christ of Latter-day Saints view Joseph Smith as a charlatan, a lunatic, a fanatic, or at very best a mystic. To those who have read the Book of Mormon and have a testimony of it, Joseph Smith is a prophet, seer, revelator, and translator (see D&C 21:1). I approach the Prophet Joseph Smith as a believer; I am one who has benefited from the positive impact he has had upon the world.

Joseph Smith has been compared to many prophets and leaders, and only One surpassed him. Elder Francis M. Gibbons, in a recent general conference address, reiterated John Taylor's famous statement found in D&C 135:3 that Joseph Smith did more than anyone else except the Savior Jesus Christ "for the salvation of men in this world" (32–33). Parley P. Pratt equated Joseph with John the Baptist as an Elias (80–82). And I would like to draw parallels between the lives of Joseph Smith and the prophet Mormon.

In the Church we speak of Jesus Christ as the author and finisher of our faith (Moroni 6:4; Heb 12:2). This paper examines and compares Mormon as an "author" and Joseph Smith as a "finisher" of the

John M. Butler is a PhD candidate at the University of Virginia.

Book of Mormon. Perhaps no other prophet personifies the preparation and achievements of Joseph Smith better than the prophet Mormon. He was a type for the Prophet Joseph—foreshadowing Joseph's life and important mission.

We first meet Mormon as a young boy of ten as he is visited by the prophet Ammaron, who perceives that Mormon is a "sober child" and "quick to observe" (Mormon 1:2). An alert and reverent child must have been as unusual in those days as it is in ours. Lucy Mack Smith, Joseph Smith's mother, records that Joseph was "a remarkably quiet, well-disposed child" (67). From his own history, we see that Joseph is quick to observe the religious excitement around him and takes an active role in calling upon God for direction. Thus, both these men who became prophets were alert, reverent, and attentive to the nudgings of the Lord as boys. The Lord used them because they were spiritually awake and had learned in their youths to keep the commandments of God (see Alma 37:35).

Both Mormon and Joseph Smith had noble heritages with a common lineage. Mormon was "a pure descendant of Lehi" (3 Nephi 5:20) through Nephi (Mormon 1:5)—and thus from Joseph of Egypt (1 Nephi 5:14; 2 Nephi 3:4). He also notes that he was named after his father (Mormon 1:5). From 2 Nephi 3:15, we learn that Joseph Smith was also a descendant of Joseph of Egypt and named "after the name of his father." In other words, Mormon is really Mormon, Jr., in the same way that Joseph Smith is Joseph Smith, Jr.

Both prophets were seen in vision by their ancestors. No doubt Nephi saw his future descendant, Mormon, when he recorded the vision of the final destruction of the Nephite nation in 1 Nephi 12:14–19. Joseph of Egypt saw the future and prophesied of his posterity (2 Nephi 3:5). He also recorded the name of a major role player, stating, "And his name shall be called after me; and it shall be after the name of his father" (2 Nephi 3:15). As direct descendants of Joseph of Egypt, Mormon and Joseph Smith should naturally be major contributors to the "stick of Joseph" (Ezek 37:19). Moroni, the author, and Joseph Smith, the finisher, were bringing forth to the world their family records—the Book of Mormon, the record of the tribe of Joseph.

Next, in Mormon's introduction of himself, we learn that he "was carried by [his] father into the land southward" when he was 11 years old (Mormon 1:6). Here again Joseph Smith's life follows Mormon's motif. Joseph went south with his father from Vermont to New York in his "tenth year or thereabouts" (JS-H 1:3).

Not long after moving to Zarahemla, Mormon saw that "there were no gifts from the Lord [among the people], and the Holy Ghost did not come upon any, because of their wickedness and unbelief" (Mormon 1:14). Being of "a sober mind," he called upon God when he was 15 years of age and "was visited of the Lord, and tasted and knew of the goodness of Jesus" (v 15). Mormon experienced a personal visit from the Lord, like Samuel at Shiloh (see 1 Sam 3). Joseph Smith states that he was visited of the Lord in his fifteenth year (JS-H 1:7). He, too, "tasted and knew of the goodness of Jesus." He saw and spoke with God the Father and God the Son (vv 13–20). Joseph had gone to the Lord in prayer seeking direction regarding his spiritual life (see vv 10–14), and his result was the same as Mormon's. They were both visited by the Lord in their teenage years. Was it by accident that Joseph Smith and Mormon had their "First Visions" at the same age? Perhaps, for Joseph, it was preparation to becoming literally a Mormon prophet, or in other words, a prophet like Mormon.

Both men were instructed by older prophets as to their role in the Church and kingdom of God. The prophet Ammaron visited Mormon to prepare him for his life's work and mission (Mormon 1:2–4). And while Joseph was yet in his youth, he was visited by the angel-prophet Moroni, who taught him of his life's work and future mission (JS-H 1:27–54). Both received this message from a prophet who had hidden up records in the ground for their future use.

While we know only that Mormon was ministered unto by the Three Nephites (Mormon 8:10–11), Joseph was tutored by numerous heavenly messengers. H. Donl Peterson has listed 59 such personages who appeared to the Prophet Joseph or were seen by him in vision (184–86). In fact, President John Taylor stated, "When Joseph Smith was raised up as a Prophet of God, Mormon, Moroni, Nephi and others . . . came to him and communicated to him certain principles pertaining to the Gospel of the Son of God" (*Journal of Discourses* 17:374; hereafter *JD*). And he later said that Joseph "seemed to be as familiar with these people as we are with one another" (*JD* 21:94). Visits by the authors of the words he translated prepared Joseph to bring forth the Book of Mormon. In compiling the plates which bore his name, Mormon may have likewise been visited by the authors of the words he abridged.

Both Mormon and Joseph were men of large stature (Mormon 2:1 and Cannon 19). Having physical strength was possibly a prerequisite to prevent the records they protected from falling into the hands of the adversary's agents (see Mormon 6:6). And although they were both large and physically fit as youths, neither Mormon nor Joseph received the plates appointed them until they were spiritually mature enough to perform the labors required by them. Several years of testing and training went by after Ammaron and Moroni revealed to their respective charges the missions they were to fulfill regarding the record of the Nephites.

Their 24th year was an important one in the lives of both these prophets. Mormon was told to record his observations of Nephite society on the plates when he was 24 (Mormon 1:3–4). Joseph translated those words when he was in his 24th year (see JS-H 1:66–67) and published them to the world in March of 1830, shortly after his 24th birthday.

The adversary constantly struggled against both these men of Christ. Both gathered their people into one body trying to escape persecution. Mormon fled to the Hill Cumorah area before the hordes of Lamanites and assembled the Nephites for the final battles. Joseph, after suffering from his neighbors in New York, the apostates in Kirtland, and the mobs in Missouri and Illinois, gathered the Saints at Nauvoo seeking refuge from the hostile world. An "Extermination Order" faced them on every front, yet they never wavered in their faith. In the end, they both sealed their testimonies with their blood as they were martyred by enemies of Christ (Mormon 8:3; D&C 135:1; 136:39). They "lived great, and [they] died great in the eyes of God and [their] people" (Moroni 5:11; 8:3; D&C 135:3).

Both men had charisma which made them natural leaders. Mormon served as the chief captain of the Nephite armies almost all of his adult life. While speaking of Mormon's leadership qualities, Sterling W. Sill wrote the following:

> Mormon impresses his greatness upon us in many ways. He was a greater general than Washington. Washington led a little Revolutionary army for just a few months, and the total American dead was 4,435. The total American dead in World War I was 116,563. The total American dead in World War II was 407,828. Mormon lost 230,000 in one single encounter. . . . Mormon led this great national army for 58 years, . . . and he was able to offer them victory at

any moment, providing only they would obey God, which they continually declined to do. (253)

With the organization of the Nauvoo Legion in 1841, Joseph Smith consented to serve as lieutenant general, in other words, the chief captain of his army. Protection of his people by military service was foremost on his mind when Joseph accepted that position. In his book, *Life of Joseph Smith the Prophet*, George Q. Cannon wrote, "His conduct in this respect is a reminder that, notwithstanding his divine appointment, he held himself amenable to every law and every regulation of his country" (365). Joseph and Mormon were always ready to help their people in time of need. They led from the front, and served and suffered with their soldiers and Saints in the trenches of war and before the mistreatment of mobs.

Both gave poignant farewell addresses. Over his slain people at Cumorah, Mormon cried, "O ye fair ones, how could ye have departed from the ways of the Lord! O ye fair ones, how could ye have rejected that Jesus, who stood with open arms to receive you!" (Mormon 6:17). The Prophet Joseph's farewell to the Nauvoo Legion was a little more optimistic but no less heart-rending. "God has tried you. You are a good people; therefore I love you with all my heart. Greater love hath no man than that he should lay down his life for his friends. You have stood by me in the hour of trouble, and I am willing to sacrifice my life for your preservation" (Cannon 498). Both spoke to their armies with feelings of melancholy: Mormon for what had just happened—Joseph for what was about to happen.

In spite of all the evil that raged about them, both men maintained charity and forgiveness towards those who had harmed them. Mormon spent his entire life with "a continual scene of wickedness and abominations" before him and yet never lost charity, unlike so many of those around him (Mormon 2:18; Moroni 9:5). Joseph likewise endured much, yet never lost his love for others. Once when asked why he had so many followers, Joseph replied, "It is because I possess the principle of love. All that I offer the world is a good heart and a good hand" (Cannon 528). Mormon and Joseph possessed "the pure love of Christ" and showed that charity can endure forever (see Moroni 7:47; see also *Teachings of the Prophet Joseph Smith* 9; hereafter *TPJS*).

From the time that they were called to their ministries, both prophets never ceased to labor. From age 16 to his death sometime after age 74, Mormon struggled to aid his people militarily and spiritually. Joseph Smith similarly was in the service of God and his people from his teenage years to his death at age 38. They "labor[ed] diligently," knowing that "should [they] cease to labor, [they] should be brought under condemnation" (Moroni 9:6; see also *TPJS* 258).

Lifelong service is not always the norm for the Lord's leaders. David was called of God in his youth but afterwards lost favor with the Lord through transgression. On the other hand, the Apostle Paul and Alma the Younger championed the gospel cause in their later lives but spent their early years in opposition to the Church. Mormon and Joseph Smith never wavered in their faith or righteousness. "Mormon was faithful in the beginning of his life; he was faithful in the middle of his life; he was faithful in the end of his life" (Sill 250). The same can be said of the Prophet Joseph Smith: "He lived great, and he died great" (D&C 135:3).

The diligence of Mormon and Joseph Smith seems to have been rewarded with their having their callings and elections made sure while yet in the flesh. Mormon mentions in Mormon 2:19, "Nevertheless, I know that I shall be lifted up at the last day." Joseph's promise came in stronger words when the Lord said "I seal upon you your exaltation, and prepare a throne for you in the kingdom of my Father" (D&C 132:49). They had followed the Lord's commands, and they sealed their missions and their testimonies of the Savior with their blood and continue their work on the other side of the veil (138:57).

Mormon saw the end of a great civilization whereas Joseph Smith's ministry was at the beginning of a new civilization, The Church of Jesus Christ of Latter-day Saints, which shall stand in the promised land through the Millennium. Mormon saw the Dark Ages begin; Joseph Smith saw them end.

It is not by accident that Mormon, the author, and Joseph Smith, the finisher of the Book of Mormon, have so many parallels in their lives. Being among the noble and great ones before the foundation of this earth, they were chosen before they were born to perform the work they did for God (see Abr 3:22–23; D&C 138:38, 53; *JD* 7:290). Both their lives centered around preparing and bringing forth the stick of Joseph so the world might know that "Jesus is the Christ" and "get nearer to God by abiding by its precepts" (see Book of Mormon Title Page and Introduction). Mormon and Joseph Smith sacrificed all that they had, even their own lives, in sustaining and defending the kingdom of God.

We are to be judged by how we respond to the message authored by Mormon and finished by Joseph. Mormon wrote, "Ye must all stand before the judgment-seat of Christ . . . to be judged" (Mormon 3:20). Mormon and Joseph will undoubtedly also meet us before the bar of God that we may know that they have been "commanded of [Christ] to write these things" (see 2 Nephi 33:11; see also Jacob 6:13; Ether 12:38). Brigham Young told the Saints in his day, "Joseph Smith holds the keys of this last dispensation, and is now engaged behind the vail [*sic*] in the great work of the last days. . . . [N]o man or woman in this dispensation will ever enter into the celestial kingdom of God without the consent of Joseph Smith" (*JD* 7:289). In our day, President Ezra Taft Benson has warned us that we are on trial to see what we will do with the Book of Mormon (see Benson, *A Witness* 13). We will answer for our response to this second witness of Jesus Christ. Should not we do more to make the Book of Mormon a larger part of our lives?

No other latter-day prophet matches Mormon as well as the Prophet Joseph. Perhaps he possessed many of Mormon's attributes so that he could be more in tune with the compiler of the Book of Mormon as he translated it. Or, as James E. Talmage put it in his book *The Articles of Faith*, "The translator must have the spirit of the prophet if he would render in another tongue the prophet's words" (237). The attributes, character, and even many of the activities of Mormon can be considered a type which foreshadowed the future translator. In this manner, the author and the finisher of the Book of Mormon have more in common than just the book which they helped bring forth.

Today we may draw nearer to Christ—"the author and the finisher of [our] faith" (Moroni 6:4)—because of the efforts of Mormon and Joseph Smith—the "author" and the "finisher" of the Book of Mormon.

BIBLIOGRAPHY

Benson, Ezra Taft. *A Witness and a Warning*. Salt Lake City: Deseret Book, 1988.

————. *The Teachings of Ezra Taft Benson*. Salt Lake City: Bookcraft, 1988.

Cannon, George Q. *Life of Joseph Smith the Prophet*. Salt Lake City: Deseret Book, 1964.

Gibbons, Francis M. "The Savior and Joseph Smith—Alike Yet Unlike." *Ensign* (May 1991) 21:32–33; also in *Conference Report* (Apr 1991) 39-42..

Journal of Discourses. 26 vols. 1854–86.

Peterson, H. Donl. "Personages Who Appeared to the Prophet Joseph Smith." *Joseph Smith: The Prophet, The Man*. Eds. Susan Easton Black and Charles D. Tate, Jr. Provo, UT: Religious Studies Center, Brigham Young Univ, 1993. 184–86.

Pratt, Parley P. *Key to the Science of Theology*. Salt Lake City: Deseret Book, 1973.

Sill, Sterling W. "Mormon." *The Upward Reach*. Salt Lake City: Bookcraft, 1962. 249–54.

Smith, Lucy Mack. *History of Joseph Smith by His Mother*. Salt Lake City: Bookcraft, 1979.

Talmage, James E. *The Articles of Faith*. Salt Lake City: Deseret Book, 1977.

Teachings of the Prophet Joseph Smith. Comp. Joseph Fielding Smith. Salt Lake City: Deseret Book, 1976.

The Plates of Ether and the Covenant of the Book of Mormon

6

Lee L. Donaldson

*I*f the books of the Book of Mormon were placed in chronological order, the first book would be the book of Ether, the story of the brother of Jared at the tower of Babel. However, this story is placed after the reader has encountered the rise and fall of the Nephite nation. Why is the book of Ether positioned exactly where it is?

Imbedded in that question is the faith and understanding that there is always a purpose in the Lord's patterns and so there must be a divine purpose in concluding with the plates of Ether. The Lord told the Elders of this last dispensation, "I will give unto you a pattern in all things, that ye may not be deceived" (D&C 52:14). Elder Marvin J. Ashton noted that the "'pattern in all things' is one of the Lord's greatest gifts and promises." He continued, "There are patterns for all worthy things if we will search for them. 'And behold, it must be done according to the pattern which I have given unto you' (D&C 94:2). There is no other proven way" (21).

To understand the pattern of the structure in the Book of Mormon, we must first appreciate the essence of the book. The Lord, in chastising the elders of this dispensation, called the Book of Mormon a covenant: "And they shall remain under this condemnation until they repent and remember the new covenant, even the Book of Mormon" (D&C 84:57). How is the Book of Mormon a covenant, and what is there in this sacred volume that makes it a covenant? Fundamentally, a scriptural covenant is a contractual promise between God and man. President Joseph Fielding Smith said, "A

Lee L. Donaldson is a coordinator in the Church Educational System, Chicago, Illinois.

covenant is a contract and an agreement between at least two parties. In the case of gospel covenants, the parties are the Lord in heaven and men on earth. Men agree to keep the commandments and the Lord promises to reward them accordingly" (26). Anciently, these covenants that man made with God were entered into with a specific formula which bound both parties. The biblical scholar George Mendenhall identified six common steps in ancient covenants and treaties (*Interpreter's Dictionary* 1:714). These elements are as follows: (1) the preamble, (2) historical prologue, (3) stipulations, (4) blessings and curses, (5) witnesses, and (6) deposit and public reading of the covenant.

Each element of the covenant making process is vital. For instance, the preamble demonstrates the authority of the people making the covenant. The historical prologue to the covenant forms the foundation for the history of a covenant people. The stipulations lay out the requirements of the covenant for both parties. The blessings and curses graphically illustrate the consequences of keeping or breaking the pact. The witnesses serve to show God's people that all his actions were done without secret covenants. Finally, the deposit and public reading remind God's people of their promises and illustrate that his covenants stretch beyond an isolated time and people.

The overarching Book of Mormon covenant to obey Jesus Christ as the God of the land fits this very old pattern. A close look at the second chapter of Ether illustrates each of the six elements (see table on page 73). First, the preamble, like all ancient preambles, contains the names of both parties to the covenant. This preamble also mentions the physical location where the covenant is established. The tying together of time and place is important to lift the covenant beyond a metaphysical notion to a bond between mortals and a living God. Such a covenant affects people's lives in time and space.

The plates of Ether open with a specific historical event, the tower of Babel. The Jaredites, led by the brother of Jared, fled this ancient type of Babylon and came "down into the valley of Nimrod [and] the Lord came down and talked with the brother of Jared; and he was in a cloud" (Ether 2:4). The record carefully mentions both time and place. Furthermore, this covenant was formally created between the two authority figures: the king of this land, Jesus Christ, and the representative of the covenant people, the brother of Jared.

Anciently, the preamble also contained a token of the superior authority of the one setting the terms of the covenant. The same is true with the Book of Mormon covenant to serve the God of the land, as found in the book of Ether. Moroni noted that the Lord came down in a cloud. The cloud was a divine token of the power and glory of the king of heaven. For instance, this was the same token of authority that the Lord used in creating the preamble to the Sinai covenant with Moses (Ex 19:9). The cloud also led the covenant people through the wilderness (13:21) and was a heavenly sign of the Lord's authority in the Savior's transfiguration (Matt 17:5). Additionally, the Doctrine and Covenants equates the clouds of heaven with "the glory of the Lord" (D&C 84:5).

Second, the historical prologue of a covenant focuses the people's minds and hearts as they remember their history. Ancient Israel, for instance, always remembered the Exodus and the Sinai covenant as they recited their history. The brother of Jared's covenant to serve the God of the land became the focal point of Jaredite historiography. In fact, the whole Jaredite history was an account of how well the people kept their covenant to serve Jesus Christ, the God of the land. The covenant was put in force at the beginning of the Jaredite record (Ether 2:8), and throughout Jaredite history prophets warned the people to remember the covenant. For instance, Moroni notes that "the Lord did pour out his blessings upon this land" after Omer and Emer cast out the secret combinations and returned to serving Jesus Christ (9:13–21). Finally, Moroni concludes this tragic record with Coriantumr remembering "the words [concerning the covenant] which had been spoken by the mouth of all the prophets, and he saw them that they were fulfilled thus far, every whit" (15:3).

Third, the Lord clearly states the stipulations of this covenant. The record notes, "whoso should possess this land of promise, from that time henceforth and forever, should serve him, the true and only God" (Ether 2:8). The text clearly states that the true and only God of this land "is Jesus Christ" (v 12). This service to the Savior is to be full and complete. The Lord does not allow divided loyalties from his people in the promised land. Moroni's final assessment of the Jaredites revolves around their refusal to fulfill the stipulations of the covenant. He wrote, "For behold, they rejected all the words of Ether; for he truly told them of all things, from the beginning of man; and that after the waters had receded from off the face of this land it became a choice land above all other lands, a chosen land of the Lord; wherefore the Lord would have that all men should serve him who dwell upon the face thereof" (Ether 13:2).

The fourth covenantal element suggested by Mendenhall, the blessings and curses, is also laid out in the covenant the Lord established with the Jaredites. Obedience to this covenant insures that the inhabitants of this land will "be free from bondage, and from captivity, and from all other nations under heaven" (Ether 2:12). Disobedience brings down the judgments of God so that "they should be swept off" the face of the land (v 8). Total destruction occurs when the people are "ripened in iniquity" (v 9).

Fifth, this covenant is made with witnesses. The prophet Ether personally stood as an eyewitness to the terrible fulfillment of the curses of the covenant and "beheld that the words of the Lord had all been fulfilled; and he finished his record" (Ether 15:33). In fact, we also become witnesses to this covenant as we read the Book of Mormon. Moroni notes as he records the account of the covenant, "we can behold the decrees of God concerning this land" (2:9).

Lastly, this covenant is deposited and read publicly for every nation that comes to the promised land. Prophets sent to the Jaredites either read or quoted the covenant to them frequently (Ether 7:23; 9:28; 11:1, 12, 20). They reminded the Jaredites to serve the Lord or "the Lord God would send or bring forth another people to possess the land, by his power, after the manner by which he brought their fathers" (11:21). Furthermore, Moroni promises that each nation possessing the promised land will have access to the words of the covenant: "Whatsoever nation shall possess it shall be free from bondage, and from captivity, and from all other nations under heaven, if they will but serve the God of the land, who is Jesus Christ, who hath been manifested by the things which we have written" (2:12). The Jaredite covenant was also read during the reign of king Mosiah (Mosiah 28:17–19). The final recorded act of Ether's life was to deposit the record "in a manner that the people of Limhi did find them" (Ether 15:33).

A broader look at the Book of Mormon reveals that this same covenant to serve Jesus Christ as the God of this land is also part of the plates of Nephi and the plates of Mormon. This covenant has the same elements as the Jaredite covenant. Below, in Figure 1, the elements of the Book of Mormon covenant are listed with the parallels from the plates of Nephi, Mormon, and Ether.

Figure 1

Elements	Plates of Nephi	Plates of Mormon	Plates of Ether
Preamble	2 Ne 1:5–6	Alma 36:1	2:7
Historical Prologue	2 Ne 1:9	Alma 36:2	2:12
Stipulations	2 Ne 1:7	Alma 36:1	2:8–10
Blessings and Curses	2 Ne 1:7	Alma 36:1, 30	2:8–10
Witness	2 Ne 1:9	Alma 36:5	2:9
Deposit of the Covenant	2 Ne 1:9–12	Alma 37:1–2	2:12

An interesting motif in this covenant is a right to inherit a promised land. Why is the promised land emphasized? We must realize that this promised land motif extends beyond the American continent. The promised land is a type for the promised reward of the faithful. The only way an individual can obtain the celestial land of promise is to enter into a covenant to serve the true God of this earth—Jesus Christ. This quest for the celestial land of promise is the focus of the covenant of the Book of Mormon. Why is this same covenant given in all three sets of plates? Is it significant that the Lord selected three different sets of plates to establish his covenant? Finally, what sets the Jaredite record apart, that it was placed at the end of the Book of Mormon?

First, having a set of three in making covenants is an ancient pattern. For instance, the baptismal covenant is made "in the name of the Father, and of the Son, and of the Holy Ghost" (3 Nephi 11:25). Abraham divided three animals as he entered into the Abrahamic covenant (Gen 15:9). Each of these animals needed to be three years old. Three times Peter was shown the same vision of the unclean animals which represented that the gospel covenants were to be taken to the gentiles (Acts 10:16).

The ancient covenantal pattern of repeating or having something done three times or three ways is also fulfilled in multiple ways in the Book of Mormon. Moroni, in the middle of his abridgment of the Jaredite record, prophesies that "in the mouth of three witnesses shall these things be established; and the testimony of three . . . shall stand against the world at the last day" (Ether 5:4). This "new covenant, even the Book of Mormon" (D&C 84:57) has been established like other covenants by having three witnesses.

Traditionally, we think of the three witnesses to the Book of Mormon as Oliver Cowdery, Martin Harris, and David Whitmer. Certainly, they do stand as latter-day witnesses to the divine origin of the Book of Mormon. However, there are additional sets of three witnesses to this sacred record. Moroni declared that the "Father, and the Son, and the Holy Ghost bear record" (Ether 5:4). Also, three branches of the House of Israel, the Jews, the Nephites, and the lost tribes, each kept a record, and each branch will eventually receive the others' records (2 Nephi 29:12–14). These three branches of the House of Israel will also become a set of three witnesses in the latter-days.

However, another set of three witnesses, the three sets of plates that make up the Book of Mormon, is in the forefront in establishing the Book of Mormon. The plates of Nephi, the plates of Mormon, and those of Ether stand as vital components in establishing the Book of Mormon covenant. Each set of plates contains each of the six elements of the ancient covenant and also serves to illustrate the ramifications of the covenant to a different nation.

The first set, the plates of Nephi, contains the story of a family and their struggles to keep their covenants. The second set, the plates of Mormon, records the Nephite nation's struggles to keep those same covenants. The third set, the plates of Ether, merges the plates of Nephi and Mormon. It begins, like the plates of Nephi, with the story of a family and develops, like the plates of Mormon, into the story of a nation.

Figure 2

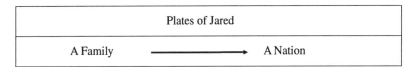

From this we can begin to understand why the plates of Ether were placed after the plates of Nephi and Mormon. They serve as the final element of the covenant process and recapitulate the Book of Mormon covenant. The recapitulation or covenant renewal element, consistent with the ancient pattern, contains all the parts of the covenant. Therefore, it was important for Moroni to place the book of Ether at the end of the Book of Mormon record to place our dispensation under covenant. The Ether summary to the Nephite record underscores the constant theme that a covenant family and nation must obey the God of this land or be destroyed.

The book of Ether testifies of the same message as the other two sets of plates: keep your covenant to serve the God of this land and be blessed, or break your covenant and be destroyed. This covenant applies to both family and nation. Beyond the covenant, the Jaredite story summarizes the Nephite account in two additional ways: the Jaredite civilization passes through the same tragic cycle of prosperity, pride, and plague as the Nephites, and the Jaredites share a parallel record with their Nephite counterparts.

First, the tragic cycle of prosperity, pride, and plague is a supporting theme to remind the people to keep their covenants. The Lord always sends prophets and plagues before he totally destroys his covenant people. He also withdraws peace from the land. This theme pervades both the Jaredite and Nephite records. God continues striving to reclaim his people by sending prophets and plagues to stir them up in remembrance of the covenant. The Lord never completely destroys the people until they are "ripened in iniquity" (Ether 2:9) and can no longer keep the covenant.

Ether's record, like the records of Nephi and Mormon, graphically paints the same vivid picture of this cycle of God calling back his chosen people. The people alternate between keeping and breaking their covenants to the Lord. The cycle begins with the people being delivered by the hand of the Lord, then they prosper in the land, they grow in pride and wickedness, and they are finally brought down by their own iniquities. Interestingly, this same pattern is repeated six times in the book of Ether before the complete destruction of the Jaredites.

Figure 3: Six Tragic Cycles in the Book of Ether

	Delivered	Prosper	Pride & Iniquity	Brought Down
Cycle 1	1:33–6:12	6:18, 28	7:4–19	7:20–25
Cycle 2	7:26	7:27	8:2–17	9:1, 12
Cycle 3	9:2–3	9:16–20	9:26–29	9:30–34
Cycle 4	9:35	9:35–10:4	10:5–10	10:11–15
Cycle 5	10:15	10:16–29	10:30	11:7
Cycle 6	11:8		11:10–15	11:19–12:3; 13:15–15:31

Second, the Book of Mormon authors paint a similar picture between the Nephites and Jaredites so we can see the effects of the covenant in both civilizations. For instance, the Jaredite record begins, like the Nephite record, with a family being delivered from imminent destruction by the hand of the Lord. Lehi's homeland was about to be captured by the Babylonians, and Jared's fellow citizens were about to be scattered at the tower of Babel. Both Babel and

Babylon share the same Hebrew root word which means *confusion.* Both Lehi and the brother of Jared were saved from this confusion or chaos by divine intervention.

The family of Jared, like the Lehites, received divine instructions on how to construct a vessel to cross the ocean (1 Nephi 17:8; Ether 2:16). Their ships' design came from the Lord and not man. This same divine help protected the two different families as they crossed the ocean. This ocean was described by the same term, many waters, in both texts (1 Nephi 17:5; Ether 6:7). *Many waters* is "an Old Testament expression which often designates the waters of chaos" (*Interpreter's Dictionary* 4:816). The Lord was the only one who could help both families pass through the chaos to the promised land.

They also gathered provisions for the trip in a similar manner, and both groups were told to gather seeds of every kind (1 Nephi 8:1; Ether 1:41). This gathering was followed by a vision concerning Lehi's seed and a blessing on the seed of the Jaredites. The blessings for the seed of these two nations were contingent on keeping covenants. Both parties were then placed under the same covenant to worship God or be swept off the face of the promised land (2 Nephi 1:1–12; Ether 2:8).

The Jaredites and the Lehites also spent a preparatory time in the wilderness (1 Nephi 17:4; Ether 2:13), which was punctuated for both groups by multiple visions (1 Nephi 10–14; Ether 2–3). Finally, both groups were divinely protected as they crossed the ocean (1 Nephi 18:8–23; Ether 6:4–11).

These parallels continued throughout the records of both civilizations. There was a division in both groups. The Nephites broke off from the Lamanites, and the kingdoms of Shule and Cohor also broke off from each other. Additionally, there was the continual rise and fall of wicked governments. Riplakish, like wicked king Noah, had many wives and concubines, laid a grievous tax on his people, built spacious buildings, and eventually suffered a violent death (Ether 10:4–8).

The Jaredites, like their Nephite counterparts, also had prophets come among them to call them to repentance. This repentance was followed by prosperity (Ether 7:23–26). Unfortunately, this prosperity, like the Nephite success, was followed by someone coming with cunning words to gain power (Ether 8:2). This power grabbing divided both nations.

Finally, both groups were destroyed by the same insidious secret oaths and combinations. Moroni points out, "Their oaths and combinations . . . have caused the destruction of this people of whom I am now speaking, and also the destruction of the people of Nephi" (Ether 8:20–21). Thus, both accounts are records of a fallen people (D&C 20:9) and serve as two witnesses to our nation and generation.

The book of Ether is at the end of the Book of Mormon to serve as the third leg in the covenantal triad and testify to Book of Mormon readers that they must serve God or be swept off the face of the land. The record of the Jaredite nation in the 15 chapters of Ether summarizes the tragic theme of the 15 books of the Book of Mormon and is a prophetic reminder that our own survival depends on our ability to make and keep covenants.

In conclusion, the Lord has provided three sets of plates to establish his covenant with our dispensation. These three sets of plates show that God's plan are the same for both the Nephites and the Jaredites. The Book of Mormon is divinely designed to prove "to the world that the holy scriptures are true, and that God does inspire men and call them to his holy work in this age and generation, as well as in generations of old; Thereby showing that he is the same God yesterday, today, and forever" (D&C 20:11–12). The plates of Ether are divinely placed to establish the covenant with latter-day readers and to warn them away from a similar fall.

The Nephite and Jaredite voices come from the dust to call our own dispensation to repentance. President Marion G. Romney declared,

> In America two great civilizations, the Jaredite and the Nephite, were completely annihilated because of their rejection of the laws of righteousness which God revealed unto them. In both cases, the Lord, through His prophets, pointed out their iniquities, warned them, and predicted their destruction if they did not repent. This they did not do. Consequently they were totally destroyed. We today are approaching the close of a similar cycle. We have been warned that we are ripening in iniquity and that we will be destroyed if we do not repent. (14–15)

We become the third Book of Mormon civilization to enter into the covenant to serve Jesus Christ, the God of this land. The Book of Mormon record of the covenant becomes our own record. Our civilization's survival, like that of the Nephite and Jaredite nations, depends on our keeping the covenant to serve Jesus Christ as the God of this land.

The plates of Ether, like the plates of Nephi and Mormon, witness of the great latter-day Book of Mormon covenant of the Eternal God. We may choose to keep our covenants and prosper or break these sacred oaths and be destroyed. This covenant has been established, like ancient covenants, by three separate sets of plates within the Book of Mormon. Moroni promised that these plates would be shown "unto those who shall assist to bring forth this work" (Ether 5:2). Figuratively, we are shown these plates as we ponder the Book of Mormon so that we can "know of a surety that these things are true. And in the mouth of three witnesses shall these things be established; and the testimony of three, and this work, in the which shall be shown forth the power of God and also his word, of which the Father, and the Son, and the Holy Ghost bear record—and all this shall stand as a testimony against the world at the last day" (vv 3–4).

BIBLIOGRAPHY

Ashton, Marvin J. "A Pattern in All Things." *Ensign* (Nov 1990) 20:20–22; also in *Conference Report* (Oct 1990) 23-27.

The Interpreter's Dictionary of the Bible. 5 vols. Nashville, TN: Abingdon Press, 1962.

Romney, Marion G. "The Tragic Cycle." *Ensign* (Nov 1977) 7:14–16; also in *Conference Report* (Oct 1977) 19-23.

Smith, Joseph Fielding. "The Oath and Covenant of the Priesthood." *Improvement Era* (Dec 1970) 73:26–27.

Light in Our Vessels: Faith, Hope, and Charity

7

H. Dean Garrett

God's commandment that the brother of Jared build vessels to cross the oceans to the new land presented many difficult and seemingly insurmountable problems. However, through diligence and obedience, the prophet overcame the arising problems until he was faced with the challenge of providing light for vessels which could have no windows. This problem seemed unsolvable for the brother of Jared and he cried, "O Lord, behold, I have done even as thou hast commanded me; and I have prepared the vessels for my people, and behold there is no light in them. Behold, O Lord, wilt thou suffer that we shall cross this great water in darkness?" (Ether 2:22). The Lord's response to him is very revealing, because it placed the responsibility of providing possible solutions squarely on the brother of Jared: "What will ye that I should do that ye may have light in your vessels?" (v 23).

Like the brother of Jared, each of us faces challenges in life. At times we may plead with the Lord: "Will ye have me go through this life without light to understand why things are the way they are?" His answer to us might be the same question he asked the brother of Jared: "What would ye that I should do to put light into your spiritual vessels?" The brother of Jared provided stones and asked the Lord to touch them with his fingers to produce light for their vessels. We, too, must provide stones that the Lord can touch to give light to our spiritual vessels. The Book of Mormon teaches that the foundation stones for our spiritual growth are faith, hope, and charity. Mormon indicates that without these three qualities, especially charity, we are

H. Dean Garrett is associate professor of Church History and Doctrine at Brigham Young University.

nothing (Moroni 7:44). It is through faith, hope, and charity that we are brought to Christ (Ether 12:28). Having these three characteristics enabled the brother of Jared, not only to solve his problem, but also qualified him to see the finger of the Lord and to have the extraordinary experience of viewing the spiritual body of the Lord as no other person had. If we are to return to God's presence, we, too, like the brother of Jared, must develop the qualities of faith, hope, and charity.

Faith

Faith was the foundation for the spiritual development that led the brother of Jared to success. Through faith he saw the finger of God (Ether 12:21). Because of the faith that the brother of Jared developed "the Lord could not withhold anything from his sight, wherefore he showed him all things, for he could no longer be kept without the veil" (v 21). It was by this same powerful faith that he was able to say to the mountain Zerin, "Remove—and it was removed. And if he had not had faith it would not have moved" (v 30).

To have faith is "not to have a perfect knowledge of things" (Alma 32:21), but rather it is the power by which things which "are hoped for and not seen" (Ether 12:6). True faith is focused in and on God and his Son, Jesus Christ. "Faith in Him is more than mere acknowledgment that He Lives. It is more than professing belief. Faith in Jesus Christ consists of complete reliance on Him. . . . Faith in Him means believing that even though we do not understand all things, He does" (Benson, *Teachings* 66). We, therefore, should look to Him "in every thought," for by so doing we doubt not, neither do we fear (D&C 6:36).

Alma taught that faith comes from a desire for knowledge, a hope that things are true. Cultivation of that desire leads to a confirmation of truth which then turns to faith, which, as Elder Oaks has said, "is developed in a setting where we cannot see what lies ahead" (122). It rests on the experience of the past while it focuses on the hope of the future. As we develop faith, it becomes an assurance that the events that transpire will, in the end, produce the desired results. True faith must be centered in that Being who is unmovable and totally reliable. The Prophet Joseph Smith taught that three things are necessary for an individual to exercise faith that will lead to salvation.

First, the idea that he [God] actually exists. Secondly, a *correct* idea of his character, perfections, and attributes. Thirdly, an actual knowledge that the course of life which he is pursuing is according to his [God's] will. For without an acquaintance with these three important facts, the faith of every rational being must be imperfect and unproductive; but with this understanding, it can become perfect and fruitful abounding in righteousness, unto the praise and glory of God the Father, and the Lord Jesus Christ." (*Lectures on Faith* 3:3–5; hereafter *LF*)

This faith is exemplified in the life of the brother of Jared. Because the brother of Jared knew the characteristics and qualities of God and understood that his life was in accordance with God's will, the Lord showed himself unto him and said: "Because thou knowest these things, ye are redeemed from the fall; therefore, ye are brought back into my presence; therefore, I show myself unto you" (Ether 3:13).

Moroni teaches that God works in the lives of people after they have faith in him (Ether 12:30-31). He testifies that "it was by faith that Christ showed himself unto our fathers, after he had risen from the dead." However, the Lord did not show "himself unto them until *after* they had faith in him; wherefore, it must needs be that some had faith in him, for he showed Himself not unto the world" (v 7; emphasis added). This same qualification of faith also applied to the Savior's disciples. Moroni tells us that only "after they had faith and did speak in [his] name, [Christ] didst show [himself] unto them in great power" (v 31). The brother of Jared also had to show his faith before he could see the Lord. After he showed him his finger, the Lord asked him: "Sawest thou more than this?" He answered: "Nay, Lord, show thyself unto me." The Lord responded: "Believest thou the words which I shall speak?" The brother of Jared answered: "Yea, Lord, I know thou speakest the truth, for thou art a God of truth, and canst not lie" (3:9–12). His faith allowed the veil to be lifted and the brother of Jared to see the spirit body of the Lord.

Faith becomes "the principle of action in all intelligent beings" (*LF* 1:9). It is the power by which things happen. "Christ hath said: If ye will have faith in me ye shall have power to do whatsoever thing is expedient in me" (Moroni 7:33). Moroni taught that it was by faith that the law of Moses was given and that Christ also appeared to the Nephites because of their great faith (Ether 12:1, 7). In addition, "it was the faith of Alma and Amulek that caused the prison to tumble to the earth. Behold, it was the faith of Nephi and Lehi that wrought the change upon the Lamanites, that they were baptized with fire and with the Holy Ghost" (Ether 12:13–14). Miracles transpire because of faith (v 12), and men of old were called to "the holy order of God" (v 10) by faith. Above all, it was by faith that the "more excellent way" (the Atonement) was fulfilled (v 11).

Moreover, modern scripture notes that without faith "no man can please God" (D&C 63:11). The reason for this is that "we are saved by faith in his name; and by faith [we] become the sons [and daughters] of God" (Moroni 7:26). Those who have faith in Christ "will cleave unto every good thing" (v 28). Therefore, Moroni forcefully states: "If ye have not faith in him then ye are not fit to be numbered among the people of his church" (v 39). Faith is the foundation stone for all of our spiritual growth.

Hope

The brother of Jared received through his faith an assurance of his relationship with the Savior. Through his faith-building experiences, he developed a hope in Christ. True faith becomes the foundation for hope. "If a man has faith he must needs have hope; for without faith there cannot be any hope" (Moroni 7:42). Moroni understood this when he stated that those who "believeth in God might with surety hope for a better world, yea, even a place at the right hand of God, which hope cometh of faith, maketh an anchor to the souls of men, which would make them sure and steadfast, always abounding in good works, being led to glorify God" (Ether 12:4). He also realized that faith leads to an understanding of the future in such a way that a personal assurance of possibilities exists for individuals.

The hope spoken of in the Book of Mormon is very personal. It is one thing to believe that we humans can gain exaltation; it is an altogether different thing to believe that you, personally, can achieve exaltation. When we transfer that belief and faith from the general to the personal, then we function by hope. Notice, both Paul and Moroni teach that hope comes of faith and is the anchor of the soul (Heb 6:19; Ether 12:4).

Moreover, hope is centered "through the atonement of Christ and the power of his resurrection, to be raised unto life eternal, and this because of your faith in him according to the promise" (Moroni 7:41).

Once we come to the knowledge that Jesus Christ is our personal Savior and that we are proceeding along the path that leads to exaltation, there comes an assurance—a hope—that we can achieve exaltation. Thus, hope is not "a flimsy, ethereal desire, one without assurance that the desired consummation will be received but a desire coupled with full expectation of receiving the coveted reward" (McConkie 365).

Moroni recognized that this type of hope would become the "anchor to the souls of men which would make them sure and steadfast" (Ether 12:4). This hope does not allow for wavering or hesitation. In fact, once we have an "unshaken faith in him, relying wholly upon the merits of him who is mighty to save," then it is necessary that we "press forward with a steadfastness in Christ, having a perfect brightness of hope" (2 Nephi 31:19–20).

This hope in Christ strengthens us through our trials and tribulations. It is the hope that allows us to be "patient in tribulation" (D&C 54:10). In all that comes into our lives, such brightness of hope allows the growth and development of the soul. This is possible because it is based on goodness and righteousness. It is centered on the source of all goodness. One of the fruits of this type of hope is the desire "to do good continually" (Mosiah 5:2). Elder Neal A. Maxwell has taught, "Since, for instance, despair cometh because of iniquity, then true hope cometh because of righteousness" ("Not Withstanding" 48). Moroni concludes, "If ye have no hope ye must be in despair; and despair cometh because of iniquity" (Moroni 10:22). Because it results from righteousness, hope reinforces the faith that allows us to face the trials and challenges of life. Thus, we are able to press forward with a brightness of hope.

In his own personal life, Moroni relied on his hope in Christ that came from his great faith. He was very concerned that the Gentiles would mock his writings which he viewed as weak. Through his hope, or the assurance of his own relationship with Christ, he accepted the Lord's response that he would make "weak things become strong" unto those who have faith in him; and Moroni was not to worry about the Gentiles (Ether 12:27).

We must have this hope, which Moroni called "a more excellent hope," or we "cannot receive an inheritance in the place which [God] hast prepared" for us (Ether 12:32). This type of hope is the product of a "meek and lowly" heart (Moroni 7:43). Pride is a destroyer of hope, for pride is centered in self and worldly things, things that are temporary and fleeting. To be righteous and full of hope, we must consider ourselves "fools before God, and come down in the depths of humility" (2 Nephi 9:42). This depth of humility allows us to reach out of ourselves to God and his children and to develop love like that that Christ possesses. This Christlike love becomes the motivator of our actions. It comes from the faith and hope that we have in the mission and atonement of Christ. Moroni understood this when he "prayed unto the Lord that he would give unto the Gentiles grace, that they might have charity" (Ether 12:36). Increased faith and hope allows the atonement of Christ to function in our lives, and that develops charity in us.

Charity

Faith and hope lead to the development of charity, the third part of the triad of spiritual growth. Charity, which is focused on the Savior and our love for him, cannot be developed in any sense without the foundation of faith and hope. By definition, charity is "the highest, noblest, strongest kind of love not merely affection" (Bible Dictionary 632.) This love is more than just a willingness to share time or possessions with another human being; rather, it is a deep and lasting devotion for and to God and his Son (Mormon 7:47). Thus, more than an act, charity is an attitude, a state of heart and mind that accompanies our works and is proffered unceasingly (1 Cor 13:4–7; D&C 121:45). It follows faith and hope, but surpasses them in importance (1 Cor 13:13; *Encyclopedia of Mormonism* 1:264). Charity is best illustrated by Christ's own actions, for he so loved his Father that he did whatsoever his Father required, even to the suffering and giving of his own life for the spiritual lives of his Father's children. Mormon characterizes charity as "the pure love of Christ" (Moroni 7:47).

Moroni further explains the pure love of Christ or charity when he declares:

> I remember that thou hast said that thou hast loved the world, even unto the laying down of thy life for the world, that thou mightest take it again to prepare a place for the children of men. And now I know that this love which thou hast had for the children of men is charity; wherefore, except men shall have charity they cannot inherit that place which thou hast prepared in the mansions of thy Father. (Ether 12:33–34)

For us to acquire charity requires at least two things. First, we must "love the Lord thy God with all [our] heart, with all [our] might, mind and strength; and in the name of Jesus Christ [we] shalt serve him." The second requirement is like unto the first: "[We] shalt love [our] neighbor as [ourselves]" (D&C 59:5–6; Matt 12:37–40). True charity develops from love—love for God, the Lawgiver, and for his children. Without this basis of love, we cannot possess charity. Even if we were to give all that we have, if we do not give for the love of God, it is not charity. Consequently, an atheist, although he may love, cannot have charity.

Therefore, Mormon counsels that we should "pray unto the Father with all the energy of heart, that [we] may be filled with this love, which he hath bestowed upon all who are true followers of his Son, Jesus Christ" (Moroni 7:48). Certain characteristics accompany this gift from God:

> Charity suffereth long, and is kind, and envieth not, and is not puffed up, seeketh not her own, is not easily provoked, thinketh no evil, and rejoiceth not in iniquity but rejoiceth in the truth, beareth all things, believeth all things, hopeth all things, endureth all things. (Moroni 7:45)

These characteristics are all fruits of the love that we have for God and his children. This love is completely different from the love spoken of in the world. President Benson observed:

> The world today speaks a great deal about love, and it is sought for by many. But the pure love of Christ differs greatly from what the world thinks of love. Charity never seeks selfish gratification. The pure love of Christ seeks only the eternal growth and joy of others. ("Godly Characteristics" 47)

Because this love is focused on the Eternal God, it endures forever and never fails (Moroni 7:46–47).

Having charity is so critical for spiritual growth that Mormon declares that if we do not have it, we are "nothing" (Moroni 7:44). Without charity, or the pure love of Christ, we "can in nowise be saved in the kingdom of God" (10:21). We are, therefore, commanded to "clothe [ourselves] with the bond of charity, as with a mantle, which is the bond of perfectness and peace" (D&C 88:125). The Joseph Smith Translation of the Bible helps us see that Peter's counsel to the Former-day Saints echoes this command when he wrote, "And above all things have fervent charity among yourselves, for charity preventeth a multitude of sins" (JST 1 Peter 4:8).

Moroni's charity motivated him to plead that if the Gentiles have the privilege of reading his words, the Lord would give them "grace that they might have charity" (Ether 12:36-37). The Lord's response to this request was very comforting for He informed Moroni not to worry whether the Gentiles had charity because he had "been faithful, wherefore thy garments shall be made clean. And because thou hast seen thy weakness thou shalt be made strong, even unto the sitting down in the place which I have prepared in the mansions of my Father" (v 37). Thus, the fruits of his charity became a reality in the life of Moroni.

The centrality of charity to spiritual growth led Hugh Nibley to ask the following questions:

> What, then is holding us back? Why are so few willing to let faith and hope lead them? There is a serious obstacle here, for a man "cannot have faith and hope, save he shall be meek, and lowly of heart . . . and if a man be meek and lowly in heart . . . he must have charity; for if he have not charity he is nothing; wherefore he must needs have charity" (Moroni 7:43–44). Both Mormon and Moroni come back unerringly to charity as the key to the whole business; it was for lack of charity that their people were destroyed, charity is "the greatest of all" without which "all things must fail" (Moroni 7:46). No demonstration of its existence is necessary; it "is the pure love of Christ," the irreducible quantity in the universe, as mysterious and undeniable as consciousness itself; without it we are impatient, unkind, envious, puffed up, self-seeking, touchy, suspicious, irritable, distrustful, skeptical, and intolerant (Moroni 7:47), in a word, incapable of seeking truth in any field. (7:404)

The Light of Our Vessels

Not only were the Jaredite sailing vessels filled with light, but the brother of Jared's spiritual vessel was also illuminated with the light of Christ which filled his whole body (D&C 88:67). Because of his great faith, hope, and charity, the brother of Jared was able to face the challenges of his life, although he lived a difficult one. The wicked environment from which the family of Jared had to flee, the challenges of traveling through the wilderness "into that quarter where there never had man been" (Ether 2:5) are just two of the challenges he and his family faced. Because of his charity, his pure love of Christ, he was able to bear, believe, hope, and endure all things (Moroni 7:45). In addition, it may have been through the things that the brother of Jared suffered that he developed his strong faith. The Prophet Joseph Smith understood this principle:

> Let us here observe that a religion that does not require the sacrifice of all things never has power sufficient to produce the faith necessary unto life and salvation. . . . When a man has offered in sacrifice all that he has for the truth's sake, not even withholding his life, and believing before God that he has been called to make this sacrifice because he seeks to do His will, he does know, most assuredly, that God does and will accept his sacrifice and offering and that he has not sought nor will he seek His face in vain. Under these circumstances, then, he can obtain the faith necessary for him to lay hold on eternal life. (*LF* 6:7)

Paul affirmed this by declaring, "tribulation worketh patience; and patience, experience; and experience, hope" (Rom 5:3–4). Submitting to whatsoever God placed upon him showed the brother of Jared to be "meek and lowly in heart"; and "if a man be meek and lowly in heart, and confesses by the power of the Holy Ghost that Jesus is the Christ, he must have charity" (Moroni 7:44).

The brother of Jared's faith, hope, and charity brought many blessings into his life. So great was his faith that the Savior could not keep the veil between them. The Lord also answered his pleading not to confound the language of the families and friends of Jared. The Lord spoke to the brother of Jared in the valley of Nimrod and guided him and his family to a land of promise. It may even have been these same qualities of faith, hope, and charity that allowed the Lord to talk with the brother of Jared for three hours, and chasten him "because he remembered not to call upon the name of the Lord" (Ether 2:14). These are the same qualities that allowed the Lord to show him "all the inhabitants of the earth which had been, and also all that would be; and he withheld them not from his sights, even unto the ends of the earth" (3:25). Elder Neal A. Maxwell notes that, "Great faith, born of doing simple things, is the key to much that matters. When we give place in our lives for developing such faith, this faith facilitates the development of other vital qualities [such as hope and charity] and outcomes as well" (*Men and Women of Christ* 96).

Like the brother of Jared, we can also follow the pattern that will develop the triad of faith, hope, and charity. We can develop the faith that will allow our eyes to be single to the glory of God. We can come to understand that "only Jesus Christ is uniquely qualified to provide that hope, that confidence, and that strength to overcome the world and rise above our human failings. To do that, we must place our faith in [Christ] and live by His laws and teachings" (Benson, "Jesus Christ" 5). The strength of our faith from which our hope and charity will spring determines greatly the wellsprings of our spiritual understanding and commitment.

Development of Faith, Hope, and Charity

The development of faith, hope, and charity is a very personal endeavor based on our testimony of God, the Father, and his Son, Jesus Christ. It is focused on the atonement of Christ as a personal atonement. Therefore, the development of these three characteristics comes by personal effort. Jacob declared: "Wherefore, we search the prophets, and we have many revelations and the spirit of prophecy; and having all these witnesses, we obtain a hope; and our faith becometh unshaken, insomuch that we truly can command in the name of Jesus and the very trees obey us, or the mountains, or the waves of the seas" (Jacob 4:6). This personal search of the writings of the prophets and the reception of the revelation leads to a development and strengthening of faith, hope, and charity. Elder Marion G. Romney affirms this when he promises:

> I feel certain that if, in our homes, parents will read from the Book of Mormon prayerfully and regularly, both by themselves and with their children, the spirit of that great book will come to permeate our homes and all who dwell therein. The spirit of reverence will increase, mutual respect and consideration for each other will grow. The spirit of contention will depart. Parents will counsel their children in greater love and wisdom. Children will be more responsive and submissive to that counsel. Righteousness will increase. Faith, hope, and charity—the pure love of Christ—will abound in our homes and lives, bringing in their wake peace, joy, and happiness. (436)

As we receive the blessings from this type of living, we increase in spiritual sensitivity and then become candidates for the gifts of the Spirit, including the gifts of faith, hope, and charity. It is important to note that without the Spirit, we cannot develop these characteristics. Paul taught that "the manifestation of the Spirit is given to every man to profit withal. For to one is given by the Spirit the word of wisdom; to another the word of knowledge by the same Spirit; to another faith by the same Spirit . . ." (1 Cor 12:7–9). We are taught an example of this gift in latter-day revelations: "To some it is given by the Holy

Ghost to know that Jesus Christ is the Son of God, and that he was crucified for the sins of the world. To others it is given to believe on their words, that they also might have eternal life if they continue faithful" (D&C 46:13–14). Thus, the basis for the attainment of faith, hope and charity is the Holy Ghost and the personal efforts that are required to attain the companionship of the Holy Ghost.

The more we become qualified for the companionship of the Holy Ghost through righteous living, the more we receive the gifts of faith, hope, and charity. The Lord told Hyrum Smith he had two major responsibilities to perform before he could go forth and preach the gospel. The first was "to keep my commandments, yea, with all your might, mind, and strength," and the second was to "seek to obtain my word, and then shall your tongue be loosed; then, if you desire, you shall have my Spirit and my word" (D&C 11:20–21). The combination of obedience and scripture study allows us to obtain the gifts of the Holy Ghost that develop and strengthen this triad of faith, hope, and charity. Elder Bruce R. McConkie understood this when he was quoted in the *Church News* as saying:

> I think that people who study the scriptures get a dimension to their life that nobody else gets and that can't be gained in any way except by studying the scriptures. There's an increase in faith and a desire to do what's right and a feeling of inspiration and understanding that comes to people who study the gospel—meaning particularly the standard works—who ponder the principles, that can't come in any other way. ("Spare Times's Rare" 4)

This triad of characteristics did not come to the brother of Jared without effort. Likewise, it will only become the fuel of our spiritual vessels with conscientious effort and devotion.

Conclusion

Faith, hope, and charity cannot really be separated. They act in concert, one with the others. They are the forces that enabled the brother of Jared to have light in the sailing vessels and also in his own spiritual vessel. Because the brother of Jared had great faith, he was filled with hope and perfect love. He maintained and strengthened these qualities through his prayers and diligence in keeping the commandments. Having all three kept his spiritual vessel illuminated.

Mormon understood the interrelationships between faith, hope, and charity. He taught that the first fruits of repentance is baptism:

Baptism cometh by faith unto the fulfilling the commandments; and the fulfilling the commandments bringeth remission of sins. And remission of sins bringeth meekness, and lowliness of heart; and because of meekness and lowliness of heart cometh the visitation of the Holy Ghost, which comforter filleth with hope and perfect love, which love endureth by diligence unto prayer, until the end shall come, when all the saints shall dwell with God. (Moroni 7:25–26)

Having faith, hope, and charity will also give light to our vessels, and power, direction, and progression in our lives. These characteristics become the seedbed of all our good qualities. "Thus we see not only centrality but also the needed constancy of these qualities" (Maxwell, "Men and Women of Christ" 53).

In a despairing world that lacks faith and where "the love of men shall wax cold and iniquity shall abound" (D&C 45:27), developing faith, hope, and charity to provide spiritual light in our personal vessels is a necessity. "Events can shake us, bring on despair, and cause us to shrivel up in our capacity to love—unless we have faith and love based on truths that are relevant not only now but in eternity!" (Maxwell, "For the Power" 61–62).

The desire to know eternal truths leads to faith; and if we develop faith, we will have hope in Christ. With hope, we become candidates for charity—the pure love of Christ. The brother of Jared followed this path as did Mormon and Moroni. No single event is recorded that illustrates the charity of the brother of Jared. However, the relationship that he developed with the Lord expresses that quality. The brother of Jared exhibited great love for the Savior by his devotion and commitment to serve and obey him. So must we. We must

pray unto the Father with all the energy of heart, that [we] may be filled with this love, which he hath bestowed upon all who are true followers of his Son, Jesus Christ; that [we] may become the [children] of God; that when he shall appear we shall be like him, for we shall see him as he is; that we may have this hope; that we may be purified even as he is pure. (Moroni 7:48)

Above all things, "[we must] clothe [ourselves] with the bond of charity, as with a mantle, which is the bond of perfectness and peace" (D&C 88:125) so that we, like the brother of Jared, can enjoy the presence of the Lord.

BIBLIOGRAPHY

Benson, Ezra Taft. "Jesus Christ: Our Savior and Redeemer." *Ensign* (Nov 1983) 13:6–8; also in *Conference Report* (Oct 1983) 5–8.

———. "Godly Characteristics of the Master." *Ensign* (Nov 1986) 16:45–48; also in *Conference Report* (Oct 1986) 59–64.

———. *The Teachings of Ezra Taft Benson.* Salt Lake City: Bookcraft, 1988.

Encyclopedia of Mormonism. 5 vols. New York: Macmillan Publishing Co., 1992.

The Lectures on Faith In Historical Perspective. Eds. Larry E. Dahl and Charles D. Tate, Jr. Provo, UT: Religious Study Center, Brigham Young University, 1990.

Maxwell, Neal A. *For the Power is in Them.* Salt Lake City: Bookcraft, 1978.

———. *Men and Women of Christ.* Salt Lake City: Bookcraft, 1991.

———. *Not Withstanding My Weakness.* Salt Lake City: Bookcraft, 1981.

McConkie, Bruce R. *Mormon Doctrine.* Salt Lake City: Bookcraft, 1966.

Nibley, Hugh. *Since Cumorah.* Provo, UT: F.A.R.M.S. and Deseret Book, 1988.

Oaks, Dallin H. *Pure In Heart.* Salt Lake City: Bookcraft, 1988.

Romney, Marion G. "Drink Deeply From the Divine Fountain." *Improvement Era* (June 1960) 63:435–36; also in *Conference Report.* (Apr 1960) 112–13.

"Spare Time's Rare to Apostle." *Church News* (24 Jan 1976) 4.

Preparing for the Judgment 8

Gerald Hansen, Jr.

*T*he power of the Book of Mormon to move us closer to God comes largely from the stark contrast of its two main messages. On almost every page, the prophets preach the positive and preeminent message of overcoming the world through hope in Christ. On the other hand, their constant reminder of judgment for the wicked never allows us to relax or be comfortable in sin. These two messages reach their greatest intensity in the nine chapters known also as the book of Mormon in the Book of Mormon. (To avoid confusion with the Book of Mormon, these nine chapters will hereafter be referred to as Mormon's book.) Mormon's book demands that we pay attention to the teachings of the entire Book of Mormon because it contains the account of the final destruction of the Nephites—a terrifying symbol that men and women will be judged for their sins. More specifically, Mormon's book pushes us to examine the types of materialism that caused the Nephites to be destroyed. It presses us to use the Book of Mormon to see through the lies of this world, while urging us to find hope in Christ. Without Mormon's book, the teachings on materialism in the rest of the Book of Mormon, though correct, lack leverage, much like a parent who constantly threatens to discipline but never does. With Mormon's book we are brought to acknowledge that God will hold us accountable for the choices we make, just as he did the Nephites. Our analysis of the power of Mormon's book to move us to acknowledge the Book of Mormon's attack on materialism must begin with the destruction of the Nephites.

Mormon does not record the Nephites' destruction just because it fulfills prophecy or for his readers' information only (see 1 Nephi 12:20; Alma 45:10–11). Rather, his description of the extinction of

---

Gerald Hansen, Jr., is an instructor of Religion at Ricks College, Rexburg, Idaho.

95

his people at Cumorah graphically illustrates the truth that "the wages of sin [are] death" (Rom 6:23). It rouses our curiosity to look for the exact cause of their annihilation and, thereby, stimulates us to pay attention to the portrait Mormon paints of his own people. He says his society was one in which the Holy Ghost did not function and, consequently, there were no spiritual gifts. Secret combinations seeking power and money abounded. People sought answers to life's questions from unholy sources such as sorcery. The power of evil (probably meaning false philosophies and life-styles) was rampant everywhere (Mormon 1:14–19). Because of the wars and atrocities, caused by gangs within and the Lamanites without, the entire nation of Nephites began to complain and mourn. They were terrified by the problems they faced and sorry that they had to face them. But they would not turn to God or seek the real solution, which is repentance. They sought for happiness in wickedness, but life became miserable, and some felt it was not worth living. They blamed God for their problems and did not have access to his spirit (2:8–26). After success in a couple of wars they bragged about their military abilities and even swore to avenge themselves against their enemies with military solutions (3:9). All in all, Nephite society during this time was a sick one, heading to its death.

In case we missed the point of Mormon's description of the Nephites' wickedness, Moroni adds a second witness of our need for repentance by prophesying of the most problematic types of wickedness existing in our day. He says our day is one of secret combinations, pride and envying in churches, wars, pollutions, murders, robbing, lying, deceivings, and whoredoms; it is a day of false philosophies that excuse sin and build churches to get gain; it is a day where men and women love money and fine apparel, which causes envying, strife, malice and persecutions; it is a day where we care more about adorning churches than we do about taking care of the poor, needy, sick, and afflicted; a day where we seek the praise of the world, and oppress the downtrodden and the righteous (Mormon 8:24–41). Moroni's teaching is clear: just as the Nephites were destroyed because they did not repent of the wickedness described by Mormon, we face destruction and judgment unless we repent of our sins, some of which Moroni described.

The account of the destruction of the Nephites insists that we see the consequences of following the world's enticements instead of

God's commandments. As a result, this destruction is not meant to be read as just historical fact, but as a metaphor of judgment, a shadow of the everlasting destruction known as second death (see Alma 12:16–17). Mormon makes it obvious that he wants us to understand and feel the destruction of the Nephites on a personal level. For one thing, he spends much more time on their decline and fall than is necessary for a simple history, in contrast to Amaron, who describes an earlier but similar destruction of the Nephites in four verses (Omni 1:4–7). Mormon chooses to use his entire personal record to describe the Nephites' plunge to destruction at Cumorah with an account that moves with the cadence of a funeral dirge. He seems determined that we personally experience a degree of the horror that he felt as he watched his own society deteriorate in wickedness, hoping that we will do all we can to prevent our own destruction. A more obvious key to Mormon's intention is his own words. He tells us point blank that he wants us to repent and prepare for judgment. Addressing both Gentile and Israelite, he says: "And for this cause I write unto you, that ye may know that ye must all stand before the judgment-seat of Christ . . . [and] ye must stand to be judged of your works, whether they be good or evil. . . . And I would that I could persuade all ye ends of the earth to repent and prepare to stand before the judgement-seat of Christ" (Mormon 3:20–22). The depth of Mormon's concern for us comes through not only in this admonition, but also in the fact that he repeats it three more times, twice directly and once indirectly, as he mourns for and chastises the destroyed Nephites (5:12–24; 6:16–22; 7:1–10). As though four warnings are not enough, Moroni, in his portion of Mormon's book, admonishes us in tones even more severe than his father's, demanding to know how we as a society and as individuals can continue in wickedness and still expect a joyful judgment (8:33–41; 9:1–14).

As we read these admonitions today, the most important thing for us to remember, if not the most disturbing, is that the Nephites could have avoided their destruction at Cumorah. They should have known better than to fall into the traps that led to their doom. They not only received continual exhortations from the prophets to repent, but, like us, they also had a record, a warning really, of a people who destroyed themselves through wickedness. The Jaredite record showed that the penalty for disobedience to God for peoples who live on the American continent is destruction (see Alma 37:21–32). With all these warnings available, one wonders what went wrong. Why didn't the Nephites listen? Did they read their own book? Did they miss its message? Did they take the Jaredite record seriously, or did they view it only as a history book, a record of God's dealings with the people in the ancient promised land? Whatever their attitude, they evidently did not view the record as a warning to themselves. Given the fact that the Nephites neglected to learn from their scriptures, the Book of Mormon becomes for us a double warning, a second witness, a record of two civilizations that God allowed to be destroyed because they disregarded the prophets and records he gave them.

Because the Book of Mormon contains such a warning, any group which has access to it is enormously accountable. The scriptures themselves accentuate this accountability in at least two powerful ways. First, the Doctrine and Covenants reveals that Nephite prophets spent their faith and effort to bring forth the Book of Mormon (D&C 10:46–52). It also reveals that the Book of Mormon was purchased for us at no small cost but by the blood of the modern prophets, Joseph and Hyrum Smith, who died to seal its testimony (135:1, 6). At the judgment bar, God will not lightly dismiss the high price paid to bring the book forth. Second, the Book of Mormon testifies that God will judge the nations that possess the things he writes according to that record (2 Nephi 25:22). In fact, Nephi, Jacob, Mormon, and Moroni, the four most prominent writers of the book, all testify in sobering farewell statements that we will stand with them at the judgment bar of God to answer for what we have done with the teachings of the Book of Mormon (see 2 Nephi 33:10–15; Jacob 6:5–13; Mormon 7:5–10; Moroni 10:24–34). These prophets want us to know that part of our judgment will be based on how well we have used their teachings in our lives.

The high seriousness of the Book of Mormon prophets' warnings should push us to search their record for what led the Nephites to their destruction. From the beginning of the book to the end, these prophets denounce materialism as the source of Nephite wickedness. They said it was materialism more than anything else that caused the wars, persecutions, apostasy, and secret combinations which led finally to annihilation. It seems, for example, to have been the reason for Laman and Lemuel's pride (1 Nephi 2:11; 17:21–22). The Isaiah chapters Nephi quotes attack materialistic attitudes again and again (see 2 Nephi chapters 12–24). Materialism was the source of the wars and wickedness that caused Alma's abdication as chief judge so he could preach full time (Alma 1:16; 4:8–19). The same is true of the wars and wickedness that caused Nephi₂ to resign as chief judge (Hel 3:33–36; 4:11–12). Mormon says it was this sin that caused the destruction among the Nephites just before the Savior came (3 Nephi 6:10–15), and caused the Nephite slide to wickedness after 200 years of peace (4 Nephi 1:24). Moroni says it, along with pride, was the motivation behind the secret combinations that led to the destruction of the Jaredites and Nephites (Ether 8:21–22).

The value of the Book of Mormon on this issue is hard to overstate. According to President Ezra Taft Benson, the Book of Mormon teaches the perils of materialism better than any other source:

> From the Book of Mormon we learn how disciples of Christ live in times of war. From the Book of Mormon we see the evils of secret combinations portrayed in graphic and chilling reality. In the Book of Mormon we find lessons for dealing with persecution and apostasy. We learn much about how to do missionary work. And more than anywhere else, we see in the Book of Mormon the dangers of materialism and setting our hearts on the things of the world. ("The Book" 7)

As this quotation indicates, while the writings of the prophets of the Book of Mormon show great concern for many different problems relevant to our society, they reserve their greatest and most consistent condemnation for those who set their hearts on the things of this world.

We can better understand the inherent danger in this temptation if we first note that the Book of Mormon prophets do not condemn money itself, nor do they expect us to live in poverty. Having enough for our needs, even having more than enough, is not the problem, if we use it for others (see Jacob 2:18–19). God expects us to be responsible in financial affairs and, in most cases, to be self-supporting. This is what the Savior means when he says "make unto yourselves friends with the mammon of unrighteousness, and they will not destroy you" (D&C 82:22). King Benjamin also gives excellent counsel on establishing priorities in monetary matters and governing ourselves with order and wisdom (Mosiah 4:14–27). The problem with wealth is not the money itself, but how easily having wealth distracts us from centering our hearts in Christ.

The distraction that money causes can happen so naturally and so easily that it is hardly noticeable. One reason for this is that we do have to live in this world and we do have to take care of our finances. But the Book of Mormon prophets show us that the fine line between being industriously self-supporting and setting our hearts on riches is treacherously easy to cross. It is far too easy to begin spending most of our time thinking about money and the things it can buy. Joseph Smith taught that our concern for riches, as much as anything, will keep us from being exalted. Focusing our attention on the things of this world keeps us from focusing on God and from learning the lessons of righteousness that we have to know in order to be exalted (D&C 121:34–36). This focus generally leads to compromises of integrity that good people would not otherwise make. These compromises can be as large as fraud, but can also show up in smaller ways, such as infringing on a friendship in order to make money.

To soothe the conscience of those who cross the line, or, as Nephi says, those who are "[lulled] into carnal security" (2 Nephi 28:21), the world offers a whole set of silly notions and rationalizations. It teaches that the mere making of money means we are serving God; that we cannot really serve God unless we have money; that being blessed with wealth is a sure sign of God's love for us; and that since God requires us to work, working automatically makes us righteous. The world convinces us that we worked hard for what we have and, therefore, we have the right to spend our money the way we want to, rather than use it to build up the kingdom of God; it encourages us to believe the poor are somehow inferior, or unworthy, or unrighteous and deserve their poverty. With a handful of such ready-made rationalizations to support us, we sin with minimal guilt, oppressing the poor in a multitude of ways, as Moroni prophesied (Mormon 8:31–37). He says the general attitude of our day will be "Do this, or do that, and it mattereth not, for the Lord will uphold such at the last day"; he also says that such are in the bonds of iniquity (v 31). Moroni helps us understand that the danger in materialism is not so much a formal decision to be wicked as it is fuzzy thinking which leads us to unrighteous behavior.

The treachery of seeking wealth can be especially perilous for religious people because the outward respectability that comes from the combination of wealth and religious devotions can camouflage the need to constantly seek Christ. As John the Revelator points out, this combination among the members in ancient Laodicea prevented them from realizing that they were spiritually "wretched, and miserable, and poor, and blind, and naked" (Rev 3:17). They did not know they needed Christ because they were respectable people. Professor Hugh Nibley explains this phenomenon in historical terms:

> As the Romans became ever more corrupted by wealth . . . they became more and more fascinated with the image of themselves as honest, hard-working, straight-forward, tough-minded citizens: *Hic est Ausonia* . . . ["Here is Ausonia"], they said: "The Western world of clean, fresh, simple, unspoiled pioneers." This fiction became the very cornerstone of the official doctrine. "Rome was great because Rome was good, giving expression to the old Roman belief in the close association between piety and success." This was the rhetoric of wealth, and it was inevitable—it always follows in such a situation, because people simply can't live virtuously and viciously at the same time. Yet they want to be good and rich at the same time, and so they reach a compromise called respectability, which is nothing less than Babylon masquerading as Zion. (45–46)

As Nibley implies, respectability is not always possible to the followers of Christ (see Hel 3:33–35; John 15:19) and must not be used to determine whether or not we are right with God.

The antidote to the slow poison of materialism is the Book of Mormon. Its particular power on this issue stems from its ability to unmask the false notions that confuse us. It does not just label and condemn the seeking of riches and worldly things; it forces us to "unthink" faulty reasoning. The Book of Mormon disabuses us of false materialistic attitudes by attacking them head on and revealing what God really expects of us. As with the Zoramites, it shows us the dangers of a religious albeit materialistic people who, while thanking God for their blessings, look down upon and mistreat others because their clothing does not conform to the latest fashion or namebrand (Alma 31:12–24). In the book of Helaman, it shows that materialistic persecution happens within the Church (Hel 3:33–36); that even righteous people can be seduced into ridiculous beliefs concerning money (6:38–39); and that materialism can cause spiritual blindness even when warning signals are all around us, even when prophets chastise us (7:15–21). In the book of Mosiah, king Benjamin reminds us that we must find a way to help the needy even if their own poor decisions are responsible for their extreme circumstances (Mosiah 4:16–23). King Benjamin also teaches us that the amount we must charitably give depends on how much we have—that God judges us on the intent of our hearts, not on the amount given (Mosiah 4:23–25). In the book of Jacob, the Book of Mormon informs us that helping others is the only reason for having wealth beyond our needs (Jacob 2:18–19). Most important of all, the resurrected Savior, Jesus Christ, teaches us that we must not spend all our time thinking about ourselves and how we can get ahead; rather we must keep our eyes single to God's glory (3 Nephi 13:19–24).

On this last issue—keeping our eyes single to God's glory—the Book of Mormon prophets are especially persistent. Throughout their records, they use an "either/or" rhetoric with metaphors, characterizations, and narrative to insist that we see the basic test of life as a choice between seeking God or seeking the world. Lehi and Nephi, for instance, portray our basic choice as either coming to and partaking of the tree of life—the love of God—or moving into the great and spacious building—the pride of the world (1 Nephi 8:10–33; 11:8–36). Elsewhere, Nephi says that there are "save two churches only; the one is the church of the Lamb of God, and the other the church of the devil" (1 Nephi 14:10). King Benjamin's lifestyle is opposed to that of king Noah's as a stark contrast between good and evil (Mosiah 2, 11), as is the Savior's command to build our houses on the rock of his doctrine rather than the sand of the world's philosophies (3 Nephi 14:24–27). In 4 Nephi, Mormon contrasts a Zion society in which there are no rich and no poor with the search for costly apparel and fine pearls that started the demise of righteousness among the Nephites (vv 3, 24). These few examples show that the Book of Mormon prophets confirm again and again the Savior's injunction that we cannot serve both God and mammon.

The prophets' persistent efforts to attack and unmask the dangers of materialism through narrative, argument, and rhetoric, could be ignored if not for the destruction at Cumorah. Mormon's use of the extinction of the Nephites is a metaphor of the final judgment. It testifies that when God warns us with scriptures and prophets, he holds us accountable according to those teachings. He will not let us off the hook—wiggle as we might. The Nephite destruction gives us pause to consider more fully President Benson's concern that the Church is collectively under condemnation because "the Book of Mormon has not been, nor is it yet, the center of our personal study, family teaching, preaching, and missionary work" ("Cleansing" 5–6).

We must read the book if we are to follow God's commandment "not only to say, but to do according to that which is written" (D&C 84:57). Further, the Nephite destruction insists that we not take lightly the Book of Mormon's expectations. It insists that we read the book not merely as a history or as a book of God's favorite sayings, but that we carefully and fully consider its messages and apply them to our lives. We must exert our faith in deep study and pondering of the Book of Mormon, and not treat it trivially (see Alma 37:38–46). We must not be intimidated by Isaiah and the harder doctrinal chapters. In all this the Book of Mormon warns us not to reject its messages just because we do not like them.

What all of the warnings, teachings, rhetoric, and prophecies finally bring us to is that we must leave behind the foolishness of the world and seek to follow Christ with our whole souls. It is not the intention of the prophets of the Book of Mormon to tell us we are doomed or damned, but, rather, to awaken us to greater repentance. They long for us to learn how to come to Christ in a world that offers hundreds of counterfeit gospels. They show in their writings that hoping in Christ is a gift God reserved for those who know his will and follow his teachings, not a self-induced state of pseudo-happiness begotten illegitimately by seminars on self-awareness, self-esteem, success, and positive mental attitude (see Ether 12:4; Moroni 7:41–42; 8:26; *Lectures on Faith* 3:5, 65–66). Hoping in Christ is a hope of eternal life, engendered by repentance and the Atonement. It is not cheaply bought, but comes from living correct principles, and receiving confirmation through the Holy Ghost that we are in harmony with God. The Book of Mormon directs us to this hope. It is a tangible guide that shows us how to live righteously in a wicked world. It expects us to pursue perfection. It expects us to keep our covenants. Mormon's book requires us to take these expectations seriously by testifying that those who use the Book of Mormon to see through the lies of this world will, like Mormon, "be lifted up at the last day" (Mormon 2:19), while those who do not will face the judgment of spiritual destruction.

BIBLIOGRAPHY

Benson, Ezra Taft. "The Book of Mormon—Keystone of Our Religion." *Ensign* (Nov 1986) 16:4–7; also in *Conference Report* (Oct 1986) 3–7.

———. "Cleansing the Inner Vessel." *Ensign* (May 1986) 16:4–7; also in *Conference Report* (Apr 1986) 3–6.

The Lectures on Faith in Historical Perspective. Eds. Larry E. Dahl and Charles D. Tate, Jr. Provo, UT: Religious Studies Center, Brigham Young Univ, 1990.

Nibley, Hugh. *Approaching Zion*. Salt Lake City: Deseret Book, 1989.

Mormon and Moroni: Father and Son

9

Gary Layne Hatch

*T*he prophet Mormon must be one of the greatest geniuses in the history of the human race. Scholar, soldier, prophet, poet— Mormon distinguished himself in a number of ways and under difficult circumstances. He was a serious scholar and careful observer, and he possessed the ability to report his observations and experiences in a concise, straightforward, objective manner. We learn from Mormon's abridgment of his own record that Ammaron, the keeper of the plates, sought him out when he was just 10 years old, because he had noticed Mormon was "a sober child, and . . . quick to observe" (Mormon 1:2). Ammaron told Mormon to remember the location of the plates so he could find them 14 years later and then record on them what he had observed about the Nephite people during those 14 years, a task difficult enough for an adult, even more so for a 10-year-old boy. Yet Mormon records his ability to perform this difficult cognitive task with the simple phrase: "And I, Mormon . . . remembered the things which Ammaron commanded me" (v 5). Because of the travels of his family, Mormon had abundant opportunity to observe the Nephite people. He reports the over-building and overpopulation of the land, the extreme wickedness of the people, and the vicious wars among the Nephites and Lamanites, all in the same spare, confident style that he uses in his abridgment of the large plates of Nephi. Indeed, he reports what must have been one of the sublime moments of his life in the following terse sentence: "And I, being fifteen years of age and being somewhat of a sober mind, therefore I

Gary Layne Hatch is assistant professor of English at Brigham Young University.

was visited of the Lord, and tasted and knew of the goodness of Jesus" (v 15).

Soberness and seriousness of mind characterize Mormon as one of the unique Book of Mormon figures. These characteristics were innate in part, and in part brought on by the "continual scene of wickedness and abominations" he had witnessed since he had been "sufficient to behold the ways of man" (Mormon 2:18).

Mormon gives no indication that he felt overwhelmed by the literary miracle he was performing in gathering and sorting out the many records of the Nephites and writing on and abridging the large plates. Many Book of Mormon authors remark that they could write only a small part of the events they witnessed. Yet, according to the testimony of Brigham Young, the Book of Mormon plates were themselves a small part of a library of plates—as many as many wagon loads (*Journal of Discourses* 19:38). Mormon had to sift through 1,000 years of history, religion, and culture to provide the abridgment that became the Book of Mormon. It might be roughly equivalent to taking all the holdings of a local library and condensing them into a 500-page book, maintaining a coherent narrative, relating the parts to one another and to the book as a whole, and commenting on the meaning and significance of many episodes and ideas.

The manner in which Mormon abridges the plates is also remarkable. He carefully selects events that will illustrate different aspects of the mercy and love of God and the need for people to come to Christ. Mormon directs the readers' attention to and comments on events with his confident "thus we see," and "now behold" phrases, but, at the same time, is able to describe the events he records in a detached voice so that readers often forget that they are reading an abridgment. He incorporates the dialogue and voices of different writers in a seamless, organic, literary whole. If Joseph Smith's achievement in translating the book was remarkable, then Mormon's abriging the plates into a unified whole must be equally remarkable, a work certifying him as one of the great literary scholars. And he was a man of God, without whose help even one as talented as he could not have completed the task. The Book of Mormon truly is Mormon's book.

Somehow Mormon was able to combine a literary life with a life of action. Like his ancestor Nephi, Mormon was large for his age and a skilled soldier. At the age of fifteen, perhaps not long after being visited by the Lord, Mormon takes command of the Nephite army and leads them into battle. A man of courage, Mormon criticizes those who flee before the Lamanites and refuse to fight (Mormon 2:3), finally winning a decisive battle against Aaron, the king of the Lamanites. Mormon must have been an inspiring leader. Even though he recognizes that the Lord is not with them and despite the crushing defeats they have sustained in the second onslaught of the Lamanites, Mormon speaks to his people "with great energy, that they would stand boldly before the Lamanites and fight for their wives, and their children, and their houses, and their homes." In this manner, he inspires his men "somewhat to vigor, insomuch that they did not flee from before the Lamanites, but did stand with boldness against them" (Mormon 2:23–24).

Frustrated with the cowardice and wickedness of his people, and with his world tumbling down around him, Mormon looked for inspiration to another young general, who lived over 400 years earlier and was able to inspire his people to victory through righteousness. Captain Moroni, chief captain of the Nephite armies, is a man Mormon greatly admired. He devotes a large part of his abridgment to the wars fought by Captain Moroni and may even have named his son after this courageous captain. The description of Captain Moroni in the book of Alma gives some insight into Mormon's personality. He admires Moroni for his skill as a general but even more for his faith in God:

> And Moroni was a strong and a mighty man; he was a man of a perfect understanding; yea, a man that did not delight in bloodshed; a man whose soul did joy in the liberty and the freedom of his country, and his brethren from bondage and slavery;
>
> Yea, a man whose heart did swell with thanksgiving to his God for the many privileges and blessings which he bestowed upon his people; a man who did labor exceedingly for the welfare and safety of his people.
>
> Yea, and he was a man who was firm in the faith of Christ, and he had sworn with an oath to defend his people, his rights, and his country, and his religion, even to the loss of his blood. . . .
>
> Yea, verily, verily I say unto you, if all men had been, and were, and ever would be, like unto Moroni, behold, the very powers of hell would have been shaken forever; yea, the devil would never have power over the hearts of the children of men. (Alma 48:11–13, 17)

One could easily substitute Mormon's name for Captain Moroni's in the above passage, for Mormon was above all else a man of God, one who also threatened to shake the very foundations of hell. He recognizes that the troubles faced by the Nephites result from their great wickedness, from their secret combinations to commit murder, and from their thievery and adultery. His heart rejoices when he witnesses the sorrow and lamentations of the Nephites because of his confidence in the mercy and patience of the Lord; however, his rejoicing turns to sorrow when he realizes that their sorrow is not Godly sorrow or sorrow for their sins, but "the sorrowing of the damned, because the Lord would not always suffer them to take happiness in sin" (Mormon 2:13). Like Nephi, Mormon feels great sorrow for the wickedness of his people and expresses it in his characteristically concise manner: "And wo is me because of their wickedness; for my heart has been filled with sorrow because of their wickedness, all my days; nevertheless, I know that I shall be lifted up at the last day" (v 19).

When Mormon is not abridging the plates or leading armies into battle, he is preaching the word of the Lord. After reaching an uneasy peace with the Lamanites and in the midst of preparations for the inevitable third onslaught, Mormon hears the voice of the Lord which commands him to preach repentance and build up the Church. Mormon shows himself a greater prophet than a general, heeding the Lord's words and preaching to the people that if they will repent they will be spared (Mormon 3:2). When the Lamanites return a third and fourth time, Mormon is ready for them and wins two stunning victories. But when the people turn to even greater wickedness, entering into devilish oaths and covenants, swearing "by all that had been forbidden them by our Lord and Savior Jesus Christ," the Lord reveals to Mormon that the Nephites are ripe for destruction (vv 10–15).[1] Mormon steps down as the Nephite commander, leaving the people to their own wickedness and destruction. Once again, Mormon becomes the sober, observant scholar, "an idle witness to manifest unto the world the things which [he] saw and heard, according to the manifestations of the Spirit which had testified of things to come" (v 16). But his great love for his people is demonstrated by the fact

---

[1] This passage clarifies the meaning of the Lord's prohibition against "swearing" in his sermon to the Nephites and in the Sermon on the Mount (3 Nephi 12:33-37; Matt 5:33-37). In these discourses the Lord is warning against entering into the oaths typical of secret combinations. For additional instances of these oaths, see Hel 1:11 and Ether 8:14.

that, despite their wickedness, he agrees to lead them into battle a final time, a hopeless cause, a battle which brings the destruction of the Nephite people.

A man of God to the end, Mormon the general knows that salvation cannot come by the sword but only through repentance and faith in Christ: "Know ye that ye must come unto repentance, or ye cannot be saved. . . . Know ye that ye must lay down your weapons of war, and delight no more in the shedding of blood, and take them not again, save it be that God shall command you. Know ye that ye must come to the knowledge of your fathers, and repent of all your sins and iniquities, and believe in Jesus Christ" (Mormon 7:3–5). Mormon ends his mortal ministry with his stirring testimony of Jesus and leaves his life's work, his abridgment of the large plates of Nephi, the Book of Mormon, in the hands of his son, Moroni.

Like his father, Moroni distinguished himself in battle. He was selected to lead a group of 10,000 men into battle. Along with his father, he was one of the 24 to survive the terrible destruction of more than 230,000 warriors at Cumorah. As 23 of those 24 are hunted down and killed by the Lamanites, Moroni finds himself alone, surrounded by death, destruction, and wickedness, and faced with the difficult task of completing his father's work.

Moroni feels the weight of this task keenly. In addition to describing the events following Cumorah and adding his own testimony to his father's, Moroni abridged and translated the record of the Jaredites (Mosiah 28:19) as a fitting parallel to the destruction of the Nephites. Moroni expected his personal contribution to the record to be small.[2] He writes: "Behold I, Moroni, do finish the record of my father, Mormon. Behold, I have but few things to write, which things I have been commanded, by my father" (Mormon 8:1).

Instead of the concise, objective style of the sober and observant Mormon, Moroni gives us glimpses into his own fears, sorrows, and misgivings. As he begins to relate the events following the great battle at Cumorah, he describes his sorrow and loneliness and resignation:

---

[2] What we have of Moroni's writings in the current Book of Mormon is small compared to Mormon's; however, the late Professor H. Donl Peterson argues in his article herein that Moroni also wrote all that is in the sealed portion of the gold plates, making his production larger than Mormon's.

> And now it came to pass that after the great and tremendous battle at Cumorah, behold, the Nephites who had escaped into the country southward were hunted by the Lamanites, until they were all destroyed.
>
> And my father also was killed by them, and I even remain alone to write the sad tale of the destruction of my people. But behold, they are gone, and I fulfil the commandment of my father. And whether they will slay me, I know not.
>
> Therefore I will write and hide up the records in the earth; and whither I go it mattereth not.
>
> Behold, my father hath made this record, and he hath written the intent thereof. And behold, I would write it also if I had room upon the plates, but I have not; and ore I have none, for I am alone. My father hath been slain in battle, and all my kinsfolk, and I have not friends nor whither to go; and how long the Lord will suffer that I may live I know not. (Mormon 8:2–5)

In his writing, Moroni also lacks the confident, concise, and detached style of Mormon. In addressing the future readers of this record, Moroni expresses his concern that others will condemn the record because of its imperfections and faults (Mormon 8:12, 17), a theme that he also states at the end of his father's record. After giving his testimony of Christ, he writes:

> Condemn me not because of mine imperfection, neither my father, because of his imperfection, neither them who have written before him; but rather give thanks unto God that he hath made manifest unto you our imperfections, that ye may learn to be more wise than we have been.
>
> And now, behold, we have written this record according to our knowledge, in the characters which are called among us the reformed Egyptian, being handed down and altered by us, according to our manner of speech.
>
> And if our plates had been sufficiently large we should have written in Hebrew; but the Hebrew hath been altered by us also; and if we could have written in Hebrew, behold, ye would have had no imperfection in our record. (Mormon 9:31–33)

Moroni seems to have two kinds of imperfections in mind: first, the human frailty of himself and his people; second, his own shortcomings as a writer, difficulties that bother him while he is completing his translation and abridgment of the record of the Jaredites. We learn that Moroni is not merely talking about the general difficulty of writing on plates in reformed Egyptian but also of his particular struggles as a writer. In describing the faith of the prophet Ether, Moroni digresses from his abridgment to discuss the power of faith. Although he directs his ideas about faith to the reader, Moroni must have received them in a conversation with the Lord because, in verse 23, he breaks back into this conversation in order to record his personal struggles with the Lord about his weakness in writing:

> And I said unto him: Lord, the Gentiles will mock at these things, because of our weakness in writing; for Lord thou hast made us mighty in word by faith, but thou hast not made us mighty in writing; for thou hast made all this people that they could speak much, because of the Holy Ghost which thou hast given them;
>
> And thou hast made us that we could write but little, because of the awkwardness of our hands. Behold, thou hast not made us mighty in writing like unto the brother of Jared, for thou madest him that the things which he wrote were mighty even as thou art, unto the overpowering of man to read them.
>
> Thou hast also made our words powerful and great, even that we cannot write them; wherefore, when we write we behold our weakness, and stumble because of the placing of our words; and I fear lest the Gentiles shall mock at our words. (Ether 12:23–25)

The weakness that troubles Moroni is his inability to express in writing what he feels inside, what he can express in speech through the power of the Spirit. He is obviously moved by the literary power and skill of the brother of Jared. His own writing pales by comparison, and he feels below the task of translating and abridging the work of this great writer and prophet. We can understand Moroni's feelings of inadequacy. A comparable task for us might be to paraphrase and abridge all 38 of Shakespeare's plays, preserving some of the continuity and brilliance of the originals. We, too, would worry that others would mock at our words.

Yet the Lord promises Moroni that his weakness in writing will become his great strength:

> Fools mock, but they shall mourn; and my grace is sufficient for the meek, that they shall take no advantage of your weakness;
>
> And if men come unto me I will show unto them their weakness. I give unto men weakness that they may be humble; and my grace is sufficient for all men that humble themselves before me; for if they humble themselves before me, and have faith in me, then will I make weak things become strong unto them. (Ether 12:26–27)

After finishing the abridgment of the record of the Jaredites and completing the writings of his father, Moroni expected that he would be finished with the book and could hide it in the earth:

> Now I, Moroni, after having made an end of abridging the account of the people of Jared, I had supposed not to have written more, but I have not as yet perished. . . .
>
> Wherefore, I write a few more things, contrary to that which I had supposed; for I had supposed not to have written any more; but I write a few more things, that perhaps they may be of worth unto my brethren. (Moroni 1:1, 4)

Moroni adds brief descriptions of procedural matters in the Church and selections from the writings of his father. H. Donl Petersen maintains that some church organization still existed in Moroni's early life and that he probably presided over a congregation. Mormon and Moroni discuss problems of church governance in their epistles, and Moroni probably would have had first-hand experience with these procedures (10). In chapter 2, Moroni also fulfills a promise made by Mormon that he would give evidence that the Lord gave the Nephite Twelve Disciples the power to give the Holy Ghost (3 Nephi 18:37). In chapter 10, Moroni adds a few of his own words, and I believe that it is in this chapter that the Lord fulfills his promise to Moroni that He will make his weaknesses into strengths. The entire chapter is moving; Moroni records his powerful testimony with confidence and grace. But a few particular passages demonstrate that the Lord has made Moroni as strong a writer as he was a speaker.

It is always difficult to discuss the literary qualities of a work in translation. It is difficult to know what to attribute to the writer and what to the translator or what may have been added or lost in the process of translation. Despite these difficulties, my sense as a critic tells me that here are some examples of powerful writing. Consider the following passage on faith, hope, and charity:

> Wherefore, there must be faith;
>   and if there must be faith there must also be hope;
>   and if there must be hope there must also be charity.
> And except ye have charity ye can in nowise be saved
>   in the kingdom of God;
>   neither can ye be saved in the kingdom of God if ye have not faith;
>   neither can ye if ye have no hope.
> And if ye have no hope ye must needs be in despair;
>   and despair cometh because of iniquity. (Moroni 10:20–22)

I have adjusted the line endings to emphasize the balance and parallelism in these lines. Note how Moroni begins coordinate sentences in the same manner to emphasize the relationships among these sentences. He also ends each balanced sentence or phrase with words he desires to emphasize: faith, hope, charity, God, not faith, no hope, despair, iniquity. These words form a mirror reflection around the word *God*, the foundations of the gospel—faith, hope, and charity— opposed by Satan's inversion of this trinity—lack of faith, despair, and iniquity.

In other passages, Moroni uses short, emphatic phrases to punctuate his writing. In the following passage, Moroni refers to the possibility of the power of God disappearing from the earth because of wickedness: "And wo be unto the children of men if this be the case; for there shall be none that doeth good among you, no not one" (Moroni 10:25-28). The final phrase of this sentence, "no not one," is a redundancy; the idea that no one would be righteous if the power of God is taken away is expressed in the previous phrase. This final phrase is added for emphasis. Moroni uses a similar emphatic phrase in the next verse: "And wo unto them who shall do these things away and die, for they die in their sins, and they cannot be saved in the kingdom of God; and I speak it according to the words of Christ; and I lie not (v 26).

In the next passage, Moroni mingles his voice with the voices of Isaiah and Nephi and uses direct reported speech to give immediacy to the scene he creates of the Lord interrogating the reader about Moroni's testimony:

> And I exhort you to remember these things; for the time speedily cometh that ye shall know that I lie not, for ye shall see me at the bar of God; and the Lord God will say unto you: Did I not declare my words unto you, which were written by this man, like as one crying from the dead, yea, even as one speaking out of the dust?
>
> I declare these things unto the fulfilling of the prophecies. And behold, they shall proceed forth out of the mouth of the everlasting God; and his word shall hiss forth from generation to generation. (Moroni 10:27–28)

Instead of merely stating that the Lord will hold us accountable for how we receive Moroni's testimony, he gives the scene presence by placing the question directly in the Lord's mouth, using the very words He might use. Moroni gives authority and elegance to these words by adopting some of the same phrases used by Isaiah and Nephi: "speaking out of the dust" and "his word shall hiss forth" (see Isa 5:26; 29:1–4; 2 Nephi 29:2–3; 33:13).

But I find the final passages particularly elegant and equal to any writing found in the scriptures:

> And again I would exhort you that ye would come unto Christ, and lay hold upon every good gift, and touch not the evil gift, nor the unclean thing.
>
> And awake, and arise from the dust, O Jerusalem; yea, and put on thy beautiful garments, O daughter of Zion; and strengthen thy stakes and enlarge thy borders forever, that thou mayest no more be confounded, that the covenants of the Eternal Father which he hath made unto thee, O house of Israel, may be fulfilled.
>
> Yea, come unto Christ, and be perfected in him, and deny yourselves of all ungodliness; and if ye shall deny yourselves of all ungodliness, and love God with all your might, mind and strength, then is his grace sufficient for you, that by his grace ye may be perfect in Christ; and if by the grace of God ye are perfect in Christ, ye can in nowise deny the power of God.
>
> And again, if ye by the grace of God are perfect in Christ, and deny not his power, then are ye sanctified in Christ by the grace of God, through the shedding of the blood of Christ, which is in the covenant of the Father unto the remission of your sins, that ye become holy, without spot.
>
> And now I bid unto all, farewell. I soon go to rest in the paradise of God, until my spirit and body shall again reunite, and I am brought forth triumphant through the air, to meet you before the pleasing bar of the great Jehovah, the Eternal Judge of both quick and dead. Amen. (Moroni 10:30–34)

The first two passages echo Isaiah 52:1–2. They are a hymn of rejoicing as well as an exhortation to Israel to return unto their God. These passages provide a poetic introduction to Moroni's more straightforward exhortation for Israel to "come unto Christ, and be perfected in him" (Moroni 10:32-33). Verses 32 and 33 are a complex interlacing of the words *Christ, grace,* and *perfection.* Note the number of times that these words are repeated in some form. These verses are punctuated with the climactic and emphatic phrase, "without spot."

In the final verse of the Book of Mormon, Moroni creates the image of himself flying through the air triumphantly to meet face to face with the reader at the judgment bar of God, an image prophesied by John and since recreated in gold-leaf statuary on the tops of many of our temples:

> And I saw another angel fly in the midst of heaven, having the everlasting gospel to preach unto them that dwell on the earth, and to every nation, and kindred, and tongue, and people,

Saying with a loud voice, Fear God, and give glory to him; for the hour of his judgment is come: and worship him that made heaven, and earth, and the sea, and the fountains of waters. (Rev 14:6–7)

Moroni truly sealed his father's testimony, adding a fitting capstone to his father's book, finally giving the same force to his own writing which he no doubt conveyed in his preaching.

Unlike Captain Moroni, neither Mormon nor Moroni could bring salvation to the Nephites, who were beyond any desire for repentance. But these last two Nephite prophets had a greater mission to fulfil than bringing the word to their contemporaries. The fragmented, violent, and evil world they found themselves in prevented them from leading normal, peaceful lives, but it also prepared them for the service of God. Mormon prepared this second witness of Jesus Christ, and Moroni delivered it to the Prophet Joseph Smith, bringing salvation to millions, truly shaking the very powers of hell forever, preparing the way for a time when "the devil would never have power over the hearts of the children of men."

BIBLIOGRAPHY

Peterson, H. Donl. "Some Church Organization Remained in Moroni's Day." *LDS Church News* (26 Feb 1994) 10.

Journal of Discourses. 26 vols. 1854–86.

Mormon, the Man and the Message

10

Richard Neitzel Holzapfel

When the angel Moroni delivered the gold plates to Joseph Smith in 1827, he fulfilled biblical prophecy (see Rev 14:6; Isa 29:11–12). The young prophet translated the unsealed portion of those plates and published that translation to the world for the first time in March 1830 as the Book of Mormon. This book contains an abridgment of the sacred records and writings of several groups of Israelites living in the Western Hemisphere. Mormon was not only the abridger of the plates, but he was a Nephite record-keeper, a general, an apostle and prophet, a father, and he may have also been a prophetic type.

Mormon as Record Keeper and Abridger

Mormon lived at the close of Nephite history (AD 310–385). The Book of Mormon bears his name because he was the major abridger—the writer of the gold plates. Although his principal effort in preparing the plates was as abridger, he also wrote the Words of Mormon, abridged the first seven chapters of his own record, the book of Mormon in the Book of Mormon, and occasionally interpolated comments into the text he was abridging.

The Words of Mormon is a short section placed between the book of Omni and the book of Mosiah. While working on his abridgment of the large plates of Nephi, Mormon discovered the small plates of Nephi, a prophetic personal second record the Lord commanded Nephi to keep (see W of M 1:3; 2 Nephi 5:30–32). Profoundly

Richard Neitzel Holzapfel is assistant professor of Church History and Doctrine at Brigham Young University.

impressed by the messianic prophecies in the small plates of Nephi and also directed by the Spirit, Mormon attached them in their entirety to his own abridgment (see W of M 1:4–6). Of course, the Lord knew already that Joseph Smith would need this record to replace the loss of the 116 manuscript pages, but Mormon did not know it, and explained, "And I do this for a wise purpose; for thus it whispereth me, according to the workings of the Spirit of the Lord which is in me. And now, I do not know all things; but the Lord knoweth all things which are to come; wherefore, he worketh in me to do according to his will" (v 7). The Words of Mormon connect the small plates to the narrative of the large plates.

Our next opportunity to examine Mormon's own writings is his abridgment of his own record that he had engraved on the large plates. He calls this abridgment the book of Mormon (see Mormon 2:18; 5:9). It is a remarkable document as it chronicles in a precise and engaging way the disintegration and final demise of Nephite civilization. Mormon's son, Moroni, lived to complete the record after his father had been killed after the great last Nephite battle. In that record, called the book of Moroni, Moroni brought together loosely related but important items, including one of Mormon's sermons (Moroni 7), and two of his letters (Moroni 8–9). In addition to these larger examples of Mormon's own writing, we have significant evidence of his masterful ability of editing sacred writings as he intrudes into the text to include interpretive commentary throughout the compilation.[1] The discovery of Mormon's usage of several apparently ancient editorial mechanisms demonstrates the magnitude of his work as a Nephite record-keeper and editor. Current academic requirements of source identification and footnoting were of course unknown in the ancient world. Nevertheless, an examination of the editorial devices used by Mormon shows his sincere concern for credibility and editorial honesty, and a sense of humility while undertaking the prophetic task of preparing another witness of Jesus Christ. Mormon continually attempts to present his message in a way that he as messenger does not get in the way. In this way Mormon stands apart from many other ancient editors and historians.

---

[1] I am indebted to several individuals for some of the insights provided in this paper; see E. Douglas Clark and Robert S. Clark, *Fathers and Sons in the Book of Mormon*; Jeffery R. Holland, "Mormon: The Man and the Book"; and Thomas W. Mackay, "Mormon's Philosophy of History: Helaman 12 in the Perspective of Mormon's Editing Procedure."

Mormon used a range of introductory and inserted notations to guide his readers: such as the names of authors for records, speeches, and epistles that are quoted or abridged—imbedded source indicators; genealogical or other authenticating information about the authors; and brief or extended summaries of contents, including subheadings for complex inserts or documents. Mormon's contribution as editor lies in the fact that he assiduously presents source documents and texts while retaining a unity of narrative flow in his historical account. Thus, even while abridging a record, Mormon would paraphrase or summarize and then return to a first-person quotation. The resultant text is clearly the product of an excellent ancient historian concerned with naming and adhering to his sources while presenting an edited account that exhibits a spiritually motivated understanding of history and purpose.

Mormon's motive for writing and editing the Nephite record seems clear. He regularly sought to draw spiritual lessons from the course of Nephite history. This was remarkable, as he often was forced to draw these lessons from works of darkness from his people's past, and, more difficult still, from his own time.

Mormon often added his own explanatory comment to the narrative. In some of these interpolations he identified himself (see W of M; 3 Nephi 5:8–26; 26:6–12; 28:24; 4 Nephi 1:23), but more often he used signals such as "thus we see," and "behold," and "I will show you" in an attempt to stress matters of particular spiritual importance to his readers (see Alma 24:19, 27; 50:19–23; Hel 3:27–30; 12:1–2).

Mormon the Man

While the focus of the Book of Mormon is not on the man Mormon, the abridgment he compiled does allow us to learn much about him and his times. Certainly he was an unpretentious man and, in many cases, too modest and concise (scarcely twelve printed pages of text deal directly with his own life). His son, Moroni, may have known how unassertive his father was, but wanted the modern reader to know him and to share some of his memories and the heritage his father had left him through two of Mormon's letters and one of his sermons, which reveal his father's doctrinal strength and devotion to God and to his people (see Moroni 7–9).

What little information we do have about the man Mormon is impressive, however. He tells us he was a pure descendant of Lehi through Nephi (see 3 Nephi 5:20; Mormon 1:5). He was named after his father, who was named after the land of Mormon (Mormon 1:5; 3 Nephi 5:12). Joseph Smith indicated that Mormon means "more good" (*History of the Church* 5:400; hereafter *HC*). Mormon was recognized by his predecessor Ammaron as being "a sober child" and one "quick to observe" (Mormon 1:2). As a young boy only ten years of age, Mormon received a charge from Ammaron that some 14 years later he should "go to the land Antum, unto a hill which shall be called Shim" and there obtain the ancient and faithfully recorded history of his people (v 3). He loyally fulfilled Ammaron's charge.

Under the guidance of his father, young Mormon moved to the land of Zarahemla when he was 11 years of age and continued to prepare for his prophetic role. But these were difficult times among the Nephites. After more than two centuries of righteousness and peace introduced on the Western Hemisphere by the Savior himself, the Nephite civilization had now greatly declined. Wickedness continued unchecked upon the whole of the land until even the disciples of Jesus stopped communing with the Nephites. This loss included the curtailment of the gifts of the Spirit among the people. Mormon added, "There were no gifts from the Lord, and the Holy Ghost did not come upon any, because of their wickedness and unbelief" (Mormon 1:13–14).

In spite of the wicked state of affairs among the Nephites, Mormon was able to maintain his beliefs and stand on holy ground— apart from those depraved souls. As a teenager, he was "visited of the Lord, and tasted and knew of the goodness of Jesus" (Mormon 1:15). Still in his teens, he tried valiantly to preach the gospel of repentance to the Nephites in an effort to turn them from wickedness: "And I did endeavor to preach unto this people, but I was forbidden; for behold they had willfully rebelled against their God" (v 16).

Mormon as General

All Mormon tells us about his call to be the commanding general of the Nephite armies is that it came "in my sixteenth year," and that, like his ancestor Nephi, he was "large in stature" (Mormon 2:1). After saying only this much, Mormon moves to comment on their wars with the Lamanites, noting that despite a devastating war, internal corruption, and wide acts of savagery, robbery, and evil among the people, the Nephites were unwilling to change their course. To be sure, there was despair at home and abroad, and great sorrow among them. However, Mormon reminded the modern reader,

> Their sorrowing was not unto repentance, because of the goodness of God; but it was rather the sorrowing of the damned, because the Lord would not always suffer them to take happiness in sin. And they did not come unto Jesus with broken hearts and contrite spirits, but they did curse God, and wish to die. . . .The day of grace was passed with them, both temporally and spiritually. (Mormon 2:13–15)

Destruction became so enormous and extensive that the bodies of the dead were "heaped up as dung upon the face of the land" (Mormon 2:15). In the midst of this kind of public and personal destruction, Mormon made his way to the hill Shim and obtained the plates of Nephi as he fulfilled Ammaron's commandment (see v 17).

Nephite history in the fourth century AD was, by any and all standards, a distasteful story to tell. Mormon did not tell everything in his abridgment, however. "And upon the plates of Nephi I did make a full account of all the wickedness and abominations; but upon these plates I did forbear to make a full account of their wickedness and abominations, for behold, a continual scene of wickedness and abominations has been before mine eyes ever since I have been sufficient to behold the ways of man" (Mormon 2:18). Yet, Mormon's task of telling part of the Nephite story was necessary, no matter how distasteful.

As the Nephite general, Mormon tried to maintain what military defense he could. Even as he recorded the inevitable demise of his people, he urged the Nephites to "stand boldly" and defend "their wives, and their children, and their houses, and their homes" (Mormon 2:23). Although there was an occasional temporary gain, Mormon faced the most hopeless of all military tasks—fighting when "the strength of the Lord was not with us." He recorded in his history, "Yea, we were left to ourselves, that the Spirit of the Lord did not abide in us; therefore we had become weak like unto our brethren" (v 26).

Yet, in the eleventh and twelfth year of his leadership, Mormon accomplished what must have seemed impossible—two stunning victories against the larger and stronger Lamanite armies (see Mormon 2:9–26). But when his people "began to boast in their own strength," and vow vengeance on their enemies, Mormon threw down his weapons of war and "did utterly refuse from this time to be a commander and a leader" (3:9, 11). Though he "had loved them" (v 12), he refused to lead their military forces and, by the Lord's command, waited "as an idle witness" for total destruction (see v 16).

Yet at such moments of despair and frustration, Mormon's compassion and charity manifested themselves. He could not abandon his own people. Notwithstanding their ugly wickedness, he once more stood as their general in defense of their very lives, and this in spite of the fact that he knew their ultimate destiny was total annihilation (Mormon 5:1–2). Mormon recorded:

> It is impossible for the tongue to describe, or for man to write a perfect description of the horrible scene of the blood and carnage which was among the people, both of the Nephites and of the Lamanites; and every heart was hardened, so that they delighted in the shedding of blood continually. And there never had been so great wickedness among all the children of Lehi, nor even among all the house of Israel, according to the words of the Lord, as was among this people. (Mormon 4:11–12)

Despite such depraved conditions, Mormon's indomitable spirit prevailed. He wrote in a letter to Moroni, "And now, my beloved son, notwithstanding their hardness, let us labor diligently . . . for we have a labor to perform" (Moroni 9:6).

Gradually, inevitably, inexorably, the Nephites lost more men, women, children, property, and possessions to the increasingly powerful Lamanites. They "began to be swept off by them even as a dew before the sun," Mormon noted (Mormon 4:18). And yet Mormon achieved a few victories and temporarily held out against all odds, but the Lamanites moved against him and his people in such force that "they did tread the people of the Nephites under their feet " (5:6). Aware of what the eventual outcome of the conflict would be, Mormon requested that the Lamanite leaders let him gather his people and armies in the land of Cumorah to wage one "last struggle" (6:2–6). Here at Cumorah Mormon hid the plates of the Nephites, except the brief, abridged record that he gave to his son, Moroni, and then went to battle. Mormon watched as his army of over 230,000 people was reduced to fewer than 25. Looking over that carnage, he cried in agony:

O ye fair ones, how could ye have departed from the ways of the Lord! O ye fair ones, how could ye have rejected that Jesus, who stood with open arms to receive you! ... O ye fair sons and daughters, ye fathers and mothers, ye husbands and wives, ye fair ones, how is it that ye could have fallen! But behold, ye are gone, and my sorrows cannot bring your return. (Mormon 6:17, 19–20)

Mormon as Apostle and Prophet

As Mormon arrived at the age of spiritual, physical, and emotional maturity, he embarked upon his sacred errand for his people and for us of abridging their sacred plates. From our perspective today, Mormon's calling as record keeper and abridger was very important. Yet in his own day, he was first and foremost an apostle and prophet among his people. We recognize Mormon as a prophet, but rarely do we say much about his calling as a disciple of Jesus, that is, as an apostle of Jesus.

While abridging the record of the period just before Jesus' appearance to the Nephite nation, Mormon stated:

And behold, I am called Mormon, being called after the land of Mormon, the land in which Alma did establish the church among the people, yea, the first church which was established among them after their transgression. And behold, *I am a disciple of Jesus Christ*, the Son of God. *I have been called of him to declare his word among his people*, that they might have everlasting life. (3 Nephi 5:10–13; emphasis added)

What a disciple of Jesus Christ is and what Mormon may have meant by the phrase is revealed a few chapters later. Following the resurrected Savior's appearance among the people, Mormon noted that 12 men were "called," given "power and authority," and instructed (see 3 Nephi 12). They were known as "disciples," a New Testament term used to describe Jesus' followers and also, on occasion, the Twelve Apostles. Mormon notes that he was *called* to declare Christ's word. An apostle is a special witness of Jesus Christ (D&C 107:23).

The Prophet Joseph Smith expanded the meaning of the Book of Mormon term "disciple" when he wrote about their church organization: "They had *Apostles*, Prophets, ... the same ordinances, gifts, powers, and blessings, as were enjoyed on the eastern continent" (*HC* 4:537; emphasis added). It seems apparent that Joseph Smith believed that the 12 disciples chosen by the resurrected Jesus were apostles. Parley P. Pratt also noted in *The Key to the Science of Theology*, "On the Western Hemisphere, the apostleship, oracles, miracles, and gifts of the Spirit, ceased from among the people in the fourth century." Later on he said, "Translated men, like Enoch, Elijah, John the Apostle, and three of the *Apostles of the Western Hemisphere*, are in these respects like the angels" (74, 112; emphasis added).

If the same organization operated among the Nephite Church as in the New Testament Church, then we can presume that succession in priesthood office also occurred. This could explain how Mormon could be an apostle hundreds of years following the advent of the Savior among the Nephites. There are other statements in the Book of Mormon itself that tend to support this interpretation. When the original apostles save the three who should tarry reached the age of 72 and had gone to the paradise of God, "there were other disciples ordained in their stead" (4 Nephi 1:14). In the book of Moroni, there are several short chapters which outline policies and procedures for the Church. He preserved for us the words Jesus spoke to the Nephite disciples when he ordained them:

> The words of Christ, which he spake unto his disciples, the twelve whom he had chosen, as he laid his hands upon them. And he called them by name, saying: Ye shall call on the Father in my name, in mighty prayer; and after ye have done this ye shall have power that to him upon whom ye shall lay your hands, ye shall give the Holy Ghost; and in my name shall ye give it, *for thus do mine apostles*. (Moroni 2:1–2; emphasis added)

Because it appears that Christ makes a parallel between the disciples and the apostles, it therefore seems reasonable to assume that Mormon was not simply a disciple in the classical sense (a follower of a great teacher), but was an apostle and prophet of the Lord among the Nephites.

Viewing Mormon from this new perspective enhances our perception of his prophetic role among the people. Paul himself said that God placed apostles first in the Church, then prophets (see 1 Cor 12:28). As an apostolic witness of the Lord and one sent by the Lord, Mormon added his witness of the Savior in the Book of Mormon. As already noted, he declared: "And I, being fifteen years of age and being somewhat of a sober mind, therefore I was visited of the Lord, and tasted and knew of the goodness of Jesus" (Mormon 1:15). It is obvious that Mormon stands as one who knew the Lord and testified of his reality.

Later, Mormon's son wrote, "And now, I would commend you to seek this Jesus of whom the prophets and apostles have written, that the grace of God the Father, and also the Lord Jesus Christ, and the Holy Ghost, which beareth record of them, may be and abide in you forever. Amen" (Ether 12:41). It is natural to think of the Old Testament prophets and New Testament apostles at this point, but Moroni was probably painting a larger picture. While it includes biblical prophets and apostles, it also seems to include the Book of Mormon prophets and apostles, of whom Mormon was one.

The writings to which Moroni referred included the New Testament and the Book of Mormon. In this case, Mormon stands as one of the few apostles who left a written record of Jesus. And when we compare his writings to other apostles' work, he stands out by the amount of material he wrote. Unlike the New Testament disciples, most of Mormon's efforts are directed to the modern reader.

Actually, Mormon had two audiences in mind when he wrote. While it is certain that all scripture was applicable to his current setting, Mormon focused on our day. For certain, he was concerned with those among whom he lived, patiently pleading with them to repent and return to God. Yet, he also spoke to unborn generations. As he concludes his editing of 3 Nephi, he adds an exhortation to the modern reader. In it he sounds like an ancient Israelite prophet: "Hearken, O ye Gentiles, and hear the words of Jesus Christ, the Son of the living God, which he hath commanded me that I should speak concerning you, for, behold he commandeth me that I should write, saying: Turn, all ye Gentiles, from your wicked ways; and repent of your evil doings" (3 Nephi 30:1–2).

As we have shown, Mormon, as the Lord's apostle and prophet, called his people to repentance, but it was his son who preserved some of his apostolic teachings. Mormon's sermon in Moroni chapter 7 focuses on the principles of faith, hope, and charity and includes teachings on how to distinguish between good and evil, the necessity of spiritual gifts, the nature of miracles, and instruction on how to obtain charity, "the pure love of Christ" (Moroni 7:47).

In two frank and straightforward letters to his son (Moroni chapters 8–9), Mormon, with authority from God, first condemns infant baptism as "solemn mockery before God" (8:9, 16). He instructed his son that children are made pure through the atonement of Christ and do not need the cleansing power of baptism until they are old enough to be accountable for their own actions and are capable of repenting of their own sins. Second, he describes the level of depravity to which the Nephites and Lamanites had fallen, offering reasons for their prophesied destruction—"they are without principle, and past feeling" (Moroni 9:20). He concluded this letter by charging his son to remain faithful to Christ in spite of society's wickedness.

Mormon stands as a bridge between the modern reader and those ancient people. He was a special witness or an apostle and prophet to both as evidenced above.

Mormon as Father

In the midst of devastation and depravity, a loving and intimate portrait of a father and son is revealed in the books of Mormon and Moroni. The glaring contrast between the world in which Mormon and Moroni lived and their own lives and relationship with each other is a fitting end to the Book of Mormon. Of course, it was in the end a team effort that allowed the modern reader to have the sacred record at all. The pattern set by Lehi and Nephi at the beginning of the record is followed and repeated at the end of the book by a righteous son following his father. Mormon and Moroni's love, respect and tenderness towards each other is made all the more poignant by the fact that they lived in such a brutal and wicked society.

The legacy of this father-and-son relationship is shown by a careful reading of the closing pages of the sacred record they were so instrumental in preserving and preparing to come forth in our day. Upon careful examination of Moroni's introduction to his own writing found in Mormon 8, we discover a son longing for his father. It should be noted that Moroni was himself already a capable leader, having led an army of 10,000 men into battle. We later learn that he had also already had a ministry in the Church. Moroni was well-seasoned by the time his father died. As one of the last survivors of the Nephite civilization, Moroni took up his father's record. In summarizing for the modern reader the events that had overtaken his people, he revealed his deep sense of loss for his father and his acute loneliness. In Mormon 8 he tells us twice that his father had been killed and adds additional insights to his relationship with him:

Behold I, Moroni, do finish the record of *my father*, Mormon. Behold, I have but few things to write, which things I have been commanded by *my father*. And now it came to pass that after the great and tremendous battle at Cumorah, behold, the Nephites who had escaped into the country southward were hunted by the Lamanites, until they were all destroyed. And *my father* also was killed by them, and I even remain alone to write the sad tale of the destruction of my people. But behold, they are gone, and I fulfil the commandment of *my father*. (Mormon 8:1–3; emphasis added)

Mormon and Moroni's combined efforts in preserving and preparing the record for us are no better evidenced than in the Jaredite record. In abridging the entire span of Nephite history up through his own day, Mormon promises that an account of the earlier inhabitants would be "written hereafter; for behold, it is expedient that all people should know the things which are written in this account" (Mosiah 28:19). Mormon's death prevented him from fulfilling this promise, but his son faithfully filled in for him and abridged the book of Ether.

Moroni seems to exhibit a deep sense of love and admiration for his father. The inclusion of two letters and a sermon by his father in his own record shows this respect and admiration. He is also fiercely loyal to the charge his father gave him concerning the record, as already noted.

Moroni was also an articulate writer. It is obvious from Ether 12 that he could compose doctrinal discourses, yet, surprisingly, he quotes his father in Moroni 7. I believe Moroni could have written Moroni 7 himself, but chose not to. This is not to say that Moroni was not a great doctrinal writer like his father, it is only to say that he recognized his father's significant contributions.

All in all, the letters provide more evidence of a powerful parental bond between father and son as Mormon honors his son by addressing him, "my beloved son" (see Moroni 8:1, 9). In this letter, Mormon addresses Moroni six times as "my son" (see vv 6, 24, 27–30).

In a second letter, Mormon again addresses Moroni as "my beloved son" three times (Moroni 9:1, 6, 11). In this last letter, he encourages his son to "be faithful in Christ, and may not the things which I have written grieve thee, to weigh thee down unto death; but may Christ lift thee up, and may his sufferings and death, and the showing his body unto our fathers, and his mercy and long-suffering, and the hope of his glory and of eternal life, rest in your mind forever"

(Moroni 9:25). Mormon's teachings and example inspired his son to be faithful to the end.

Mormon as Prophetic Type

If Mormon was a type, then his life and mission may have represented other prophets' lives and missions, including the life of Jesus Christ. While translating the Book of Mormon, Joseph Smith must have been impressed with the life and mission of Nephi and of Mormon. He may have felt an immediate affinity between himself and these two historical personalities, as he would have had with other Book of Mormon prophets. But these two men seem to have had particular experiences that relate to Joseph Smith.

Both Nephi and Mormon led similar lives. Possibly even Mormon was aware of this pattern and similarity. Both Mormon and Nephi were young when they were visited by the Lord. Both young men were large in stature. Each was entrusted with sacred plates. Each was called by the Lord to be the spiritual and temporal leader of their people. Each wrote important doctrinal and historical pieces themselves and each bore witness of the divinity of Jesus Christ.

Young Joseph Smith may have seen this common thread within their lives; a thread he could see being woven into his own life's fabric. We may never know what lessons Joseph was discovering about his own prophetic career while learning about Nephi and Mormon as he worked on the translation of the Book of Mormon.

Both Mormon and Joseph were named after their fathers. Both had a vision of the Lord as teenagers. Both Mormon and Joseph Smith rejected the wickedness of their day. As young men, both Joseph and Mormon were chosen to receive the ancient plates of the Nephites. Both of them wrote of their struggles in proclaiming the word during their ministry among the people. Both were apostles and prophets of the Lord. Whatever parallels the Prophet Joseph noticed during the translation period may have been heightened as the Prophet matured at the close of his ministry in Nauvoo, where he became the temporal leader of the people when he was elected city mayor. He had already been nominated and commissioned a general in the Nauvoo Legion by the Illinois state governor earlier. Like Nephi and Mormon before, Joseph was the spiritual and temporal leader of the people.

The way Joseph Smith's life may have been patterned after Mormon's is seen in one final detail. Dramatically, Joseph's life paralleled Mormon's life even in death. Both died for their religion and in defense of their people's rights; one while imprisoned and the other on the battlefield, yet both as martyrs. This approach doesn't assume, of course, that the younger was a carbon copy of the older man: Mormon had the best education his culture could furnish, whereas Joseph Smith was raised in frontier poverty without training beyond basic skills. But in spite of that personal difference, there are dramatic common denominators. It matters little that one spoke English and the other the language of the Nephites, provided they both spoke as inspired by the Holy Ghost. Ultimately, we can not be sure that these parallels have any significance. We have no evidence to suggest that Joseph Smith noticed them. If these parallels were not coincidental, however, then Mormon's influence may be more significant for Joseph Smith than has otherwise been noted before.[2]

Conclusion

In reference to the record that Mormon helped to produce, Joseph Smith stated in Nauvoo, "I told the brethren that the Book of Mormon was the most correct of any book on earth, and the keystone of our religion, and a man would get nearer to God by abiding by its precepts, than by any other book" (*HC* 4:461). Who can estimate Mormon's contribution to the salvation of the modern world? As an apostle of the Lord, Mormon is capable of putting the Savior's ministry among the Nephites in proper perspective. He has an intimacy with the resurrected Lord that few have experienced. He stands as a witness of Jesus and therefore is an example of discipleship in the truest sense.

---

[2]   One secular historian has suggested that some of the stories and personalities found in the Book of Mormon reflected Joseph's own life (see Fawn M. Brodie, *No Man Knows My History*). Joseph, according to this Freudian interpretation, simply projected his own life and experiences into the lives of certain Book of Mormon characters, including Mormon. While Brodie identified a few parallels between Joseph and Mormon, others exist as indicated above. This secular interpretation does not adequately explain all the parallels. How would Joseph Smith know in 1829 (when the translation of the Book of Mormon was completed) that he would become the political and military leader of a people (mayor of Nauvoo and Nauvoo Legion general) as Mormon? How could he know that he would die for his beliefs and in defense of the rights of his people as Mormon? If parallels exist, then all of them must be considered.

As a father, Mormon's efforts are reflected in the life of his son, Moroni—a son whose ultimate mission was seen by John the Revelator. In a most cruel and hostile world filled with all manner of evil and destruction, Mormon and Moroni weld a living and tender link with the teachings of Christ's pure gospel. As a possible prophetic type, Mormon's life may well have brought understanding to Joseph Smith. Mormon's own experiences may have cast a long shadow into the future—the life of Joseph Smith.

As a record keeper, both as Nephite historian and abridger, Mormon's impact may never really be known. The Book of Mormon is a complex record, astutely edited by Mormon. He did not of course have the use of such modern inventions as footnotes, tables of contents, indices, or hypertext links to help the readers. The brilliance and precision of his mind led him to utilize an extensive system of internal source references, while the magnitude of his vision is evident in the scope and composition of the Book of Mormon as a whole. Doctrine and Covenants section 20 states the following regarding this sacred document:

> [It] contains a record of a fallen people, and the fulness of the gospel of Jesus Christ to the Gentiles and to the Jews also . . . proving to the world that the holy scriptures are true . . . and those who receive it in faith, and work righteousness, shall receive a crown of eternal life. (D&C 20:9, 11, 14)

Thus the Book of Mormon stands as a witness to Mormon's prophetic call to complete the record for us today. It stands on its own—an ancient record for a modern world, a record that can bring us closer to God than any other book. Through its pages we meet the man Mormon, whom the Lord chose to create the "marvelous work and wonder." By reading it, we can learn the message he preserved for us today.

BIBLIOGRAPHY

Brodie, Fawn M. *No Man Knows My History.* New York: Alfred Knopf, 1947.

Clark, E. Douglas and Robert S. Clark. *Fathers and Sons in the Book of Mormon.* Salt Lake City: Deseret Book, 1991.

History of the Church. 7 vols. Salt Lake City: Deseret Book, 1980.

Holland, Jeffery R. "Mormon: The Man and the Book." *Ensign* (Mar 1978) 8:15–18.

Mackay, Thomas W. "Mormon's Philosophy of History: Helaman 12 In the Perspective of Mormon's Editing Procedures." *The Book of Mormon: Helaman Through 3 Nephi 8, According To Thy Word.* Ed. Monte S. Nyman, and Charles D. Tate, Jr. Provo, UT: Brigham Young Univ, Religious Studies Center, 1992. 129–46.

Pratt, Parley P. *The Key to the Science of Theology.* Salt Lake City: Deseret Book, 1965.

The Spirit of Christ: A Light Amidst the Darkness

11

Daniel K Judd

*T*hose prophets who wrote, compiled, and abridged the Book of Mormon did so with the inhabitants of our day in mind. President Ezra Taft Benson has stated:

> We must make the Book of Mormon a center focus of study because it was written for our day. The Nephites never had the book, neither did the Lamanites of ancient times. It was meant for us. Mormon wrote near the end of the Nephite civilization. Under the inspiration of God, who sees all things from the beginning, he abridged centuries of records, choosing the stories, speeches, and events that would be most helpful to us. (58)

Moroni, the last of the Book of Mormon prophets, saw our day:

> The Lord hath shown unto me great and marvelous things concerning that which must shortly come, at that day when these things shall come forth among you. Behold, I speak unto you as if ye were present, and yet ye are not. But behold, Jesus Christ hath shown you unto me, and I know your doing . . . the pride of your hearts . . . envying, and strifes, and malice, and persecutions, and all manner of iniquities. (Mormon 8:34–35)

From the *Wall Street Journal*, we read a sobering description of the problems in today's society which is consistent with Moroni's vision:

> Since 1960 . . . there has been a 560% increase in violent crime; a 419% increase in illegitimate births; a quadrupling in divorce rates; a tripling of the percentage of children living in single-parent homes; more than a 200% increase in the teenage suicide rate. (Bennet 59)

Daniel K Judd is assistant professor of Ancient Scripture at Brigham Young University.

We live in difficult times, and my heart goes out to all those whose lives embody these statistics in any way. While some of the problems of our day do not involve questions of morality, most do. We have all been influenced in some way by the moral decay of our culture. Many things which were once considered evil are now celebrated as "good," and numerous things which were once reverenced as good are now called inappropriate or evil. Isaiah has written: "Wo unto them that call evil good, and good evil, that put darkness for light, and light for darkness, that put bitter for sweet, and sweet for bitter!" (Isa 5:20; also 2 Nephi 15:20).

A Light in the Darkness

Not only have prophets provided descriptions of the problems of our day, but they have also given counsel as to how to address them. As part of his record, the prophet Moroni included his father's teaching on the most fundamental means by which God sustains man: the Spirit of Christ: "For behold, the *Spirit of Christ* is given to every man, that he may know good from evil; wherefore, I show unto you the way to judge; for every thing which inviteth to do good, and to persuade to believe in Christ, is sent forth by the power and gift of Christ; wherefore ye may know with a perfect knowledge it is of God" (Moroni 7:16; emphasis added). The Spirit of Christ is not merely a source of truth, it is an integral part of what we are as human beings (see John 14:6, 20; D&C 93:29).

The Spirit of Christ Described

While the Book of Mormon does not provide detailed information concerning the Spirit of Christ, it does describe its purposes and its influence upon the lives of people. From modern scriptures, we learn that the Spirit of Christ is the *power* that "proceedeth forth from the presence of God to fill the immensity of space" (D&C 88:12; see also 2 Nephi 16:3). It is the *light* of the sun, the moon, and the stars, and the *power* by which all things were made (D&C 88:7–10). It is a *spirit* that "giveth life to all things" and the "*law* by which all things are governed" (v 13; emphasis added). Also, this spirit is the power which enables God to comprehend all things (v 41). The Spirit of Christ is also that which "giveth light to every man that cometh into the world" (D&C 88:46) and is given to everyone that they "may know good from evil" (Moroni 7:15).

The Spirit of Christ and the Holy Ghost

The Spirit of Christ is often confused with the Holy Ghost, the Gift of the Holy Ghost, and the spirit personage of Jesus Christ. Some of the confusion obviously comes because terms such as "Spirit of the Lord," "Spirit of God," and "Spirit of Christ" are often used interchangeably in both scripture and conversation, and it is often difficult to determine to which personage or gift the passage refers. The term "Spirit of Christ" is used only twice in the Book of Mormon (Moroni 7:16 and 10:17) while the term "Holy Ghost" is used 95 times. The term "Spirit of the Lord" is used 40 times, "Spirit of God" 20 times, and the expression "Power of God" is utilized 54 times. An analysis of the use of these terms reveals that only in a few instances is the differentiation of these terms made clear.

It is from the prophets of this dispensation that we learn that the Spirit of Christ is neither the Holy Ghost, the Gift of the Holy Ghost, nor the spirit personage of Jesus Christ; but it is the primary means by which each of these entities operate. President Joseph F. Smith taught:

> The question is often asked, Is there any difference between the Spirit of the Lord and the Holy Ghost? The terms are frequently used synonymously. We often say the Spirit of God when we mean the Holy Ghost; we likewise say the Holy Ghost when we mean the Spirit of God. The Holy Ghost is a personage in the Godhead, and is not that which lighteth every man that cometh into the world. It is the Spirit of God which proceeds through Christ to the world, that enlightens every man that comes into the world, and that strives with the children of men, and will continue to strive with them, until it brings them to a knowledge of the truth and the possession of the greater light and testimony of the Holy Ghost. (67–68)

Elder James E. Talmage taught that the Spirit of Christ is the "divine essence" by means of which the Godhead operates upon man and in nature (488).

The Gift of the Holy Ghost has been likened to the "continuing blaze of the sun at noonday," and the Holy Ghost as "a flash of lightning blazing forth in a dark and stormy night" (McConkie 262). Perhaps it would be appropriate to liken the Spirit of Christ to the faint and yet fixed light of the moon and stars which precedes the brighter light of dawn.

Prophets, both ancient and modern, have taught that the Spirit of Christ is *preparatory* in purpose. It prepares God's children to receive the temporary witness of the Holy Ghost, followed by the more constant Gift of the Holy Ghost, which is bestowed upon those who are baptized (see D&C 130:23). An example of this progression can be identified in the Book of Mormon account of the conversion of king Lamoni. Even though Lamoni had the autocratic authority of a king and had been taught that "whatsoever [he] did was right," the text suggests that he still knew it was wrong to slay those servants he judged had not served him well: "Notwithstanding [king Lamoni and his father] believed in a Great Spirit, they supposed that whatsoever they did was right; nevertheless, Lamoni began to fear exceedingly, with fear lest he had done wrong in slaying his servants" (Alma 18:5).

We may conclude from this verse that the Spirit of the Lord is *not* simply the internalization of the expectations of the culture in which one lives (see JST John 7:24), but it is a part of what we are as human beings (see also Rom 2:14). Though the truth was eclipsed by tradition and sin, a spirit was working upon king Lamoni that revived his sense of right and wrong.

King Lamoni's experience continued and intensified as he "fell unto the earth, as if he were dead" (Alma 18:42). Note the description of Lamoni's experience during the time he was overcome:

> Ammon . . . knew that king Lamoni was under the power of God; he knew that the dark veil of unbelief was being cast away from his mind, and the *light* which did *light* up his mind, which was the *light* of the glory of God, which was a marvelous *light* of his goodness—yea, this *light* had infused such joy into his soul, the cloud of darkness having been dispelled, and that the *light* of everlasting life was lit up in his soul, yea, he knew that this had overcome his natural frame, and he was carried away in God. (Alma 19:6; emphasis added)

Ammon seems to be describing the light of Christ that was working on the king, preparing him to receive the constant companionship of the Holy Ghost. King Lamoni and all of his servants were then baptized and even though it is not detailed in this scriptural account, we can be confident that precedent was followed and, after being baptized, they were given the Gift of the Holy Ghost (see 2 Nephi 31:14).

The additional light which comes with the reception of the Gift of the Holy Ghost is demonstrated by Ammon's experiences as he worked with king Lamoni. In addition to the great physical power demonstrated by Ammon, he was also "filled with the *Spirit of God*, therefore he *perceived . . . the thoughts of the king*" (Alma 18:16; emphasis added). Ammon also described additional blessings in the following: "I am called by his *Holy Spirit* to teach these things unto this people, that they may be brought to a knowledge of that which is just and true; And a portion of that *Spirit* dwelleth in me, which giveth me knowledge, and also power according to my faith and desires which are in God" (Alma 18:34–35; emphasis added).

The Light of Creation

The scriptures also teach us that one of the fundamental functions of the Spirit of Christ was in the creation of the earth (D&C 88:7–9). This strongly suggests that the Spirit of God that "moved upon the face of the water" mentioned by Moses in the various Creation accounts was the Spirit of Christ (see Moses 2:2–5; Gen 1:2–5). Parley P. Pratt wrote that it is the "true light" or the Spirit of Christ that permeates all nature and provides the life-sustaining instincts found in both men and animals (41). As stated earlier, the Spirit of Christ is not always something that is external to us; it is also a part of what we are as living creatures. The scriptures imply that without the Spirit of Christ, which gives us life "from one moment to another," life would cease to exist (Mosiah 2:21; see also D&C 88:50).

The Light of Discovery and Intellect

The Spirit of Christ is also the power that enlightens our intellects as we seek to discover the mysteries of heaven and earth (D&C 88:11). Nephi tells us that "the *Spirit of God* . . . wrought upon the man" Columbus in his discovery of the new world and that "the *Spirit of God* . . . wrought upon other Gentiles [ie, Pilgrims]; and they went forth out of captivity, upon the many waters" (1 Nephi 13:12–13; emphasis added). We also read of the Lord's promise to Nephi to be his "*light* in the wilderness" as he sought to find the promised land (17:13; emphasis added).

Alma wrote of hearts being changed and souls being "illuminated by the *light* of the everlasting word" (Alma 5:7; emphasis added). He also described the "discernible" nature of light in the following passage: "O then, is not this real? I say unto you, Yea, because it is *light*; and whatsoever is *light*, is good, because it is discernible, therefore ye must know that it is good" (Alma 32:35; emphasis added).

Many of the world's great leaders, scientists, artists and philosophers have also been influenced by "a portion of God's light." In 1978, the First Presidency stated:

> The great religious leaders of the world such as Mohammed, Confucius, and the Reformers, as well as philosophers including Socrates, Plato, and others, received a portion of God's light. Moral truths were given to them by God to enlighten whole nations and to bring a higher level of understanding to individuals. (Faust 12)

It was also the Spirit of Christ that led to the scientific discoveries of Gutenberg, Edison, and Bell, and others. Joseph Fielding Smith wrote:

> Those who make these discoveries are inspired of God or they would never make them. The Lord gave inspiration to Edison, to Franklin, to Morse, to Whitney and to all of the inventors and discoverers, and through their inspiration they obtained the necessary knowledge and were able to manufacture and invent as they have done for the benefit of the world. Without the help of the Lord they would have been just as helpless as the people were in other ages. (1:147)

The Light of Conscience

While the Spirit of Christ is manifest in a multitude of ways, the remainder of this chapter will be dedicated to the dimension of the Spirit of Christ which deals with conscience, the knowing of "good from evil." In addition to what was stated earlier concerning "every thing which inviteth to do good" being "sent forth by the power and gift of Christ" (Moroni 7:16), Mormon also teaches us about discerning that which is evil:

> But whatsoever thing persuadeth men to do evil, and believe not in Christ, and deny him, and serve not God, then ye may know with a perfect knowledge it is of the devil; for after this manner doth the devil work, for he persuadeth no

man to do good, no, not one; neither do his angels; neither do they who subject themselves unto him. (Moroni 7:17)

Though we live in marvelous times when the gospel of Christ has been restored to the earth in its fulness, many have come to a distorted view of good and evil for they "denieth the *power* of God" because of the "precepts of men" (2 Nephi 28:26; emphasis added). The good and evil spoken of in scripture has been replaced by the dogmatism of some and the relativism of others. The Book of Mormon anti-Christ, Korihor, taught that "every man prospered according to his genius" and justified his own evil deeds and those of others by teaching that "whatsoever a man did was no crime" (Alma 30:17). The Apostle Paul warned of those who would come to associate righteousness with prosperity and competence (see 1 Tim 6:5). All of these false philosophies lead to serious distortions of conscience.

The Lord has warned us that the day would come when men would "perceive not the light" (D&C 45:29) and reject the fulness of the gospel because they would come to believe in false philosophies. President Joseph Fielding Smith warned of relying solely on the power of intellect:

> *The worship of reason, of false philosophy*, is greater now than it was [in the days of the Son of God]. Men are depending upon their own research to find out God, and that which they cannot discover and which they cannot demonstrate to their satisfaction through their own research and their *natural senses*, they reject. They are not seeking for the Spirit of the Lord; they are not striving to know God in the manner in which he has marked out by which he may be known; but they are walking in their own way, believing in their own man-made philosophies, teaching the doctrines of devils and not the doctrines of the Son of God. (3:275)

We ought not interpret this to say that reason and intellect should be rejected, but rather that reason should not be exercised without regard to the morality of which it is inextricably a part. Nephi taught that we should not "hearken unto the precepts of men, *save their precepts shall be given by the power of the Holy Ghost*" (2 Nephi 28:31; emphasis added). His brother, Jacob, taught that "to be learned is good if [the learned] hearken unto the counsels of God" (9:29). Note the following counsel from Elder Hugh B. Brown:

> The Church of Jesus Christ of Latter-day Saints accepts newly revealed truth, whether it comes through direct revelation or from study and research. We deny the common conception of reality that distinguishes radically between the

natural and the supernatural, between the temporal and the eternal, between the sacred and the secular. For us, there is no order of reality that is utterly different in character from the world of which we are a part, that is separated from us by an impassable gulf. We do not separate our daily mundane tasks and interests from the meaning and substance of religion. We recognize the spiritual in all phases and aspects of living and realize that this life is an important part of eternal life. (458)

We need to make "righteous judgment[s]" (JST Matt 7:2) concerning the knowledge we obtain, whether it comes from secular or sacred sources. Mormon teaches us that the way to make these judgments is as plain as day and night: "For every thing which inviteth to do good, and to persuade to believe in Christ, is sent forth by the power and gift of Christ; wherefore ye may know with a perfect knowledge it is of God" (Moroni 7:16). However, this does not say that we will always be able to discern right from wrong in the present moment. From the Doctrine and Covenants we read: "But as you cannot always judge the righteous, or as you cannot always tell the wicked from the righteous, therefore I say unto you, hold your peace until I shall see fit to make all things known unto the world concerning the matter" (D&C 10:37). There will be times when we must exercise patience and faith as we "wait upon the Lord" for the understanding that is sought (2 Nephi 18:17).

Moral Agency

We live in a day when many are claiming that all truth is relative and there are no absolutes. Moral agency, which invites the choice between right and wrong, has been replaced by a distorted notion of free agency—the choice between alternatives. Elder Boyd K. Packer clarifies this point of doctrine in his discussion of the "pro-choice" philosophy in his conference talk entitled "Our Moral Environment":

Regardless of how lofty and moral the "pro-choice" argument sounds, it is badly flawed. With that same logic one could argue that all traffic signs and barriers which keep the careless from danger should be pulled down on the theory that each individual must be free to choose how close to the edge he will go. . . . The phrase "*free* agency" does not appear in scripture. The only agency spoken of there is *moral agency*, "which," the Lord said, "I have given unto him, that every man may be *accountable* for his own sins in the day of judgment" (D&C 101:78; emphasis added). (66-67)

Just as the scriptures contain accounts of lives being changed for the better in days of old, lives continue to be changed in the present as we come to understand and exercise the moral agency we have been given. Elder Spencer J. Condie has shared the following story of a man whose life was changed as he was true to the light within:

> I know [a] good man who was reared in a family without the blessings of the gospel. Through a series of unfortunate events in his early youth, he was introduced to homosexuality, and gradually he became a prisoner of this addictive behavior.
>
> One day two young missionaries knocked on his door and asked if he would be interested in learning of the restored gospel of Jesus Christ. In his heart of hearts he wanted to be freed from his prison of uncleanness, but feeling unable to change the direction his life had taken, he terminated the missionary discussions. Before leaving his apartment, the two elders left a copy of the Book of Mormon with him, and testified of its truthfulness.
>
> My friend placed the book on his bookshelf and forgot about it for several years. He continued acting out his homosexual tendencies, assuming that such relationships would bring him happiness. But alas, with each passing year, his misery increased.
>
> One day in the depths of despair, he scanned his bookshelf for something to read which might edify and uplift him and restore his self-worth. His eye caught hold of the book with a dark-blue cover, which the missionaries had given him several years before. He began to read. On the second page of this book, he read of Father Lehi's vision in which he was given a book to read, and "as he read, he was filled with the Spirit of the Lord" (1 Nephi 1:12). And as my good friend continued reading, he too was filled with the Spirit of the Lord.
>
> He read King Benjamin's benedictory challenge to undergo a mighty change of heart—not a little change, but a mighty change. He was given hope by the comforting conversion stories of Enos, Alma, Ammon, and Aaron. He was also inspired by the account of the Savior's visit to the ancient Nephites. By the time he reached the final page of the Book of Mormon, he was prepared to accept Moroni's loving invitation to "come unto Christ, and be perfected in him, and deny yourselves of all ungodliness" (Moroni 10:32).
>
> My friend contacted the Church and was taught the gospel and was baptized. Within a relatively short time, he married a lovely young woman, and they are the parents of several beautiful children. He and his wife are very dynamic and committed servants of the Lord, influencing many others for good. (15–17)

In the following passage, the prophet Mormon summarizes for us the great sorrow of those who reject the light of Christ, and the great rejoicing experienced by all who follow him: "And thus we see the great reason of sorrow, and also of rejoicing—sorrow because of death and destruction among men, and joy because of the *light of Christ* unto life" (Alma 28:14; emphasis added).

Promptings of Conscience

It is through our conscience we first come to perceive the love of a Father in Heaven who does "all things for the welfare and happiness of his people" (Hel 12:2). The word "conscience" literally means to know within oneself. Elder Boyd K. Packer has written about the word conscience:

> It is made up of the prefix *con*, meaning "with," and the word *science*, meaning "to know." The *Oxford English Dictionary* says it comes from the Latin *conscientia*, meaning "knowledge [knowing] within oneself." The first definition listed there is "inward knowledge, consciousness, inmost thought, mind." The second one is "consciousness of right and wrong," or in just two words, "moral sense."
>
> Our conscience might be described as a memory, a residual awareness of who we really are, of our true identity. *It is perhaps the best example of the fact that we can become aware of truths because we feel them rather than by knowing them because we perceive them through the physical senses.* ("The Law and the Light" 2–3)

We can experience our conscience, *or* "light of Christ" or "Spirit of Christ"—in different ways. If we are living truth-full-y (consistent with light and truth), we will experience our conscience as a gentle invitation persuading us to follow its prompting to do good. We may have even reached a point of self-less-ness, where we aren't even cognizant that we are being prompted or acting upon the prompting. When this is the case, we will live spontaneously, without self-regard (see 3 Nephi 9:20). When we are not living truthfully, we will experience our conscience as a demanding and irritating mandate.

Following our conscience leads us to peace and greater understanding, while acting against what we know to be right leads to distress and confusion and is often the beginning of greater problems. Large, ominous problems typically begin as small, simple ones. While the problems most of us face are neither as dramatic as Lamoni's nor as complicated as the individual's described by Elder Condie, we still confront them on a daily basis. A friend told me the following example of a prompting of conscience with which most of us can identify:

My wife had asked if I would rock the baby to sleep. I knew I should, but I really wanted to watch the football game. I quickly settled on a compromise, I could take the baby into my room, watch the football game on the portable television and rock her to sleep at the same time. A real "win/win" situation! I would miss the color screen, but what a small price to pay for being a good Dad.

The problem came after about two minutes of watching the game. My daughter began to fuss. The thought came in my mind that if I turned the television off, walked with her and sang to her, she might be soothed. I knew it was the right thing to do, but did I do it? No, I spent the next thirty minutes struggling to watch the game and rock my child, all the while resenting the fact that I couldn't do what I wanted to!

One of the characteristics of persons who go against their conscience is that they have to justify their actions. These justifications come in the forms of rationalizations, thoughts, blaming emotions, and in some cases, physiological responses. In Proverbs we read, "The way of a fool is right in his own eyes" (12:15). Having discussed this story with the individual who lived it, I can detail for you what his self-justifications were: (1) "I've been working with difficult situations all day, I need some time to myself"; (2) "My wife is much better suited to deal with children than I am, she should be doing this"; (3) "My wife doesn't appreciate all that I do, it's really unfair she would have me do this"; (4) "I'm so tired, I need to lie down"; and finally, (5) "Why did we have all these kids anyway?"

We often think of "sin" as being something grievous like murder, adultery, or some other form of gross immorality, and while they are among the most serious of sins, the scriptures teach that anytime we "knoweth to do good, and doeth it not, . . . it is sin" (James 4:17). When my friend didn't arise and walk with his child, he went against that which he knew was right (conscience), and that in a word is sin.

I know from personal, professional, and ecclesiastical experience that most of the problems we face in life begin when we deny the promptings of conscience we experience daily. President Spencer W. Kimball made this same observation in the following:

> There are many causes for human suffering—including war, disease, and poverty—and the suffering that proceeds from each of these is very real, but I would not be true to my trust if I did not say that *the most persistent cause of human suffering, that suffering which causes the deepest pain, is sin*—the violation of the commandments given to us by God. . . . If any of us wish to have more precise prescriptions for ourselves in terms of what we can do to

have more abundant lives, all we usually need to do is to consult our conscience. (155)

While many of us go against our conscience by not doing those things we know are right, others of us confuse conscience with societal expectations and get lost in the artificial light of perfectionism. Consider the following story of Esther, published in the Sunday School manual, *Teach Them Correct Principles*:

> Esther was trying to be the perfect wife and mother. Every morning she woke up announcing to herself: "This is the day I will be perfect. The house will be organized, I will not yell at my children, and I will finish everything important I have planned." Every night she went to bed discouraged, because she had failed to accomplish her goal. She became irritable with everyone, including herself, and she began to wonder what she was doing wrong.
>
> One night Esther knelt in prayer and asked for guidance. Afterward, while lying awake, a startling thought came to her. She realized that in focusing on her own perfection she was focusing on herself and failing to love others, particularly her husband and children. She was being not loving, therefore not Christlike, but essentially selfish. She was trying to be sweet to her children, but not freely, out of love for them, but because she saw it as a necessary part of *her* perfection. Furthermore, she was trying to get a feeling of righteousness by forcing her husband and children to meet her ideal of perfection. When her children got in the way of her "perfect" routine, she blamed them for making her feel "imperfect," and she became irritated with them and treated them in a most unloving way. Likewise, if her husband did not meet her idea of perfection when he came home from work, she judged him as failing and was critical of him as a way of reinforcing her sense of her own righteousness.
>
> Esther remembered the Savior's commandment to be perfect *as he is perfect* (see 3 Nephi 12:48). She realized that this perfection includes loving as he loved (John 13:34), and realized she had been pursuing the wrong goal. (7)

As with Esther, most of us who have challenges with perfectionism are not committed to selflessly serving others, but in serving ourselves by showing the world how competent we are. We are constantly on the run, doing a lot of things for a lot of people and, sometimes, becoming physically ill in the process. Like Martha of New Testament times, those who struggle with perfectionism are "careful and troubled about many things" (Luke 10:41). A perfectionist's flurry of activity is often a type of "virtuous" excuse for not being true to simple promptings of conscience.

It is through these simple promptings of conscience that the Lord continually attempts to get us to be one with him. He will never invite us to fall short or go "beyond the mark" (see Jacob 4:14). He promises us that if we are true to the light given us, he will give us greater light: "That which is of God is light; and he that receiveth light, and continueth in God, receiveth more light; and that light groweth brighter and brighter until the perfect day" (D&C 50:24).

Conclusion

In conclusion, I give you my own witness that I have felt the love and direction of my Father in Heaven through both the Spirit of Christ and the Holy Ghost. I have also been privileged to work with many people who have experienced a "mighty change" (Mosiah 5:2) by first coming to recognize and then by being true to the Spirit of Christ within them. I know that if we are true to the portion of the Light given us, we will receive more. "Wherefore, I beseech of you, brethren [and sisters], that ye should search diligently in the light of Christ that ye may know good from evil; and if ye will lay hold upon every good thing, and condemn it not, ye certainly will be a child of Christ" (Moroni 7:19).

BIBLIOGRAPHY

Benson, Ezra Taft. *The Teachings of Ezra Taft Benson*. Salt Lake City: Bookcraft, 1988.

Bennet, William J. "Quantifying America's Decline." *Wall Street Journal* (15 Mar 1993) as cited in Gordon B. Hinckley's "Conference Address." *Ensign* (Nov 1993) 23:54-60; also in *Conference Report* (Oct 1993) 75–80.

Brown, Hugh B. "They Call for New Light." *Improvement Era* (Jun 1964) 67:457–59; also in *Conference Report* (Apr 1964) 81–82.

Condie, Spencer J. "A Mighty Change of Heart." *Ensign* (Nov 1993) 23:15–17; also in *Conference Report* (Oct 1993) 18–22.

Faust, James E. "Communion with the Holy Spirit." *Ensign* (May 1980) 10:12-15; also in *Conference Report* (Apr 1980) 14–19.

Kimball, Spencer W. *The Teachings of Spencer W. Kimball*. Ed. Edward L. Kimball. Salt Lake City: Bookcraft, 1982.

McConkie, Bruce R. *A New Witness for the Articles of Faith*. Salt Lake City: Deseret Book, 1984.

Packer, Boyd K. "The Law and the Light." *The Book of Mormon: Jacob through Words of Mormon, to Learn with Joy.* Provo, UT: Religious Studies Center, Brigham Young Univ, 1990. 1–27.

————. "Our Moral Development" *Ensign* (May 1992) 22:66–68; also in *Conference Report* (Apr 1992) 91–95.

Pratt, Parley P. *Key To The Science of Theology.* Salt Lake City: George Q. Cannon & Sons, 1891.

Smith, Joseph F. *Gospel Doctrine.,* Salt Lake City, UT: Deseret Book, 1973.

Smith, Joseph Fielding. *Doctrines of Salvation.* 3 vols. Salt Lake City: Bookcraft, 1954.

Talmage, James E. *Articles of Faith.* Salt Lake City: The Church of Jesus Christ of Latter-day Saints, 1949.

Teach Them Correct Principles: A Study in Family Relations. Salt Lake City: The Church of Jesus Christ of Latter-day Saints, 1987.

Jaredite Zion Societies: Hope for a Better World

12

Frank F. Judd, Jr.

Introduction

When people think of the book of Ether in the Book of Mormon, they often remember scenes of deception, darkness, and bloodshed. This is not all that surprising, for indeed the book of Ether contains much of these kinds of things. The text speaks of a time of terrible wickedness when "all the people upon the face of the land were shedding blood, and there was none to restrain them" (Ether 13:31). All the men kept their swords in their hands and no one would lend anything to another because no one was trustworthy in all the land (14:1–2). These unrestrained contentions led to so much bloodshed "that the whole face of the land was covered with the bodies of the dead. And so swift and speedy was the war that there was none left to bury the dead, . . . leaving the bodies of both men, women, and children strewed upon the face of the land, to become prey to the worms of the flesh. And the scent thereof went forth upon the face of the land" (vv 21–23). Because "the Spirit of the Lord had ceased striving with them, and Satan had full power over the hearts of the people; for they were given up unto the hardness of their hearts, and the blindness of their minds that they might be destroyed," all the Jaredites "were drunken with anger, even as a man who is drunken with wine" (15:19, 22). The final bloodbath culminated when Coriantumr decapitated Shiz, leaving only Coriantumr and Ether alive (vv 30–34).

Frank F. Judd, Jr., is a part-time instructor of Ancient Scripture at Brigham Young University.

Why All That Wickedness?

When we read the bloody conclusion of Ether, the following statement by the Lord to the brother of Jared at the commencement of the record seems strange: "There [in the promised land] will I bless thee and thy seed, and raise up unto me . . . a seed, upon all the face of the earth" (Ether 1:43). We wonder why Moroni included all that wickedness if the Jaredites were such a "great nation" and whether the record contained on the gold plates was, as Moroni said, "of great worth" (Mormon 8:14).

First, to read the book of Ether as a record of only wickedness is to miss Moroni's intent in placing it in the Book of Mormon record. Moroni knew that the Jaredites, like his own people, had been destroyed because of wickedness. Consequently, the Jaredite record stands as a second witness with the Nephite record to the fact that if the inhabitants of the promised land do not serve the God of that land, who is Jesus Christ, they will be destroyed (Ether 2:8). Together, these two records witness to latter-day readers in the Western Hemisphere that they must also serve Jesus Christ or suffer a similar fate. Perhaps this is what Moroni meant when he said he included certain events in his abridgment so that we, his readers, "may learn to be more wise" than they (Mormon 9:31).

Second, amidst his description of the scenes of frightening carnage and bloodshed in the book of Ether, Moroni said that it is important for these things to come to us, "that thereby ye may repent of your sins, and suffer not that these murderous combinations shall get above you" (Ether 8:23). Moroni therefore included examples of people who were able to overcome these "murderous combinations." In addition to the incredible spiritual experiences of the brother of Jared recorded in the first chapters of the book of Ether, there are at least four more examples of righteousness among the terrible wickedness. Just as the Lord provided for the brother of Jared "stones to shine in darkness" (Ether 6:3), Moroni provided in his abridgment of the Jaredite record the experiences of a few righteous societies, which show the modern reader how to overcome the darkness. These Zion-like societies were primarily under the leadership of Orihah, Shule, Emer, and Lib (Ether chapters 6, 7, 9 and 10).

Orihah

When the people of Jared desired to have a king, with acute prophetic foresight the brother of Jared warned, "Surely this thing leadeth to captivity" (Ether 6:23). All of his sons and all of the sons of his brother Jared declined the throne save one. Luckily for the Jaredites, the remaining son Orihah proved to be a good man and a righteous king. The record states, "Orihah did walk humbly before the Lord, and did remember how great things the Lord had done for his father [Jared], and also taught his people how great things the Lord had done for their fathers" (Ether 6:30). Just as were the righteous Nephites, the Jaredites were blessed by the Lord with all manner of riches, and they prospered in the land under Orihah (v 28). He lived to a ripe old age and "did execute judgment upon the land in righteousness all his days." Orihah prospered personally and was blessed with a large posterity of 31 children, including 23 sons (7:1–2). But this peace and prosperity did not last long. Following Orihah's death, rival factions arose and spread discord and captivity until Shule restored peace and order to the kingdom (vv 3–9).

Shule

Shule "did execute judgment in righteousness" (Ether 7:11). He punished all those who "did revile against the prophets, and did mock them" (v 24). Because Shule was so determined to defend righteousness, "the people were brought unto repentance" (v 25). The Lord saw the sincerity of their repentance, spared them from a terrible destruction, and blessed them. Shule prospered and was blessed with a great posterity, and the people prospered under the care of God. Additionally, "there were no more wars in the days of Shule; and he remembered the great things that the Lord had done for his fathers in bringing them across the great deep into the promised land" (v 27). Both Orihah and Shule remembered the great things that God had done for their fathers, which brings to mind one of the original purposes of the Book of Mormon stated on the title page:

> An abridgment taken from the book of Ether also, which is a record of the people of Jared, who were scattered at the time the Lord confounded the language of the people, when they were building a tower to get to heaven—Which is to show unto the remnant of the House of Israel *what great things the Lord hath done for their fathers.* (Title Page; emphasis added)

Unfortunately, after the reign of Shule, the Jaredite people once again slipped into their previous ways of wickedness. These wicked practices were characterized by the people of Akish, who "were desirous for gain, even as Akish was desirous for power" (Ether 9:11). Following a period of apostasy and deception, however, Emer was anointed king over the land.

Emer

When Emer reigned as king in righteousness, "the Lord began again to take the curse from off the land, and the house of Emer did prosper exceedingly under the reign of Emer; and in the space of sixty and two years they had become exceedingly strong, insomuch that they became exceedingly rich" (Ether 9:16). In his abridgment of this part of the Jaredite record, Moroni specifically states that the people of Emer were blessed with an abundance of precious metals (gold and silver), other fine materials (silk and linen), food (grain, fruit, and beasts), and domestic stock animals (vv 17–19). Additionally, Emer was blessed with many sons and daughters (v 21). As these verses indicate, not only did Emer prosper, but his whole household prospered, similar to the conditions described in 4 Nephi.

Not only did the people of Emer prosper materially, but they were able to live in peace during his reign. The experiences of Emer are some of the most promising moments in these chapters of rampant wickedness among the Jaredites. As a very righteous leader of his people, Emer was privileged to have the veil parted and see the Lord Himself. The text says, "Emer did execute judgment in righteousness all his days . . . ; and he saw peace in the land; yea, and he even saw the Son of Righteousness, and did rejoice and glory in his day" (Ether 9:21–22). Emer seems to have exercised faith comparable to that of the brother of Jared and to have been granted similar holy experiences. Moroni said the following concerning the sacred experience when the brother of Jared saw the Lord: "And because of the knowledge of this man he could not be kept from beholding within the veil; and he saw the finger of Jesus, which, when he saw, he fell with fear; for he knew that it was the finger of the Lord; and he had faith no longer, for he knew, nothing doubting" (3:19). Moroni may have desired to show us through Emer that not only righteousness but perfect faith is possible in a world sandwiched in on all sides by wickedness.

Likewise, Emer's son Coriantum "did walk in the steps of his father" and treated his subjects very well. They prospered and built "many mighty cities" (Ether 9:23). Again similar to the 4 Nephi account, these Jaredites remained righteous for at least two generations (4 Nephi 1:22). Following the reign of Coriantum, certain Jaredites "began to embrace the secret plans again of old" (Ether 9:26). The land which had been greatly blessed under the reigns of Emer and Coriantum became cursed, insomuch that famine spread and poisonous serpents plagued the inhabitants of the land (see vv 28–32). Moroni recorded that "when the people saw that they must perish they began to repent of their iniquities and cry unto the Lord" (v 34). But this repentance was only temporary and wickedness soon prevailed again.

Lib

Not until the days of a king named Lib, many years later, were the poisonous serpents finally destroyed (Ether 10:19). Lib was a righteous ruler like Orihah, Shule, and Emer. He "did that which was good in the sight of the Lord" (v 19). Lib was blessed for his righteousness and begat many children. Under the leadership of Lib the people became "exceedingly industrious, and they did buy and sell and traffic one with another, that they might get gain" (v 22). Moroni recorded that these people prospered as they worked inside the earth and mined ore such as gold, silver, brass, iron, and copper. Just like the people of Emer, they obtained fine cloth such as silk and linen. Additionally, they worked the soil to sow and reap bounteous harvests. There is a big difference between the way this people prospered compared with the deceptive and bloodthirsty means by which previous wicked men murdered to get gain. Moroni said of the people of Lib, "And [there] never could be a people more blessed than were they, and more prospered by the hand of the Lord" (v 28). The language which Moroni used to describe the state of the people of Lib is remarkably similar to the language his father Mormon used to describe the Zion society of the Nephites in 4 Nephi. Mormon wrote concerning them, "Surely there could not be a happier people among all the people who had been created by the hand of God" (4 Nephi 1:16). It seems possible that Moroni was trying to bring to our memory the precious experiences of those Nephites as he describes the righteousness among the people of Lib.

Conclusion

Moroni included the accounts of incredible wickedness in his abridgment of the Jaredite record for important reasons. While preparing an abridgment of the wickedness that was among the Jaredites, he was also preparing a pattern of the type of society in which we would be living in the last days. As Moroni himself said, "Jesus Christ hath shown you unto me, and I know your doing. And I know that ye walk in the pride of your hearts; and there are none *save a few only* who do not lift themselves up in the pride of their hearts" (Mormon 8:35–36; emphasis added). Moroni shows in the book of Ether that those "few" righteous people can indeed beat the incredible odds, overcome wickedness, and live in righteousness similar to the near perfect Zion society of the Nephite Saints in 4 Nephi. The account in the book of Ether provides a map for us, that we might *not* end up like Coriantumr and Shiz, but that we might follow the examples of righteous men such as Jared and his brother, Orihah, Shule, Emer, and Lib. Moroni stated plainly, "This cometh unto you, O ye Gentiles, that ye may know the decrees of God—that ye may repent, and not continue in your iniquities until the fulness come, that ye may not bring down the fulness of the wrath of God upon you as the inhabitants of the land have hitherto done" (Ether 2:11). As we hearken to this wise counsel we also "might with surety hope for a better world, yea, even a place at the right hand of God, which hope cometh of faith, maketh an anchor to the souls of men, which would make them sure and steadfast, always abounding in good works, being led to glorify God" (12:4).

Ether and Mormon: Parallel Prophets of Warning and Witness

13

E. Dale LeBaron

*T*he Book of Mormon is a record of two fallen nations. Both the Jaredites and the Nephites achieved marvelous heights spiritually and temporally, but then fell to spiritual depths and eventual destruction. The prophet Nephi testifies that God does not destroy a chosen people "save it were foretold them by the prophets of the Lord" (2 Nephi 25:9). The destructions of the Jaredites and Nephites were foretold by prophets. Both Ether (a Jaredite prophet) and Mormon (a Nephite prophet) filled their divine appointment by warning their respective people, witnessing their destruction, and documenting the fulfillment of rejected prophecies.

The purpose of this paper is to show the similarities and differences of these two prophets and ministries. Ether and Mormon were different in their backgrounds and situations, and similar in their missions and convictions. How different they might have been in personalities cannot be fully determined from the present record because in its edited form it lacks much of the detail of their lives. However, since the gospel of Jesus Christ is based upon eternal principles and not personalities, the similarities are particularly significant. To recognize a similarity is often to recognize an eternal principle. The differences between Ether and Mormon show how eternal truths can be manifest in differing circumstances, making the Book of Mormon eternally and individually significant to all who read it. This all illustrates how the Lord can use a diversity of people to

E. Dale LeBaron is associate professor of Church History and Doctrine at Brigham Young University.

bring about a unity with him by accepting his prophets and the eternal principles which he reveals through them.

Differences Between Ether and Mormon

Ether and Mormon came from vastly different family and social backgrounds. Ether was a direct descendant of Jared and was the last in a long line of royalty. His grandfather, Moron, was overthrown as king of the Jaredites and spent many of his days in captivity; and his father, Coriantor, spent all his days as a political prisoner (Ether 11:23). We do not know whether Ether's father was righteous, but the record does state that Ether's grandfather, Moron, and the three previous kings were wicked. We also know that Ether lived during the reign of Coriantumr, the last Jaredite king.

The prophet Mormon was a "pure descendant of Lehi" (3 Nephi 5:20), and his name means "more good" (*Teachings of the Prophet Joseph Smith* 299–300; hereafter *TPJS*). He was named after his father and also after the land where Alma established the Church (Mormon 1:5; 3 Nephi 5:12), which suggests a spiritual commitment on the part of Mormon's parents. There is no indication that Mormon's family had either wealth or station.

Ether was deprived of social status whereas Mormon was granted it by the Nephites. Ether, the heir apparent to the Jaredite throne, was rejected by the people in power, and they even tried to kill him. The fact that Ether was the grandson of a deposed king and that he was making accusations against king Coriantumr must have created a strong bias against him. Because both his person and his message were unwelcome in Coriantumr's court, Ether had to flee for his life (Ether 13:20–22). He lived without influence among the people rather than as a king in a castle. In fact, he was considered to be an enemy, and lived as a recluse in a cave. He warned the people, observed the war by night, and recorded the tragic events (Ether 13:13–14).

By contrast, Mormon was elevated to perhaps the highest position of power and responsibility in Nephite society—that of commander over their armies. The Nephites gave him this honor twice. Even though Mormon warned the people they had to repent, they still considered him a hero, not an enemy. He lived at the center of Nephite political life, not as a recluse.

Such differences between Ether and Mormon illustrate how the Lord works through a diversity of people. Because different people may be inspired and impressed by different things, through diversity in the prophets, some messages may touch the hearts and minds of some readers whereas another's writings may impact others. What is critical, of course, is for everyone to recognize the Lord's divine message and His eternal voice. He said: "Mine elect hear my voice and harden not their hearts" (D&C 29:7). Ether and Mormon both heard the Lord's voice, which brought similarities into their very different lives.

Similarities Between Ether and Mormon

1. *The Timing of Their Mortal Mission—A Final Witness*

The birth of a prophet comes according to the Lord's time-table. Elder Spencer W. Kimball said: "When clouds of error need dissipating and spiritual darkness needs penetrating and heavens need opening, a little infant is born" ("A Prophet is Born" 426–27). Both Ether and Mormon entered the world after their societies had fallen to unprecedented lows from unparalleled heights. Their missions included being final witnesses and giving final warnings to their people.

The Jaredite civilization had reached its temporal apex prior to Ether's birth. According to chapter 10 of Ether, the Jaredites became a vast population of people who were "exceedingly industrious." The record states that there "never could be a people more blessed than were they, and more prospered by the hand of the Lord. And they were in a land that was choice above all lands, for the Lord had spoken it" (Ether 10:21–28; see also Ludlow 323).

Yet in these times of great prosperity there was wickedness and war, and the Lord sent many prophets to call the people to repentance (Ether 11:1–6, 12–13, 20–22). However, they rejected the prophets and killed them. This was followed by "a great destruction, such an one as never had been known upon the face of the earth" (v 7) and a warning that, "except they should repent the Lord God would execute judgment against them to their utter destruction; and the Lord God would send or bring forth another people to possess the land" (vv 20–21). Still the people rejected all the words of the prophets because of their secret societies and wicked abominations (Ether 11:22). It was into this situation that the prophet Ether was born.

Mormon was also born in a time of spiritual decadence. After nearly two centuries of celestial peace and righteousness among the Nephites, that came about from the Savior's post-resurrection ministry among them, the people had turned from the glorious gospel light to evil and darkness. At the time of Mormon's birth, they had slipped into self-indulgence, superstitions, and secret combinations. They sought sorceries, witchcrafts, and magic instead of their God and "the power of the evil one was wrought upon all the face of the land" (Mormon 1:19).

Thus, both Ether and Mormon filled their mortal missions at most difficult and demanding times when their societies were disintegrating, destroying themselves spiritually and temporally.

2. A Divine Calling and Spiritual Preparation

The Prophet Joseph Smith taught that "every man who has a calling to minister to the inhabitants of the world was ordained to that very purpose" in his premortal existence (*TPJS* 365). Along with being foreordained, Ether and Mormon received careful preparation for their divine callings as prophets and seers.

Although the Book of Mormon gives little information about Ether's life prior to his call as a prophet, we can be certain that he was spiritually prepared for his calling. The record states: "Ether was a prophet of the Lord; wherefore Ether came forth in the days of Coriantumr, and began to prophesy unto the people" (Ether 12:2). Ether was blessed with the godly powers of seership. He saw from the beginning to the end of the world, including the ministry of Christ. He prophesied of the last days, the rebuilding of old Jerusalem, the building of the New Jerusalem, the return of the city of Enoch, and the ushering in of the millennial era (Ether 13:2–12). Of his prophetic powers, Elder Neal A. Maxwell has said the following:

> Ether is a classic example of a prophet who devoted his whole life to the cause of the Savior. . . . Because his righteousness removed the restraints that otherwise hold each of us back, Ether actually saw high points of the future—centuries before these were to occur. . . . Other things Ether saw were simply too "great and marvelous" for Moroni to record (Ether 13:13). How marvelous these must have been—in view of the great things Moroni was able to record! (6–7)

Like Ether, Mormon devoted his life to service of the Savior and was prepared spiritually for his divine calling. Although Nephite society had sunk into spiritual quicksand, he exercised the faith and courage to build on the Rock of Christ. From that foundation, Mormon excelled in ways rarely equalled in history as a military leader, an editor-historian, and as a prophet.

Few prophets have received their divine appointment at such a young age. When he was ten years old Mormon was given a charge by Ammaron, who had kept the Nephite records for the previous fifteen years. Just as Ammaron was "constrained by the Holy Ghost" to hide up all the sacred records (4 Nephi 1:48), he must have also been constrained by that Spirit in selecting a ten-year-old boy to have responsibility for these records at this most critical time in Nephite history. Ammaron was impressed that Mormon was "a sober child, and . . . quick to observe." He instructed Mormon to go get the plates in some 14 years time (Mormon 1:2–4).

At the age of 15 years, Mormon "was visited of the Lord, and tasted and knew of the goodness of Jesus" (Mormon 1:15). Surely this heavenly visitation must have been one of the greatest experiences of Mormon's life and a spiritual anchor to his soul. In his ministry, Mormon also seems to have been given the power and authority of an apostle of Christ. While editing the Nephite records, he identified himself as "a disciple of Jesus Christ, the Son of God. I have been called of him to declare his word among His people that they might have everlasting life" (3 Nephi 5:13). The twelve disciples chosen by Jesus as he ministered to the Nephites were ordained apostles according to the Prophet Joseph Smith (*History of the Church* 4:538). Mormon's designation of himself as a disciple called of Jesus Christ strongly supports this thesis (Moroni 2:2).

From his early years, Mormon must have been an impressive young man spiritually, physically, socially, and mentally. Mormon, who was now large in stature, was selected to be the commander-in-chief of all the Nephite armies in his sixteenth year (Mormon 2:1). This began one of the greatest military careers in history, stretching over the rest of his life, a period of 58 years. Of this, Elder Sterling W. Sill has said:

> If you think it an inspiration that a 16 year old boy could win the leadership of a great national army, what would you think of a man between the ages of 65 and 74 who was still the best man among his entire people for this top position

of leadership, and in those days the general marched at the head and not in the rear of his troops (Mormon 6:11). (Sill 248–49, 252–54)

Although Ether and Mormon differed in their backgrounds, circumstances, and personalities, they were both prophets. They were both called and schooled by the Lord. The Lord's influence was manifest in their lives, spiritually and temporally.

3. Writer, Abridger, Editor, and Historian

From the beginning the Lord appointed some of His servants to "write by the spirit of inspiration" so a record could be kept for the blessing of mankind (Moses 6:4–9). Because many prophets have carried out this task, we are blessed with a rich treasure of scriptures. From the voluminous records kept by the Jaredites and Nephites, Ether and Mormon abridged the entire histories of their people from the time the Lord brought them to the promised land until their final destruction (Ether 1:6; W of M 1:3, 9). Although Ether and Mormon were blessed with the godly power of seership, their individual personalities and backgrounds undoubtedly impacted their records.

Although Ether's abridgment of the Jaredite history was later abridged by Moroni, some of Ether's background and circumstance are reflected in the Jaredite record. Perhaps because his grandfather and father were dethroned monarchs who spent much of their lives in prison, the record draws particular attention to the imprisonment of deposed royalty (Ether 7:7; 8:3; 10:14, 30; 11:18). It suggests strong feelings about abusive and corrupt rulers, and frequently focuses on kings being rebuked by prophets because of their wickedness (Ether 7:23; 9:28; 11:1, 12, 20). Surely, Ether saw much political corruption, war, and violence.

Mormon, who spent most of his life involved with warfare, focused on war throughout most of his writings. He devotes 20 chapters (Alma 43–62) detailing the Nephite-Lamanite battles fought by Captain Moroni. He gave Captain Moroni one of the greatest tributes of any person in Nephite history: "He was a man who was firm in the faith of Christ. . . . If all men had been, and were, and ever would be, like unto Moroni, behold, the very powers of hell would have been shaken forever" (Alma 48:11–17). It is also evident that the Book of Mormon was prepared by a knowledgeable military strategist (Hamblin 241–55).

Mormon edited the materials from Lehi through 4 Nephi, periodically writing editorial comments such as Helaman 12. He also wrote the Words of Mormon. Mormon chapters 1–7 is an abridgment of a larger record he had written on the large plates of Nephi (Mormon 2:18). From his letters included in the record by Moroni (Moroni 7–9), we can see the power of revelation which rested upon Mormon and the clarity with which he expounded doctrine, such as baptism of little children, translated beings, and faith, hope and charity. Mormon's great faith and hope and charity are evident in his final message, directed to the posterity of those who had destroyed his people (Mormon 7).

As an editor, Mormon selected material, wrote, and drew conclusions that would bring people to Christ (Hardy 15; Tvedtness 31). He had a constant vision before him of those who would receive this record in the last days. It was to us that he was writing, for he said:

> I write unto you, Gentiles, and also unto you, house of Israel . . . Yea, behold, I write unto all the ends of the earth, yea, unto you, twelve tribes of Israel . . . And I write also unto the remnant of this people . . . And these things doth the Spirit manifest unto me, therefore I write unto you all. (Mormon 3:17–20)

President Ezra Taft Benson has said the following:

> The Book of Mormon was written for us today. God is the author of the book. . . . Mormon, the ancient prophet after whom the book is named, abridged centuries of records. God, who knows the end from the beginning, told him what to include in his abridgment that we would need for our day. (63)

4. A Warning Voice

As previously noted, the Lord will always send prophets to warn his covenant children before he allows them to destroy themselves (2 Nephi 25:9). Both Ether and Mormon courageously testified of the people's wickedness and warned of their pending destruction if they did not repent. Ether's dedication to his responsibility is described as follows: "He could not be restrained because of the Spirit of the Lord which was in him. For he did cry from the morning even until the going down of the sun, exhorting the people to believe in God unto repentance lest they should be destroyed" (Ether 12:2–3). In the second year of Ether's ministry, the Lord commanded him to deliver a final warning to king Coriantumr face to face:

> The word of the Lord came to Ether, that he should go and prophesy unto Coriantumr that, if he would repent, and all his household, the Lord would give unto him his kingdom and spare the people—Otherwise they should be destroyed, and all his household save it were himself. And he should only live to see the fulfilling of the prophecies which had been spoken concerning another people receiving the land for their inheritance; and Coriantumr should receive a burial by them; and every soul should be destroyed save it were Coriantumr. (Ether 13:20–21)

The Lord's final plea and opportunity for the king and his people to be spared was not only rejected by them, but they sought to kill Ether, and he made a hasty retreat to his cave.

Early in Mormon's life, the Lord forbade him to preach to the Nephites because they had willfully rebelled and hardened their hearts (Mormon 1:16–17). However, over three decades later, the Lord commanded him to give the Nephite people a final warning and plea. They were told to repent, be baptized, and build up the Church, and the Lord would spare them (3:2). However, his missionary efforts were in vain and the people hardened their hearts against the Lord. Soon thereafter the Lord assured Mormon that the Nephites "shall be cut off from the face of the earth" (vv 13–15).

The Lord gives prophets an eternal perspective and a "knowledge that the course they are pursuing is according to the will of God"; otherwise, they would "grow weary in their minds and faint" (*Lectures on Faith* 6:4). Mormon wrote to Moroni:

> And now, my beloved son, notwithstanding their hardness, let us labor diligently; for if we should cease to labor, we should be brought under condemnation; for we have a labor to perform whilst in this tabernacle of clay, that we may conquer the enemy of all righteousness, and rest our souls in the kingdom of God. (Moroni 9:6)

Both Mormon and Ether persevered in their ministry regardless of how the people responded.

5. A Witness to Prophecies Fulfilled

It is an awesome responsibility to prophesy in the name of the Lord, but for Ether and Mormon to prophesy regarding the pending destructions to come to their own people if they did not repent was even more so. And they witnessed the fulfillment of what they prophesied. This, too, came with their callings. They were special witnesses that every word had been fulfilled.

A vivid description of the total collapse of the Jaredite civilization is reflected in these words:

> The Spirit of the Lord had ceased striving with them, and Satan had full power over the hearts of the people; for they were given up unto the hardness of their hearts, and the blindness of their minds that they might be destroyed. . . . They were drunken with anger, even as a man who is drunken with wine. (Ether 15:19, 21)

The final struggle between Coriantumr and his arch-enemy Shiz illustrates the ultimate tragedy of a self-destructing society. Driven by revenge and vengeance towards Coriantumr, Shiz overthrew many cities and "he did slay both women and children, and he did burn the cities" (Ether 14:17). This scorched-earth policy created a dreaded fear among the people, who cried: "Who can stand before the army of Shiz? Behold, he sweepeth the earth before him!" (v 18).

The Jaredite war of extinction may have been the bloodiest war ever fought on the American continents (Ludlow 327–28). Even before the final battle, king Coriantumr had lost two million "mighty men, and also their wives and their children" (Ether 15:2), and this represents only one side of the conflict. In preparation for this final battle the two sides spent four years gathering "all who were upon the face of the land" so that every man, woman and child were on one side or the other, determined to fight to the end (vv 14–15). And they fought to the end.

As with the Jaredites, the Nephites had fallen to such a spiritual low that they were "without principle, and past feeling" (Moroni 9:20). Hence, "the day of grace was past with them both temporally and spiritually" (Mormon 2:13–15).

When the Nephites began an offensive warfare, Mormon refused to lead them. Thirteen years later, at age 64, he repented of his oath and agreed to command their armies once again because the Nephites "looked upon me as though I could deliver them from their afflictions" (Mormon 5:1–2). However, because of their continued wickedness, he knew what the future held for them.

The Lamanites now began a scorched-earth policy of warfare, as Shiz had among the Jaredites. As the Lamanite army moved forward, they burned Nephite cities and killed the people who could not escape. Mormon was sickened by the "awful scene of blood and carnage" which was before his eyes (Mormon 5:5–8), and chose to spare us a graphic description of the carnage he witnessed. He wrote that some things were "impossible for the tongue to describe," for "there never had been so great wickedness among all the children of Lehi" (4:11–12). He does tell that Lamanites offered captive Nephite women and children as human sacrifices to Lamanite idol gods (v 14), and fed them the flesh of their husbands or fathers as their rations (Moroni 9:8). But the Nephites were doing worse things as they raped the daughters of the Lamanites, tortured and murdered them, and then ate their flesh like wild beasts. He concludes: "O the depravity of my people! They are without order and without mercy. . . . They have become strong in their perversion. . . . They are without principle, and past feeling" (vv 18–20).

The Nephites, as the Jaredites before them, arranged a period of time to gather all the people together for one final battle. Their battle site was also the same—a hill named Ramah by the Jaredites and Cumorah by the Nephites (Ether 15:11; Mormon 6:2).

After hiding the records in Cumorah, Mormon joined his people as the vast armies of the Lamanites marched towards them. The Nephites experienced "that awful fear of death which fills the breasts of all the wicked" (Mormon 6:7). Mormon then records that 230,000 of his people died in senseless slaughter.

6. The Record is Completed

It is important for the scriptures to be complete and accurate. The Savior taught this to the Nephites by having them correct their record to testify that every prophecy given by Samuel had been fulfilled (3 Nephi 23:6–13). As the fighting ended and the destruction was finished, both Ether and Mormon completed their records as witnesses that every word of the Lord had been fulfilled. This also concluded the mortal mission of both prophets.

Ether observed and recorded the final scenes of extermination which left only two Jaredite survivors: Coriantumr and himself. His last recorded directive from the Lord was to "go forth," and he "beheld that the words of the Lord had all been fulfilled; and he finished his record" (Ether 15:33). He then hid the record so the people of Limhi would find it. We are left to wonder if there was any contact or communication between Ether and Coriantumr at this point. The record does confirm the fulfillment of the final part of the Lord's promise to Coriantumr, in that he was found by the people of Zara-hemla and lived with them for "nine moons" (Omni 1:21).

As with the Jaredites, the Nephites were destroyed as a people (Mormon 6:15). Mormon completed his record and testimony of the events which he witnessed. He and his son Moroni were among 24 Nephite survivors. A heart-wrenching outpouring of deep sadness is recorded by Mormon as he views the lifeless bodies of his people strewn across the bloody landscape of Cumorah:

> O ye fair ones, how could ye have departed from the ways of the Lord! O ye fair ones, how could ye have rejected that Jesus, who stood with open arms to receive you! Behold, if ye had not done this, ye would not have fallen. But behold, ye are fallen, and I mourn your loss. O ye fair sons and daughters, ye fathers and mothers, ye husbands and wives, ye fair ones, how is it that ye could have fallen! But behold, ye are gone, and my sorrows cannot bring your return. (Mormon 6:17–20)

We do not know how long Mormon lived after the final battle, but Moroni records that his father was killed by the Lamanites. Moroni, who was given the keys to the Book of Mormon (D&C 27:5), was left to finish the record and bury it in Cumorah. In the end, he, like Ether, faced a future alone in the hands of the Lord (Mormon 8:1–5; Moroni 10:34).

7. Well Done, Thou Good and Faithful Servants

Because of their faithfulness in giving their lives to Christ, both Ether and Mormon received the assurance of an eternal reward. Ether's final words on the plates reflect his complete trust in and love for the Lord, when he writes: "Whether the Lord will that I be translated, or that I suffer the will of the Lord in the flesh, it mattereth not, if it so be that I am saved in the kingdom of God" (Ether 15:34). Elder Neal A. Maxwell has stated that "this very special prophet might have been translated" (9).

As Mormon reflected upon a life fraught with spiritual and physical destruction, he expressed contrasting feelings of pain for his people, and feelings of joy for his promise of eternal life:

> A continual scene of wickedness and abominations has been before mine eyes ever since I have been sufficient to behold the ways of man. And wo is me because of their wickedness; for my heart has been filled with sorrow because

of their wickedness, all my days; nevertheless, I know that I shall be lifted up at the last day. (Mormon 2:18–19)

Thus, although Ether and Mormon were different people with diverse experiences, they were brought together through Christ.

Conclusion

The Book of Mormon was written by many prophets who had a variety of backgrounds, personalities, and experiences. The Jaredite and Nephite records were written or edited by two prophets— different people who in some ways seem like polar opposites. Clearly, the Lord can accomplish his purposes using all of his children, different as they may be. Surely these differences enhance and strengthen the Lord's work, for they demonstrate that the Lord's principles are eternal. The similarities between Ether and Mormon center on things that matter most: eternal principles of Jesus Christ.

Elder Marion G. Romney compared our day with that of the Jaredites and Nephites, and he sounded this warning to us:

> Fifteen and a half centuries ago, because of their unrighteousness, the remnants of the Nephite race were in a death grapple upon this land with their brethren, the Lamanites. Among them stood the mighty prophet-leader Mormon. . . . They as well as the Jaredites, were wiped off this land. This was true notwithstanding the glorious promises made in the Book of Mormon. . . .
>
> The world in which we live today is sick nigh unto death. The disease of which it suffers is not a new one. It is as old as history. Its name is unrighteousness. The cure for it is repentance. The Lord foresaw our present extremity long ago and prescribed the remedy. On November 1, 1831, he said:
>
> "I the Lord, knowing the calamity which should come upon the inhabitants of the earth, called upon my servant Joseph Smith, Jun., and spake unto him from heaven, and gave him commandments; and also gave commandments to others, that they should proclaim these things unto the world" (D&C 1:17–18). (430)

Elder Romney's statement bears the subtle stamp of his personality. However, the Lord's eternal voice can also be heard, and his warning is consistent and unmistakable. President Kimball taught at the December 1973, Johannesburg, South Africa Stake Conference, "If we will just follow the Lord's prophets we will arrive at where they are going" (Author's personal note). Surely, that was the desire of Ether and Mormon, for all of their people—and for us.

BIBLIOGRAPHY

Benson, Ezra Taft. "The Book of Mormon is the Word of God." *Ensign* (May 1975) 5:63–65; also in *Conference Report* (Apr 1975) 93–97.

Hamblin, William J. "Warfare in the Book of Mormon." *Rediscovering the Book of Mormon.* Eds. John L. Sorenson and Melvin J. Thornel. Salt Lake City: Deseret Book, 1991. 241–55.

Hardy, Grant R. "Mormon as Editor." *Rediscovering the Book of Mormon.* Eds. John L. Sorenson and Melvin J. Thornel. Salt Lake City: Deseret Book, 1991. 15–28.

History of the Church. 7 vols. Salt lake City: Deseret Book, 1980.

Kimball, Spencer W. "A Prophet is Born." *Improvement Era* (June 1960) 63:426–27.

———. Johannesburg, South Africa Stake Conference (Dec 1973). Recorded by author.

Lectures on Faith in Historical Perspective. Eds. Larry E. Dahl and Charles D. Tate, Jr. Provo, UT: Religious Studies Center, Brigham Young Univ, 1990.

Ludlow, Daniel H. *A Companion to Your Study of the Book of Mormon.* Salt Lake City: Deseret Book, 1976.

Maxwell, Neal A. "Three Jaredites: Contrasting Contemporaries." *Ensign* (Aug 1978) 8:6–7.

Romney, Marion G. "Hearken and Obey." *Improvement Era* (May 1950) 53:385-432.

Sill, Sterling W. *The Upward Reach.* Salt Lake City: Bookcraft, 1962.

Sorenson, John L. "Seasons of War, Seasons of Peace in the Book of Mormon." *Rediscovering the Book of Mormon.* Eds. John L. Sorenson and Melvin J. Thornel. Salt Lake City: Deseret Book, 1991. 249–55.

Teachings of the Prophet Joseph Smith. Comp. Joseph Fielding Smith. Salt Lake City: Deseret Book, 1976.

Tvedtnes, John A. "Mormon's Editorial Promises." *Rediscovering the Book of Mormon.* Eds. John L. Sorensen and Melvin J. Thornel. Salt Lake City: Deseret Book, 1991. 29–31.

There Was No Contention　　14

Byron R. Merrill

Introduction

*A*ppearing repeatedly in the book of 4 Nephi is a phrase which speaks to the heart of what Zion was and will be. Occurring three times in its singular form and once in the plural within the first 18 verses, this phrase explains a primary reason for the blessed state enjoyed by the Nephites as well as the results which flowed therefrom. The phrase simply reads: "There was no contention." In its simplicity lies a pattern for reestablishing Zion which encompasses both a warning of what must be avoided and a promise of what can, with the Lord's help, be achieved.

Early in the Lord's visit to the Nephites, as recorded in 3 Nephi, he taught the people this principle:

> And there shall be no disputations among you, as there have hitherto been; neither shall there be disputations among you concerning the points of my doctrine, as there have hitherto been.
>
> For verily, verily I say unto you, he that hath the spirit of contention is not of me, but is of the devil, who is the father of contention, and he stirreth up the hearts of men to contend with anger, one with another.
>
> Behold, this is not my doctrine, to stir up the hearts of men with anger, one against another; but this is my doctrine, that such things should be done away. (11:28–30)

The people in 4 Nephi received, internalized, and lived this commandment for a lengthy time. Verses 2 and 15 detail the reasons for their success in eradicating contention: "The people were all converted unto the Lord, upon all the face of the land, both Nephites and Lamanites, and there were no contentions and disputations among

Byron R. Merrill is assistant professor of Ancient Scripture at Brigham Young University.

them, and every man did deal justly one with another"; and "there was no contention in the land, because of the love of God which did dwell in the hearts of the people" (4 Nephi 1:2, 15). Two other verses disclose the blessings arising from this condition:

> And it came to pass that there was no contention among all the people, in all the land; but there were mighty miracles wrought among the disciples of Jesus.
> And how blessed were they! For the Lord did bless them in all their doings; yea, even they were blessed and prospered until an hundred and ten years had passed away; and the first generation from Christ had passed away, and there was no contention in all the land. (vv 13, 18)

Contention

In order to better understand why the Lord so sharply condemned contention during his visit to the Nephites and why it is absent from such a blessed state, we must seek the true meaning of the word and examine its use. One definition of *contend* is "to assert or to maintain in argument." It seems to be this meaning that the Lord used in a modern revelation: "Contend thou, therefore, morning by morning; and day after day let thy warning voice go forth" (D&C 112:5). Likewise, this meaning may be inferred when Jude admonishes us to "earnestly contend for the faith" (1:3) or when Paul says he was bold "to speak unto you the gospel of God with much contention" (1 Thes 2:2). Similarly, the command to "contend against no church, save it be the church of the devil" (D&C 18:20) may be read in this context. But this last verse may also advance a different definition of *contend*, namely "to struggle." Read thus, there is still no suggestion that we *contend* against another person. The implication seems to be to struggle against evil or to fight the powers of darkness.

In the Book of Mormon, *contention* invariably carries this latter meaning of struggling or fighting, equating it with Webster's definition, "violent effort or struggle to obtain, resist or compete." What is it that causes *contention* to always be used in this negative manner? The Lord incorporates into *contention* an added ingredient when he indicates that the devil "stirreth up the hearts of men to contend with anger, one with another" (3 Nephi 11:29). *Contention*, then, as used in the Book of Mormon, is not just a matter of asserting or defending a position, but of doing so with anger as the added element. The Saints may honestly and forthrightly differ in opinion on ideas, insights, or approaches while still remaining calm; but it is when hostile feelings are added that disagreement turns into contention. Thus, while it is possible to disagree without anger, *contention*, as used in the Book of Mormon, means disagreeing in anger. Once this more complete definition is understood, it is easier to comprehend why Nephi declared, "The Lord God hath commanded that men . . . should not contend one with another" (2 Nephi 26:32), and why the Lord promised: "I will contend with him that contendeth with thee, and I will save thy children" (1 Nephi 21:25).

Therefore, without exception in the Book of Mormon, the word *contention* refers to conflict in which heated passions play a part. The word is modified by adjectives such as "serious" (Hel 1:2), "warm" (Alma 50:26), "exceedingly sharp" (19:28), "much" (Hel 1:18) and "great" (Mosiah 19:3; Alma 22:22; Hel 3:19; 3 Nephi 7:7). The modifier "wonderful" in Alma 2:5 is used in conjunction with the phrase "much dispute" and seems to denote "astonishing" or "surprising." Even more instructive as to its meaning are other words with which it is coupled. It regularly appears in phrases like "much contention and many dissensions" (W of M 1:16; Hel 3:3) and is often found in conjunction with such companions as "disturbance(s)" (Alma 22:22; Hel 3:17), "difficulty" (Hel 1:18), "dispute" (Alma 2:5), "destructions" (Enos 1:23), "quarrelings" (Alma 50:21), and "bloodsheds" (35:15). It is remarkably telling that this word was engraved by Book of Mormon authors in almost the same stroke with "war(s)" a full 31 times.

On the other hand, the only positive references to contention in the entire Book of Mormon are to its absence. Unfortunately, recorded periods of Nephite history without contention are few and their duration short (Mosiah 1:1; 6:7; Alma 4:1; 16:1; Hel 3:1–2). With periods of peace being so scarce in the narrative, having a time with no contention must have seemed to Mormon a virtually unattainable condition. Considering the circumstances of his day in combination with all the history he had reviewed, Mormon mentions the absence of contention four times in 17 verses as if to convince himself of such a wonderment, to dispel the belief that this is only a heavenly goal, and to reenforce the possibility of a contentionless people. No wonder he exclaimed: "Surely there could not be a happier people among all the people who had been created by the hand of God. . . . And how blessed were they!" (4 Nephi 1:16, 18).

Anger

To fully understand the Lord's depth of condemnation of contention, it is necessary to examine the negative underpinning of anger, which is defined as "a feeling of sudden and strong displeasure and antagonism directed against the cause of an assumed wrong or injury" (Funk and Wagnells). Note that it is a feeling or emotion. One group of authors indicates that research in physiology shows "all strong emotions [grow] out of the same physical reaction . . . stress response" (McKay 22), and that "the sole function of anger is to stop stress" (44). Contrary to popular opinions that this emotion is biologically determined or instinctive or that its expression is a healthy release, these authors conclude that "anger is nothing more than a learned response to certain kinds of stress" (50). Whereas we may have learned to use it in an attempt to control stress, we are not compelled to do so because we "have a choice" (51). Thus, these authors propose that the individual is ultimately responsible for his anger: "There is a pleasure in blaming. . . . But there's a problem with the habit of finding others responsible for your pain. It isn't true. You are solely responsible for the quality of your life. Whether you are in pain or not, whether your needs are met or not, whether your relationships feel good or not is entirely determined by the choices you make" (58). Similarly, another author indicates that we largely bring on these hostile feelings ourselves "and have the responsibility for continuing to feel them or for giving them up" (Ellis 183).

Carol Tavris writes that anger involves conscious, split-second judgments "that an injustice, insult or idiocy has been committed, and a choice of reactions" (35). She concludes: "Judgment and choice are the hallmarks of anger" (36). Another writer agrees, stating: "Angry people are experts, truly experts, on what they believe *ought to be*" (Doty 15). Thus, anger requires the ability to reason, to make judgments, and to choose to respond with hostile emotions instead of forbearance or charity. Uncomfortable as it may seem to some, all this analysis points to the conclusion that anger is a conscious act, not, as some would rationalize, an uncontrollable emotion.

It is instructive to see how closely the findings of such writers conform to Lehi's witness that because the Messiah has redeemed all men and women from the Fall, "They have become free forever, knowing good from evil; to act for themselves and not to be acted upon" (2 Nephi 2:26). While we may not be able to determine our circumstances, we are free to choose our responses to them. Should we choose to ignore the option we have to act with patience, understanding, and love, and react instead with anger, have we not, to a certain degree, relinquished that freedom so dearly purchased by the Redeemer's blood? Satan cannot destroy our agency, and God will not abridge it; but we may, by blaming others for our actions, diminish our capacity to choose freely and "by persisting long enough, reach the point of no return" (Romney 45). We may blind ourselves into accusing others for our failings and feelings, but we cannot escape the assigned consequences which will surely flow from our acts and attitudes.

A careful examination of the Old Testament verses dealing with anger, or its alternative rendering, "wrath," reveals the impression that it is a natural—or perhaps more accurately, a "natural man" (Mosiah 3:19)—response to stressful situations. However, when the risen Lord discussed the fulfillment of the Old Testament Mosaic law with the Nephites and Lamanites, he used several examples to indicate that carefully following the law would only elevate people to the status of honorable men and women of the earth. In order for them to become celestial, they had to take a further step, and move from obedience of Mosaic law to a higher level of sanctification where basic motivations were purified. Not committing adultery would bring one to a terrestrial plateau; but only by eradicating lust could one come to harmony with celestial law. From this standpoint Jesus indicated the new, higher commandment relating to anger in these words: "Whosoever is angry with his brother shall be in danger of his judgment" (3 Nephi 12:22). Clearly, this passage contains no old law qualifications for anger such as whosoever *is quick* to anger, *cannot control* anger, *continues* in anger, or even the rationalization of one who is angry *without a cause* that appears in the King James Version. These qualifications are conspicuously absent in the Book of Mormon, the Joseph Smith Translation, and even in many of the early manuscripts from which the gospel of Matthew was translated (for a more detailed discussion, see Welch 161–63).

But some will counter that the Lord did not mean to condemn the emotion altogether. Yet is that not exactly what he said? Did he not direct Paul to utter this blanket condemnation: "Can ye be angry, and not sin?" (JST Eph 4:26). "But the anger or wrath of God is often spoken of in scripture. Are we not to follow His example?" Reference has already been made to the fact that our anger is the result of judgments quickly made and that it is a chosen response. While we have been commanded to "judge not unrighteously" (JST Matt 7:2), the realities of life often prompt us to judge people by their words or actions. We are not in a position to judge others' motivations and certainly not to render a verdict on the status of their hearts, even though we sometimes think otherwise. Only the Lord can do that. He taught the prophet Samuel, "For the Lord seeth not as man seeth; for man looketh on the outward appearance, but the Lord looketh on the heart" (1 Sam 16:7). The only recorded instance of attributing anger to the Lord during his earthly sojourn speaks of his judging the heart. It is written that he looked upon the Pharisees "with anger, being grieved for the hardness of their hearts" (Mark 3:5). While the Lord's anger or wrath is often referred to in scripture, it is usually spoken of in terms of the judgment resulting from his justice, often in the context of the Lord's people having broken their covenant with him. A definition of his anger, different from that ascribed to mortals, might be "a feeling of strong displeasure toward persons who have hardened their hearts against light and truth." It is his all-seeing, all-knowing judgment of people's hearts which evokes his perfect justice (D&C 84:24; 1 Kings 11:9).

Mortals, on the other hand, are simply not in a position to make such judgments. Therefore, human anger is not acceptable. The only exception seems to be when the Lord's Spirit moves us to know his will and to act in his behalf. Unless and until that happens, human anger, not just its outward expression, but its existence, is unjustifiable. The Lord has indicated we should "reprov[e] betimes with sharpness," but only in those rare instances "when moved upon by the Holy Ghost" (D&C 121:43). It is in that context that Lehi steps in to defend Nephi from the accusations of Laman and Lemuel: "And ye have murmured because he hath been plain unto you. Ye say that he hath used sharpness; ye say that he hath been angry with you; but behold, his sharpness was the sharpness of the power of the word of God, which was in him; and that which ye call anger was the truth, according to that which is in God" (2 Nephi 1:26). Notice Lehi's approving use of the word "sharpness," identical to the use thereof in Doctrine and Covenants 121:43, where the meaning seems to indicate preciseness or accuracy, not harshness or overbearance.

Perhaps the permissibility of anger in our lives could be compared to the Lord's instructions regarding forgiveness: "I, the Lord, will forgive whom I will forgive, but of you it is required to forgive all men" (D&C 64:10). While he, who is from everlasting to everlasting and who knows the thoughts and intents of all our hearts, can look upon us and render righteous judgments, we, who "see through a glass, darkly" (1 Cor 13:12), who understand so imperfectly, dare not venture blindly onto the stand, declaring ourselves to be the judge. Yet, that is precisely what we are doing when we feel anger—we are declaring ourselves judge, jury, and often, in the flash of the moment, executioner. Perhaps we could paraphrase the Lord's directive to us regarding this matter in these terms: "I, the Lord, will feel anger [ie, render judgment] toward whom I will; but of you it is required not to feel anger toward anyone."

Attitudes Leading to Contention

If contention and anger are so strongly condemned by the Lord, what underlying attitudes tempt us to embrace them? One of the foremost is pride. The book of Proverbs tells us that "only by pride cometh contention" (13:10). In Doctrine and Covenants 64:8, the Lord indicates that, in days of old, his disciples "sought occasion against one another and forgave not one another in their hearts." One such moment may have been the occasion of the Last Supper. Elder Bruce R. McConkie speaks of contention in the upper room as a result of the apostles' order of seating. Judas, who was "more of a Pharisee than a Christian" by both inclination and custom, sought for himself the seat of honor. Were there those at the table who, when "Jesus rebuked the contention" (4:31–33), might have harbored ill feelings toward Judas for his claiming preeminence? Was it not pride that prompted Judas to take the undeserved seat and the same motivation that may have prompted any resentment for his doing so? Neither seeking position nor reacting in anger or by lack of forgiveness is becoming of Saints.

Perhaps our anger is sometimes generated by our being offended. Speaking of mortality, Elder Boyd K. Packer has stated that each person "will have a test sufficient to his needs; how each responds is the test" ("The Mystery of Life" 18). For some of us, our test may be whether we respond to offenses with anger. The opposite response was displayed in instances when the righteous Nephites were persecuted. They responded not by taking offense but by fasting and praying often, and "yielding their hearts unto God" (Hel 3:35). At another time, it was recorded that they would "receive railing and persecution and all manner of afflictions, and would not turn and revile again, but were humble and penitent before God" (3 Nephi 6:13). At times it may be as sinful to take offense and respond negatively as to give the offense. Certainly, the Zion of 4 Nephi could never have been established if people were regularly taking offense and responding with anger.

It is relatively easy to see contentious feelings coming to the fore as a defensive mechanism, when we know we are doing wrong but object to being told so. A more subtle excuse often expressed for such feelings is the frustration and fear which result from losing face or a sense of selfworth, a recognition of who we really are in the midst of a confusing and insecure world. The milieu of competition which so pervades society adds to this sense of frustration, anger and, ultimately, contention. Competition frequently combines several of the contention-causing attitudes just discussed. If it is defined as "mutually exclusive goal attainment," it means that "my success requires your failure. Our fates are negatively linked" (Kohn 4). There is a significant difference between the desire to do well and the desire to do better than someone else. C. S. Lewis wrote: "Pride gets no pleasure out of having something, only out of having more of it than the next man. . . . It is the comparison that makes you proud: the pleasure of being above the rest. Once the element of competition has gone, pride has gone" (109–110). Is this not the goal of contention, to be above, to be better, to be victor or conqueror? When we exclusively live by the rules of competition, we tend to look sideways and compare ourselves to others, instead of looking up to God.

On a personal, internal level, many of us have come to believe that we only have selfworth if we are successful. We live in a world which preaches, at every turn, that you are only successful if you are a "winner," which, in worldly terms, means you must prove your worth by "beating" someone else. "Ultimately, this strategy reveals itself as futile, since making our self-esteem contingent on winning means that it will always be in doubt. The more we compete, the more we need to compete" (Kohn 183). Thanks be to God for a prophet who has told us that we need not get caught up in this maelstrom of combative comparison and resulting contention. President Benson has stated: "If we love God, do His will, and fear His judgments more than men's, we will have self-esteem" ("Beware of Pride" 6). To paraphrase, "The essence of self-esteem is the approval of God."

From a gospel perspective, something seems intrinsically wrong with a system where somebody must lose, which is the espoused desire of Satan and an often overlooked facet of contention. Elder Packer has stated:

> In this life we are constantly confronted with a spirit of competition. Teams contest one against another in an adversary relationship in order that one will be chosen a winner. We come to believe that wherever there is a winner there must also be a loser. To believe that is to be misled. In the eyes of the Lord, everyone may be a winner. Now it is true that we must earn it; but if there is competition in His work, it is not with another soul—it's with our own former selves. (*That All May be Edified* 84)

The operative phrase in this last sentence is "If there is competition in His work." If competition is defined as "mutually exclusive goal attainment," then focusing our efforts on reaching the standard the Lord has set, by striving to perfect ourselves, does not qualify as competition since no one need lose. In a class where the discussion of the Nephite Zion raised questions about the promised latter-day Zion, a student queried, "Will there be competition in Zion?" My immediate thoughts turned to a recent "fun run" held as part of our stake's July 24th celebration. Most of the members of my family had participated, some walking, some jogging, and some actually running. All finished, each received some ribbon or other token, but none had been trying to outdo someone else. I was grateful not to sense the desire to "beat" another person, to be proclaimed winner at the expense of the loser(s), since such an attitude speaks more of contention than of the spirit of cooperation and oneness which is a prerequisite to Zion. After some reflection, I responded to my student with this thought: "I feel sure we will participate in wonderful activities in Zion; but I rather doubt anyone will be interested in keeping score."

Good Contention?

Having discussed contention, anger, and some of the attitudes which lead us to both, we must address the question, "Is there such a thing as good contention?" Some have rationalized that it is justifiable to enter into contention when defending the truth. However, the Prophet Joseph Smith said: "Avoid contentions and vain disputes. . . . Remember that 'it is a day of warning, and not a day of many words.' If they receive not your testimony in one place, flee to another, remembering to cast no reflections, nor throw out any bitter sayings. If you do your duty, it will be just as well with you, as though all men embraced the Gospel" (*Teachings of the Prophet Joseph Smith* 43). Even when we have a spiritual witness that something is true, it is unwise to argue to prove a point. For example, regarding an issue as provocative of heated debate as the theory of organic evolution as the explanation for the origin of man, Elder Packer has wisely cautioned that we present the scriptural view and then let the Spirit work: "Do not be contentious. Speak of conscience, values, moral law" ("The Law and the Light" 25).

As people engage in contention, they tend to become more and more entrenched in the positions espoused, increasingly solidified in the points of view taken, until they become so hardened they can hardly feel the promptings of the Spirit. Inspiration, light, and truth are locked out. Even those supposedly arguing for the right may become so puffed up in their learning (2 Nephi 9:28; 28:4) or so engrossed in their interpretation of doctrine, history, or prophecy as to preclude any illumination from the Spirit which might temper or even change their strongly forged opinions. While the Spirit can and does bear witness to the truth, the Spirit is rarely called to witness when contending parties are busy throwing proofs and epithets at each other. Speaking of this problem, Elder Theodore M. Burton said:

> Whenever you get red in the face, whenever you raise your voice, whenever you get "hot under the collar," or angry, rebellious, or negative in spirit, then know that the Spirit of God is leaving you and the spirit of Satan is beginning to take over. At times we may feel justified in arguing or fighting for truth by contentious words and actions. Do not be deceived. Satan would rather have you contend for evil if he could, but he rejoices when we contend with one another even when we think we are doing it in the cause of righteousness. He knows and recognizes the self-destructive nature of contention under any guise. (56)

The Savior told the Nephites that if they remembered anyone had aught against them, they should first be reconciled with them and then return to worship the Lord (3 Nephi 12:23–24). Who might be right or wrong in such a case is not relevant to that command. Elder Dallin H. Oaks has written, "We are obliged to 'be reconciled to [our] brother' even when he is wrong and we are only the victim of the grievance. . . . Reconciliation seeks the restoration of relationships, not the adjudication of differences" (142–143). He further stated, "It is noteworthy that the Savior did not limit his teaching about disputations and contention to those who had wrong ideas about doctrine or procedure. He forbade disputations and contention by everyone. The commandment to avoid contention applies to those who are right as well as to those who are wrong" (142).

The following words of President Joseph F. Smith confirm that "positive contention" is a contradiction in terms:

> You find the spirit of contention only among apostates and those who have denied the faith, those who have turned away from the truth and have become enemies to God and his work. There you will find the spirit of contention, the spirit of strife. There you will find them wanting to "argue the question," and to dispute with you all the time. Their food, their meat, and their drink is contention which is abominable in the sight of the Lord. We do not contend. We are not contentious, for if we were we would grieve the Spirit of the Lord from us, just as apostates do and have always done. (372)

President Ezra Taft Benson has succinctly summarized: "Contention must cease" (*Teachings* 527). And cease it must; but how?

Faith

In order to have the peace which the gospel promises, we must move positively toward change. While we may not be able to alter all the "negative" circumstances in our lives, we can and must change our attitude concerning them. This is the starting place. The Lord grants unto us according to our desires (Alma 29:4; D&C 137:9) and, therefore, our first goal should be to purify our desires. What is required of us to eradicate contention from our lives, our homes, our communities? It will take faith in Christ, hope in Christ, and the charity that Christ freely bestows on those who seek him with all their hearts.

The first major step to overcoming contention is to come to truly believe that it is possible to do so. Many of us, from our expressed attitudes and actions, seem to disbelieve that such a world could really exist—our lip service to such a desire aside. It is not uncommon to brush off such a suggestion by labeling it an "unrealistic dream." When our children bicker and fight with each other we say, "Well, what do you expect; they're only children," or "Boys will be boys," indicating a deep-seated belief that such actions are inherent in human nature and cannot be modified. By reacting so, we effectively absolve ourselves of the responsibility of teaching the truth and bringing about change. King Benjamin taught: "And ye will not suffer your children that they go hungry, or naked; neither will ye suffer that they transgress the laws of God, and fight and quarrel one with another, and serve the devil. . . . But ye will teach them to walk in the ways of truth and soberness; ye will teach them to love one another, and to serve one another" (Mosiah 4:14–15). There are some who can testify that by obeying those very verses they have been able to teach children from an early age that, because of the constraints that God has placed upon them as parents, they cannot allow fighting and quarrelling in the home. It is possible to live in a home devoid of such contention. Until we begin to exercise our faith in the words of Christ and adhere to his commandments, how can we expect a changed result? Miracles follow only the faithful and obedient.

When we decry the responsibility to bring about change with excuses such as "That's just the way it is," we are acknowledging the doubt that a better condition could really exist. The real question is "Do we believe Christ?" It is one thing to believe in him and quite another to believe him (Robinson 8–12). Mormon's record in 4 Nephi indicates that "The people were all converted unto the Lord" (1:2). Is it possible that being "converted unto the Lord" has stronger connotations than being converted to the Church? To be truly converted to him is to truly believe him. By contrast, some of us react to his injunction to "turn the other cheek" as an altruistic, but unreachable, goal. Should we not, instead, believe him? Did he really mean that we should forgo the lawsuit even when we feel justified in pursuing it? Did he mean that we must work and pray and struggle toward truly forgiving another who has offended us, even when that person has not asked our forgiveness? He could not possibly have meant that when we are rudely cut off by another driver on the freeway, we should respond by hitting our brake instead of our horn. Or could he? There is a tendency to believe that intrinsic goodness can only be experienced when the world is a better place.

If we mistakenly rationalize that such innate goodness will have to wait until the Millennium when all others will act similarly, have we not missed the point? Is not the Savior asking us to act that way *now*, in the midst of offense and confrontation, so that we might be counted worthy to continue acting that way *then*? Mormon's day cannot have been so different from the era into which we are rapidly moving, which is perhaps why he marveled so much at the lack of contention he reads about during the period after Christ's ministry. We too can live peacefully in a turbulent world if we will, like him, follow the Savior's teachings and example. Elder Dallin H. Oaks has indicated that the current leaders of the Lord's church are living proof. He has "marveled at how effectively they live the commandment to avoid disputation and contention. They are not always in agreement, but they are always in harmony. They are not uniform in opinions, but they are united in effort. They are many, but they are one" (150).

Hope

If we can come to believe that it is truly possible for some to live without contention, not just in the abstract but in reality, then the next issue becomes, "but what about me? It may be possible for some, but is it possible for me?" Hope in Christ adds the personal dimension, "I believe it can exist for me." Amulek said that "Now is the time and the day of your salvation; and therefore, if ye will repent and harden not your hearts, immediately shall the great plan of redemption be brought about unto you" (Alma 34:31). Does that not include the elimination of contention? The ethical theorist Immanuel Kant wrote: "Duty demands nothing of us which we cannot do. . . . When the moral law commands that we *ought* now to be better men, it follows inevitably that we must *be able* to be better men" (43, 46). The same idea expressed in a prophetic voice is, "I will go and do the things which the Lord hath commanded, for I know that the Lord giveth no commandments unto the children of men, save he shall prepare a way for them that they may accomplish the thing which he commandeth them" (1 Nephi 3:7).

The Lord promised: "Whatsoever ye shall ask the Father in my name, which is right, believing that ye shall receive, behold it shall be given unto you" (3 Nephi 18:20). That brings us back to the question of whether I really believe him. Do I trust him? If I do, will not my prayers be answered as he has promised if I humbly put myself in his care? I must work and pray to avoid disputations and deal justly with others as the Nephites did (4 Nephi 1:2, 15). While there may seem to be no end to the stresses and offenses that could give rise to my justification for a contentious attitude, there is also no end to the assistance that will be freely offered me to overcome such an attitude, if I seek the Lord with faith and hope.

What if I have made some terrible errors? How can I ever forgive myself? Are we not commanded "to forgive all men"? (D&C 64:10). Does not that require that I forgive myself as well? A major danger of anger is that it is often turned inward. When we have erred, it is appropriate for us to experience that "godly sorrow" which leads to true repentance. But to feel hostile emotions toward ourselves is to become both aggressor and victim. The resultant two-edged injury—suffering from acting as judge on the one hand and feeling the sting of being attacked on the other—leads us away from God instead of toward him and can severely damage our sense of selfworth. God knows our hearts far better than even we do. Why not let him be the judge? President Spencer W. Kimball said we must "lean heavily upon the Lord and trust in him, acknowledging that 'with God all things are possible'" (339).

As we apply this hope personally, the "them," "you," and "they" of the Lord's counsel become "I" and "me." I must hope in Christ for the miracles that attended the people of 4 Nephi to attend *me*, realizing that before contention will depart from my home it must depart from my soul. As I rid myself of those attitudes which promote anger, and thereby purify my emotions, I must be prepared for miracles to become my reality as well. George Q. Cannon promised:

> By the Saints refusing to be led by the influences of Satan and not yielding to his seductive temptations, he is virtually bound so far as they are concerned; and, when the head of the family can attain unto this power and persuade his wife and family to do likewise, the power of Satan will be bound in that habitation, and the Millennium will have commenced in that household. (1:88)

Charity

Unless we are "meek, and lowly of heart," Mormon says our "faith and hope [are] vain" (Moroni 7:43–44). But if we have exercised our faith in Christ and have felt the wellsprings of hope in him, then we "must needs have charity" (v 44), which is "the greatest of all" (v 46). In the first part of 4 Nephi, there was no contention "because of the love of God which did dwell in the hearts of the people" (1:15). It is in the heart where Zion must begin. Elder Orson F. Whitney wrote: "The redemption of Zion is more than the purchase or recovery of lands, the building of cities, or even the founding of nations. It is the conquest of the heart, the subjugation of the soul, the sanctifying of the flesh, the purifying and ennobling of the passions" (65).

Contention, while separating persons or groups, also drives a wedge between our natural selves and our celestial reconciliation with God. It causes a blockage in the heart, for the love of God cannot coexist with contention. If we fully love God, our turning the other cheek cannot be a mere outward show, it will be the outward expression of an inner conviction. The Savior commanded "Love one another; as I have loved you" (John 13:34). If he is truly our example, why do we not act charitably toward others even when confronted with hostility? Certainly he showed us the way when he absorbed all the hurt and evil of the world in Gethsemane and on Golgotha, yet returned only good (Robinson 122–23).

We must be filled with the pure love of Christ. It is both the cleansing agent and the resultant blessing of becoming clean. Therefore, it is incumbent upon us to "pray unto the Father with all the energy of heart, that [we] may be filled with this love, which he hath bestowed upon all who are true followers of his Son, Jesus Christ" (Moroni 7:48). One who is endowed with this promised gift "suffereth long, and is kind, and envieth not, and is not puffed up, seeketh not her own, [and] is not easily provoked" (v 45). How opposite these attributes are to a contentious attitude!

Conclusion

Alma the Elder commanded his people that "there should be no contention one with another, but that they should look forward with one eye, having one faith and one baptism, having their hearts knit together in unity and in love one towards another" (Mosiah 18:21). Sadly, the success of the people to follow his command was short-lived. There were brief periods of righteousness; but not until the record reaches 4 Nephi was there a sustained period which resulted in the full establishment of Zion. There were no "Lamanites, nor any manner of -ites; but they were in one, the children of Christ, and heirs to the kingdom of God" (1:17). Undoubtedly that blessed people, like those of Enoch's day, were "of one heart and one mind" (Moses 7:18). By definition, "one heart and one mind" can not be characterized by disputations, divisions, "ites," or any of a myriad of related evils which constitute contention, for all of these poison righteous unity.

Mormon tells us what will come from obedience: "And it came to pass that there was no contention among all the people, in all the land; but there were mighty miracles wrought among the disciples of Jesus. . . . And how blessed were they! For the Lord did bless them in all their doings; yea, even they were blessed and prospered" (4 Nephi 1:13, 18). Imagine the marvels and wonders, the knowledge and majesty which the Lord bestowed upon this people because of their righteousness. It takes faith, hope, and charity to obtain such bounteous blessings and participate in such mighty miracles. It will require opening our hearts to Christ without reservation for us to so partake; for the same promises and possibilities are extended to us by that same Lord, conditioned on obedience to the same commandments. We will be ready and willing to love so that we will have no contention but will live with surpassing joy. Then will it also be written of us: "Surely there could not be a happier people among all the people who had been created by the hand of God" (4 Nephi 1:16).

BIBLIOGRAPHY

Benson, Ezra Taft. "Beware of Pride." *Ensign* (May 1989) 19:4–6; also in *Conference Report* (Apr 1989) 3–7.

———. *The Teachings of Ezra Taft Benson*. Salt Lake City: Bookcraft, 1988.

Burton, Theodore M. "Blessed are the Peacemakers." *Ensign* (Nov 1974) 4:54–56; also in *Conference Report* (Oct 1974) 74–77.

Cannon, George Q. *Gospel Truth*. 2 vols. Ed. Jerreld Newquist. Salt Lake City: Deseret Book, 1974.

Doty, Betty, and Pat Rooney. *The Anger Puzzle*. Redding: Bookery Publishing, 1986.

Ellis, Albert. *Anger: How to Live With and Without It*. Secaucus, NJ: Citadel Press, 1977.

Kant, Immanuel. *Religion Within the Limits of Reason Alone*. New York: Harper & Row, 1960.

Kimball, Spencer W. *The Miracle of Forgiveness*. Salt Lake City: Bookcraft, 1969.

Kohn, Alfie. *No Contest: The Case Against Competition*. New York: Houghton Mifflin Company, 1992.

Lewis, C. S. *Mere Christianity*. New York: Macmillan, 1960.

McConkie, Bruce R. *Mortal Messiah*. 4 vols. Salt Lake City: Deseret Book, 1979.

McKay, Matthew, Peter D. Rogers, and Judith McKay. *When Anger Hurts*. Ed. Kirk Johnson. Oakland: New Harbinger Publications, 1989.

Oaks, Dallin H. *The Lord's Way*. Salt Lake City: Deseret Book, 1991.

Packer, Boyd K. *That All May be Edified*. Salt Lake City: Bookcraft, 1982.

———. "The Law and the Light." *The Book of Mormon: Jacob through Words of Mormon, To Learn with Joy*. Provo, UT: Religious Studies Center, Brigham Young Univ, 1990. 1–31.

———. "The Mystery of Life." *Ensign* (Nov 1983) 13:16–18; also in *Conference Report* (Oct 1983) 19–23.

Robinson, Stephen E. *Believing Christ*. Salt Lake City: Deseret Book, 1992.

Romney, Marion G. "The Perfect Law of Liberty." *Ensign* (Nov 1981) 11:43–45; also in *Conference Report* (Oct 1981) 60–64.

Smith, Joseph F. *Gospel Doctrine*. Salt Lake City: Deseret Book, 1973.

Tavris, Carol. *Anger: The Misunderstood Emotion*. New York: Simon and Schuster, 1982.

Teachings of the Prophet Joseph Smith. Comp. Joseph Fielding Smith. Salt Lake City: Deseret Book, 1976.

Welch, John W. *The Sermon at the Temple and the Sermon on the Mount*. Salt Lake City: Deseret Book, 1990.

Whitney, Orson F. *Life of Heber C. Kimball, an Apostle*. Salt Lake City: Bookcraft, 1967.

Gatherings in the Last Days: Saved in Sheaves, Burned in Bundles

15

Michael W. Middleton

*T*he great gatherings and subtle siftings by which God has separated grain from chaff in individual lives, and the wheat from the tares in the fields of the promised land, are as ubiquitous as any Book of Mormon themes. Such accounts are particularly poignant in its last four books, as centuries of sifting and gathering culminate in the destruction of two civilizations. While the Book of Mormon recounts the peace and progress of righteous societies in the promised land, it also records their descent into evil and their decline into oblivion. Both Jaredite and Nephite histories record numerous events that demonstrate the gathering power of God: the righteous united and readied for the heavenly harvest—the wicked fully ripened and gathered for destruction.

Yet the history of the American continent is only a preview of its future. Mormon's description of the Nephites' last days and Moroni's account of the Jaredites' destruction contain important parallels to the horror and the glory that will precede and accompany the second coming of the Savior Jesus Christ. Discussing the "subject of gathering," the Prophet Joseph Smith wrote, "It is a principle I esteem to be of the greatest importance to those who are looking for salvation in this generation, or in these, that may be called, 'the latter times.' All that the prophets have written, from the days of righteous Abel, down to the last man that has left any testimony on record for our consideration, in speaking of the salvation of Israel in the last days, goes

Michael W. Middleton is public communication manager of Brigham Young University's Cougar Club.

directly to show that it consists in the work of the gathering" (*Teachings of the Prophet Joseph Smith* 83; hereafter *TPJS*).

The Book of Mormon is the record of great gatherings, both to salvation and to destruction. Using the overlay of the parable of the wheat and the tares, we can contrast the Zion societies established when righteous individuals came to Christ with the destruction that befell millions of the wicked when they rejected Christ and turned their minds and hearts to do evil. This all has application to our day because the latter times and the last days will be seasons of gathering: the righteous will be gathered to safety and salvation while the wicked punish and destroy themselves amidst wars and calamities (Mormon 4:5). The principle of gatherings to salvation and to destruction in the promised land follows an important pattern that is best illustrated by the parable of the wheat and the tares (Matt 13:24–43; D&C 86:1–7). There are four main aspects to that parable: (1) separating the righteous from the wicked, (2) planting the good seed in a promised land, (3) introducing the tares, and (4) finally, gathering before the harvest.

Out of the Midst of Wickedness: Sifting and Separation

In gathering his people the Lord always gathers the righteous by separating them out from the wicked, never vice versa. This distinction is important enough that the Joseph Smith Translation of Matthew 13 corrects the King James Bible order of the Lord's command to the reapers in verse 30 from "Gather ye together first the tares, and bind them in bundles to burn them" to read "Gather ye together *first* the wheat into my barn; and the tares . . . to be burned" (JST Matt 13:29; emphasis added). The Doctrine and Covenants clarifies and confirms this order: "Ye shall *first* gather out the wheat from among the tares, and *after* the gathering of the wheat, behold and lo, the tares are bound in bundles, and the field remaineth to be burned" (D&C 86:7; emphasis added).

Such siftings and gatherings are apparent throughout the Book of Mormon. The Jaredite record opens with a gathering for a wicked purpose—building the tower of Babel. Unworthy to be invited into God's kingdom and unwilling to change their ways, the people in the days of the brother of Jared concocted their own ideas about exaltation. Inspired by Satan, "they attempted to build a tower sufficiently high that they might get to heaven" (Hel 6:28; see also Gen 11:4).

After observing for himself the misbegotten designs of his children (Gen 11:5), "the Lord confounded the language of the people, and swore in his wrath that they should be scattered upon all the face of the earth" (Ether 1:33). Yet, while the wicked were scattered and confounded, a colony of righteous individuals was gathered and led away from the others to the promised land because of their faithfulness. Under the direction of the Lord, the brother of Jared and his followers were separated from the confounding curse that fell upon the builders of Babel. From that day to ours, Babel, or Babylon, the ancient capital of Babylonia, has been a symbol of all that is corrupt and confused; specifically, it connotes the false religion of all schemes or denominations that promise an entrance into heaven which they cannot deliver.

Like the Jaredite account, Nephite history begins with a separation. The Lord commands the prophet Lehi to leave Jerusalem and journey into the wilderness. Gathered by God to be a "peculiar treasure" (Ex 19:5), the Jews had become workers of wickedness and worshipers of idols. Though dedicated to the Lord, Solomon's temple had become like the tower of Babel—an edifice which pretended a relationship with deity it was incapable of providing. So egregious was Judah's sin that Jeremiah declared it to be "written with a pen of iron and with the point of a diamond" on individual hearts and engraved on the horns of the temple altars (Jer 17:1). Jerusalem would be destroyed just over a decade later, but Lehi's colony was gathered and spared, separated from the wicked, and led to the promised land because of their faithfulness.

Once recognized, God's pattern of separating the good from the evil can be found in many places in the scriptures, including nearly every book of the Book of Mormon. Consider the following examples. Shortly after their arrival in the promised land, the Lord directed Nephi and the righteous to depart from his wicked brothers (2 Nephi 5). Warned of the Lord, Mosiah led his people out of the land of Nephi (Omni 1:12). Converted by Abinadi's teaching, Alma the Elder prompted the believers to withdraw from Noah's kingdom and to gather at the waters of Mormon; then, divinely "apprised of the coming of the king's army," the colony left their homes behind and began their own city (Mosiah 18:4–7, 34). The Anti-Nephi-Lehies, who were converted by the sons of Mosiah, hearkened to the Lord's commandment to leave the Lamanites and established a righteous society in Jershon (Alma 27:12–14).

Analyzing these examples and those of the colonies of Lehi and of the brother of Jared, we see three parallels. First, in each case a righteous people were warned by God, under the direction of a prophet, to separate themselves from the wicked. Second, in each case the chosen group was led into a "wilderness" where they were prepared and proven. As section 86 of the Doctrine and Covenants suggests, it is the tares that "choke the wheat and drive the church into the wilderness" (v 3). And, third, in each case the chosen people eventually received their rest in a promised land where they began to build a Zion society. The rise of The Church of Jesus Christ of Latter-day Saints also followed this pattern; a series of siftings, gatherings, and journeyings in the wilderness led from New York through Ohio to Missouri. Unprepared to build Zion at that time, the Church passed through a series of purges and divisions. As a result, a colony of pioneers departed into the wilderness to endure a "little season" of chastening, growth, and refinement in order that Zion may be redeemed (D&C 100:13; 101:3–4).

Until Zion is redeemed, Christ will continue to separate the good from the evil, the righteous from the wicked. He who separated the light from the darkness at creation's dawn will also divide the sheep from the goats during the final judgment (Moses 2:4; Matt 25:32). The shadow of Christ's second coming could not be more clearly portrayed than it is by his Book of Mormon ministry; in the midst of calamities and destruction, the "more righteous" in the meridian of time were separated and spared (3 Nephi 9:13). Preserved through God's catastrophic judgments, many of the "more righteous" later gathered to a temple site in the land of Bountiful where they became personal witnesses of the resurrected Christ (11:1–17).

The Sower of the Seed

In the parable of the wheat and the tares, the sower of the seed is Christ himself (Matt 13:37) or the apostles who continued his work, acting in his name (see D&C 86:2); it is Christ who plants the people in a field that is his own—his to give and his to take away. The inhabitants of the promised land are not there by chance; individually and collectively they have been separated from others, brought through a wilderness of testing, and planted in a land choice above all other lands. Expressing sentiments as applicable to us as they were to the Nephites or the Jaredites, Lehi taught, "There shall none come into this land save they shall be brought by the hand of the Lord. Wherefore, this land is consecrated unto him whom [the Lord] shall bring" (2 Nephi 1:6–7).

In many instances where wickedness prevails, the Lord covenants with the righteous and guides them to a land of promise where their inheritance includes the opportunity and responsibility to build Zion. Their land of promise is not taken away until they reject the promise of Zion and are fully ripened in their iniquity. Possession of a land of promise is always predicated upon hearkening to the voice of the Lord (Abr 2:6) and serving "the God of the land, who is Jesus Christ" (Ether 2:12).

Before they arrived in the promised land, the Lord revealed to both the Nephites and the Jaredites the blessings and correlative responsibilities associated with being gathered to the promised land. Expressing his "thoughts upon the land" that he would soon give the Jaredites, the Lord's warning is forcefully redundant (Ether 2:15). Three times in four verses he repeats a vital couplet concerning the American continents: first, this is a choice land of promise; second, the inhabitants will be swept off if they become fully ripened in iniquity (vv 7–10).

Grave responsibilities are associated with being good seed planted in a promised land. The Book of Mormon reiterates more than a dozen times the idea that the American continents are a land choice above all other lands (1 Nephi 2:20; Ether 9:20); as Jesus taught, "Unto whomsoever much is given, of him shall be much required" (Luke 12:48; see also D&C 82:3). Because of the unparalleled opportunities and rich blessings extended to the righteous in the promised land, they incur the severest penalties if they rebel against their God. Alma taught that if his people, after being "highly favored . . . of the Lord," transgressed contrary to the light and knowledge which they had received, "it would be far more tolerable for the Lamanites than for them" (Alma 9:20, 23). He admonished his people to repent, reminding them that "the Lord expressly promised and firmly decreed, that if ye will rebel against him that ye shall utterly be destroyed from off the face of the earth" (v 24).

The Lord extended three promises to Nephi even before his family left the land of Palestine. If he were obedient to the commandments of the Lord, he would prosper in the land of promise (1 Nephi 2:20; 1 Nephi 4:14); he would be a "ruler and a teacher over [his] brethren" (1 Nephi 2:22); and he, and his righteous posterity, would never be under the power of their enemies (v 23). The blessings that the Lord promised to the Nephites have also been offered to the current inhabitants of the promised land —prosperity for the obedient (Omni 1:6; Mosiah 1:7), possession of a land of liberty (2 Nephi 1:7), freedom from the oppressive rule of others (2 Nephi 10:11; D&C 101:77, 80), and protection from foreign powers (1 Nephi 13:19; Alma 44:3–4). However, if we reject these promises and become fully ripened in iniquity, we will not escape the curses and judgments that befell the former inhabitants of the Americas.

An Enemy Hath Done This: Opposition from Opposites

Satan always seeks to sow tares in the midst of the wheat on many levels—in the world, in the Church, in the family, and in individual souls. By describing the children of the wicked one as the tares (Matt 13:38), the Savior teaches a powerful lesson: while evil is the opposite of good, it often appears as a counterfeit. The father of lies has learned that one of his most effective schemes is to present what sounds and looks like the truth even though it lacks substance and authority. As defined by God, evil is anything that is either more or less than the doctrine of Christ (3 Nephi 11:40); it is just as destructive to look beyond the mark as it is to stop short of it (Jacob 4:14).

Without the aid of the Holy Ghost or the light of Christ, the natural man cannot distinguish the righteous from the wicked prior to the time of separation. Worthless tares and wholesome wheat seem identical until the harvest. Using words he gave to Malachi, the Savior taught the Nephites that prior to every time of separation many will call the proud happy, workers of wickedness will seem "set up," and tempters of God will appear delivered. Not until the Lord of Hosts returns to make up his jewels in judgment "shall ye return and discern between the righteous and the wicked, between him that serveth God and him that serveth him not" (3 Nephi 24:14–18).

As in the parable of the wheat and the tares, the Lord is not the source of evil. The tares are sown among the righteous during his absence. The Lord, as the sower of good seed, permits the tares to grow with the wheat so that agency may exist, creating an arena of opposites where the righteous may earn their exaltation. Exaltation is not about appearance or association; as in other eras, eventually every shaft of grain in the promised land will be judged on its own merits. Neither tithing receipts, temple marriages, nor Church membership can save those who choose to be gathered into Satan's fold. We can claim only one name; only one shepherd can seal us his (Mosiah 5:14–15; Alma 34:35).

Mormon taught the Saints of his day that they were either a good or a bitter fountain. Certainly there are different degrees of bitterness, but the dichotomy is complete and discrete: a servant of the devil cannot follow Christ, neither can a follower of Christ be a servant of the devil (Moroni 7:11). Even actions that appear to be righteous, such as saying prayers or offering gifts to God, are not counted as acts of righteousness if they are not done with real intent (v 6). In fact, "A man being evil cannot do that which is good"; faithless and grudging efforts leave both the individual and his acts "counted evil before God" (vv 6, 8–9). Consider Cain's offering; the same Satan commands and the same consequences await in our day (Moses 5:18–24).

And so Satan revels in his role as the creator of counterfeits and the father of lies. The rejection of his offer in the premortal council has not weakened his resolve. Since shrieking at Moses "I am the Only Begotten, worship me" (Moses 1:19), he has not slackened his efforts to substitute priestcraft for priesthood, to supplant love with lust, and to replace true worship with idle ritual. Fittingly, Nephi classifies the church of the devil as a "harlot," for while the lips of Satan's servants may claim a relationship with the bridegroom, their hearts are far from him. Though they may perform the ordained duties of the Church of the Lamb—for money—their actions are always without authority.

Such is the sum and substance of apostasy: false claims of authority, perverted doctrines, the modification or deletion of saving ordinances, and the introduction of paid ministers. Prophesying of our day, Moroni decried the universal apostasy of "every one" of the pre-restoration churches; they had become polluted by pride, priestcraft, and perversions (Mormon 8:31–41). Although he had "supposed not to have written more" (Moroni 1:1) after abridging the Jaredite record, Moroni devotedly uses his own book in the Book of Mormon to attempt to repair the effects of the great apostasy he had predicted. It is hard to imagine a more concise cure for the ills of apostasy than the content of the book of Moroni. Chapters 2 and 3 describe how the Nephite apostles received their authority and the manner by which priests and teachers were ordained in the true Church. Chapters 4 and 5 describe the ordinance of the sacrament, including verbatim records of the sacramental prayers. And chapter 6 gives instructions concerning church meetings and how repentant individuals were accepted for baptism and fellowshipped into the Church. Writing to our day, Moroni concludes his book with two epistles written by his father, Mormon, and with his own explanation of the long-absent gifts of the Spirit (Moroni 10:8–19). Certainly Mormon spoke and wrote many things, but Moroni chose to include his father's doctrinal exposition on how to use the Spirit of Christ to judge between good and evil (Moroni 7) and his epistle against infant baptism (Moroni 8).

Nothing could be more important to the inhabitants of the promised land in the last days than to be able to distinguish between good and evil. Foretelling the signs preceding his second coming, the Savior explained that there would arise "false Christs, and false prophets," who would show such great signs and wonders "that, if possible, they shall deceive the very elect, who are elect according to the covenant" (JST Matt 1:22). Though both the power of God and the influence of Satan will grow in this last dispensation, distinguishing between them will not necessarily become easier. Speaking "against the devil" in the 1987 October general conference, Elder James E. Faust taught, "We will witness increasing evidence of Satan's power as the kingdom of God grows stronger. . . . In the future the opposition will be both more subtle and more open" (33). Trying to prepare us against this time of shifting standards and subtle deceptions, President Ezra Taft Benson has exercised keys held only by the living prophet on our behalf. Speaking in the April 1986 general conference, he said: "Now, in the authority of the sacred priesthood in me vested, I invoke my blessing upon the Latter-day Saints and upon good people every-where. I bless you with increased discernment to judge between Christ and anti-Christ. I bless you with increased power to do good and to resist evil. I bless you with increased *understanding* of the

Book of Mormon" (78). These three specific blessings bestowed by a prophet of God—increased discernment, wisely-exercised agency, and improved understanding of the Book of Mormon—are related necessities for survival in the last days.

The Great Gatherings: Saved in Sheaves, Burned in Bundles

Before the destruction of any people, Christ and his servants always gather all who are worthy and willing unto salvation. Satan claims all those who reject the name of the good shepherd (Mosiah 5:9–10). When those invited to come unto him refuse his willing arms, the Savior sorrows. Before leaving mortality, Christ wept over Jerusalem: "O Jerusalem, Jerusalem . . . how often would I have gathered thy children together . . . and ye would not!" (Matt 23:37). Similar sentiment flows from the words of the master of the vineyard recorded in Jacob chapter 5: "What could I have done more in my vineyard? Have I slackened my hand, that I have not nourished it? Nay . . . I have stretched forth mine hand almost all the day long, and the end draweth nigh" (v 47).

When the field is fully ripe, the wheat is gathered into the master's barn, and then the tares are destroyed. During the slow process of ripening in iniquity that precedes the rapid harvest, servants of the Lord always warn all those with ears to hear of the impending judgments; no people is ever destroyed without ample warning from the Lord. Concerning the Jews, Nephi taught, "Never hath any of them been destroyed save it were foretold them by the prophets of the Lord" (2 Nephi 25:9). Once righteous, two great civilizations on this continent declined until they labored in iniquity. In each instance, they rejected and persecuted the prophets and servants the Lord sent until he withdrew them (Ether 13:22; Mormon 8:10). Deceived by Satan, these two societies were hardened and past feeling when chastened by the hand of God (Mormon 9:20; D&C 43:23–26). Eventually, even the Lord's Spirit ceased striving with them (Mormon 5:16; Ether 15:19) and destruction was unavoidable and immediate. To paraphrase Samuel the Lamanite, their falling and rejection was made sure (Hel 13:37–38; Ether 14:25).

To a civilization fully ripened in iniquity, judgment and destruction become the kindest gifts God can give; once decreed, such judgments come quickly (D&C 99:5). The Jaredites' war of extinction was "swift and speedy" (Ether 14:22); likewise, the Nephites were swept off the land before the Lamanites "even as a dew before the sun" (Mormon 4:18). Either of these Book of Mormon civilizations could have been described by Jeremiah's lament over Judah, "Destruction upon destruction is cried; for the whole land is spoiled: suddenly are my tents spoiled, and my curtains in a moment" (Jer 4:20). Although divine destruction is rapid, it is never slipshod. Unquestionably, God has the power to take one and leave another in any circumstance (Matt 24:40–41), and often the righteous are spared. However, at times the Lord does not stretch forth his hand to protect his people from suffering or even death (see Alma 14:10–11), if such circumstances allow the wicked to be punished and the righteous to enter into his rest (Alma 60:12–13; *TPJS* 34). Also indicative of God's discretion in destruction is the way that two or more witnesses are always left to attest to his justice in judgment.

When the Jaredites were fully ripened in their iniquity, the final "gatherings" began. In spite of the warnings of prophets (Ether 7:23; 11:20) and their growing, obvious peril, every citizen of this greatest of all nations (1:43) was gathered to destruction. With hardened hearts and blinded minds, the Jaredites still spent "four years gathering" for battle even after the deaths of "two millions" of Coriantumr's mighty men (15:14). In the end, the names of leaders such as Shiz, Lib, and Coriantumr were little more than threads by which bundles of tares were bound before the burning.

After three generations of righteous wheat were gathered into the rest of the Lord, the remaining Nephites ripened in iniquity. Mormon mentions the gathering of the Nephites into one body as early as 327 AD: "We did gather in our people as fast as it were possible" (Mormon 2:7). After 58 years of fighting and fleeing, all the while striving to "gather in our people as much as it were possible, that perhaps we might save them from destruction" (v 21), the Nephites gather one final time. "And I, Mormon, wrote an epistle unto the king of the Lamanites, and desired of him that he would grant unto us that we might gather together our people unto the land of Cumorah, by a hill which was called Cumorah" (Mormon 6:2).

There can be no land of promise for mortals who will not keep their covenants. After Enoch and his city were gathered into the heavenly barn and this land was cleansed of all with whom the Spirit had ceased to strive, the American continents "became a choice land above all other lands, a chosen land of the Lord"; God decreed that all who inhabited this promised land shall serve him or they will fall (Ether 13:2). The Jaredites came, but several thousand years later the Lord of the vineyard reluctantly removed the once mighty tree that then "cumbered this spot of land" (Jacob 5:44). Later, the Nephites abandoned Zion's united order of "no contentions and disputations" (4 Nephi 1:2) for a world "without order and without mercy" (Moroni 9:18) where the only things combatants had in common were hearts equally filled with hate and hands similarly stained with blood. Three times the Lord has cleansed the promised land; each day we are determining, both collectively and individually, how extensive the fourth purging will be.

The Book of Mormon is the record of great gatherings: the righteous gathered to lands of promise and the wicked gathered to destruction. However, both the Jaredite and Nephite prophets promise that a series of separations will occur as the Lord waits for the wheat and the tares to grow until the harvest. This pattern of great gatherings will be a characteristic of the last days until the second coming of Christ. Collectively and individually we are each, unavoidably, being gathered. The scriptures powerfully suggest that there are gatherings for which we will want to prepare ourselves and others we should plan to avoid, for Adam-ondi-Ahman will be as real as Armageddon.

The righteous will be gathered to stakes of Zion, while the wicked gather to battle among themselves and against the kingdom of God. Physically and spiritually, both Christ and Satan will assemble their hosts for the battle that will end what the war in heaven began. Armed with "truth . . . out of the earth," the Church of God will grow as we use the Book of Mormon to "gather [the Lord's] elect from the four quarters of the earth, unto a place which [he] shall prepare" (Moses 7:62). The Book of Mormon is the great gathering and sifting tool of the last days.

Meanwhile, the followers of Satan will assemble in evil armies and secret combinations that will overtly and covertly "make war with the saints" (Rev 13:7). These two groups will continue to polarize the earth's population until the words of the First Presidency's declaration of 1845 are fulfilled, "As this work progresses in its onward course . . . no king, ruler, or subject, no community or individual, will stand *neutral*. All will at length be influenced by one spirit or the other; and will take sides either for or against the kingdom of God" (*Messages of the First Presidency* 1:257).

In spite of all that the world knows of the last days, all that we fear and all that we anticipate, we will be gathered—some to majestic glory and some to sudden destruction. The great gatherings of the last days are imminent, neither our ignorance nor our trepidation will slow their arrival. But each of us determines where he or she will be found; we individually determine the direction of our destiny. Nearly 2,000 years ago, on the day the resurrected Christ appeared on the American continent, it was not by chance that "there were a great multitude gathered together, of the people of Nephi, round about the temple which was in the land Bountiful" (see 3 Nephi 11:1; Ether 12:7). It is not coincidence that those worthy souls were conversing about Jesus Christ at the very moment of his coming.

The Book of Mormon, the most beautiful and the most correct of any book on the earth, provides the perfect template for the second coming of the Savior. For if we desire to meet him when he comes again, we must endure the sifting that will precede his appearance to the world. Each day we are choosing either the barn or the burning. As we select our associations for the approaching harvest that will accompany the Lord's return, it will not be enough to bask in our lighted vessels; eventually we must each climb the high mountain where, at great length and through great effort, we too will hear and see and know for ourselves (3 Nephi 11:14–15). To prepare for the harvest, we must gather to stand in holy places and separate ourselves from the world. In our closets, our secret places, and our wildernesses, we must come to know Him whom all the world one day shall see. For in that moment, when every knee bows and every tongue confesses that Jesus Christ is the Lord (Philip 2:10–11), some knees will need no practice and some lips will recite words that are willing and familiar. To be gathered into the celestial fold, we must each depart from Babylon, live worthy of the promises of the promised land, distinguish between the wheat and the tares, and do all in our power to establish Zion.

BIBLIOGRAPHY

Benson, Ezra Taft. "A Sacred Responsibility." *Ensign* (May 1986) 16:77–78; also in *Conference Report* (Apr 1986) 98–100.

Faust, James E. "The Great Imitator." *Ensign* (Nov 1987) 17:33–36; also in *Conference Report* (Oct 1987) 40–44.

Messages of the First Presidency. Comp. James R. Clark. 6 vols. Salt Lake City: Bookcraft, 1965.

Teachings of the Prophet Joseph Smith. Comp. Joseph Fielding Smith. Salt Lake City: Deseret Book, 1976.

The Judgment Seat of Christ

16

Monte S. Nyman

*I*n the New Testament we read the promise given to the Twelve Apostles by Jesus: "Ye also shall sit upon twelve thrones, judging the twelve tribes of Israel" (Matt 19:28). This promise to the Twelve is verified in both the Book of Mormon (1 Nephi 12:9; Mormon 3:18) and the Doctrine and Covenants (29:12). However, only the Book of Mormon clarifies and enlarges the doctrine of the judgment by the apostles.

The word *judgment* may be misleading. The usual meaning of the word to us in the twentieth century is to pass sentence or determine innocence or guilt. This interpretation, however, gives only half of the broader meaning as used in the Book of Mormon concerning the judgment of Christ. It speaks of the judgment of Christ as a time of reward as well as a time of accountability for the acts of mortals. It is similar to the biblical injunction of "being weighed in the balances" (Dan 5:27), where consideration is given to both the positive and the negative acts of the individual. It further clarifies that there will be apostles or special witnesses at the judgment seat of Christ to testify in behalf of or against the persons being judged.

In his great sermon on the atonement of Christ, Jacob warned his brethren of reviling against the truth and then invited them to "come unto the Lord, the Holy One. Remember that his paths are righteous. Behold, the way for man is narrow, but it lieth in a straight course before him, and the keeper of the gate is the Holy One of Israel; and he employeth no servant there; and there is none other way save it be

Monte S. Nyman is professor of Ancient Scripture at Brigham Young University.

by the gate; for he cannot be deceived, for the Lord God is his name" (2 Nephi 9:41). Jacob's warning is consistent with Jesus' declaration at the pool of Bethesda during his earthly ministry, "For the Father judgeth no man, but hath committed all judgment unto the Son" (John 5:22). Jacob went on to testify: "O, my beloved brethren, remember my words. Behold, I take off my garments, and I shake them before you; I pray the God of my salvation that he view me with his all-searching eye; wherefore, ye shall know at the last day, when all men shall be judged of their works, that the God of Israel did witness that I shook your iniquities from my soul, and that I stand with brightness before him, and am rid of your blood" (2 Nephi 9:44). Jacob's testimony is significant in understanding the role of the apostles at the judgment bar. His testimony to those listening to his sermon will not only rid him of his accountability for their sins, but it will make them accountable for the testimony he has borne. He will stand as a witness of God and they will be judged either positively or negatively by their response in word and actions to his declaration of truth. Just as Jacob will stand as a witness for or against his people at the day they stand at the judgment bar of Christ, the Twelve Apostles will be witnesses for or against all people at the judgment bar of Christ.

The apostles are "special witnesses of the name of Christ in all the world—thus differing from other officers in the church in the duties of their calling" (D&C 107:23). Thus, they are Christ's representatives, and all people who hear their testimony or have an opportunity to hear it will be responsible for accepting what they were taught and will be blessed or held accountable at the judgment bar or judgment-seat of Christ for what they do with it. Understanding the apostles' roles in various times and places enables us to know how they will serve as judges of the house of Israel and all the world.

The Jerusalem Twelve

Mormon addressed his writings "unto all the ends of the earth; yea, unto you, twelve tribes of Israel, who shall be judged according to your works by the twelve whom Jesus chose to be his disciples in the land of Jerusalem" (Mormon 3:18). As already noted, Jesus had said that his Twelve Apostles chosen in Jerusalem would judge the twelve tribes of Israel (Matt 19:28). The Doctrine and Covenants notes that they will judge the whole house of Israel.

> And again, verily, verily, I say unto you, and it hath gone forth in a firm decree, by the will of the Father, that mine apostles, the Twelve which were with me in my ministry at Jerusalem, shall stand at my right hand at the day of my coming in a pillar of fire, being clothed with robes of righteousness, with crowns upon their heads, in glory even as I am, to judge the whole house of Israel, even as many as have loved me and kept my commandments, and none else. (D&C 29:12)

This says the same thing in another way because the twelve tribes are the whole house of Israel.

The ending of the above verse may also be misleading. Why will the Twelve judge only "as many as have loved me and kept my commandments, and none else"? The answer to that question is given in the following verse: "For a trump shall sound both long and loud, even as upon Mount Sinai, and all the earth shall quake, and they shall come forth—yea, even the dead which died in me, to receive a crown of righteousness, and to be clothed upon, even as I am, to be with me, that we may be one" (D&C 29:13). In this context, the Twelve are to be with Christ at his second coming. Those who are called forth by the trump of God to be resurrected and come forth to meet Christ at his coming (45:44–46) will be judged by the Twelve at that time. They will later judge others of the house of Israel who are not worthy to be raised up at Christ's coming and those of the world who would not come to him. Those who have accepted and followed the testimony or witness of the Twelve will be raised at the time of Christ's coming and will thus receive the blessing of the resurrection.

Why would these Twelve Apostles judge all of the tribes of Israel when they primarily ministered to the Jewish people? The answer is that they were special witnesses of the ministry, atonement, crucifixion and resurrection of the Lord Jesus Christ. Their written testimonies, like Mormon's, were to go to all the world, and recorded the events of Christ's coming to earth to redeem his people, the house of Israel, and all who would accept his gospel. These Twelve Apostles were chosen from among those disciples who responded to Jesus' invitation to follow him to be eye witnesses from the beginning of his ministry (Matt 4:18–22; John 1:35–51). Being such witnesses was important because when Judas, one of the original Twelve, apostatized, Peter instructed the other apostles concerning Judas' replacement: "Wherefore of these men which have companied with us all the time that the Lord Jesus went in and out among us, beginning from the baptism of John, unto that same day that he was taken up from us, must one be ordained to be a witness with us of his resurrection" (Acts 1:21–22). Thus these twelve men were eye witnesses of his earthly ministry from the beginning to the end. They stood as special witnesses of Christ to the whole house of Israel and to all the world, in life to many and in writings to many, many more.

Although the New Testament does not tell us the lineage of the Twelve Apostles, it is possible they represented all the twelve tribes. All but one of the Jerusalem Twelve were from the area of Galilee which was earlier occupied by the northern 10 tribes of Israel. The people of Galilee claimed to be Israelites although they had intermarried with Gentiles (2 Kings 17:24; John 4; Jacob 5:7–14). The Lord gave the commandment to harvest these souls (John 4:35–45) long before he gave the revelation to go to the Gentiles (Acts 10). It is possible that the Twelve came from those remnants of the lost tribes who had not been taken captive by the Assyrians. Whatever their lineage, the twelve tribes will eventually receive the testimony of the Jerusalem Twelve (2 Nephi 29:12–13) and at the judgment bar will be accountable for and blessed by the degree of their acceptance of that testimony.

The Nephite Apostles

In vision, Nephi saw his people at the meridian of time, and part of what he saw was the calling of the Nephite Twelve Disciples (apostles) by Christ as he walked among them: "And I saw the heavens open, and the Lamb of God descending out of heaven; and he came down and showed himself unto them. And I also saw and bear record that the Holy Ghost fell upon twelve others; and they were ordained of God, and chosen" (1 Nephi 12:6–7).[1] Nephi also saw that these Nephite Twelve Apostles were chosen to minister to the seed of Nephi and his brethren or to be special witnesses to them (v 8). In their role as special witnesses, they would be judges of the Nephite

---

[1] Although the Book of Mormon calls the Nephite Twelve "disciples," the Prophet Joseph Smith declared that they were ordained "apostles" (*History of the Church* 4:538).

people: "And these twelve ministers whom thou beholdest shall judge thy seed. And, behold, they are righteous forever; for because of their faith in the Lamb of God their garments are made white in his blood" (1 Nephi 12:10). What Nephi saw in vision did take place when the resurrected Jesus Christ called and ordained twelve apostles among the Nephites as he ministered among them, and admonished and promised blessings if they would give heed to their words (3 Nephi 11:18–12:2).

The Lord commanded Mormon to "stand as an idle witness to manifest unto the world the things which [he] saw and heard, according to the manifestations of the Spirit which had testified of things to come" (Mormon 3:16). As shown by the following verse, his being an idle witness was through his writing: "Therefore I write unto you, Gentiles, and also unto you, house of Israel, when the work shall commence, that ye shall be about to prepare to return to the land of your inheritance" (v 17). Mormon's words were addressed to people in the latter days, when the gathering of Israel would be beginning.

As indicated by the word "yea" in the beginning of the next verse, Mormon apparently understood that his words would go forth in conjunction with the records of the Twelve Apostles chosen in Jerusalem. "Yea, behold, I write unto all the ends of the earth; yea, unto you, twelve tribes of Israel, who shall be judged according to your works by the twelve whom Jesus chose to be his disciples in the land of Jerusalem" (Mormon 3:18). The second use of the word "yea" indicates a knowledge that the twelve tribes of Israel had been scattered to the ends of the earth. The above verse also gives another testimony of the judgment of the twelve tribes by the Jerusalem Twelve. Mormon also wrote to the remnant of the Nephites and testified that they would be judged by the Twelve Apostles among them: "And I write also unto the remnant of this people, who shall also be judged by the twelve whom Jesus chose in this land" (v 19).

He further declared that the Nephite Twelve "shall be judged by the other twelve whom Jesus chose in the land of Jerusalem" (Mormon 3:19). Nephi was also told by the angel as he saw his seed in vision, "Thou rememberest the twelve apostles of the Lamb? Behold they are they who shall judge the twelve tribes of Israel; wherefore, the twelve ministers of thy seed shall be judged of them; for ye are of the house of Israel" (1 Nephi 12:9). The Nephites had been taught of Christ's coming ministry, crucifixion, atonement and resurrection

(Mosiah 3:5–11; Alma 7:10–13). The witness of the Jerusalem Twelve was verified in person to the Nephites, among whom were the Nephite Twelve Apostles, when Christ ministered among them. He testified that he was the light and life of the world, that he had drunk of the bitter cup (made the Atonement), and that he had been resurrected (3 Nephi 11:11). Those who accept or reject this testimony of Jesus' Jerusalem ministry to the Nephites will be accountable at the judgment seat of Christ and will be blessed to the degree they have merited. Thus the Nephite Twelve and the people will be judged by the testimony of the Twelve in Jerusalem that Christ came to the earth, ministered, was crucified and resurrected, and atoned for the sins of all mankind.

The people to whom Mormon wrote will also be accountable when they appear at the judgment bar for what he recorded on the plates that were translated into the Book of Mormon. Mormon continued to testify: "And these things doth the Spirit manifest unto me; therefore I write unto you all. And for this cause I write unto you, that ye may know that ye must all stand before the judgment-seat of Christ, yea, every soul who belongs to the whole human family of Adam; and ye must stand to be judged of your works, whether they be good or evil; And also that ye may believe the gospel of Jesus Christ, which ye shall have among you" (Mormon 3:20–21). All will be judged by the words written by Mormon.

Three Nephite Apostles

Three of the Nephite Twelve had their ministry extended until the second coming of Christ (3 Nephi 28:4–9). Their ministry was to all nations:

> And it shall come to pass, when the Lord seeth fit in his wisdom that they shall minister unto all the scattered tribes of Israel, and unto all nations, kindreds, tongues and people, and shall bring out of them unto Jesus many souls, that their desire may be fulfilled, and also because of the convincing power of God which is in them. And they are as the angels of God, and if they shall pray unto the Father in the name of Jesus they can show themselves unto whatsoever man it seemeth them good. Therefore, great and marvelous works shall be wrought by them, before the great and coming day when all people must surely stand before the judgment-seat of Christ; Yea even among the Gentiles shall there be a great and marvelous work wrought by them, before that judgment day. (3 Nephi 28:29–32)

Having been on the earth for approximately 2,000 years, working among all nations, these three disciples will have done extensive work, although many may not recognize the source of the miracles they performed. This teaching is strongly implied by the declaration "when all people must surely stand before the judgment seat of Christ" that people who witness any part of the three transfigured Nephites' great and marvelous ministry will be accountable for that part of the work.

The Four Nephite Abridgers

Mormon also wrote in order that "the Jews, the covenant people of the Lord, shall have other witness besides him whom they saw and heard, that Jesus, whom they slew, was the very Christ and the very God" (Mormon 3:21). The other witness to the Jews would in general be the Book of Mormon and the yet to come forth record of the lost tribes which Nephi foretold would come to the Jews (2 Nephi 29:13). But the Book of Mormon promises final witnesses in addition to the written word. Nephi concluded his record upon the small plates with this testimony:

> And if they are not the words of Christ, judge ye—for Christ will show unto you, with power and great glory, that they are his words, at the last day; and you and I shall stand face to face before his bar; and ye shall know that I have been commanded of him to write these things, notwithstanding my weakness. And I pray the Father in the name of Christ that many of us, if not all, may be saved in his kingdom at that great and last day. And now, my beloved brethren, all those who are of the house of Israel, and all ye ends of the earth, I speak unto you as the voice of one crying from the dust: Farewell until that great day shall come. And you that will not partake of the goodness of God, and respect the words of the Jews, and also my words, and the words which shall proceed forth out of the mouth of the Lamb of God, behold, I bid you an everlasting farewell, for these words shall condemn you at the last day. For what I seal on earth, shall be brought against you at the judgment bar; for thus hath the Lord commanded me, and I must obey. Amen. (2 Nephi 33:11–15)

The Book of Mormon will go to every nation, kindred, tongue, and people (Rev 14:6–7; D&C 88:103–04). Every nation that possesses it will be judged by it (2 Nephi 25:22; D&C 5:4–10). The individuals of those nations who accept Nephi's words will see him at the judgment bar as a confirmation of his writings, and he bade them farewell until that day. Those who reject his words will be judged and condemned by them, and Nephi bade them an everlasting farewell.

After recording the great allegory of the destiny of the house of Israel (Jacob 5), Jacob also bore his testimony of a final meeting with the readers of the Book of Mormon: "I bid you farewell, until I shall meet you before the pleasing bar of God, which bar striketh the wicked with awful dread and fear. Amen" (Jacob 6:13). Jacob had previously invited his brethren to come through the narrow way and obtain eternal life. There will be both joy and fear at the judgment bar.

Mormon does not say he will see his readers at the judgment bar, but he does "write unto you, that ye may know that ye must all stand before the judgment-seat of Christ" (Mormon 3:20). He also wrote that they might "believe the gospel of Jesus Christ, which ye shall have among you" (v 21). Their opportunity to believe the gospel will come through their reading the Book of Mormon, which will go to all the ends of the earth. Mormon's final plea to the reader speaks again of the judgment bar: "And I would that I could persuade all ye ends of the earth to repent and prepare to stand before the judgment-seat of Christ" (v 22). Since Nephi and Jacob say they will be at the judgment bar, Mormon's two references to the judgment-seat are strong indications that he will be there as well. This is more evident from Moroni's testimony. As he abridged the Jaredite record, he foretold of meeting his readers at the judgment bar: "And now I, Moroni, bid farewell unto the Gentiles, yea, and also unto my brethren whom I love, until we shall meet before the judgment-seat of Christ, where all men shall know that my garments are not spotted with your blood. And then shall ye know that I have seen Jesus, and that he hath talked with me face to face, and that he told me in plain humility, even as a man telleth another in mine own language, concerning these things" (Ether 12:38–39).

By fulfilling his mission, Moroni was no longer held accountable for his reader's sins; neither was Jacob (2 Nephi 9:44). Moroni bore his testimony to the principle that the messenger must give his message as he concluded his father's record (Mormon 9:35–37), and at the close of his own book he gave this exhortation: "Remember these things; for the time speedily cometh that ye shall know that I lie not, for ye shall see me at the bar of God; and the Lord God will say unto you: Did I not declare my words unto you, which were written by this man, like as one crying from the dead, yea, even as one speaking out of the dust?" (Moroni 10:27). His cry from the dust will continue to go to the earth's inhabitants as long as the earth remains in its mortal state. When people leave this mortal probation, they will meet Moroni personally: "And now I bid unto all, farewell. I soon go to rest in the paradise of God, until my spirit and body shall again reunite, and I am brought forth triumphant through the air, to meet you before the pleasing bar of the great Jehovah, the Eternal Judge of both quick and dead. Amen" (v 34).

Thus three of the major contributors to the Book of Mormon record bear witness that they will be at the judgment bar of God, and the implication is that the fourth will be there, too. These men are also special witnesses of Christ, prophets and apostles of their own day and eternal judges of the dead as they meet them at the bar of Christ (see 3 Nephi 5:13).

There is an interesting reference in the Doctrine and Covenants that may possibly apply to these four Nephite abridgers. As Joseph Smith was translating the Bible, he was given several explanations of verses in the book of Revelation of St. John. One of these explanations regarded Revelation 7:1: "And after these things I saw four angels standing on the four corners of the earth, holding the four winds of the earth, that the wind should not blow on the earth, nor on the sea, nor on any tree." The question and the explanation given to Joseph Smith were as follows:

> Q. What are we to understand by the four angels, spoken of in the 7th chapter and 1st verse of Revelation?
>
> A. We are to understand that they are four angels sent forth from God, to whom is given power over the four parts of the earth, to save life and to destroy; these are they who have the everlasting gospel to commit to every nation, kindred, tongue, and people; having power to shut up the heavens, to seal up unto life, or to cast down to the regions of darkness (D&C 77:8).

The eternal role of Nephi, Jacob, Mormon, and Moroni fits the Doctrine and Covenants explanation for the following reasons. First, their message, the Book of Mormon, was to go to all the ends of the world or the four quarters of the earth. Secondly, the mission of the four angels was to save life or to destroy it spiritually through the coming forth of their message. In their testimonies that they will be at the judgment bar, the four abridgers speak of both salvation and condemnation coming from the words they had recorded upon the plates. Furthermore, the Doctrine and Covenants bears testimony that the Book of Mormon will judge the world, "even as many as shall hereafter come to a knowledge of this work. And those who receive it in faith, and work righteousness, shall receive a crown of eternal life; But those who harden their hearts in unbelief, and reject it, it shall turn to their own condemnation" (D&C 20:13–15). The third reason these four men fit the Doctrine and Covenants explanation is that the four angels have "the everlasting gospel to commit to every nation, kindred, tongue, and people." This is the same message as Revelation 14:6 that there was "another angel fly[ing] in the midst of heaven, having the everlasting gospel to preach to them that dwell on the earth, and to every nation, and kindred, and tongue, and people." The angel referred to in this verse is not limited to but certainly includes the angel Moroni revealing the Book of Mormon to Joseph. The work of this angel (Moroni) is not completed until the fifth trump is sounded at the Second Coming announcing that the everlasting gospel has been taken to every nation, kindred, tongue and people (D&C 88:103–04). As the last overseer of the Book of Mormon records, Moroni's assignment was apparently to continue that assignment through the latter days. Therefore, it seems quite evident that Moroni would be one of the four angels. Who would the others logically be other than Mormon, Jacob, and Nephi?

While there may be other interpretations of the Doctrine and Covenants' explanation of Revelation 7:1, the fact that there were four men who did most of the recording on the plates from which the Book of Mormon was translated, which plates contain the everlasting gospel, forms an interesting parallel. Add to it the fact that four angels would commit the everlasting gospel to every nation, kindred, tongue, and people in the explanation of the verse, and the parallel gets stronger. Suffice it to say that the four abridgers hold an important role in bringing either salvation or condemnation to the inhabitants of the earth depending on how they receive or reject their message. They are special witnesses who will be at the judgment-seat of Christ.

Who Are the Apostles?

As already stated, the Apostles are special witnesses of Christ, called and ordained upon the earth. Their mission began before their mortal probation and extends beyond this world. Lehi saw in a vision a glorified being at the time he was called to warn the inhabitants of

Jerusalem in 600 BC (1 Nephi 1:9). This was obviously the pre-mortal Christ; "And he also saw twelve others following him, and their brightness did exceed that of the stars in the firmament" (v 10). The brightness of the twelve others not only indicates their righteousness in the premortal state, but also that they held important callings and responsibilities there. They were undoubtedly among the noble and great intelligences (spirits) shown to Abraham of whom the Lord said, "These I will make my rulers; for he stood among those that were spirits, and he saw that they were good; and he said unto me: Abraham, thou art one of them; thou wast chosen before thou wast born" (Abr 3:23). These choice spirits are also Christ's representatives when they come to earth. They are those against whom the world gathers to fight: "And after he was slain I saw the multitudes of the earth, that they were gathered together to fight against the apostles of the Lamb; for thus were the twelve called by the angel of the Lord" (1 Nephi 11:34). The world is still fighting the apostles of the Lamb because they represent the truth and the world rejects the truth. Even those of the house of Israel at times will gather to fight against the twelve: "And the angel of the Lord spake unto me again saying: Behold the world and the wisdom thereof; yea, behold the house of Israel hath gathered together to fight against the twelve apostles of the Lamb" (v 35). This verse describes the apostasy following Christ's ministry in Jerusalem. The Apostasy was caused by the pride and wisdom of the world, but it will not stand forever: "And it came to pass that I saw and bear record, that the great and spacious building was the pride of the world; and it fell, and the fall thereof was exceedingly great. And the angel of the Lord spake unto me again, saying: Thus shall be the destruction of all nations, kindreds, tongues, and people, that shall fight against the twelve apostles of the Lamb" (v 36). The world still fights the Twelve Apostles and their teaching with its own wisdom, but it will eventually fall, and the pride that motivates the fight will be the cause of that fall.

Joseph Smith and the Three Witnesses

Apostles have also been called to be special witnesses in these last days, which Paul calls the dispensation of the fulness of times (Eph 1:10). In a revelation commemorating the organization of the Church on 6 April 1830, the Lord spoke of Joseph Smith as one "who was called of God, and ordained an apostle of Jesus Christ, to be the first elder of this church" (D&C 20:2). He then revealed that He "gave [Joseph] power from on high, by the means which were before prepared, to translate the Book of Mormon" (v 8).

The translation of the Book of Mormon was Joseph's primary responsibility in the latter-day restoration. In March 1829, the Lord told him: "And you have a gift to translate the plates; and this is the first gift that I bestowed upon you; and I have commanded that you should pretend to no other gift until my purpose is fulfilled in this; for I will grant unto you no other gift until it is finished. Verily, I say unto you, that woe shall come unto the inhabitants of the earth if they will not hearken unto my words" (D&C 5:4–5).

The warning to the world who will not hearken to "my words" is obviously a reference to the Book of Mormon, which Joseph translated from the plates. As an apostle, Joseph was to be a special witness to the inhabitants of the earth of his translation of the Book of Mormon. The Lord further declared in this same revelation, "But this generation shall have my word [the Book of Mormon] through you" (D&C 5:10). Oliver Cowdery, the scribe for the majority of the translation, also an apostle and the second elder of the Church (20:3), was chosen by the Lord to hold the keys of translation with the Prophet Joseph. "And now, behold, I give unto you, and also unto my servant Joseph, the keys of this gift, which shall bring to light this ministry; and in the mouth of two or three witnesses shall every word be established" (6:28). Thus there are at least two special witnesses of the translation of the Book of Mormon. Although there is no specific declaration that these two men will be at the judgment bar, the following verses of the revelation warn against rejecting the Lord's words they would translate and promise blessings to those who do not reject the Lord's words from the translation "which shall be established by the testimony which shall be given" (vv 29–31).

The testimony which shall be given undoubtedly has reference to the testimony of the three special witnesses promised in the Book of Mormon (2 Nephi 27:12; Ether 5:4), and to the revelation previously cited, that designates that Joseph is to bring forth the Lord's word to this generation. On that occasion, the Lord said to Joseph:

And in addition to your testimony, the testimony of three of my servants, whom I shall call and ordain, unto whom I will show these things, and they shall go forth with my words that are given through you. Yea, they shall know of a surety that these things are true, for from heaven will I declare it unto them. I will give them power that they may behold and view these things as they are. (D&C 5:11–13)

Oliver Cowdery was also one of these three special witnesses along with David Whitmer and Martin Harris. Oliver and David, in a later revelation, are called apostles (D&C 18:9-37, 39) and are commissioned to search out the original Twelve Apostles of this generation and, when found, to show them "these things" (vv 37, 39). The phrase "these things" seems to refer to the things that qualify them to be special witnesses or members of the Twelve as given previously in the revelation (vv 10–36).

The promise given in section five of the Doctrine and Covenants that the three special witnesses would "know of a surety" from heaven and view the things associated with the Book of Mormon (D&C 17:1) was fulfilled, and their testimony to this effect is recorded in every copy of the Book of Mormon. They were indeed apostles and special witnesses of the Book of Mormon. They heard the voice of the Lord declare that it had been translated by the gift and power of God, and they saw the plates and the engravings on them (The Testimony of Three Witnesses). Those who read the Book of Mormon will certainly be held responsible at the judgment seat of Christ for the testimony of Joseph Smith and the three witnesses and be blessed accordingly.

Apostles of the Restoration

The original Twelve Apostles in this dispensation have testified and will yet testify of Christ,[2] and we will be accountable for hearing their testimonies at the judgment bar of Christ. Those apostles who have succeeded them and have testified to us will also be at the judgment bar to testify either for or against us. If we will heed their testimonies and the testimonies of the Jerusalem and Nephite Twelve, we may come under the class of people described by Nephi: "I have

---

[2] The question may be raised concerning those of the original twelve who apostatized from the Church being at the judgment bar. It is interesting to note that those who were "appointed to supply the place of those who had fallen," John Taylor, John E. Page, Wilford Woodruff, and Willard Richards (D&C 118:1, 6), appointed in 1838, had been witnesses of most, if not all, of the events of the Restoration that the original twelve, appointed in 1835, had observed. The Lord will determine which of all those will be witnesses of the Restoration at the judgment bar.

charity for my people, and great faith in Christ that I shall meet many souls spotless at his judgment-seat" (2 Nephi 33:7).

The choice of whether we will become spotless or remain filthy to receive a torment that shall be "as a lake of fire and brimstone, whose flame ascendeth up forever and ever and has no end" is ours (2 Nephi 9:16).

> Wherefore, we shall have a perfect knowledge of all our guilt, and our uncleanness, and our nakedness; and the righteous shall have a perfect knowledge of their enjoyment, and their righteousness, being clothed with purity, yea, even with the robe of righteousness. And it shall come to pass that when all men shall have passed from this first death unto life, insomuch as they have become immortal, they must appear before the judgment-seat of the Holy One of Israel; and then cometh the judgment, and then must they be judged according to the holy judgment of God. (2 Nephi 9:14–15)

The knowledge of the joy spoken of by Jacob seems to be the knowledge that the Atonement has paid for our sins and cleansed us so that we might return to the presence of God. In contrast, those who have not qualified for the blessings of the Atonement will remember all of their wicked acts, and will know their judgment, for no unclean thing can dwell in His presence (Alma 7:21).

Conclusion

Jacob teaches that the Lord "employeth no servant" at the gate to eternal life (2 Nephi 9:41). He will have his chosen servants, the prophets and apostles, stand as special witnesses for or against us. We will see all of these, perhaps only in vision, but we will have a bright recollection of how we have received or rejected their words. We will see the Jerusalem Twelve and know of Christ's ministry, atonement, crucifixion, and resurrection. We will see the Nephite Twelve, and Nephi, Jacob, Mormon, Moroni, and perhaps others, and know of Christ's ministry in America, and of the truthfulness of the Book of Mormon. We will see Joseph Smith and his original Twelve, and will know of the restoration of the gospel in these latter days through them. Finally, we will see the Twelve of our day and know of their teachings.

When it was decided in 1831 to compile and publish selected revelations of the restoration of the gospel as the Book of Commandments, the Lord revealed to Joseph Smith a "preface to the doctrines, covenants, and commandments given in this dispensation" (Heading of D&C 1). At the conclusion of this revelation, the Lord declared: "What I the Lord have spoken, I have spoken, and I excuse not myself; and though the heavens and the earth pass away, my word shall not pass away, but shall all be fulfilled, whether by mine own voice or by the voice of my servants, it is the same" (D&C 1:38).

The Lord has spoken to us through his servants in this dispensation both by voice and the written word. He has also revealed, through the first apostle of this dispensation, Joseph Smith, the record of the prophets and apostles in the Book of Mormon. We will be accountable for the words of these servants as we come to the judgment bar of Christ and be blessed accordingly. If we have hearkened to these words, we will "have a perfect knowledge of [our] enjoyment" and be clothed "even with the robe of righteousness" (2 Nephi 9:14).

Part of the responsibility of hearkening to these words is to share them with others and testify of their truthfulness. Through our bearing testimony of the words of the prophets and apostles, the "God of Israel [will] witness that [we] shook [the people's] iniquities from [our] soul[s]" (2 Nephi 9:44). However, we will answer "the sins of the people [our friends and neighbors] upon our own heads if we did not teach them the word of God with all diligence" (Jacob 1:19). The word of God includes the words of the apostles and prophets of all dispensations that are available to us, but particularly our dispensation. As taught by Jacob, we can thus "prepare [our] souls for that glorious day when justice shall be administered unto the righteous, even the day of judgment, that [we] may not shrink with awful fear; that [we] may not remember [our] awful guilt in perfectness, and be constrained to exclaim: Holy, holy are thy judgments, O Lord God Almighty—but I know my guilt; I transgressed thy law, and my transgressions are mine; and the devil hath obtained me, that I am a prey to his awful misery" (2 Nephi 9:46). May we prize the written and spoken words of the prophets and apostles, and so follow them that we may look forward to the day when we will meet them at the judgment bar of Christ.

Zion Zion Zion: Keys to Understanding Ether 13

17

Jeff O'Driscoll

Introduction

Gospel study requires careful attention to context, as context is often essential in establishing which of many possible meanings the writer intends to convey. Attention to context is crucial to gaining an appropriate mental image of Zion. The bulk of the comments that follow, therefore, deal with the study of Zion in a few specific verses of scripture, the context of those verses, and comments made by various modern prophets which are directly pertinent to understanding Zion. Certain verses are rather ambiguous, but by considering each possibility we hope to be enlightened.

Zion in Context

Clearly the concept of Zion refers to a lifestyle, a social structure (4 Nephi; Moses 7:18; D&C 105:5), and a state of mind (D&C 97:21; Moses 7:18). Whether in the time of Enoch, among the Nephites after the Savior's visit, or in this dispensation, a Zion people are "pure in heart" (D&C 97:21). They are "of one heart and one mind, and [dwell] in righteousness," and among them are found "no poor" (Moses 7:18). Neither is there any manner of sin "nor any manner of -ites; but they [are] in one the children of Christ, and heirs to the kingdom of God" (4 Nephi 1:15–17). These blessings came to Zion people because they

Jeff O'Driscoll is a physician in Salt Lake City, Utah.

built Zion in the only way possible—"by the principles of the law of the celestial kingdom" (D&C 105:5).

In this dispensation, "Zion" also refers to various geographic locations. For example, many revelations refer to Zion in Jackson County, Missouri (D&C 57:2–3). Specifically, "Independence is the center place" of Zion, and therein is the designated site, already dedicated, for the temple-complex of Zion (v 3; see also *History of the Church* 1:196–99; hereafter *HC*). The Prophet Joseph Smith provided a detailed plat of the city and, using that plat as a pattern, instructed the Saints, "When this square is thus laid off and supplied, lay off another in the same way, and so fill up the world in these last days; and let every man live in the city, for this is the city of Zion" (*HC* 1:358). This is consistent with the Lord's counsel found in a subsequent revelation concerning Zion:

> There is none other place appointed than that which I have appointed; neither shall there be any other place appointed than that which I have appointed, for the work of the gathering of my saints—Until the day cometh when there is found no more room for them; and then I have other places which I will appoint unto them, and they shall be called stakes, for the curtains or the strength of Zion. (D&C 101:20–21)

When we consider such instruction, we can more easily understand the Prophet's declaration that "the whole of America is Zion itself from north to south. . . . It is the Zion where the mountain of the Lord should be" (*HC* 6:318). Brigham Young notes that "Zion will extend eventually, all over this earth. There will be no nook or corner upon the earth but what will be in Zion. It will all be Zion" (*Journal of Discourses* 9:138; hereafter *JD*). Elder Matthew Cowley further explained, "In your homes where the priesthood of God exists, there is Zion. And to you whose lives are committed to righteousness, I say unto you, You are Zion" (441). The incumbency under which the Saints labor is, as President Brigham Young said, to "begin and make Zion in our own hearts, and then extend it to our neighborhoods, and so continue until the Lord shall reign upon the earth" (*JD* 1:245). Note the Lord's declaration, "This is Zion—THE PURE IN HEART" (D&C 97:21).

Whether we discuss the nature of Zion's sociotheocratic system, its people, or its geography, the value of establishing context to elucidate meaning is demonstrated. Nowhere is this more true than in

Ether chapter 13 where the cities of Zion are mentioned. As will be seen, only context can determine the different cities Ether refers to by the same name, as do other prophets. While most of the verses are quite clear, some concepts require additional study. In preface to the study of those verses, we must note some facts.

Three Holy Cities

President Joseph Fielding Smith spoke of three holy cities:

> In the day of regeneration, when all things are made new, there will be three great cities that will be holy. One will be the Jerusalem of old which shall be rebuilt according to the prophecy of Ezekiel. One will be the city of Zion, or of Enoch, which was taken from the earth when Enoch was translated and which will be restored; and the city Zion, or New Jerusalem, which is to be built by the seed of Joseph on this the American continent. (*Answers to Gospel Questions* 2:105; hereafter *Answers*)

Note that two of these cities are called Zion. They are distinguished by reference to Enoch and Joseph and events which are unique to their identification. Context makes the reference clear. We shall see, however, that there is yet another holy city, a composite Zion, which consists of the united and combined cities of Enoch and the New Jerusalem. This city is also called Zion, and knowledge of it comes to us through the book of Moses in the Pearl of Great Price.

Two Zions Become One Zion

The prophet Enoch may be best known among Latter-day Saints for his success in establishing a Zion community. He thus seems the appropriate recipient and disseminator of any special revelation on the subject. Indeed, such revelation came; and we are fortunate to have a glimpse into the same. The Lord spoke to Enoch: "And righteousness will I send down out of heaven; and truth will I send forth out of the earth, to bear testimony of mine Only Begotten . . . and righteousness and truth will I cause to sweep the earth as with a flood, to gather out mine elect from the four quarters of the earth" (Moses 7:62). President Ezra Taft Benson, on one occasion, quoted this verse and explained, "The Book of Mormon is the instrument that God designed to 'sweep the earth as with a flood, to gather out [His] elect' (Moses 7:62)" (4). This verse clearly refers to our time—the dispensation of the fulness of times. Where will the elect be gathered? That gathering, said the Lord, is "unto a place which I shall prepare, an Holy City . . . for there shall be my tabernacle, and it shall be called Zion, a New Jerusalem" (Moses 7:62). To Enoch, the archetypal Zionist prophet, the Lord continued:

> Then shalt thou and all thy city meet *them there* [that is, Enoch's city Zion, meets Zion, the New Jerusalem, in this land], and we will receive them into our bosom, and they shall see us; and we will fall upon their necks, and they shall fall upon our necks, and we will kiss each other; And *there shall be mine abode, and it shall be Zion,* which shall come forth out of all the creations which I have made; and *for the space of a thousand years the earth shall rest.* (Moses 7:63–64; emphasis added)

The Lord granted this knowledge to Enoch while he yet dwelt upon the earth, and while still living in the city of Zion over which he presided. Enoch was blessed with this vision of what would happen to his city—it would return to earth to meet and embrace the New Jerusalem, and they will become one city, also called Zion, and serve as the home of the Lord during the Millennium.

The above verses suggest that the Lord will physically be with Enoch in that city of Zion when it returns to earth. Joseph Smith taught that "Christ and the resurrected Saints will reign over the earth during the thousand years. They will not probably dwell upon the earth, but will visit it when they please, or when it is necessary to govern it" (*HC* 5:212). He clarified the words of the psalmist, saying, "Zion shall come, and God shall be in the midst of her" (JST Ps 46:5). Whether God's presence in Zion will be literal or figurative or both, Enoch's description of the union of these two holy cities notes the return of Zion *before* the Millennium is ushered in. This may give insight into the Saints' millennial song, "The Lord hath brought down Zion from above. The Lord hath brought up Zion from beneath" (D&C 84:100).[1] By uniting these two cities, the Lord will fulfill his sworn oath that in Enoch's city "the heavens and the earth should come together" (JST Gen 14:35).

---

[1] Elder Orson Pratt commented that "the Zion which was built up by Enoch . . . will come down again at the commencement of the Millennium to meet the Zion here, according to the song in the Book of Covenants, 'The Lord has brought up Zion from beneath, the Lord has brought down Zion from above,' and they shall gaze upon each other's countenances, and see eye to eye" (*JD* 2:103).

Zion After the Millennium, the Bride

In contrast to the return of Zion *before* the Millennium, certain scriptural passages clearly seem to refer to a city of God descending from heaven to a celestialized earth *after* the Millennium (Rev 21:10–27). Specifically answering a question as to the interpretation of Revelation 21:1–2, Elder Joseph Fielding Smith referred to and quoted Ether 13:2–11. He said, "We read in the Book of Ether that the Lord revealed to him many of the same things which were seen by John. . . . In his vision, in many respects similar to that given to John, [Ether][2] saw the old city of Jerusalem and also the new city which has not yet been built" (*Answers* 2:103). Perusal of the references in Ether and Revelation confirms that they do, for the most part, refer to the same events. These passages will, therefore, be considered together in the discussion to follow.

Ether spoke of "a new heaven and a new earth" to which the "New Jerusalem" would come (13:9–10). Clearly the Apostle John described this same setting in the first two verses of Revelation chapter 21. The terminology, "a new heaven and a new earth," is applicable to the earth whether in its paradisiacal and millennial state or in its exalted and celestial state (see McConkie, *Mormon Doctrine* 531; hereafter *MD*). Also, when the "bride, the Lamb's wife . . . that great city, the holy Jerusalem" descends from heaven as described in Revelation 21:9–10, it will descend to a celestial earth. Elder McConkie cites these later verses in Revelation and comments, "When this earth becomes a celestial sphere 'that great city, the holy Jerusalem,' shall *again* descend 'out of heaven from God,' as this earth becomes the abode of celestial beings forever (Rev 21:10–27)" (*Doctrinal New Testament Commentary* 3:582; emphasis added; hereafter *DNTC*).

Though less certain context is found, the city described in Revelation 21:9–10 may be the same "holy city, new Jerusalem, coming down from God out of heaven, prepared as a bride adorned for her husband" described by John earlier in the same chapter (Rev 21:2). This seems to be the intent of Elder Joseph Fielding Smith's explanation of those verses (*Answers* 2:103–06). On the other hand,

---

2   The cited reference reads "Enoch," but from the context it appears that this may have been an error. It seems that Elder Smith intended to refer to Ether.

Elder Bruce R. McConkie has said verses 1–4 clearly refer to millennial earth (*The Millennial Messiah* 306; hereafter *MM*). Perhaps these verses refer to both times and circumstances in a dual-meaning prophecy. Regardless of how one interprets these verses, it is quite clear that a holy city shall twice descend, once as the Millennium is ushered in and again after the 1,000 years and a "little season" (Rev 20:3; D&C 88:110–11). Elder McConkie says, "Events to transpire after the millennial era and before the earth becomes a celestial sphere have not been revealed. We do have an account, however, of 'the holy Jerusalem, descending out of heaven from God' a second time, that is, after the earth has become a celestial planet" (*MD* 533; citing Rev 3:12, 21 as references).

The Preservation of Zion

Although it is clear that this earth will see a city of God descend at two different times and under two different sets of circumstances, just how this will occur is not clearly explained. If that holy city is to descend "a second time," it is reasonable to surmise that it must have been taken back to heaven in the interim. Elder Joseph Fielding Smith explained it as follows:

> After the close of the millennial reign we are informed that Satan, who was bound during the millennium, shall be loosed and go forth to deceive the nations. Then will come the end. The earth will die and be purified and receive its resurrection. During this cleansing period the city Zion, or New Jerusalem [the combined city Zion which existed throughout the Millennium], will be taken from the earth; and when the earth is prepared for the celestial glory, the city will come down according to the prediction in the Book of Revelation. (*Answers* 2:106)

Apparently, God is interested in preserving Zion. When Melchizedek and his people "sought for the city of Enoch," they found that "God had before taken [it], separating it from the earth, having reserved it unto the latter days, or the end of the world" (JST Gen 14:34). It seems that the pattern set by Enoch's people—that of being taken from the earth during its cleansing period—will again be observed. In Enoch's day the earth was cleansed by water, and after the earth is again cleansed, that city will return. The composite Zion, however, will likewise be taken from the earth during its final sanctification, and when that cleansing is complete, she will return to a celestial sphere, the home of the exalted.[3]

Consider just two reasons why Zion must be preserved: first, the inhabitants of those cities and, second, in Enoch's case at least, the temples therein. We read that the exalted Saints

> are priests of the Most High, after the order of Melchizedek, which was after the order of Enoch, which was after the order of the Only Begotten Son. . . . These are they who are come unto Mount Zion, and unto the city of the living God, the heavenly place, the holiest of all. These are they who have come to an innumerable company of angels, to the general assembly and church of Enoch, and of the Firstborn. (D&C 76:57)

Note that Enoch is mentioned along with Melchizedek and the Savior when referring to the Holy Priesthood. He is again mentioned with the Savior in reference to the church of the Saints. These verses refer to the celestial reward promised each of the translated inhabitants of Enoch's city. The Lord, himself, refers to Enoch's city as "the general assembly of the church of the first-born" (JST Gen 9:23; see also *MD* 136).

Enoch's relationship with the Lord is reflected in his declaration, "Forasmuch as thou art God, and I know thee. . . . Thou hast made me, and given unto me a right to thy throne" (Moses 7:59). In response, the Lord promised, "Great tribulations shall be among the children of men, but *my people will I preserve* . . . to gather out mine elect from the four quarters of the earth, unto a place which I shall prepare, an Holy City . . . and it shall be called Zion, a New Jerusalem" (vv 61–62; emphasis added). As mentioned previously, this gathering will be accomplished through the instrumentality of the Book of Mormon in this dispensation. Thus the protection or preservation the Lord promised the people of Enoch—"my people will I preserve"—may also be applicable to the Saints in these last days.

---

[3] The exact order of events is not entirely clear. Elder Joseph Fielding Smith taught that "when the earth is prepared for the celestial glory, the city will come down according to the prediction in the Book of Revelation" (*Answers* 2:106), but this is not to say that the holy city will miss out on such sanctification. Joseph Young, Sr., brother of President Brigham Young and one of the first Presidents of the Seventy, reported that the Prophet Joseph Smith taught "that inasmuch as they [Enoch's city] did not pass through all the refinement which was necessary, as the Lord lives, they would return to the earth, when they and the city would pass through the same fiery ordeals that yet await the earth; when it shall be transformed into a sea of glass, mingled with fire, and their preparations for a celestial abode of the glorified Saints shall be perfected" (11–12).

Enoch said, "Surely Zion shall dwell in safety forever"; to which the Lord responded, "Zion have I blessed" (Moses 7:20). Those who attain the status of a Zion-people are entitled to the Lord's protection. They are they who walk with God literally and/or figuratively (v 69; Smith, *Doctrines of Salvation* 1:4). Joseph Smith said that "this Enoch, God reserved unto Himself, that he should not die at that time, and appointed unto him a ministry unto terrestrial bodies. . . . He is reserved also unto the Presidency of a dispensation" (*HC* 4:209). Although the inhabitants of Enoch's city, being translated, are yet terrestrial beings (see *Teachings of the Prophet Joseph Smith* 170; hereafter *TPJS*), they abide a celestial law (D&C 105:5). As Elder Joseph Fielding Smith pointed out, "they were living the celestial law in a telestial world" and for them "it was no longer expedient that they should remain on the earth" (*Church History and Modern Revelation* 1:195). They simply no longer needed to be subject to the things of this world, and it seems they were entitled to protection and preservation from the same. I believe this is one reason the Lord takes his holy cities from the earth.

The second reason Zion is preserved is that it is the center of temple work, the work of the Millennium. Ether points out that when the city of Enoch returns to earth, it will contain "the holy sanctuary of the Lord" (Ether 13:3). Likewise, John notes that when "the holy city, new Jerusalem, [comes] down from God out of heaven . . . the tabernacle of God is with men, and he will dwell with them" (Rev 21:2–3). Enoch saw the same thing (Moses 7:62). Elder Franklin D. Richards said he wished

> to speak a word in reference to the three Nephites. They wanted to tarry until Jesus came, and that they might He took them into the heavens and endowed them with the power of translation, probably in one of Enoch's temples, and brought them back to the earth. Thus they received power to live until the coming of the Son of Man. I believe He took them to Enoch's city and gave them their endowments there. I expect that in the city of Enoch there are temples; and when Enoch and his people come back, they will come back with their city, their temples, blessings and powers. (*JD* 25:236–37)

Remember that Enoch's people, being translated, retain physical bodies and thus remain in a position to utilize temples to further the work. Similarly, Zion on this continent will include temples of the Most High. Joseph Smith explained that in the center place of Zion there would be 24 temples; 12 for the work of the Aaronic Priesthood and 12 for the work of the Melchizedek Priesthood. These temples are to have divinely inspired names as revealed to the Prophet. On three of those edifices shall be found the name, "House of the Lord for the Presidency of the High and most Holy Priesthood, after the order of Melchizedek, which was after the order of the Son of God, upon Mount Zion, City of the New Jerusalem." And on each house is to also be written, "Holiness to the Lord" (*HC* 1:359).

This work of building temples engages the Saints in Mount Zion (D&C 97:10–12); it is the work of the Mountain of the Lord's house (Isa 2:2–3), and those who labor therein are "saviours . . . on mount Zion" (Obad 1:21). The Prophet Joseph Smith taught that when Zion is built and the Saints gathered, they will "come up as saviours on Mount Zion." He further stated:

> But how are they to become saviors on Mount Zion? By building their temples, erecting their baptismal fonts, and going forth and receiving all the ordinances, baptisms, confirmations, washings, anointings, ordinations and sealing powers upon their heads, in behalf of all their progenitors who are dead, and redeem them that they may come forth in the first resurrection and be exalted to thrones of glory with them; and herein is the chain that binds the hearts of the fathers to the children, and the children to the fathers, which fulfills the mission of Elijah. (*TPJS* 330; see also 191, 366)

Clearly there is an intimate cooperation among the Saints in this work, whether living, dead, or translated.[4] Quoting from the afore-mentioned prophecies of Enoch, Joseph Smith commented, "And now, I ask, how righteousness and truth are going to sweep the earth as with a flood? I will answer. Men and angels are to be co-workers in bringing to pass this great work, and Zion is to be prepared, even a new Jerusalem, for the elect that are to be gathered from the four quarters of the earth, and to be established an holy city, for the tabernacle of the Lord shall be with them" (*HC* 2:260). That coopera-tion will continue when the cities of Zion become one.

At the end of the 1,000-year labor, when the temple work is complete, the need for those temples will be obviated. Of that time, John said of the holy city, "I saw no temple therein: for the Lord God Almighty and the Lamb are the temple of it" (Rev 21:22). This is one reason that it seems the first few verses of Revelation chapter 21 refer

---

4 See also Brigham Young 321-22; M. Russell Ballard 200–02; *The Manti Temple* 53; George Albert Smith 564; Orson Pratt 141.

to Enoch's city descending to millennial earth, while later verses seem to refer to the composite Zion returning to celestial earth. In the first instance, John notes that "the tabernacle of God is with men" (v 3), while in the latter case he comments that "I saw no temple therein; for the Lord God Almighty and the Lamb are the temple of it" (v 22). Elder McConkie notes that "temples, now and during the millennium, are to prepare men for a celestial inheritance. When that glorious goal is gained, heaven itself becomes a temple" (*DNTC* 3:588).

There may be other reasons why the Lord so jealously preserves his Zions (see Zech 8:1–3), but clearly the progress of and the promises made to the inhabitants of Zion as well as the temples therein are two such reasons. Understanding this helps us to appreciate why the Lord took Enoch and his city to heaven and why he will yet take that composite Zion back into heaven.

Review of Ether 13

Let us now review the observations and prophecies of Ether. In doing this, we should remember that Moroni, while conveying to us these words of Ether, fell under a restriction known well by the prophets. He said, "I was about to write more, but I am forbidden; but great and marvelous were the prophecies of Ether" (Ether 13:13). Similarly, Nephi saw a great many things which he was instructed not to write because the stewardship of that record-keeping was to fall upon John the Apostle and Revelator (1 Nephi 14:20–30). Perhaps the same was true in the case of Moroni's editing responsibilities, for it seems that Ether and John beheld similar visions, and perhaps it was again John's responsibility to provide the record. Elder McConkie notes, however, that "we might surmise [that] the sealed portion of the Book of Mormon contains a full and complete account of all things pertaining to the New Jerusalem and the second coming of Christ. From the writings of Ether, preserved in full on those plates, Moroni digested for us a few salient facts that enable us to glimpse what is to be" (*MM* 304).

Verses 1–4

First, we are told that the American continent is "a choice land above all other lands, a chosen land of the Lord" (Ether 13:2; see also

MM 304) and this land is "the place of the New Jerusalem, *which should come down out of heaven*, and the holy sanctuary of the Lord. Behold, Ether saw *the days of Christ*, and he spake concerning a New Jerusalem upon this land" (Ether 13:3–4; emphasis added). These two New Jerusalems, both to be found on the American continent, are mentioned in two consecutive verses, but refer to two entirely different cities. Context is key. One is to "come down out of heaven"[5] while the other shall be built *in situ* in the promised land in "the days of Christ." The first is the city of Enoch, and the sanctuary mentioned is the temple of the Lord (see *MM* 304). The second is the Zion yet to be built. As Latter-day Saints, we believe "that Zion (the New Jerusalem) will be built upon the American continent" (AF 10). Enoch's city will return to this place, and Elder Orson Pratt said it may be that "all the Zions God has taken out of His creations to heaven" will also come to this place (*JD* 2:103).

Some may note that "Ether saw the days of Christ" when he spoke of "a New Jerusalem upon this land" (Ether 13:4). In a sense, the Zion society built by the Nephites after the Savior's visit (4 Nephi) could be considered a fulfillment of those words, but Elder McConkie points out that the days of Christ seen by Ether on that occasion were "the days of his glorious Second Coming" and the "New Jerusalem seems to be the one built by the saints in the latter days" (*MM* 304).

It is interesting to note that when code names were used in certain revelations, the Zion to be built in our day was referred to as "the city of Enoch" and its presiding founder, Joseph Smith, Jr., as "Enoch" (see *HC* 1:255–57). The reason for those intentionally obscure designations has passed, and the designations themselves have been discontinued. The analogy of the latter-day Zion and the city of Enoch is, however, worth remembering.

Verse 5

Moroni continues to point out that Ether speaks of "the Jerusalem from whence Lehi should come—after it should be destroyed it should be built up again, a holy city unto the Lord" (Ether 13:3–5).

---

[5] One may reasonably ask to where this city will return. Joseph Young Sr. notes that "Joseph Smith said . . . in the hearing of some of the saints still surviving, that the City of Enoch would again take its place in the identical spot from which it had been detached, now forming that chasm of the earth, filled with water, called the Gulf of Mexico" (12; see also Widtsoe 365).

In three short verses (vv 3–5), then, we have reference to each of the three holy cities mentioned by Joseph Fielding Smith. Ether calls them all "Jerusalem" and refers to both of the first two as New Jerusalem. Consider, however, that neither John nor Ether, in these so often referred to chapters, uses the word *Zion*. Nevertheless, the meaning is clear. Each of the New Jerusalems, each properly titled Zion, is separate and distinct in geography and in temporal existence until that time in the future when they become one.

Elder Orson Pratt indicates that the Jerusalem from which Lehi came will find a like fate as we have described for the New Jerusalem. Speaking of the final celestialization of the earth, he said,

> As the earth passes through its great last change, two of its principal cities—the Old Jerusalem of the eastern continent, and the New Jerusalem of the western continent, will be preserved from the general conflagration, being caught up into heaven. These two cities, with all their glorified throng, will descend upon the redeemed earth, being the grand capitals of the new creation. (*JD* 1:332)

Speaking of this same ancient Jerusalem that will yet be rebuilt, Elder Franklin D. Richards said, "She is yet to take an important part in the great work of the latter days. Like the New Jerusalem of the American continent, this city will descend out of heaven, after the final change of the earth to its celestial condition (Rev 21:10–27). It is often called Zion in the Old Testament, and will be the capital city of gathered Israel on the Eastern hemisphere, in the latter days" (172).

Verses 6–8

In verses 6–8, Ether refers again to the "New Jerusalem [which] should be built up upon this land, unto the remnant of the seed of Joseph, for which things there has been a type" (Ether 13:6). He explains this typology as follows:

> For as Joseph brought his father down into the land of Egypt . . . the Lord brought a remnant of the seed of Joseph out of the land of Jerusalem, that he might be merciful unto the seed of Joseph that they should perish not. . . . Wherefore, the remnant of the house of Joseph shall be built upon this land; and it shall be a land of their inheritance; and they shall build up a holy city unto the Lord, like unto the Jerusalem of old; and they shall no more be confounded, until the end come when the earth shall pass away. (Ether 13:7–8)

As already noted, God moves his people from place to place to preserve and protect them, and as they have built a holy city in one land, so shall they build one in another. With this explanation from Ether and in fulfillment of such a portent, the Zion in America should be called a *New* Jerusalem. Elder McConkie explained that "we who are of Ephraim (and of Manasseh) into whose hands the Church and kingdom has now been given shall build the city in due course, and we and our children after us [as prophesied by Ether] shall never be confounded or lose the faith; for [to] our dispensation, the promise is that the gospel shall remain with us to prepare a people for the second coming of Him whose servants we are" (*MM* 305).

Verses 9–11

Continuing on, Ether describes a time when

> the end come[s] when the earth shall pass away. And there shall be a new heaven and a new earth . . . and then cometh the New Jerusalem; and blessed are they who dwell therein, for it is they whose garments are white through the blood of the Lamb. . . . And then also cometh the Jerusalem of old; and the inhabitants thereof, blessed are they, for they have been washed in the blood of the Lamb; and they are they who were scattered and gathered in from the four quarters of the earth . . . fulfilling . . . the covenant which God made with their father, Abraham. (Ether 13:8–11)

Verses 9–11 along with Revelation 21:1–2 potentially have more than one meaning and fulfillment. If Ether, like John, placed importance on referring to the presence of the temple of the Lord among the people, it should be noted that in verse 3 he clearly refers to Enoch's city and the "holy sanctuary of the Lord" found therein. In contradistinction, verse 10 mentions no temple and may, therefore, refer to a future time when the composite Zion returns to earth and God and the Lamb are the temple of that city.[6] Not wanting to wrest the intent of these verses, let me simply say here that the terminology of "a new heaven and a new earth" is twice applicable; once at the beginning of the Millennium and again at the end (see *MD* 531). The New Jerusalem referred to in Ether 13:10 may be Enoch's Zion returning to millennial earth; or it may be the Zion built by the Saints

---

[6] Though the temple may not be in the city after the Millennium, it is interesting to note Orson Pratt, who spoke of a time after "Jesus has been on the earth a thousand years, [when] God himself is to be on the new earth. . . . The tree of life will be on the earth in the midst of that city that will descend on the earth, and whoever eats of the fruit of that tree will live forever, just the same as the tree of life [which] was placed upon the earth before Adam transgressed" (*JD* 21:327–28).

in Jackson; or the composite Zion returning to celestial earth. Perhaps it is all of these.

Verse 12

Having referred to scattered Israel and the oft-mentioned "gather[ing] in from the four quarters of the earth" in fulfillment of the Abrahamic covenant (v 11), Ether explains that "when these things come, [they] bringeth to pass the scripture which saith, there are they who were first, who shall be last; and there are they who were last, who shall be first" (Ether 13:12). The Savior similarly taught that "there are last which shall be first, and there are first which shall be last" (JST Luke 13:30). Elder Bruce R. McConkie paraphrased these words of Christ, saying, "There are those Gentiles in all nations to whom the gospel is offered *last* who shall be saved ahead of you Jews to whom the word of God came *first*, and there are those among you who *first* had opportunity to hear the truth who shall be *last* as to honor, preference, and salvation hereafter" (*DNTC* 1:497).

While Zenos spoke allegorically of Israel and a time when "the last . . . may be first, and . . . the first may be last" (Jacob 5:63), Nephi spoke more literally of a time when Christ "shall manifest himself unto all nations, both unto the Jews and also unto the Gentiles; and after he has manifested himself unto the Jews and also unto the Gentiles, then he shall manifest himself unto the Gentiles and also unto the Jews, and the last shall be first, and the first shall be last" (1 Nephi 13:42). In the meridian of time, the gospel went first to the Jews and then to the Gentiles. In this dispensation the gospel goes first to the Gentiles and then to the Jews; hence, the first shall be last and the last shall be first.

Our record of Ether's writings on Zion concludes with Moroni's editorial comment, "I was about to write more, but I am forbidden" (Ether 13:13).

Conclusions

What then of these dozen verses in the book of Ether in the Book of Mormon? What are we to conclude? Consider that these verses are Joseph Smith's translation of Moroni's abridgment of Ether's words. The product of at least three prophets' labors in at least three different dispensations must have some import to us. We are also told of three holy cities in three dispensations, and perhaps we are told of a fourth city in yet another time. When we add to this the words of so many additional prophets, both ancient and modern, the inestimable value of the message of Zion is impressive. Indeed, it seems we are under obligation to seek an understanding of these things.

Perhaps we can conclude at least three points from Ether's writings: First, Zion is a worthy and a significant theme consistently found throughout the cannon of scripture. Second, Zion, the New Jerusalem, is to be built in this dispensation on the American continent with its center place in Jackson County, Missouri, and faithful Latter-day Saints should plan to participate. Third, the preservation of Zion has necessitated its being removed from the earth in the past and will require it in the future. Let us briefly consider each of these.

The Message of Zion

Nearly every prophet of whom we have record has discussed Zion. The message of Zion is the message of salvation. The cities of Zion are the cities of God. The church of Enoch is the Church of the Firstborn (D&C 76:67) and is composed of those whose "callings and elections were made sure, and they were all assured of . . . an inheritance of exaltation in the eternal worlds . . . and all those who gain exaltation will be joined with them" (*MD* 136). In his covenant with Enoch, God stated that

> when men should keep all my commandments, Zion should again come on the earth, the city of Enoch which I have caught up unto myself. And this is mine everlasting covenant, that when thy posterity shall embrace the truth, and look upward, then shall Zion look downward. . . . And the general assembly of the church of the first-born shall come down out of heaven, and possess the earth, and shall have place until the end come. And this is mine everlasting covenant, which I made with . . . Enoch. (JST Gen 9:21–23)

It seems an appropriate goal for every Former-day Saint and Latter-day Saint to become worthy of Zion. In *Lectures on Faith* we read "that after any members of the human family are made acquainted with the important fact that there is a God . . . the extent of their knowledge respecting his character and glory will depend upon their diligence and faithfulness in seeking after him, until, like Enoch

. . . they shall obtain faith in God, and power with him to behold him
face to face" (2:55).

Enoch and his people were translated to a terrestrial state (*TPJS*
170), but they abide the laws of the celestial kingdom (D&C 105:5).
The doctrines, messages, and spirit of Zion take us to, through, and
beyond terrestrial glory to a celestial exaltation. The inhabitants of
the holy cities are, as Ether said, those "whose garments are white
through the blood of the Lamb. . . . They have been washed in the
blood of the Lamb" (Ether 13:10–11) and, as John points out, "they
. . . are written in the Lamb's book of life" (Rev 21:27).

Zion in America

Heber C. Kimball taught that "the spot chosen for the garden of
Eden [the first Zion Community] was Jackson County, in the State
of Missouri, where Independence now stands" (*JD* 10:235). So shall
it be again. Regarding Zion in America, there is much to consider. We
now live in the time for "which our forefathers have awaited with
anxious expectation," a time "which their minds were pointed to by
the angels" (D&C 121:27). That "time to come in the which nothing
shall be withheld" (D&C 121:28) has come upon us[7] and as this
greater light is being shed upon the Latter-day Saints, so is their
responsibility increasing (D&C 82:3). Never, to our knowledge, since
the days of Enoch have the Saints had such an abundant compilation
of promises regarding their role in actively participating in the building of Zion, not in a future, but in the present dispensation. This
participation may take several forms.

One interesting responsibility we may not often consider is our
governmental responsibility. President George Albert Smith, in the
dedicatory prayer of the Idaho Falls Temple, said, "We thank thee that
thou hast revealed to us that those who gave us our constitutional form
of government were men wise in thy sight and that thou didst raise
them up for the very purpose of putting forth that sacred document"

---

[7] Wilford Woodruff said, "The day has already dawned when the light of heaven is to fill the
earth; the day in which the Lord has said that nothing should be kept hidden, whether it be the things
pertaining to one God, or many Gods, or to thrones, principalities or powers; the day in which
everything that has been kept from the knowledge of man ever since the foundation of the earth,
must be revealed; and it is a day in which the ancient prophets looked forward to with a great deal
of interest and anxiety" (*JD* 24:52).

(see also D&C 101:79–80). He then spoke of the three branches of government and asked "that all may function fully and courageously in their respective branches completely independent of each other to the preservation of our constitutional form of government forever." He also asked that "kings and rulers and the peoples of all nations under heaven" might look and be persuaded "to adopt similar governmental systems, thus to fulfill the ancient prophecy of Isaiah that 'out of Zion shall go forth the law and the word of the Lord from Jerusalem'" (564).

Similarly, George Washington, in his presidential farewell address, expressed gratitude for the support of the people and said,

> Profoundly penetrated with this idea, I shall carry it with me to my grave as a strong incitement to unceasing vows that Heaven may continue to you the choicest tokens of its beneficence; that your union and brotherly affection may be perpetual; that the free Constitution which is the work of your hands may be *sacredly* maintained; that its administration *in every department* may be stamped with wisdom and virtue; that, in fine, the happiness of the people of these States, under the auspices of liberty, may be made complete by so careful a preservation and so prudent a use of this blessing as will acquire to them the glory of recommending it to the applause, the affection, and *adoption of every nation* which is yet a stranger to it. (1:206; emphasis added)

If the influence of this constitutional form of government is to lead to the adoption of similar forms of government throughout the world,[8] we are uniquely responsible for participation in the same. If this is to be one of the means by which Isaiah's prophecy is to be fulfilled, we should be involved. We need also to support the independent administration of each branch of government as mentioned by these great men of God, a prophet and a statesman.

When the cities of Zion are united, the earth shall again see a theocracy. We are now commanded to "be subject to the powers that be, until he reigns whose right it is to reign" (D&C 58:22); but of that future time the Lord said, "Ye shall have no king nor ruler, for I will be your king and watch over you . . . and ye shall have no laws but my laws when I come, for I am your lawgiver" (D&C 38:21–22). Elder McConkie said that such is a "government by the immediate direction of God through his ministers and representatives. . . . This

---

[8] Elder Parley P. Pratt also clearly taught that the Declaration of Independence and the Constitution of the United States of America would have a worldwide influence upon the destiny of the human race (*JD* 1:138).

type of government apparently continued among the righteous portion of mankind from the days of Adam to Enoch . . . [and] when Christ comes to reign personally on earth during the millennial era, a perfect theocratic government will prevail" (*MD* 789). Zion is as pervasive in concept as it is in geography. We are not only responsible to support our constitutional government, but we are likewise responsible for building Zion in preparation for the theocracy which will supplant our present system.

Zion Preserved

Consider the removal and return of Zion to earth. Recognizing that Zion now exists in many stakes and homes throughout the world, let us acknowledge that the center place and the city are yet to be built. The city of Enoch is our model and has been for generations. Many have sought this city of God. The great high priest Melchizedek and his people "sought for the city of Enoch" (JST Gen 14:34). Likewise, Abraham "looked for a city which hath foundations, whose builder and maker is God" (Heb 11:8–10). Speaking of the transcendent events which transpired at the valley of Adam-ondi-Ahman, the Prophet Joseph Smith said, "This is why Adam blessed his posterity; he wanted to bring them into the presence of God. They looked for a city, etc., 'whose builder and maker is God' (Heb 11:10). Moses sought to bring the children of Israel into the presence of God, through the power of the Priesthood, but he could not" (*TPJS* 159). If Adam, Melchizedek, Abraham, and Moses sought this holy city, should we not seek the same? Indeed, we should; "For God having sworn unto Enoch and unto his seed with an oath by himself; that every one being ordained after this order and calling should have power, by faith . . . to stand in the presence of God" (JST Gen 14:30–31) has in these days restored this oath and covenant and priesthood which "holdeth the key of the mysteries of the kingdom, even the key of the knowledge of God" (D&C 84:19, 39). Brigham Young said of Joseph Smith:

> Did he not accomplish all that was in his heart to accomplish in his day? He did, to my certain knowledge, and I have many witnesses here that heard him declare that he had done everything he could do—he had revealed everything that could be revealed at present, he had prepared the way for the people to walk in, and no man or woman should be deprived of going into the presence

of the Father and the Son, and enjoying an eternal exaltation, if they would walk in the path he had pointed out. (*JD* 1:132)

Though I have stressed context to identify the various cities of Zion or New Jerusalem, such identification has little effect on our present obligation. Becoming a Zion people requires the same in all dispensations. We must be engaged in preparing to build the city of Zion according to the Lord's plan and timetable. As President Brigham Young said, "We must begin and make Zion in our own hearts, and then extend it to our neighborhoods, and so continue until the Lord shall reign upon the earth" (*JD* 1:245). When Zion is established, Enoch and his people and their temples shall return as part of the ushering in of the Millennium. Following that era, the worthy shall be inhabitants of that composite city, Zion, when it is removed again to heaven. Finally, when the earth is sanctified and celestialized, that Zion and its inhabitants will return, and if we qualify because of our personal righteousness, we will there be present when "the Lord God Almighty and the Lamb are the temple of [that city] . . . and the Lamb is the light thereof" (Rev 21:22–23).

BIBLIOGRAPHY

Ballard, M. Russell. *Melvin J. Ballard: Crusader for Righteousness.* Salt Lake City: Bookcraft, 1966.

Benson, Ezra Taft. "Flooding the Earth with the Book of Mormon." *Ensign* (Nov 1988) 18:4–6; also in *Conference Report* (Oct 1988) 3–5.

Cowley, Matthew. "You Are the Leaven." *Improvement Era* (Jun 1952) 55:441–42, also in *Conference Report* (Apr 1952) 102–04.

History of the Church. 7 vols. Salt Lake City: Deseret Book, 1980.

Journal of Discourses. 26 vols. 1854–86.

The Lectures on Faith in Historical Perspective. Eds. Larry E. Dahl and Charles D. Tate, Jr. Provo, UT: Religious Studies Center, Brigham Young Univ, 1990.

The Manti Temple. Provo, UT: Community Press, 1988.

McConkie, Bruce R. *Doctrinal New Testament Commentary.* Salt Lake City: Bookcraft, 1973.

———. *The Millennial Messiah.* Salt Lake City: Deseret Book, 1982.

———. *Mormon Doctrine.* Salt Lake City: Bookcraft, 1966.

Pratt, Orson. *The Seer*. Orem, UT: Grandin Book, 1990.

Richards, Franklin D. *A Compendium of the Doctrines of the Gospel*. Salt Lake City: Deseret News Company Printers, 1882.

Smith, George Albert. "Dedicatory Prayer—Idaho Falls Temple" *Improvement Era* (Oct 1945) 48:462–65.

Smith, Joseph Fielding. *Answers to Gospel Questions*. 5 vols. Salt Lake City: Deseret Book, 1960.

———. *Church History and Modern Revelation*. 4 vols. Salt Lake City: Council of the Twelve Apostles of The Church of Jesus Christ of Latter-day Saints, 1947.

———. *Doctrines of Salvation*. 3 vols. Salt Lake City: Bookcraft, 1954.

Teachings of the Prophet Joseph Smith. Comp. Joseph Fielding Smith. Salt Lake City: Deseret Book, 1961.

Washington, George. "Farewell Address." *A Compilation of the Messages and Papers of the Presidents*. 20 vols. New York: Bureau of National Literature, 1897–1917. 1:205–16.

Widtsoe, John A. "Enoch." *Juvenile Instructor* (Jun 1901) 36:363–66.

Young, Brigham. "Preaching to Spirits in Prison." *The Contributor* (Jul 1889) 10:321–22.

Young, Joseph, Sr. "Enoch and His City." *History of the Organization of the Seventies*. Salt Lake City: Deseret News, 1878.

Moroni, the Last of the Nephite Prophets   18

H. Donl Peterson

*T*he Lord chose Moroni to complete the Nephite dispensation of the gospel of Jesus Christ. He finished his father's inspired abridgment of the Nephite millennial-long history; he commanded 10,000 soldiers at Cumorah in their final battles with the Lamanites; he abridged the writings of Ether, the record of the Jaredites, a once mighty civilization that preceded his own on this western hemisphere; and he recorded the lengthy writings of the brother of Jared on the gold plates and sealed them up. He wandered alone about the land for many years, not only concerned about his personal safety, but also fully aware of his responsibility to preserve the plates until he was commanded to hide them in the earth. Finally, after traveling extensively and fulfilling priesthood responsibilities, he deposited the plates in a hillside in what is now western New York state. What Moroni accomplished has blessed many people and will yet bless many more. This chapter attempts to highlight his illustrative and productive life.

The Formative Years

Moroni was probably born close to the middle of the fourth century AD. The only other member of his family mentioned is his father Mormon, the Nephite military commander-in-chief and the Lord's chosen prophet. We do not know his mother's name or whether he had siblings or was married. Mormon, who was well aware of the prophecies about his people, knew that his newly-born son would

The late H. Donl Peterson was a professor emeritus of Ancient Scripture at Brigham Young University.

experience a lifetime of bloodshed, turmoil, and strife. Prophecies in the scriptures were clear that the once-mighty Nephite civilization would deteriorate, divide, and finally end in tragic destruction during Moroni's lifetime (see 1 Nephi 12:11–15; Alma 45:9–14; Hel 13:5–10).

Moroni's Name

Mormon, a brilliant student of the scriptures, realized that their prophecies foretelling the destruction of his people would soon be fulfilled because they were not willing to humble themselves before the Lord. He aptly described the people of his day as being "past feeling" (Moroni 9:20). Knowing the difficulties his son would encounter, Mormon, no doubt, named his infant son after the legendary prophet and military leader Captain Moroni, whose history he had abridged (see Alma 43:16–62:43).

Moroni—A Church Leader

The size, organization, and prominence of the Church of Jesus Christ as Moroni was maturing is not clear from the Book of Mormon. It is clear that Mormon was the prophet and that some organization of the Church was still intact. Moroni included a letter in his writings that his father had sent to him on the occasion of his first call to the ministry. It begins: "My beloved son, Moroni, I rejoice exceedingly that your Lord Jesus Christ hath been mindful of you, and hath called you to his ministry, and to his holy work" (Moroni 8:2, 6). After expressing additional words of hope, Mormon directed his remarks to a problem that had been reported to him relative to an apostate practice being carried out in Moroni's area of authority—that of infant baptism. Mormon exhorts Moroni, as the newly ordained leader, to "labor diligently, that this gross error should be removed from among you" (v 6). He further tells Moroni that where he was "in this part of the land they are also seeking to put down all power and authority which cometh from God; and they are denying the Holy Ghost" (v 28). This correspondence suggests that Moroni presided over a body of believers, some of whom were perverting the ways of the Lord. Mormon also admonishes Moroni to "teach—repentance and baptism unto those who are accountable and capable of committing sin . . ." (Moroni 8:10). We can conclude that some semblance of church organization still existed when Moroni was a young man.

In a second epistle, Mormon reports on the despicable level to which the Nephites had degenerated and exhorts Moroni, thus:

> Notwithstanding their hardness, let us labor diligently; for if we should cease to labor we should be brought under condemnation; for we have a labor, to perform whilst in this tabernacle of clay, that we may conquer the enemy of all righteousness, and rest our souls in the kingdom of God. (Moroni 9:6)

Moroni's Military Career

Mormon spares his readers most of the horrid, graphic details of the annihilation of his godless society who only a few generations before he had described as follows: "Surely there could not be a happier people among all the people who had been created by the hand of God. . . . They were in one, the children of Christ, and heirs of the kingdom of God. And how blessed were they!" (4 Nephi 1:16–18).

In preparation for the final battles with the Lamanites, Mormon led the badly outnumbered Nephites to the land of Cumorah, where they gathered to face their more powerful foes in a setting they hoped would give them advantage over the Lamanites (see Mormon 6:4). There were 23 Nephite captains at Cumorah, each commanding 10,000 troops in the final battle. Moroni and Mormon were two of these military leaders (vv 10–15).

In the horrendous slaughter at Cumorah, Mormon was wounded and left for dead, the Lamanites passing him by, assuming he was dead. Only 24 Nephites survived the final battle at Cumorah, and they included Mormon and Moroni, who observed the mutilated bodies of the Nephite soldiers and their wives and children. In his last two entries on the plates, Mormon laments over the Nephite's utter destruction (Mormon 6:16–22) and leaves a final message of hope to the posterity of the Lamanites (Mormon 7:1–10).

Moroni Was Entrusted
with the Plates of Mormon

To complete and preserve the great abridgment of the Nephite history from destruction, Mormon asked Moroni to finish it and then "hide up the records in the earth" until the Lord would have them discovered (Mormon 8:4). Moroni's entry is brief and factual. Writing 400 years after the birth of Christ, Moroni states that the remaining Nephites, including his father, were hunted down and killed until they were "no more" (v 7). He alone remained "to write the sad tale of the destruction of [his] people" (v 3). And although he desired to bear testimony of the worth of the plates, there was no room on them to do so, and he had no ore with which to make additional plates.

Moroni testifies in closing the record that if readers would not belittle the abridgment for its imperfections they would be given even more. Finally, he finishes the record about his people by engraving this closing sentence: "Behold, I make an end of speaking concerning this people. I am the son of Mormon, my father was a descendant of Nephi" (Mormon 8:13). We assume at this time Moroni also wrote the following on the last leaf of the gold plates:

> The Book of Mormon an account written by the hand of Mormon upon plates taken from the plates of Nephi. Wherefore, it is an abridgement of the record of the people of Nephi and also the Lamanites—Written to the Lamanites, who are a remnant of the house of Israel; and also to Jew and Gentile—Written by way of commandment, and also by the spirit of prophecy and of revelation—Written and sealed up, and hid up unto the Lord, that they might not be destroyed—To come forth by the gift and power of God unto the interpretation thereof—Sealed by the hand of Moroni, and hid up unto the Lord, to come forth in due time by way of the Gentile—The interpretation thereof by the gift of God.
>
> An abridgment taken from the Book of Ether also, which is a record of the people of Jared,w ho were scattered at the time the Lord confounded the language of the people, when they were building a tower to get to heaven—Which is to show unto the remnant of the House of Israel what great things the Lord hath done for their fathers; and that they may know the covenants of the Lord, that they are not cast off forever—And also to the convincing of the Jew and Gentile that JESUS is the CHRIST, the ETERNAL GOD, manifesting himself unto all nations—And now, if there are faults they are the mistakes of men; wherefore, condemn not the things of God, that ye may be found spotless at the judgment-seat of Christ. (Book of Mormon Title Page)

A New Beginning

We assume that at the time Moroni wrote the title page to the Book of Mormon he thought his work with the plates was completed and all he needed to do further was to bury them, but the Lord had other things for him to do. Called to a new assignment, Moroni returned to the plates once again to write upon them. He also had somehow acquired new plates upon which to write since his father's record was full. In the time between burying his father's record, and beginning a new, Moroni had been shown several visions of the future importance of the sacred Nephite record. Sometime in these years the Lord gave Moroni the "keys of the record of the stick of Ephraim" (D&C 27:5). Moroni's new calling extended beyond the grave to the glorious last dispensation in which he would give the sacred text to a new, young prophet.

The Prophecies of Moroni

As the Lord unfolded the events in this last dispensation to him, Moroni recorded them upon the plates. The following list comprises Moroni's prophecies contained in the last three books within the Book of Mormon:

1. No one shall have the plates to get financial gain even though the plates contain a considerable amount of gold (Mormon 8:14).

2. Whoever brings the plates to light will be blessed of the Lord (vv 14, 15).

3. The golden plates shall be brought out of darkness and will shine forth by the power of God (v 26).

4. In the day the plates are revealed it will be taught that miracles are done away (v 26).

5. The plates shall come as one will speak from the dead (v 26).

6. The era in which the plates will come forth will be troubled by secret combinations and works of darkness (v 27).

7. The book will come forth at a time that the power of God is denied (v 28).

8. Churches will be defiled because of pride (v 28).

9. Church leaders and teachers will envy those who belong to their churches (Mormon 8:28-37).

10. There will be great destruction, e.g. fires, tempests and vapors of smoke, in foreign lands (v 29).

11. There will be wars and rumors of wars and earthquakes in divers locations (v 30).

12. There will be great pollutions upon the face of the earth, e.g., murders, robbing, lying, deceivings, whoredoms, and all manner of abominations. It will be taught that God will uphold such at the last day (v 31).

13. Sins will be forgiven for money (v 32).

14. Very fine apparel will be a mark of the day because of pride and all manner of iniquities (v 36).

15. Every church has become polluted because of pride (v 36).

16. They love their money, substance, fine apparel and the adorning of their churches more than they love the poor and they needy, the sick and afflicted (v 37).

17. When the Lord comes, the earth shall be rolled as a scroll and the elements shall melt with fervent heat (9:2).

18. "This is a choice land, and whatsoever nation shall possess it shall be free from bondage . . . captivity, and from all other nations . . . if they will serve the God of the land, who is Jesus Christ . . ." (Ether 2:12).

19. The future translator (Joseph Smith) may be privileged to "show the plates unto those who shall assist to bring forth this work" (5:1-5).

20. Three witnesses shall be shown the plates by the power of God (vv 1–5).

21. Three sets of witnesses, the three witnesses, the eight witnesses, and the Godhead, shall all stand as a testimony against the world at the last day who reject this work (v 4).

22. Whatever nation shall uphold secret combinations until they get power and gain and spread over that nation shall be destroyed (8:22).

23. Moroni prophesied of a specific wicked combination in the last days that would attempt to overthrow the freedom of all lands. It will bring to pass destruction (Ether 8:25).

24. The Lamanites shall receive the Holy Ghost (Moroni 10:1–7).

25. Moroni shall be at the judgment bar of God where God shall ask the world's inhabitants, "Did I not declare my words unto you, which were written by this man?" (Moroni 10:27).

It is significant to note how many prophecies are directly related to Moroni's continued service in the last days.

Moroni Abridges the Book of Ether

After Moroni's return, he writes nearly two more chapters on his fathers record, Mormon 8:14–9:37, which contain many prophecies that he had seen of this last dispensation. He then seems to assume that this then really completes his work with the plates and once again ends his writings with an appropriate conclusion. But sometime later he returns and abridges the book of Ether, which itself is an abridgment of the 2,000-year history of the Jaredite civilization, made on 24 plates of gold by Ether, the last Jaredite prophet. The book of Ether was discovered by the Nephites about 92 BC, and translated by the prophet Mosiah with the aid of the Urim and Thummim (see Mosiah 28:11–19). The 24 plates containing Ether's abridgment appear to have been passed down, along with Mosiah's translation of them, from prophet to prophet until they came into Mormon's hands.

In wondering why Moroni included his abridgment of Ether's work on the plates of Mormon, we have to assume Mormon told him that he had intended to include those things "hereafter; for behold, it is expedient that all people should know the things which are written in this account" (Mosiah 28:19). Moroni completed the abridgment of the book of Ether on the plates of Mormon, which we often call the Gold Plates.

The Sealed Portion of the Book of Mormon

While abridging the Jaredite records, Moroni was so impressed with the writings of the first prophet of that gospel dispensation, referred to in the Book of Mormon as "the brother of Jared," that he wrote, "There never were greater things made manifest than those which were made manifest unto the brother of Jared" (Ether 4:4).

Prior to leading his people from the tower of Babel to the New World, the brother of Jared received a series of revelations, the Lord personally talking with him from a cloud (Ether 2:4). The premortal Savior explained that the Jaredites' inheritance "is a land which is choice above all other lands; wherefore he that doth possess it shall serve God or shall be swept off" (v 10).

As the brother of Jared grew spiritually, the Lord taught him greater truths. He said to him, "never has man come before me with such exceeding faith as thou hast" (Ether 3:9). Finally, the Lord showed himself to the brother of Jared explaining "for never has man believed in me as thou hast" (v 15). In addition to this great theophany, Jesus showed him "all the inhabitants of the earth which had been, and also all that would be; and he, withheld them not from his sight, even unto the ends of the earth" (v 25). The Lord commanded the brother of Jared to write the visions in a language that could not be read and seal them up (v 22). The Lord gave his prophet two stones to enable a future translator to read the language which had been confounded (see vv 22–27).

The Lord told the brother of Jared that the things which he saw and heard should not be revealed to the world until after Jesus should glorify his name in the flesh (Ether 3:21). In keeping with this command these great revelations were not revealed to the Nephites by king Mosiah in 92 BC. They were made available to the Nephites after Jesus ascended to heaven in AD 34, and they enjoyed them for several generations. Moroni was also commanded to write his own words and seal them all up with the interpreters (4:4–5). The Lord told Moroni that when the Gentiles in the last days exercise faith in Christ even as the brother of Jared did, then will they have the words of the brother of Jared "even to the unfolding unto them all my revelations" (v 7).

The Size of the Sealed Portion of the Book of Mormon

We are not told specifically how many of the Book of Mormon plates were sealed, but Elder Orson Pratt stated that it was two-thirds of them. This figure has been widely accepted because of the popularity of Elder Pratt's writings (see *Journal of Discourses* 3:347). David Whitmer, one of the three special witnesses who actually saw the plates is reported to have said that "about the half of the book was sealed" (Poulson 2). Elder George Q. Cannon wrote that one-third of the plates were sealed (25), while the Prophet Joseph

Smith simply stated, "The volume was something near six inches in thickness, a part of which was sealed" (*History of the Church* 4:537). If the highest estimate is correct and two-thirds of the plates were sealed, that would mean there are the equivalent of 1,062 pages sealed since there are 531 pages in the current Book of Mormon. That would make a total of 1,593 possible pages had the whole set of plates been translated. Since Moroni engraved the sealed-portion plates as well as 51 pages in the Book of Mormon, his total of 1,113 pages written would be about 70 percent of the total plates delivered to Joseph Smith.

If the smaller estimate is correct, then the numbers would be lower with about 266 pages sealed, making a total of 797 pages. Moroni would then have written 317 pages, or approximately 40 percent of the plates handed to Joseph Smith (see Peterson 47). However much Moroni wrote, he clearly fulfilled a very important writing assignment, possibly even larger than father.

Many Miles Traveled and Many Sites Dedicated

Book of Mormon geography is not an exact science, and Church leaders do not often specify exact locations of Book of Mormon sites. Relationship-type maps are found in Church manuals and periodicals, showing, for example, the land of Zarahemla was north of the land of Lehi-Nephi, and the land of Desolation was north of the narrow neck of land, but we are not instructed just where those lands are presently located. In the last fifty years theories of the geography and archeology of the Book of Mormon have proliferated. With the increased participation in travel to Central and South America, and with the popularity of antiquities, ancient history, and geographical documents, many Latter-day Saints have turned their interests to the external evidences of the Book of Mormon. But those theories remain theories, and there is no hard evidence of specific Book of Mormon lands.

Moroni in Manti, Utah

Some members of the Church are aware that at the dedication of the site for the temple in Manti, Utah, the following incident took place:

At a conference held in Ephraim, Sanpete County, June 25th, 1875, nearly all the speakers expressed their feelings to have a temple built in Sanpete County, and gave their views as to what point and where to build it, and to show the union that existed, Elder Daniel H. Wells said "Manti," George Q. Cannon, Brigham Young, Jr., John Taylor, Orson Hyde, Erastus Snow, Franklin D. Richards, Lorenzo Young, and A. M. Musse said "Manti stone quarry. " I have given the names in the order in which they spoke. At 4 p.m. that day President Brigham Young said: "The Temple should be build on Manti stone quarry." Early on the morning of April 25, 1877, President Brigham Young asked Brother Warren S. Snow to go with him to the Temple hill. Brother Snow says: "We two were alone: President Young took me to the spot where the Temple was to stand; we went to the southeast corner, and President Young said: "Here is the spot where the prophet Moroni stood and dedicated this piece of land for a Temple site, and that is the reason why the location is made here, and we can't move it from this spot; and if you and I are the only persons that come here at high noon today, we will dedicate this ground." (Whitney 436)

That Moroni dedicated the Manti Temple site is one of the few statements the Brethren have made connecting a Book of Mormon figure with a specific current place and action. This aids us in documenting one of Moroni's travels and priesthood assignments. Another reference happened when William McBride, patriarch from the Richfield Utah Stake, spoke at a prayer meeting in St. George in January 1881. After recalling many experiences from the Nauvoo period and quoting the Prophet Joseph Smith on many issues, Patriarch McBride referred to

the Route the old Nephites took travelling to Cumorah from the south and south west; of having to bury their tr[e]asures as they journeyed and finally burying the Records and precious things in the Hill Cumorah; of Moroni dedicating the Temple site of what we now call St. George, Nauvoo, Jackson Co., Kirtland, and others we know not of as yet. (Walker 2:525–26)

Two Interesting Maps

Several years ago, I came across two copies of a map in the Archives Division of the Historical Department of the Church relative to Moroni's North American journeys (see Figures 1 and 2). On the back of the map in Figure 1 is written the following:

A chart, and description of Moroni's travels through this country. Got it from Br. Robert Dickson. He got it from Patriarch Wm. McBride at Richfield in the Sevier and also from Andrew M. Hamilton of same place. And they got it from Joseph Smith the Prophet.

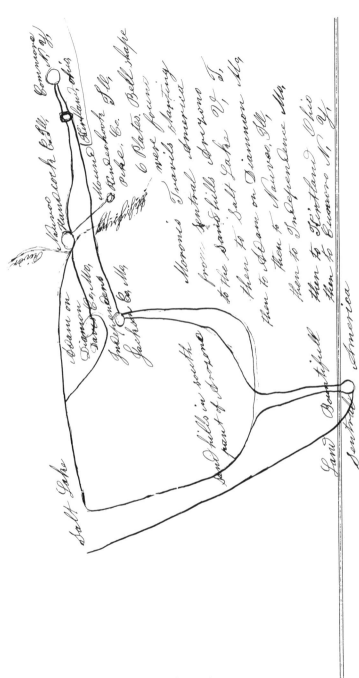

Figure 1

245

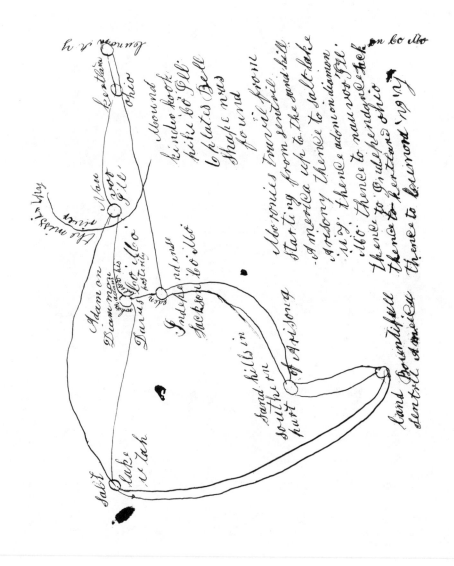

Figure 2

On the map "land Bountifull [sic]" is listed in "Sentral [sic] America." The cartographer wrote "starting point" below the reference to Central America. Above the "land Bountifull" is "Sand hills in south part of Arizona," and above it to the left is "Salt Lake." To the right is "Independens, Jackson Co, Mo," and above that is "Adam on Diamon, Davis Co, Mo." To the right of that is "Nauvoo, Hancock C. Ill." Below that is "Mound Kinderhook, Pike, Co, Ill, 6 Plates Bell shape were found" (*were* was *was* on one copy). Then to the right and above that is "Kirtland, Ohio," and to the right of that is "Commorre [Cumorah], N.Y." Below this on the right-hand side of the map is written: "Moroni's Travels starting from Sentral America to the Sand hills Arizona then to Salt Lake U[tah], T[erritory], then to Adam on Diammon Mo, then to Nauvoo, Ill, then to Independence Mo, then to Kirtland Ohio then to Cumoro NY."

The second map appears to have been drawn by the same hand and is quite similar to the first, though it twice spells Arizona as Arisony (one "y" has an "a" written over it); "eden" is written near the circle identifying "Independense"; "where adam blessed his posterity" is written near the circle identifying "Adam on Diammon"; the "missisipy river" is listed near Nauvoo; Kirtland is twice misspelled "kertland"; and Cumorah is misspelled "Cunora" and "Cumora."

It is interesting to note that the brethren mentioned on these documents were contemporaries of the Prophet Joseph Smith, and they credited him with the notion that the travels of Moroni began in the land Bountiful, which was in Central America, and went through the western Great Basin area prior to going east to Cumorah in western New York. Why Moroni took the route he did is still without answers. These men stated that the Prophet Joseph believed Bountiful is in Central America while the Hill Cumorah, the burial place of the plates, is in New York State.

The Plates of the Book of Mormon Are Buried

Sometime around AD 421, Moroni took the sacred plates, the breastplate, and the Urim and Thummim to the Hill Cumorah and buried them near the top of the hill in a stone box that he made for them. The box was made of flat stones laid on the bottom and sides which were cemented together to make it waterproof. When the Prophet Joseph Smith first met the angel Moroni at the hill Cumorah about 1,400 years later on the evening of 22 September 1823, Moroni showed him the sacred contents and told Joseph that the sacred objects had been "sealed by the prayer of faith" (Cowdery 198). The plates remained there until 27 September 1827, when Moroni gave them to Joseph to allow him to translate them into English.

Joseph Smith published the following in the July 1838 issue of the *Elders' Journal* in answer to the question: "How and where you obtain The Book of Mormon?" His reply:

> "Moroni, the person who deposited the plates, from whence the Book of Mormon was translated, in a hill in Manchester, Ontario County, New York, being dead, and raised again therefrom, appeared unto me, and told me where they were; and gave me directions how to obtain them" (42–43).

The Death of Moroni

I have found only one account which speaks of Moroni's death:

> At a meeting at Spanish Fork, Utah Co., in the winter of 1896, Brother Higginson stated in my presence that Thomas B. Marsh told him that the Prophet Joseph Smith told him (Thomas B. Marsh, he being then President of the Twelve), that he became very anxious to know something of the fate of Moroni, and in answer to prayer the Lord gave Joseph a vision, in which appeared a wild country and on the scene was Moroni after whom were six Indians in pursuit; he stopped and one of the Indians stepped forward and measured swords with him. Moroni smote him and he fell dead; another Indian advanced and contended with him; this Indian also fell by his sword; a third Indian then stepped forth and met the same fate; a fourth afterwards contended with him, but in the struggle with the fourth, Moroni, being exhausted, was killed. Thus ended the life of Moroni. (Evans)

Conclusion

This paper has attempted to highlight some of the lesser-known facts about the life of Moroni, one of the greatest prophets that has lived upon the earth. His contributions both during his mortal and his post-mortal ministries have affected and will yet affect the lives of literally millions of God's children.

Latter-day Saints and non-Mormons alike first identify Moroni as the angel, the "messenger sent from the presence of God" who visited the boy-prophet Joseph Smith (JS-H 1:33). He is probably the most easily identifiable person connected with the Restoration since statues representing him appear on many temple spires heralding the glorious restoration mentioned in the book of Revelation. He is the angel flying "in the midst of heaven, having the everlasting gospel to preach to them that dwell in the earth" (Rev 14:6). His picture is commonly seen on copies of the Book of Mormon, LDS jewelry, LDS military dog-tags, the official logo, and on tombstones for LDS servicemen. He is usually depicted as blowing a trumpet.

BIBLIOGRAPHY

Cannon, George Q. *The Latter-day Prophet: History of Joseph Smith.* Salt Lake City: *Juvenile Instructor*, 1900.

Cowdery, Oliver. "Letter VIII." *Messenger and Advocate* (Oct 1835) 2:195–202.

Evans, Charles David. "The Fate of Moroni, 1897." Archives Division, Church Historical Department, Salt Lake City, UT.

History of the Church. 7 vols. Salt Lake City: Deseret Book, 1980.

Journal of Discourses. 26 vols. 1854–1886.

Maps showing Moroni's travels. (No date.) Archives Division, Church Historical Department, Salt Lake City, UT.

Peterson, H. Donl. *Moroni: Ancient Prophet, Modern Messenger.* Bountiful, UT: Horizon Press, 1983.

Poulsen, P. Wilhelm. *Deseret Evening News* (16 Aug 1878) XI:2.

Smith, Joseph. *Elders' Journal* (Jul 1838) 1:42–43.

Walker, Charles Lowell. *Diary of Charles Lowell Walker.* Eds. A. Karl Larson and Katherine Miles Larson. 2 vols. Logan, UT: Utah State Univ Press, 1980.

Whitney, Orson F. *Life of Heber C. Kimball.* Salt Lake City: Bookcraft, 1967.

"Weak Things Made Strong"   19

Carolyn J. Rasmus

> And if men come unto me I will show unto them their weakness. I give unto men weakness that they may be humble; and my grace is sufficient for all men that humble themselves before me; for if they humble themselves before me, and have faith in me, then will I make weak things become strong unto them. (Ether 12:27)

I was familiar with this frequently-quoted scripture, and it had meaning to me before I joined the Church 22 years ago. The 58 words which comprise this verse are powerful and instructive; however, this verse becomes increasingly meaningful when we examine the context in which the Lord gave this instruction to Moroni, analyze other scriptures related to it, and apply the principles taught by the Lord in our own lives.

The Context

The instruction given by the Lord in Ether 12:27 comes midway through Moroni's abridgment of the record of the Jaredites. Taken from the 24 plates found by the people of Limhi during the reign of king Mosiah, this record is now known as the book of Ether (Ether 1:2). Chapter 12 begins with an account of Ether's prophecies in the days of Coriantumr (v 2). Ether prophesied "great and marvelous things" (v 5), telling the people that "by faith all things are fulfilled" (v 3) and that "whoso believeth in God might with surety hope for a better world, yea, even a place at the right hand of God, which hope cometh of faith, maketh an anchor to the souls of men, which would

Carolyn J. Rasmus is an administrative assistant to the Young Women General Presidency of The Church of Jesus Christ of Latter-day Saints in Salt Lake City, Utah.

make them sure and steadfast" (Ether 12:4). It is obvious that we do not have all of the words of Ether since Moroni noted that he could not write even a "hundredth part" of Ether's record (15:33).

Ether's testimony of the power of faith must have touched the spirit of Moroni, for he interrupts his account of Ether's teachings to insert his own thoughts: "And now, I, Moroni . . . show unto the world that faith is things which are hoped for and not seen; wherefore, dispute not because you see not, for ye receive no witness until after the trial of your faith" (Ether 12:6). Like Paul in his letter to the Hebrews, Moroni recounts the power of faith made manifest in the lives of individuals (vv 7–19). He then returns to a theme he discussed earlier: God is a God of miracles (Mormon 9:10–11) and if miracles cease among the children of men it is "because that they dwindle in unbelief" (v 20). Moroni emphasizes that miracles are wrought after faith; faith in the Son of God is always a requisite (Ether 12:17).

After recounting the great faith of the brother of Jared which faith enabled him to see the finger of God (Ether 12:20), Moroni appears to feel that his own attempts to communicate his belief in the power of faith to those who will someday read his record may be inadequate. He says, "Lord, the Gentiles will mock at these things, because of our weakness in writing; for Lord thou hast made us mighty in word by faith, but thou hast not made us mighty in writing" (v 23). Perhaps Moroni sees his own inadequacies and wonders how it is possible for him to accomplish his work or how he can represent the power of faith through the written word. He refers to the "awkwardness of our hands" and says, "When we write we behold our weakness, and stumble because of the placing of our words" (vv 24–25).

We see in Moroni what we often see in ourselves when our faith falters or when we feel incapable of accomplishing what lies before us. First, we love to absolve ourselves of any responsibility and blame others for our problems. Moroni seems to do this when he says to the Lord, "*Thou* hast made us that we could write but little" (Ether 12:24; emphasis added). Can you hear yourself in a calling or situation for which you feel unprepared? How often do we lament, "You got me into this. I never thought I could do this job?" Second, Moroni compares himself to the brother of Jared whose writings were "mighty even as [the Lord], unto the overpowering of man to read them" (v 24). Third, he fears others might ridicule or treat his work with contempt: "I fear lest the Gentiles shall mock at our words" (Ether 12:25). And so we see in Moroni what is so common in ourselves: a tendency to blame others for our feelings of inadequacy, compare ourselves to others who appear to have talents we do not, and fear what others will think of our work as opposed to what God will think.

Considering Moroni's prideful attitude, the Lord's response is not surprising. He teaches that he "give[s] unto men weakness that they may be humble" (Ether 12:27), and then, as if to make sure the point is well made, he repeats the word *humble* two more times in the same sentence. Both times it is used as a verb, suggesting action on our part. No doubt this was not the help Moroni sought. Instead of giving him an answer to specific concerns, God teaches him a principle far greater than if he had simply made him mighty in writing.

Humility

Humility has not always been my favorite topic. For many years I wanted to be the best, satisfy my own selfish ambitions, be in control, and think of myself before others. Elder Neal A. Maxwell's statement that humility and meekness rank "low on the mortal scale of things" (ix) described my attitude.

My awakening awareness of the necessity for developing humility came during general conference in April 1986. President Ezra Taft Benson taught that "pride is a 'my will' rather than 'thy will' approach to life. . . . Pride is characterized by 'What do I want out of life?' rather than by 'What would God have me do with my life?' It is self-will as opposed to God's will. It is the fear of man over fear of God. The opposite of pride is humbleness, meekness, submissiveness, teachableness" ("Cleansing the Inner Vessel" 6–7). Three years later in his April 1989 conference address, President Benson taught that "pride is the great stumbling block to Zion" ("Beware of Pride" 7). He had already noted that "God will have a humble people. Either we can choose to be humble or we can be compelled to be humble," and that "the antidote for pride is humility—meekness, submissiveness" (6).

As meaningful as President Benson's messages were to me, my real learning and understanding came by personal experience. In May 1990, I had been asked to accompany Young Women General President Ardeth G. Kapp to the Philippines to assist in presenting firesides and leadership training to young women and their leaders. When I received the plane ticket and noted the cost, I began to wonder what I could teach or do that would justify such a large expenditure of money. In the weeks before our departure, I studied about the history of the Church in the Philippines, met with people who had served there, and tried to prepare myself in every way. The night before we were to depart, my home teacher gave me a blessing. Afterwards I wrote down as much as I could remember of the blessing to keep it in my mind. Among the things I recalled and recorded was this statement, "As you ask in faith, your prayers will be answered."

The next morning as I awakened early, a hymn tune kept running through my mind, but I was unable to put words with it. Finally, I got up and began leafing through the hymnbook. Soon I was reading the words to the tune: "Be thou humble in thy weakness, and the Lord thy God shall lead thee, Shall lead thee by the hand and give thee answer to thy prayers" (*Hymns* #130). I felt as if the Lord were giving me a personal message in preparation for my travels.

Within 22 hours I arrived in the Philippines. Never have I felt more dependent on the Lord. The schedule was rigorous and demanding, the weather was hot and humid, and I was not prepared for the impoverished conditions in which we found people living. Often I had great difficulty understanding what people were saying to me because they would mix the dialect of Tagalog with English. When I worked with youth, I found myself praying constantly that I could understand what they were saying. And I did.

Toward the end of this assignment, I awoke early one morning and felt impressed to record in my journal what I described as a "significant experience":

> I've been awake for about an hour, reviewing in my mind all we have seen and experienced and learned. There is so much more than can ever be expressed. Then I knelt down to pray. I've prayed daily that I might see these people as Christ sees them; that I would be filled with the pure love of Christ as I interact with them, but this morning I found myself also praying that I'd *feel* toward them as the Savior felt. Almost immediately I was overcome by the Spirit and began weeping. I thought of the time described in 3 Nephi when Christ visited the Nephites and taught the people and prayed for them. He told them they were blessed because of their faith and that his joy was full. Then it is recorded, "He wept, . . . and he took their little children, one by one, and blessed them, and prayed unto the Father for them. And . . . he wept again." (3 Nephi 17:21–22)

For an instant I felt like I think Christ must have felt toward his lambs and I wondered if I had done enough. I thought of the great joy in the eyes of these people, of their humility, their teachability, their delight in so little. I cannot help but think about President Benson's message on pride. I've read and reread Mosiah 3:19, "For the natural man is an enemy to God, and has been from the fall of Adam, and will be, forever and ever, unless he yields to the enticings of the Holy Spirit, and putteth off the natural man and becometh a saint through the atonement of Christ the Lord, and becometh as a child, submissive, meek, humble, patient, full of love, willing to submit to all things which the Lord seeth fit to inflict upon him, even as a child doth submit to his father."

There could not be a better description of the people of the Philippines. How do we become more humble? How do we strip away the things of the world? How do we put off the natural man? (Journal Entry of 26 May 1990)

Then, within days I was home. My very ordinary home suddenly seemed palatial. I could both understand others with ease and be understood. I could regulate the temperature and change other things to ensure my comfort and ease. And I felt in control and comfortable, but I felt much less dependent on the Lord. Not only did I feel I was in charge, but also that I could handle things on my own. I soon realized that I was not nearly as receptive to the Spirit as I had been in the Philippines, and I missed the companionship of the Holy Ghost. I sensed that something had happened, and it was of great concern to me.

I made a determination to study about and seek to acquire humility. I realized my lack of dependency on the Lord and reliance in my own strength kept me from being humble, and I determined I would begin by learning more about humility. I went first to the scriptures looking up every scripture that included the word *humility, meekness, submissiveness*, and one of my favorites became Ether 12:27. I then looked at what the prophets have taught about humility. The Prophet Joseph understood the relationship between being humble and receiving the Spirit of the Lord. David Whitmer told the following story which illustrates that:

> At times when brother Joseph would attempt to translate . . . he found he was spiritually blind and could not translate. He told us that his mind dwelt too much on earthly things, and various causes would make him incapable of proceeding with the translation. When in this condition he would go out and pray, and when he became sufficiently humble before God, he could then proceed with the translation. Now we see how very strict the Lord is, and how he requires the heart of man to be just right in his sight before he can receive revelation. . . .

> To illustrate so you can see: One morning when he was getting ready to continue the translation, something went wrong about the house and he was put out about it. Something that Emma, his wife, had done. Oliver and I went upstairs and Joseph came up soon after to continue the translation but he could not do anything. He could not translate a single syllable. He went downstairs, out into the orchard, and made supplication to the Lord; was gone about an hour—came back to the house, and asked Emma's forgiveness and then came upstairs where we were and then the translation went on all right. He could do nothing save he was humble and faithful. (Roberts 1:130–31)

I also reviewed what modern-day prophets have taught us about humility. President Benson spoke about what humility does not mean. He said it does not mean weakness, lack of courage, lack of self-confidence, timidity, or fear. In fact, in *Teachings of Ezra Taft Benson*, we find the following: "A person can be humble, powerful and courageous" (369). "You can be humble and still be vigorous and strong and fearless" (119). And "Humility is an acknowledged recognition of our dependence on a higher power" (369).

President Spencer W. Kimball also spoke of humility, as a strength, and not as a weakness. He said, "One can be courageous and humble. . . . If the Lord was meek and lowly and humble, then to become humble one must do what he did in boldly denouncing evil, bravely advancing righteous works, courageously meeting every problem, becoming the master of himself and the situations about him and being near oblivious to personal credit. Humility is not pretentious, presumptuous, nor proud. It is not weak, vacillating, nor servile. . . . *Humble* and *meek* properly suggest virtues, not weaknesses" (232).

Have Faith in God and Jesus Christ to Develop Humility

To develop humility requires faith in God and in his Son, Jesus Christ. King Benjamin taught his people to "believe in God; believe that he is, and that he created all things, both in heaven and in earth; believe that he has all wisdom, and all power, both in heaven and in earth; believe that man doth not comprehend all the things which the Lord can comprehend" (Mosiah 4:9). He emphasized, "If you believe all these things see that ye do them" (v 10).

Humility also requires an acknowledgement of a higher power. We must acknowledge God's infinite wisdom, power, and presence, and see ourselves as finite and "unworthy creatures" (Mosiah 4:11).

Part of our weakness stems from the fact that we are mortal and God is immortal. Interestingly, in the Lord's instructions to Moroni, he says, "*If* men come unto me . . . then will I make weak things become strong unto them" (Ether 12:27; emphasis added). God first requires acknowledgement of his existence, his attributes, and our own nothingness. After the Lord had spoken, Moroni responded, "O Lord, thy righteous will be done, for I know that thou workest unto the children of men according to their faith" (v 29).

In some of Moroni's last writings, he chooses to quote the words of his father, Mormon, many of which deal with the importance of faith. For example, Mormon quotes Christ's words on faith: "If ye will have faith in me ye shall have power to do whatsoever thing is expedient in me" (Moroni 7:33), and then he adds his own testimony of faith: "It is by faith that miracles are wrought; and it is by faith that angels appear and minister unto men; wherefore, if these things have ceased wo be unto the children of men, for it is because of unbelief, and all is vain. For no man can be saved, according to the words of Christ, save they shall have faith in his name" (vv 37–38).

The prophet Jacob also understood the importance of faith. He speaks of his people's faith thus: "Our faith becometh unshaken, insomuch that we truly can command in the name of Jesus and the very trees obey us, or the mountains, or the waves of the sea" (Jacob 4:6). He then tells us the same thing the Lord is teaching Moroni: "Nevertheless, the Lord God showeth us our weakness that we may know that it is by his grace, and his great condescensions unto the children of men, that we have power to do these things" (v 7).

Both the Lord and Jacob use the word *grace* to describe the source of power given to the faithful. The LDS Bible Dictionary notes that "the main idea of the word *grace* is divine means of help or strength, given through the bounteous mercy and love of Jesus Christ. . . . It is likewise through the grace of the Lord that individuals, through faith in the atonement of Jesus Christ and repentance of their sins, receive strength and assistance to do good works that they otherwise would not be able to maintain if left to their own means. This grace is an enabling power" (697). Elder Gene R. Cook spoke of the doctrine of grace in the general conference of May 1993:

> We should have great hope in knowing, however unworthy we may feel or weak we may be, *that if we will do all we can,* He will come to our aid and provide for us whatever we may lack. . . . To obtain grace, one does not have

to be perfect but he does have to be trying to keep the commandments the best that he can. Then the Lord may allow him to receive that power. (80–81)

The Lord taught Moroni that his grace is "sufficient for all men that humble themselves" (Ether 12:27). This same principle was emphasized by the Apostle James: "God resisteth the proud, but he giveth grace unto the humble. Submit yourselves therefore to God" (James 4:6–7).

Fortunately, we do not have to face things alone; there is a higher source of power. When we feel weak or overwhelmed or inadequate, we must remember our dependence upon God, go to him, acknowledge his power, and ask for his grace. This is the essence of humility. King Benjamin taught this to his people: "I would that ye should remember . . . the greatness of God, and your own nothingness, and his goodness and long-suffering towards you, unworthy creatures, and humble yourselves even in the depths of humility, calling on the name of the Lord daily, and standing steadfastly in the faith of that which is to come" (Mosiah 4:11).

Ammon, the grandson of king Benjamin, recognized the power and grace of God in his own life. When he and his brothers returned from their missionary labors, he rejoiced that they had been made "instruments in the hands of God" to bring the gospel to the Lamanites (Alma 26:3). His brother Aaron feared that Ammon's joy had carried him "away unto boasting" (v 10), but Ammon was quick to set the record straight: "I do not boast in my own strength, nor in my own wisdom. . . . Yea, I know that I am nothing; as to my strength I am weak; therefore I will not boast of myself, but I will boast of my God, for in his strength I can do all things" (vv 11–12). Ammon is an example of what the Lord was teaching Moroni: weak things can become strong through His power. In a day when many people doubt the existence of God and rely on the arm of flesh, we need not only to choose to believe in God, but also to trust him in all things, for he is the source of all strength and power.

Look to the Savior's Life and Teachings to Develop Humility

To truly learn about humility, we must look at the Savior's life and teachings. He admonished us, "Take my yoke upon you, and learn of me; for I am meek and lowly in heart" (Matt 11:29). Jesus was humble in all things. Elder Neal A. Maxwell suggests that though Christ was

> actually the Creator of this world, the earth being his footstool, Jesus' willing-ness to become from birth a person of "no reputation" provides one of the great lessons in human history. He, the leader-servant, who remained of "no reputa-tion" mortally, will one day be he before whom every knee will bow and whose name every tongue will confess (see Philip 2:10–11). Jesus meekly stayed his unparalleled course. (57)

The Apostle Paul wrote to the Saints in Philippi that Christ had

> made himself of no reputation, and took upon him the form of a servant, and was made in the likeness of men: and being found in fashion as a man, he humbled himself, and became obedient unto death, even the death of the cross. Wherefore God also hath highly exalted him, and given him a name which is above every name: that at the name of Jesus every knee should bow, of *things* in heaven, and *things* in earth, and things under the earth; and that every tongue should confess that Jesus Christ is Lord, to the glory of God the Father. (Philip 2:7–11)

This is he who Isaiah said would be called "Wonderful, Counsellor, The mighty God, The everlasting Father, The Prince of Peace" (Isa 9:6).

Christ is not only the Creator, but also the Exemplar, the Head of the Church, Jehovah, the Messenger of the Covenant, and the Messiah. And yet it is also Jesus who entered into Jerusalem "meek, and sitting upon an ass" (Matt 21:5). How did Jesus, who had the power to turn water into wine, make the blind to see, the lame to walk, and the dead to rise from their grave, so meekly stay his course? Christ not only knew he was the Son of God and what his relationship to God the Father was, but he also knew what his mission was, and he never lost sight of it. Even before his birth, he knew that he would do the Father's will and give all glory unto him (Moses 4:2). Repeatedly throughout his life, he made it clear that he had come to do the will of the Father. After healing a man at the pool at Bethesda he declared, "I can of mine own self do nothing. . . . I seek not mine own will, but the will of the Father which hath sent me" (John 5:30). Even in the Garden of Gethsemane he said, "O my Father, if this cup may not pass away from me, except I drink it, thy will be done" (Matt 26:42). To the Nephites, he said, "Behold, I am the light and the life of the world; and I have drunk out of that bitter cup which he Father hath given me, and have glorified the Father in taking upon me the sins of the world, in the which I have suffered the will of the Father in all things from the beginning" (3 Nephi 11:11). Later in his ministry among the Nephites, he reemphasized, "I came into the world to do the will of my Father" (27:13). He taught us that when we pray we should say, "Thy will be done on earth as it is in heaven" (13:10). In this dispensation, he has said, "I am Jesus Christ; I came by the will of the Father, and I do his will" (D&C 19:24). Never did Christ take glory unto himself. What a lesson for each of us.

I have marveled that Christ, the Jehovah and Creator of this world, would have been placed into the world as a little child, totally dependent on others for every need. No doubt he was exemplar in all things, and perhaps it should not be surprising that there are several scriptures which speak not only of humility but couple it with our need to become as little children (Mosiah 3:18–19; Moroni 8:10). Nowhere is the statement more clear than in Matthew 18:1–5. It is interesting that Jesus' response comes after the disciples had asked a very prideful question: "Who is the greatest in the kingdom of heaven?" Jesus called a little child to him and set him in the midst of the people and said, "Verily I say unto you, Except you be converted, and become as little children, ye shall not enter into the kingdom of heaven. Whosoever therefore shall humble himself as this little child, the same is the greatest in the kingdom of heaven" (Matt 18:3–4).

King Benjamin taught that we can become Saints only "through the atonement of Christ the Lord, and [as we] becometh as a child, [we become] submissive, meek, humble, patient" (Mosiah 3:19). We have many other things to learn from children that help us become more humble. Young children are teachable and innocent, pure, genuine, and forgiving. Ardeth Kapp tells of a little girl who returned home from a neighbor's house where her little friend had died:

> "Why did you go?" questioned her father.
> "To comfort her mother," she said.
> "What could you do to comfort her?"
> "I climbed into her lap and cried with her," she said. (98)

I learned also from a 13-year-old young woman about reaching out to others. Erika Monson was in Primary Children's Hospital when she read in the *Church News* a story about a 2-year-old girl, Kirstin, fighting for her life. Finding someone who would donate bone marrow compatible with Kirstin's was the only thing that would save her life. No doubt many of us read the article. But a 13-year-old took the time to respond. She wrote to Kirstin's parents:

> Dear Brother and Sister Doxey: How is your family doing? My name is Erika Monson. I am from Ely, Nevada. I am in Primary Children's Hospital and getting better. I know how hard things are for you and your family even though I'm thirteen. I hope that your daughter Kirstin is lucky and finds the right donor so she can hopefully live to be a young woman. If I was old enough to donate and wasn't on medicine for my liver, I would see if I matched your daughter's type. If so, I would do everything to make it so she would be able to live. I hope and pray for the best for your family. Love, Erika Monson. (Kapp 107)

How much we can learn from little children!

Conclusion

If the Lord did not give us weaknesses, it would be easy to take credit for our own accomplishments and to rely on our own strength. Weaknesses are a constant reminder of our dependence upon the Lord. When we take those weaknesses to him, in humility, we can become effectively joined with him in a great work. When we have done as much as we can do, his grace, that divine means of strength and help, can move us beyond our native abilities. We overcome our weakness when we have faith in him and acknowledge we can be better with his help than we can ever be on our own.

As we seek in this life to become more like our Savior Jesus Christ, may we turn to Moroni who taught us that in the Lord weak things can become strong. He says to each of us:

> Yea, come unto Christ, and be perfected in him, and deny yourselves of all ungodliness; and if ye shall deny yourselves of all ungodliness, and love God with all your might, mind and strength, then is his grace sufficient for you, that by his grace ye may be perfect in Christ; and if by the grace of God ye are perfect in Christ, ye can in nowise deny the power of God. And again, if ye by the grace of God are perfect in Christ, and deny not his power, then are ye sanctified in Christ by the grace of God. (Moroni 10:32–33)

BIBLIOGRAPHY

Benson, Ezra Taft. "Beware of Pride." *Ensign* (May 1989) 19:4–7; also in *Conference Report* (Apr 1989) 3–7.

———. "Cleansing the Inner Vessel." *Ensign* (May 1986) 16:4–7; also in *Conference Report* (Apr 1986) 3–6.

———. *Teachings of Ezra Taft Benson.* Salt Lake City: Bookcraft, 1988.

Cook, Gene R. "Receiving Divine Assistance." *Ensign* (May 1993) 23:80–81; also in *Conference Report* (Apr 1993) 98–101.

Hymns of The Church of Jesus Christ of Latter-day Saints. Salt Lake City: The Church of Jesus Christ of Latter-day Saints, 1985.

Kapp, Ardeth Greene. *The Joy of the Journey.* Salt Lake City: Deseret Book, 1992.

Kimball, Spencer W. *The Teachings of Spencer W. Kimball.* Ed. Edward L. Kimball. Salt Lake City: Deseret Book, 1988.

Maxwell, Neal A. *Meek and Lowly.* Salt Lake City: Deseret Book, 1987.

Roberts, B. H. *A Comprehensive History of The Church of Jesus Christ of Latter-day Saints.* 6 vols. Salt Lake City: The Church of Jesus Christ of Latter-day Saints, 1977.

Unity Through the Power of Charity

20

Alvin C. Rencher

*O*ne of the highlights of 4 Nephi is a description of the unity that the people enjoyed following Christ's visit. Reaching that state seems beyond the power of mortals, as does obtaining the spiritual gifts and guidance they received. My thesis is that all of this spiritual support is available to us today and that entire groups as well as individuals can reach a level of worthiness so as to be blessed with feelings of unity with all people.

Mormon describes the unity the Nephites and Lamanites enjoyed following Christ's visit as follows:

> And it came to pass in the thirty and sixth year, the people were all converted unto the Lord, upon all the face of the land, both Nephites and Lamanites, and there were no contentions and disputations among them. . . . And they had all things common among them; therefore there were not rich and poor, bond and free, but they were all made free, and partakers of the heavenly gift. (4 Nephi 1:2–3)

By qualifying to be partakers of the heavenly gift, they received forgiveness of sins and the attendant blessings of the atonement. In this joyous state, they lived without contention:

> And it came to pass that there was no contention among all the people, in all the land; but there were mighty miracles wrought among the disciples of Jesus. And it came to pass that the seventy and first year passed away. . . yea, even an hundred years had passed away. . . . And it came to pass that *there was no contention in the land. . . .* And how blessed were they! For the Lord did bless them in all their doings; yea, even they were blessed and prospered until an hundred and ten years had passed away; and the first generation from Christ

Alvin C. Rencher is professor of Statistics at Brigham Young University.

had passed away, and there was no contention in all the land. (4 Nephi 1:13–15, 18; emphasis added)

This unity, characterized by lack of contention and the sharing of all things, lasted until about AD 200, long after the generation who stood in Christ's presence had all died. How did Christ's personal ministry have such a remarkable impact on those people? Can we tap that same power?

Many sources contributed to this unity. The people who stood in Christ's presence touched him and he taught them and ministered unto them. But the key, unifying factor that Mormon emphasizes in 4 Nephi is love: they had no contention in their lives "because of the love of God which did dwell in the hearts of the people" (4 Nephi 1:15).

The love the Nephites felt in Christ's presence continued not only with them, but also with their descendants. The degree of unity they reached comes only to those possessed of this pure love of Christ or charity. A major purpose of the Book of Mormon is to instill in its readers this same feeling of love for Christ and for one another. Before discussing how we might obtain this level of charity, let us review what Christ taught the Nephites about unity.

Christ's Teachings on Unity to the Nephites

Early in his visit to the Nephites, Christ declared his doctrine, the first principle of which was the elimination of contention and anger:

And there shall be no disputations among you, as there have hitherto been. . . . For verily, verily I say unto you, he that hath the spirit of contention is not of me, but is of the devil, who is the father of contention, and he stirreth up the hearts of men to contend with anger, one with another. . . . Behold, this is not my doctrine, to stir up the hearts of men with anger, one against another; but this is my doctrine, that such things should be done away. (3 Nephi 11:28–30)

Jesus then identified four additional principles of his gospel: repentance, faith, baptism, and remission of sins through fire and the Holy Ghost (vv 31-35). These principles relate to the Atonement and allow the people to be at one or in unity with the Lord and with each other. Immediately after stating these principles, Jesus delivered the Nephite counterpart of the Sermon on the Mount. The sermon in 3 Nephi is clearly intended for those who have complied with the first principles and received a remission of their sins. The first two verses of the sermon clarify this:

> Blessed are ye if ye shall give heed unto the words of these twelve. . . . After that ye are baptized with water, behold, I will baptize you with fire and with the Holy Ghost. . . . Yea, blessed are they who shall believe in your words, and come down into the depths of humility and be baptized, for they shall be visited with fire and with the Holy Ghost, and shall receive a remission of their sins. (3 Nephi 12:1–2)

The 3 Nephi beatitudes encourage unity through following church leaders, receiving the Holy Ghost, and sharing the gospel with others that they might come into the fold of Christ.

After his instructions on the first day, Jesus announces he is going to the Father, but the multitude implore him with their tears to "tarry a little longer with them" (3 Nephi 17:5). Moved by this silent plea, he stays with them, heals their sick, weeps with a fulness of joy over their faith, and calls down angels to minister to their children. Then, under these very special circumstances, he asks for bread and wine and institutes the sacrament. How fitting that in their apogee of feelings of oneness with the resurrected Jesus, he shows them how they can celebrate those feelings and re-create them with the sacrament: "And this shall ye always do to those who repent and are baptized in my name. . . . And if ye do always remember me ye shall have my Spirit to be with you" (18:11).

When Jesus finally does leave at the end of that unforgettable first day of his visit, he pronounces a concluding "blessed," in which he emphasizes that all of his instructions have pointed to unity: "And I give you these commandments because of the disputations which have been among you. And blessed are ye if ye have no disputations among you" (3 Nephi 18:34).

On the second day of his visit, Jesus utters three prayers unto the Father in the presence of the multitude. We are not given the words of the third prayer, but a petition for unity appears in both of the first two prayers. In his second prayer, for instance, Christ asks for the same oneness among his disciples that he asked for in his intercessory prayer at Gethsemane: "Father, I pray not for the world, but for those whom thou hast given me out of the world, because of their faith, that they may be purified in me, that I may be in them as thou, Father, art in me, that we may be one" (3 Nephi 19:29). The oneness, the unity of the Father and the Son is held out repeatedly in the scriptures as the supreme example we must emulate. In a sense, this fundamental doctrine embraces the whole of the gospel (see John 17:11, 23). In 3 Nephi 28, Jesus notes that this kind of unity will characterize relationships in the kingdom of God: "And for this cause ye shall have fulness of joy; and ye shall sit down in the kingdom of my Father; yea, your joy shall be full, even as the Father hath given me fulness of joy; and ye shall be even as I am, and I am even as the Father; and the Father and I are one" (3 Nephi 28:10; see also D&C 29:13).

Unity in Our Day

The unity Jesus spoke of is not reserved just for the Nephites in their golden age or for the future dwellers in the celestial kingdom. It is extended as a goal for the Saints in any age. In Mosiah 18, Alma taught his people the importance of unity and love, which he associated with repentance and faith: "And he commanded them that there should be no contention one with another, but that they should look forward with one eye, having one faith and one baptism, having their hearts knit together in unity and in love one towards another" (v 21).

In our own time, Jesus has also expressed an expectation of unity for his followers: "I am Jesus Christ, the Son of God, who was crucified for the sins of the world, even as many as will believe on my name, that they may become the sons of God, even one in me as I am one in the Father, as the Father is one in me, that we may be one" (D&C 35:2). The present day instruction to become one is more than a recommendation. The Lord has said, "Be one, even as I have commanded you" (51:9) and, in even stronger language, "If ye are not one ye are not mine" (38:27).

Being one and working together does more than just bless us spiritually; unity also brings us temporal blessings. A horse-pulling contest in Canada illustrates the effect of synergism especially well. The people put weights on a flat bed wagon, and a single horse pulled it a measured distance. They added 1,000 pounds at a time, until the horse could no longer pull it. The winner pulled 9,000 lbs., and the runner-up pulled 8,000 lbs. Out of curiosity, someone suggested putting those two horses together. When they hitched both horses to the wagon, they pulled 31,000 lbs. Working together the horses pulled more than three times the weight the best of them could pull alone.

And so it is with humans. When we work together, we can accomplish much more than we can separately.

Another interesting illustration of the power of unity is found in the exodus from Kirtland in 1838.

> As violence against the Saints and their leaders escalated, it was finally no longer safe for them to remain in Kirtland. The Prophet, whose life was in gravest danger, was "warned by the Spirit" and decided to move immediately to Missouri. . . . (Anderson 235)
>
> After Joseph left for Missouri, persecution of those close to him in Kirtland increased. . . . Most families with sufficient means and equipment escaped the threatening mobs. . . . (236–37)
>
> One effort to see that the Saints traveled to Missouri in safety was the organization of "Kirtland Camp," which was initiated by the seventies. . . . Zerah Pulsipher testified of divine direction to the brethren: "One evening, while we were in the attic story of the Lord's House, and while Joseph Young, I think, was at prayer, *I saw a Heavenly messenger*, who appeared to be a very tall man dressed in a white robe from head to foot. He cast his eyes on me and on the rest of the Council and said, *'Be one, and you shall have enough.'* Soon after the way was opened before us, so that we received money and means for clothing for the poor and to prepare for our removal. James Foster and Jonathan Dunham also saw the angel at the same time I did." (239)
>
> Benjamin Johnson described the company . . . as the "Kirtland Poor Camp." . . .(239)
>
> The Kirtland Camp left on July 5, 1838, with 515 members. . . . With the help of the Lord and the combined faith and strength of each other, the members of Kirtland Camp traveled 870 miles in about three months, arriving in Far West on October 2, 1838. (241)

The unity necessary for the Kirtland Camp to journey such a long distance could not have been possible had they not first had love for the Lord and for one another.

Necessity of Charity

We noted earlier that in 4 Nephi 1:15, the love of God, or charity, was identified as the foundation of Nephite unity. Only by being filled with the love of God could the people in 4 Nephi avoid all contention. Like them, we are charged to love and respect every person we associate with. These feelings must be real, not feigned or forced. Only with true charity can we enjoy the kind of friendship with others we should.

Having the gift of charity is also essential for us to progress along the strait and narrow path described by Nephi:

> And now, my beloved brethren, after ye have gotten into this strait and narrow path, I would ask if all is done? Behold, I say unto you, Nay. . . . Wherefore, ye must press forward with a steadfastness in Christ, having a perfect brightness of hope, and a love of God and of all men. (2 Nephi 31:19–20)

Missionaries, bishops, and many other church workers know that they cannot serve effectively without love. The Spirit does not operate in the absence of love: "Behold, I speak unto you . . . who have desires to bring forth and establish this work; And no one can assist in this work except he shall be humble and full of love, having faith, hope, and charity" (D&C 12:7–8).

Charity Covers and Prevents Sins

Joseph Smith made some incisive comments about the unifying power of charity:

> It is a time-honored adage that love begets love. Let us pour forth love— show forth our kindness unto all mankind and the Lord will reward us with everlasting increase; cast our bread upon the waters and we shall receive it after many days, increased to a hundredfold. Friendship is like Brother Turley in his blacksmith shop welding iron to iron; it unites the human family with its happy influence.
>
> I do not dwell upon your faults, and you shall not upon mine. Charity, which is love, covereth a multitude of sins, and I have often covered up all the faults among you. (*Teachings of the Prophet Joseph Smith* 315–16; hereafter *TPJS*)

When he noted that "charity, which is love, covereth a multitude of sins," the Prophet may have been referring to one of the following two scriptures: "Hatred stirreth up strifes: but love covereth all sins" (Prov 10:12) or "above all things have fervent charity among yourselves: for charity shall cover the multitude of sins" (1 Peter 4:8).

The Joseph Smith Translation of 1 Peter 4:8 reads "charity *preventeth* a multitude of sins." On another occasion, the Prophet clarified how charity both prevents and covers sins.

> Suppose that Jesus Christ and holy angels should object to us on frivolous things, what would become of us? We must be merciful to one another and overlook small things. . . . Nothing is so much calculated to lead people to forsake sin as to take them by the hand, and watch over them with tenderness.

> When persons manifest the least kindness and love to me, O what power it has
> over my mind, while the opposite course has a tendency to harrow up all the
> harsh feelings and depress the human mind. (*TPJS* 240)

Thus charity enables us to cover each other's sins, that is, to forgive
them and be unified in spite of each other's weaknesses and foibles.
Charity also prevents sins in that it leads us to forsake sin.

Overcoming Anger and Contention

As noted earlier, Nephite unity was characterized by the absence
of contention, and also, Jesus listed the elimination of anger and
contention as a basic principle of his gospel. He further underscored
this precept in the Nephite version of the Sermon on the Mount.

> Ye have heard that it hath been said by them of old time, and it is also written
> before you, that thou shalt not kill, and whosoever shall kill shall be in danger
> of the judgment of God; But I say unto you, that whosoever is angry with his
> brother shall be in danger of his judgment. And whosoever shall say to his
> brother, Raca, shall be in danger of the council; and whosoever shall say, Thou
> fool, shall be in danger of hell fire. (3 Nephi 12:21–22)

The Book of Mormon does not say "angry . . . without a cause,"
as in the Matthew version of the sermon; there is no qualification here.
Anger and criticism are characterized as grievous sins. A quotation
from Elder Neal A. Maxwell provides an interesting insight: "Letting
off steam always produces more heat than light" (84).

Let me give a personal illustration of how using scriptural
insights helped me overcome anger. I was praying to know what to
do about someone close to me whose frequent outbursts left me
depressed and suffering stomach pains for days at a time. As I prayed
for understanding, the words "A soft answer turneth away wrath"
(Prov 15:1) came into my mind. I immediately asked, "Whose
wrath?" And the answer was, "Yours!" Then the flood of insight came.
My problem had not been caused by the other person's anger but by
my own anger that arose because of my answering back in kind, either
defensively or in counterattack. Thus the soft answer would prevent
my anger from arising. The other person's anger by itself could not
cause me any discomfort. The result was a great miracle in my life.
When I answered the person's outbursts with neutral or even loving
words, my anger did not arise, and I felt no residual resentment. I later
found that using soft words alone was not sufficient to control my

feelings, but I had to get all bad thoughts out of my mind. I could not even think any resentful or critical thoughts.

The effectiveness of a group can be shattered by contention and anger or expanded by love and unity. This applies to all groups such as families, businesses, units of the Church, or even athletic teams. The following example illustrates the power of love in achieving unity in an organized group.

About ten years ago, while serving as chairman of the Department of Statistics at BYU, I was momentarily startled one day to look up from my desk into the eyes of the biggest blond giant I had ever seen. He announced that he had come in to change his major from physical education to statistics. I asked "Can you do the math? We require several courses beyond calculus." He said "I can do the math." His name was Larry Hamilton, and he was a starting defensive lineman on the football team. His warm congenial personality soon made him a great favorite with our faculty and students. He and his wife had joined the Church after coming to Brigham Young University. The next year, in the middle of the football season, I asked Larry to come and speak at a fireside for my BYU ward. He gave a great talk, but the thing I will always remember was his statement: "Do you know why we win all our games? It's not because we have the best quarterback or the best receivers or the best linemen, etc. It's because we love each other." They went on to win all their games. That was 1984, the year BYU went undefeated and was named National Champions.

Achieving Charity through Repentance

Charity is a gift; we seek this gift by complying with the requirements for its bestowal. In Moroni 7:48, Mormon states that charity is "bestowed upon all who are true followers of his Son, Jesus Christ." He further explains that perfect love comes after forgiveness of sins, which follows repentance:

> And the first fruits of repentance is baptism; and baptism cometh by faith unto the fulfilling the commandments; and the fulfilling the commandments bringeth remission of sins; And the remission of sins bringeth meekness, and lowliness of heart; and because of meekness and lowliness of heart cometh the visitation of the Holy Ghost, which Comforter filleth with hope and perfect

love, which love endureth by diligence unto prayer, until the end shall come, when all the saints shall dwell with God. (Moroni 8:25–26)

Alma pleaded with his people not to procrastinate the day of their repentance, so that they might "be led by the Holy Spirit . . . having the love of God always in your hearts" (Alma 13:27–29). On another occasion, he characterized the feelings that come after forgiveness as a song of redeeming love: "And now behold, I say unto you, my brethren, if ye have experienced a change of heart, and if ye have felt to sing the song of redeeming love, I would ask, can ye feel so now?" (5:26).

After we repent, as the Nephites did at the time of Christ's visit, we too can sing the song of redeeming love. Having felt the power of Christ's atonement in our lives, we love him and feel his love to a degree that we could not otherwise imagine. The Atonement is the pivotal turning point in the history of the universe. It lies at the core of human existence. We can expect to be possessed of wondrous feelings after we experience the effects of the Atonement.

Dissolution of Nephite Unity

Just as repentance leads to receiving the gift of charity, failing to repent leads to loss of divine love, and contention follows immediately. In the last part of 4 Nephi, we have a model of how to lose unity through sin and the lack of repentance, as the Nephites allowed pride and materialism to creep in unchecked: "And now, in this two hundred and first year there began to be among them those who were lifted up in pride, such as the wearing of costly apparel, and all manner of fine pearls, and of the fine things of the world. And from that time forth they did have their goods and their substance no more in common among them. And they began to be divided into classes" (4 Nephi 1:24–26).

Because they did not turn from their pride and materialism when the temptation arose, they soon began to lose their unity. "And again, there was another church which denied the Christ; and they did persecute the true church of Christ, because of their humility and their belief in Christ; and they did despise them because of the many miracles which were wrought among them" (4 Nephi 1:29).

What should these people have done when they witnessed the miracles? They should have done the same thing their ancestors did in reaction to the miracle of Jesus' visit, the same thing we should do in response to a miracle—repent. But these people did not repent; instead, they despised the righteous because of the miracles that were wrought among them. The record states that "the people did harden their hearts, for they were led by many priests and false prophets to build up many churches, and to do all manner of iniquity" (4 Nephi 1:34). Mormon emphasized, "they did not dwindle in unbelief, but they did willfully rebel against the gospel of Christ" (v 38). He further states that even "the people who were called the people of Nephi began to be proud in their hearts, because of their exceeding riches, and become vain like unto their brethren, the Lamanites" (v 43). Thus we can trace the sad consequences of failure to repent and to stay close to the Lord. The Nephites lost the Spirit that had provided them with unity and glorious feelings of charity.

Achieving Unity

How then do we achieve unity? What we must work on is *repentance*, which removes all barriers between us and Christ. Before coming down to visit with the Nephites, Jesus had instructed them from heaven: "O all ye that are spared because ye were more righteous than they, will ye not now return unto me, and *repent of your sins*, and be converted, that I may heal you?" (3 Nephi 9:13; emphasis added). They obviously obeyed this counsel, because they were prepared to stand in his presence and feel his love in full measure.

In his second prayer in 3 Nephi chapter 19, Jesus asked that the people might be purified so that they might be one with Christ. Hence, purification through repentance and forgiveness is the key to unity with him. This feeling of unity then extends to our families, our associates, and all who surround us. Seeking first to achieve unity with Christ is a better plan than to start by working on unity with others and hope for eventual unity with Him. Only after attaining unity with Jesus are we given power to truly achieve unity with others.

After king Benjamin delivered the words the angel gave him to his people in his celebrated sermon, they repented and were born again (Mosiah 3:2–4; 5:7). He then gave them further instructions about how they could remain close to the Lord:

> As ye have come to the knowledge of the glory of God . . . and have tasted of
> his love, and have received a remission of your sins, . . . I would that ye should
> remember, and always retain in remembrance, the greatness of God, . . . and
> humble yourselves even in the depths of humility, calling on the name of the
> Lord daily, and standing steadfastly in the faith of that which is to come, which
> was spoken by the mouth of the angel. (Mosiah 4:11)

Benjamin followed this counsel with the promise, "If ye do this ye shall always rejoice, and be filled with the love of God, and always retain a remission of your sins" (v 12). If we can meet the conditions and retain a remission of our sins, we, too, will be filled with the love of God and preserve a feeling of unity for others. Otherwise, we will lack the power to do it.

The building of unity is associated with enduring to the end. Enduring to the end is more than hanging on to a minimal level of performance and avoiding major transgression. It is a time of significant progress and preparation for the celestial kingdom. It is a time during which we become the kind of people who can dwell in the presence of God, the kind of people who can live in total unity with each other. To do this, we must eliminate the last vestige of pride, criticism, anger, etc. We can accomplish this refining process with the aid of the Holy Ghost.

Role of the Spirit in Maintaining Charity and Unity

Let us consider the role of the Spirit in helping us develop charity and unity. In his first prayer in 3 Nephi chapter 19, Jesus asked for the Holy Ghost to be given to the people, "that they may believe in me, . . . *that we may be one*" (3 Nephi 19:23; emphasis added). A remarkable sermon by Mormon on the role of the Spirit in perfecting ourselves and achieving a oneness with Christ is found in Moroni chapter 7. In that sermon, Mormon is speaking to those who are already well established on the path to eternal life, "the peaceable followers of Christ," who have "obtained a sufficient hope by which [they] can enter into the rest of the Lord, from this time henceforth until [they] shall rest with him in heaven" (v 3). Thus Mormon's sermon is not an elementary approach describing first steps, but an advanced course on enduring to the end and attaining a unity with Christ and with those who will dwell with him.

In Moroni 7:16–19, Mormon describes the role of the Spirit of Christ in aiding us to "know good from evil." Through this medium we are given an eternal view, and each moment prepares us for eternity. When we do wrong, we are blessed with instant godly sorrow, with loss of the Spirit. Thus even in periodic repentance, to maintain a remission of sins, we need help. We cannot do it by ourselves.

Let me illustrate how this process has worked for me. When I do something wrong or say something I should not, the Spirit turns off. Sometimes I feel it go, draining out of me like pulling the plug. By this means, he is teaching me what is truly good and comes from him and what is not.

In my case, three things that the Spirit is especially sensitive to are complaining, criticizing, and the least tinge of pride or boasting. I always lose the Spirit when I engage in those activities. I must not only not say such things aloud, I must not even think them. This is not always easy. There are times when I despair of ever learning this lesson permanently. Whenever I stumble, I immediately fall into a period of godly sorrow and repentance. I feel my hope in Christ slipping away. In its place comes the hopelessness that leads to repentance. After a time, my eternal hope comes back.

A Celestial Society

I have often wondered about the kinds of relationships we will have in the celestial kingdom. The Doctrine and Covenants tells us that the "same sociality that exists among us here will exist among us there, only it will be coupled with eternal glory, which glory we do not now enjoy" (130:2). Consequently, shouldn't we have the same feelings now that we expect to have then? Those we associate with have as much value now as they will have in the eternities to come. This life is the time for us to learn to love others, to overcome envy, to eliminate all resentments, to stop making unfavorable comparisons. This is the time for us to rise above materialism as the Nephites did for many years after the visit of Christ.

I assume that the Nephites were ordinary people, who received only the powers they earned. They obeyed precepts and made choices that are also available to all of us. They were blessed by the Spirit to change their natures: to love as Christ loves, to have the gift of a grateful heart, to experience unity, to gain an eternal perspective, to look beyond the materialistic components of this world.

As followers of Christ, we seek for a time and place where everyone loves and is loved by everyone else, where no one becomes angry or harms anyone. In short, we seek a society filled with charity, as in the "golden age" of the Nephites. We probably will not see such a time in which everyone on the earth acts that way until after this life. But, individually, we can experience feelings of unity with Christ, with our families, and in all of our associations. Each of us can have the feelings that powered the Nephite unity: "And it came to pass that there was no contention in the land, because of the love of God which did dwell in the hearts of the people" (4 Nephi 1:15).

BIBLIOGRAPHY

Anderson, Karl R. *Joseph Smith's Kirtland.* Salt Lake City: Deseret Book, 1989.

Maxwell, Neal A. "Murmur Not." *Ensign* (Nov 1989) 19:82–85; also in *Conference Report* (Sep/Oct 1989) 103–07.

Teachings of the Prophet Joseph Smith. Comp. Joseph Fielding Smith. Salt Lake City: Deseret Book, 1976.

Moroni 9–10: Remember How Merciful the Lord Hath Been

21

Bruce K. Satterfield

President Ezra Taft Benson declared, "The Book of Mormon brings men to Christ" ("The Book of Mormon" 83). In this declaration, he reaffirmed the fundamental importance of the Book of Mormon in the salvation of humankind. From its beginning to its conclusion, it bears witness of Christ and teaches of his atonement that makes possible "the plan of mercy" (Alma 42:15, 23). Through this plan we can be delivered from the power of Satan and our own imperfection. Throughout the Book of Mormon, the prophets urge everyone to come unto Christ (see 1 Nephi 6:4; 13:40; 2 Nephi 9:45, 51; 26:33; Jacob 1:7; 6:5; Omni 1:26; Alma 5:34–35; 3 Nephi 12:20; Mormon 9:27; 29:2). The last prophet to make this plea was Moroni.

In the final chapter of the Book of Mormon before he sealed up the plates from which it was translated, Moroni invited "all the ends of the earth . . . [to] come unto Christ, and be perfected in him" (Moroni 10:24, 32). However, Moroni 10 is more than just an invitation. Through a series of exhortations Moroni teaches us how to come unto Christ, and he also gives insight into the power of God that perfects and sanctifies those who do come unto him.

Moroni 10 in Context

The invitation to come unto Christ offered by Moroni in the final chapter is a fitting conclusion to this encouraging book. It is a curious thing, therefore, that Moroni included in his writings an appalling

Bruce K. Satterfield is a religion instructor at Ricks College in Rexburg, Idaho.

letter from his father. Even more striking is the fact that Moroni placed the letter immediately before his own invitation for everyone to come unto Christ.

In the letter, Mormon described in awful terms the degenerated condition of the Nephites. They had sunk to such extreme depths of brutality and perversion that rape, murder, and cannibalism were considered "a token of bravery" (Moroni 9:10). Mormon lamented this condition, saying:

> O the depravity of my people! They are without order and without mercy. . . . And they have become strong in their perversion; and they are alike brutal, sparing none, neither old nor young; and they delight in everything save that which is good; and the suffering of our women and our children upon all the face of this land doth exceed everything; yea, tongue cannot tell, neither can it be written. (Moroni 9:18–19)

Because of the Nephites' wickedness, Mormon told his son that "I cannot recommend them unto God lest he should smite me" (v 21).

The letter shocks the reader. Yet, that may well have been Moroni's intent. He offers no explanation as to why he included this letter in his writings. However, as it stands, it provides a striking contrast that enhances Moroni's invitation to come unto Christ. This is what Gerald N. Lund calls a scriptural foil: a technique used by scriptural writers who place "two contrasting principles or examples side by side to show even more clearly what they [are] trying to teach" (108). Moroni chapters 9 and 10 together contain the last of several contrasts found in the Book of Mormon that illustrate one of its major themes: we are "free to choose liberty and eternal life, through the great Mediator of all men, or to choose captivity and death, according to the captivity and power of the devil" (2 Nephi 2:27). Chapter 9 illustrates what happens when we choose "captivity and death" through the power of Satan, while chapter 10 offers hope and encouragement to those who desire "liberty and eternal life" through Christ.

Come unto Christ through the Book of Mormon

Moroni's final message is a well-designed study on the mercy and power of God that brings his children to perfection. It is built around a series of eight exhortations that show us how we can come unto Christ and receive his saving grace. The first six exhortations are directed toward the Lamanites while the last two are addressed "unto all the ends of the earth" (Moroni 10:24).

Though the first six exhortations are directed to the Lamanites, their message can be applied to all people. From the first three exhortations (Moroni 10:3–7), we learn that the Book of Mormon is a powerful instrument that brings its readers to Christ. Within these verses two steps are discussed that, if followed, will lead the readers to a testimony of the reality of Christ and the power of his mercy. Gaining a testimony of Christ is an essential ingredient in the process of coming unto him. Both steps, therefore, will be briefly discussed.

The Lord's Mercy from Adam Down

The first step is to read the Book of Mormon; however, merely reading it is not enough. Moroni exhorts us that "when ye shall read these things, if it be wisdom in God that ye should read them, that ye would remember how merciful the Lord hath been unto the children of men, from the creation of Adam even down until the time that ye should receive these things" (Moroni 10:3). The scriptures are the primary source for obtaining knowledge concerning God's mercy from Adam to the present time. This is especially true of the Bible and the Book of Mormon. Lehi quoted Joseph of Egypt to teach that these two books would "grow together" in the last days, bringing latter-day Israel "to the knowledge of their fathers" (2 Nephi 3:12), ie, a record of God's dealings with mankind from the creation of man until the coming of Christ and the establishment of his church in the old and new worlds. Found within this record is example after example of how God's mercy was extended to those who exercised faith in him, even to their temporal and spiritual salvation. It is precisely this pattern that Moroni encouraged the reader of the Book of Mormon to ponder, for it generates hope and inspires the reader to exercise faith in God.

Of all the events recorded in the Book of Mormon, the single most important event referred to is the atoning sacrifice of Jesus Christ. It was this act alone that made possible the extension of God's mercy to mankind (see Alma 42:23). Concerning the atonement, Elder Bruce R. McConkie wrote:

> The atonement is the most transcendent event that ever has occurred or ever will occur from creation's morn through all the endless ages of eternity. It is

the occasion on which a God paid the ransom to reclaim fallen man, and all created things, from the effects of Adam's fall. In it, Jesus Christ, who became the first immortal flesh, paid the penalty for the transgression of the First Adam, who was the first mortal flesh. In it, the Only Begotten made amends for a broken law, satisfied the demands of justice, and took upon himself the sins of all men on conditions of repentance. Through it, all men are raised in immortality while those who believe and obey are raised also unto eternal life in the kingdom of the Father. The atonement makes possible a reconciliation between God and man; it provides a Savior and a Redeemer for mortals; it gives man an advocate and an intercessor in the court above. The atonement is the great and eternal plan of redemption. (107)

Manifest Truth by the Power of the Holy Ghost

The second step is to receive a witness of the truthfulness of the Book of Mormon. To achieve this, Mormon exhorts us to "ask God, the Eternal Father, in the name of Christ, if these things are not true." He further states that "if ye shall ask with a sincere heart, with real intent, having faith in Christ, he will manifest the truth of it unto you, by the power of the Holy Ghost" (Moroni 10:4). Without a manifestation of the Holy Ghost, it is not possible to be truly converted to the Book of Mormon. This is true of all gospel principles. Therefore, Moroni asserts that "by the power of the Holy Ghost ye may know the truth of all things" (v 4).

When we receive a testimony of the truthfulness of the Book of Mormon, we have essentially received a testimony of the reality of Jesus Christ. "And whatsoever thing is good is just and true; wherefore, nothing that is good denieth the Christ, but acknowledgeth that he is" (Moroni 10:6). The Book of Mormon brings us to believe in Jesus Christ. However, more than just having a belief in Christ, we must know that he is. Moroni says that this knowledge can be gained only "by the power of the Holy Ghost" or "the power of God" (Moroni 10:7). This is the way God has always borne testimony to his children; "For he worketh by power [or the Holy Ghost], according to the faith of the children of men, the same today and tomorrow, and forever" (v 7).

Spiritual Gifts

The next three exhortations focus on spiritual gifts which are extended to those who, as a result of receiving a testimony of Christ, have come unto him through baptism and have received the Gift of the Holy Ghost. As has been shown, the knowledge that the Book of Mormon is true and that Jesus is the Christ comes through the manifestation of the Holy Ghost to those who receive it faithfully. However, as Elder Dallin H. Oaks has said, "We need to distinguish between a *manifestation* of the Holy Ghost and the *Gift* of the Holy Ghost. As men and women desire to believe, they develop faith in God (see Alma 32:26–43). When they have enough faith, they can receive a manifestation of the Holy Ghost." He further taught that the manifestations of the Holy Ghost "are preparatory gifts . . . given to lead earnest seekers to repentance and baptism" (68).

All those who have been led by the preparatory gifts of the Spirit to come unto Christ through baptism are promised the Gift of the Holy Ghost. "Spiritual gifts come to those who have received the gift of the Holy Ghost" (Oaks 68). These gifts play an important role in perfecting the Saints of God. Moroni's fourth exhortation is to those who have received the Gift of the Holy Ghost: "And again, I exhort you, my brethren, that ye deny not the gifts of God, for they are many; and they come from the same God. And there are different ways that these gifts are administered; but it is the same God who worketh all in all; and they are given by the manifestations of the Spirit of God unto men, to profit them" (Moroni 10:8).

Moroni then lists various spiritual gifts including teaching the word of wisdom, teaching the word of knowledge, faith, healing, working of mighty miracles, prophecy, ministering of angels, tongues, and interpretation of tongues (Moroni 10:9–16). However, Moroni's list is only a sample of the many gifts available. Elder McConkie wrote: "These gifts are infinite in number and endless in their manifestations because God himself is infinite and endless, and because the needs of those who receive them are as numerous, varied, and different as there are people in the kingdom" (270). Elder Marvin J. Ashton had this in mind when he spoke of "less-conspicuous gifts." He said:

> Taken at random, let me mention a few gifts that are not always evident or noteworthy but that are very important. . . . The gift of asking; the gift of listening; the gift of hearing and using a still, small voice; the gift of being able to weep; the gift of avoiding contention; the gift of being agreeable; the gift of avoiding vain repetition; the gift of seeking that which is righteous; the gift of not passing judgment; the gift of looking to God for guidance; the gift of being

a disciple; the gift of caring for others; the gift of being able to ponder; the gift of offering prayer; the gift of bearing a mighty testimony; and the gift of receiving the Holy Ghost. (23)

Concerning spiritual gifts, Elder Oaks has remarked: "Spiritual gifts do not come visibly, automatically, and immediately to all who have received the gift of the Holy Ghost" (69). The Prophet Joseph Smith taught that it "require[s] time and circumstances to call these gifts into operation" (*Teachings of the Prophet Joseph Smith* 246; hereafter *TPJS*). Therefore, the command of the Lord is to "seek ye earnestly the best gifts, always remembering for what they are given; For verily I say unto you, they are given for the benefit of those who love me and keep all my commandments, and him that seeketh so to do" (D&C 46:8–9).

Spiritual gifts unlock the divine potential found within the recipient and in so doing, eventually bring about perfection. Elder George Q. Cannon said:

If any of us are imperfect, it is our duty to pray for the gift that will make us perfect. Have I imperfections? I am full of them. What is my duty? To pray to God to give me the gifts that will correct these imperfections. . . . They are intended for this purpose. No man ought to say, "Oh, I cannot help this; it is my nature." He is not justified in it, for the reason that God has promised to give strength to correct these things and to give gifts that will eradicate them. . . . That is the design of God concerning His children. . . . Every defect in the human character can be corrected through the exercise of faith and pleading with the Lord for the gifts that He has said He will give unto those who believe and obey His commandments. (*Gospel Truth* 196)

Elder Oaks taught that "we should seek after spiritual gifts. They can lead us to God. They can shield us from the power of the adversary. They can compensate for our inadequacies and repair our imperfections" (72). Spiritual gifts are an important aspect of the atonement of Christ and come to us because of his mercy. Through spiritual gifts the healing of our infirmities, whether physical or spiritual, is brought about.

Our duty, then, is to do all in our own power to seek after these gifts. On another occasion, President George Q. Cannon taught:

How many of you are seeking for these gifts that God has promised to bestow? How many of you, when you bow before your Heavenly Father in your family circle or in your secret places, contend for these gifts to be bestowed upon you? How many of you ask the Father in the name of Jesus to manifest Himself to you through these powers and these gifts? Or do you go along day by day like a door turning on its hinges, without having any feeling upon the subject, without exercising any faith whatever, content to be baptized and be members of the Church and to rest there, thinking that your salvation is secure because you have done this? (*Gospel Truth* 195–96)

Elder McConkie wrote:

Is it proper to seek for spiritual gifts? . . . If spiritual gifts are interwoven with and form part of the very gospel of salvation itself, can we enjoy the fullness of that gospel without possessing the gifts that are part of it? . . . And if we are to seek the gospel, if we are to hunger and thirst after righteousness, if our whole souls must cry out for the goodness of God and his everlasting association, how can we exempt ourselves from seeking the gifts of the spirit that come from and prepare us for his presence? (369)

The reception of spiritual gifts depends upon our asking, seeking, and motive. The Lord told the Prophet Joseph Smith that spiritual gifts are given "that all may be benefited that seek or that ask of me, that ask and not for a sign that they may consume it upon their lusts" (D&C 46:9). Moroni tells us that the medium through which spiritual gifts are manifest to men is "the Spirit of Christ" (Moroni 10:17). The Spirit of Christ is the light of Christ, the same light that "giveth light to every man that cometh into the world" (D&C 84:46). Elder McConkie taught that the light of Christ is "the agency used by the Holy Ghost to manifest truth and dispense spiritual gifts to many people at one and the same time" (70).

Good Gifts Versus Evil Gifts

Moroni's fifth exhortation is a reminder of where spiritual gifts come from. "And I would exhort you, my beloved brethren, that ye remember that every good gift cometh of Christ" (Moroni 10:18). The Prophet Joseph Smith taught that spiritual gifts "are what Christ ascended into heaven to impart" (*TPJS* 245).

However, the phrase "good gift" implies that there are evil gifts. Mormon taught:

Wherefore, all things which are good cometh of God; and that which is evil cometh of the devil; for the devil is an enemy unto God, and fighteth against him continually, and inviteth and enticeth to sin, and to do that which is evil continually. But behold, that which is of God inviteth and enticeth to do good continually; wherefore, every thing which inviteth and enticeth to do good, and to love God, and to serve him, is inspired of God. (Moroni 7:12–13)

Elder McConkie has written concerning good and evil gifts in these terms: "Life itself depends upon the existence of opposites. . . . Thus, if there are good gifts that come from God, there are also evil gifts that spring forth from Satan." He then contrasted several gifts. If there is "a gift of preaching by the power of the Holy Ghost," he said, "there is a gift of intellectual persuasion, a gift of sophistry and delusion that pleases carnal men and lets them feel that they can believe what they will." Again, if there is "a gift of charity, of enjoying and possessing the pure love of Christ," then Satan offers "a gift of selfishness, of putting one's own interests first in all things." Further, "gifts of purity, of chastity, of clean thoughts, of upright living, all of which cleanse and perfect the soul of men and prepare them to be at ease in the fellowship of angels and holy beings" are opposed by "gifts of lust, of lewdness, of profane and evil speaking, of filling one's mind with carnal and evil thoughts, all of which lead to vulgar and immoral acts that prepare men for the continuing association of evil spirits in the realms ahead" (376–77).

The intent of Satan's evil gifts is to lead man away from Christ and the gifts he offers, especially the gift of eternal life. Evil gifts cause us to lose faith and abandon the path that leads to "liberty and eternal life." Those in this situation are bound by "the captivity and power of the devil." This is Satan's plan, for "he seeketh that all men might be miserable like unto himself" (2 Nephi 2:27). This is precisely the condition of the Nephites in Moroni 9 and what Moroni wants us to avoid.

Disbelief Does Away with Spiritual Gifts

Moroni's sixth exhortation comes as a warning: "Remember that [God] is the same yesterday, today, and forever, and that all these gifts of which I have spoken, which are spiritual, never will be done away, even as long as the world shall stand, only according to the unbelief of the children of men" (Moroni 10:19). It should be remembered that earlier in this chapter, Moroni taught that God works by power "according to the faith of the children of men" (v 7). When faith ceases so do spiritual gifts. Without spiritual gifts there is no perfection. Without perfection there is no possibility of exaltation. Therefore,

Moroni says, "there must be faith" (v 20). He then tells us that the proper exercise of faith produces hope, which is an expectation or anticipation of exaltation. Hope encourages the righteous to faithfully keep the commandments of God. Charity, or "the pure love of Christ" (Moroni 7:47), is the product of keeping God's commandments. Those who possess charity are "saved in the kingdom of God" (10:21). However, Moroni says, iniquity causes despair, and despair dispels hope, and without hope there is no charity (vv 21–22).

Having said this, Moroni turns his attention "unto all the ends of the earth." To them he also says, "If the day cometh that the power and gifts of God shall be done away among you, it shall be because of unbelief" (Moroni 10:24). If that happened, apostasy would rule the world. "And wo be unto the children of men if this be the case; for there shall be none that doeth good among you, no not one" (v 25). Those in this condition would "die in their sins, and they cannot be saved in the kingdom of God" (v 26). That is what happened after Moroni's death. For several hundred years the fulness of the gospel of Jesus Christ with all its spiritual gifts was not available on the earth because of unbelief.

Moroni knew that after long years of apostasy, the Book of Mormon would come forth as a witness to all the world that Jesus is the Christ. He also knew that most of the world would reject the message of the Book of Mormon. To those who reject the Book of Mormon, Moroni said, "I exhort you to remember these things; for the time speedily cometh that ye shall know that I lie not." How will we know this? Moroni continued, "For ye shall see me at the bar of God; and the Lord God will say unto you: Did I not declare my words unto you, which were written by this man, like as one crying from the dead, yea, even as one speaking out of the dust?" (Moroni 10:27). He then told them: "God shall show unto you that that which I have written is true" (v 29).

Come unto Christ and Be Perfected in Him

From the time that the Book of Mormon came forth, marking the restoration of the gospel of Jesus Christ including spiritual gifts, Satan has opposed the growth of the kingdom of God through the great and abominable church with its array of evil gifts (see 1 Nephi 14:10–17). Knowing this would happen, Moroni entreats his readers in these words: "I would exhort you that ye would come unto Christ, and lay hold upon every good gift, and touch not the evil gift, nor the unclean thing" (Moroni 10:30). Further, he paraphrases the prophet Isaiah (see Isaiah 52), and admonishes the Saints of God in the latter days to "awake, and arise from the dust, O Jerusalem; yea, and put on thy beautiful garments, O daughter of Zion; and strengthen thy stakes and enlarge thy borders forever, that thou mayest no more be confounded, that the covenants of the Eternal Father which he hath made unto thee, O house of Israel, may be fulfilled" (Moroni 10:31).

The phrase "awake, and arise from the dust" was first used in the Book of Mormon by Lehi in the context of awaking from a spiritual sleep (see 2 Nephi 1:13–14, 21–23). Moroni uses the same phrase to exhort scattered Israel in the last days to awaken from their spiritual sleep and hear the message of the restoration. The Lord uses similar language in a latter-day revelation: "For Zion must increase in beauty, and in holiness; her borders must be enlarged; her stakes must be strengthened; yea, verily I say unto you, Zion must arise and put on her beautiful garments" (D&C 82:14).

Commenting on this verse, President Harold B. Lee said:

> Zion, as used here, undoubtedly had reference to the Church. . . . To be worthy of such a sacred designation as Zion, the Church must think of itself as a bride adorned for her husband, as John the Revelator recorded when he saw in vision the Holy City where the righteous dwelled, adorned as a bride for the Lamb of God as her husband. Here is portrayed the relationship the Lord desires in his people in order to be acceptable to our Lord and Master even as a wife would adorn herself in beautiful garments for her husband.
>
> The rule by which the people of God must live in order to be worthy of acceptance in the sight of God is indicated by the text to which I have made reference. This people must increase in beauty before the world; have an inward loveliness which may be observed by mankind as a reflection in holiness and in those inherent qualities of sanctity. The borders of Zion, where the righteous and pure in heart may dwell, must now begin to be enlarged. The stakes of Zion must be strengthened. All this so that Zion may arise and shine by becoming increasingly diligent in carrying out the plan of salvation throughout the world. (3)

How can Zion "put on [her] beautiful garments" and "increase in beauty"? The answer can be found in the conclusion of Moroni's final exhortation:

> Yea, come unto Christ, and be perfected in him, and deny yourselves of all ungodliness; and if ye shall deny yourselves of all ungodliness, and love God

with all your might, mind and strength, then is his grace sufficient for you, that by his grace ye may be perfect in Christ; and if by the grace of God ye are perfect in Christ, ye can in nowise deny the power of God. And again, if ye by the grace of God are perfect in Christ, and deny not his power, then are ye sanctified in Christ by the grace of God, through the shedding of the blood of Christ, which is in the covenant of the Father unto the remission of your sins, that ye become holy, without spot. (Moroni 10:32–33)

Zion will become beautiful in the sight of the Lord when she comes unto Christ and is perfected in him. Only through Christ can we become spiritually and physically complete.

Moroni encouraged his readers to "deny yourselves of all ungodliness" (Moroni 10:32). President Benson taught, "To deny oneself of all ungodliness is to come to Christ by ordinances and covenants to repent of any sins which prevent the Spirit of the Lord from taking precedence in our lives" ("This is a Day of Sacrifice" 32). Those who come unto Christ obtain his saving grace and "are perfect in Christ." In other words, because of their complete devotion to God's work and glory, they have become at-one with Christ. Through his atonement, their sins have been remitted and their weaknesses have been made strengths. Those who have become "perfect in Christ" are "sanctified in Christ by the grace of God." To be sanctified is to be purified, to be made free from the stain and effects of sin. Those who attain this condition are "holy, without spot" (Moroni 10:31, 33). It is as if they had never committed sin. These are they who have put on their "beautiful garments" (v 31; see also Isaiah 52:1).

Summary

A dominant theme that permeates the Book of Mormon is that we are "free to choose liberty and eternal life, through the great Mediator of all men, or to choose captivity and death, according to the captivity and power of the devil" (2 Nephi 2:27). This theme is illustrated over and over again throughout the Book of Mormon. Moroni chapters 9–10, together, form a perfect conclusion both to the Book of Mormon and this theme. Chapter 9 illustrates the debilitating power Satan has over those who "choose captivity and death." On the other hand, the eight exhortations found in chapter 10 teach how God's mercy can be extended to us through his grace. We must come unto Christ through the Book of Mormon and know that he is. Then, after receiving the Gift of the Holy Ghost, we must seek for spiritual gifts that enable us and perfect our weaknesses. Having been made perfect in Christ, we will be sanctified by him. Thus, unlike the Nephites whom Mormon could not recommend unto God, those of us who come unto Christ will stand approved of God and worthy to come into his presence.

BIBLIOGRAPHY

Ashton, Marvin J. "There are Many Gifts." *Ensign* (Nov 1987) 17:20–23; also in *Conference Report* (Oct 1987) 23–26.

Benson, Ezra Taft. "The Book of Mormon and the Doctrine and Covenants." *Ensign* (May 1987) 17:83–85; also in *Conference Report* (Apr 1987) 104–08.

———. "This is a Day of Sacrifice." *Ensign* (May 1979) 9:32–34; also in *Conference Report* (Apr 1979) 45–48.

Gospel Truth: Discourse and Writings of President George Q. Cannon. 2 Vols. Ed. Jerreld L. Newquist. Salt Lake City: Deseret Book, 1974.

Lee, Harold B. "Strengthen the Stakes of Zion." *Ensign* (Jul 1973) 3:1–6.

Lund, Gerald N. "An Anti–Christ in the Book of Mormon—The Face May be Strange, but the Voice is Familiar." *The Book of Mormon: Alma, the Testimony of the Word*. Eds. Monte S. Nyman and Charles D. Tate, Jr. Provo, UT: Religious Studies Center, Brigham Young Univ, 1992. 107–28.

McConkie, Bruce R. *A New Witness for the Articles of Faith*. Salt Lake City: Deseret Book, 1985.

Oaks, Dallin H. "Spiritual Gifts." *Ensign* (Sep 1986) 16:68–72.

Teachings of the Prophet Joseph Smith. Comp. Joseph Fielding Smith. Salt Lake City: Deseret Book, 1976.

Zion Gained and Lost: Fourth Nephi as the Quintessential Model

22

Andrew C. Skinner

*T*he Book of Mormon makes it abundantly clear that God cares about establishing Zion in the last days. Through an angel, the Lord said to Nephi:

> And blessed are they who shall seek to bring forth my Zion at that day, for they shall have the gift and the power of the Holy Ghost; and if they endure unto the end they shall be lifted up at the last day, and shall be saved in the everlasting kingdom of the Lamb; and whoso shall publish peace, yea, tidings of great joy, how beautiful upon the mountains shall they be. (1 Nephi 13:37)

Perhaps even more significant than simply telling us that the Lord wants to establish Zion in the last days, the Book of Mormon also provides us in 4 Nephi with an impressive model which shows *how* Zion functions, and what benefits derive from living a Zion-like existence. As one examines the scriptural accounts which trace the history of efforts to establish Zion, none are as poignant and succinct, yet so detailed, as that in 4 Nephi. All of the components and principles of a Zion society described in various other passages of the standard works are discernible together in 4 Nephi.

Principles of Zion

Though the concept of Zion is multifaceted, God has decreed that the essential ingredients of a Zion society are the premier principles of purity, unity, and equality. In 1833 God said to Joseph Smith

Andrew C. Skinner is assistant professor of Ancient Scripture at Brigham Young University.

at Kirtland, "Let Zion rejoice, for this is Zion—THE PURE IN HEART; therefore, let Zion rejoice, while all the wicked shall mourn" (D&C 97:21).

In 1834 the Lord gave more specific instruction about the other characteristics which must be found among the pure in heart in order for a Zion society to exist as a people in a place. In essence, these characteristics are all extensions of the godly attribute of unity.

> But behold, [my people] have not learned to be obedient to the things which I required at their hands, but are full of all manner of evil, and do not impart of their substance, as becometh saints, to the poor and afflicted among them; And are not *united* according to the union required by the law of the celestial kingdom; And Zion cannot be built up unless it is by the principles of the law of the celestial kingdom; otherwise I cannot receive her unto myself. (D&C 105:3–5; emphasis added)

From this passage four things are apparent. One, a Zion society requires economic unity and material equality among its citizens. Elsewhere the Lord said, "For if ye are not equal in earthly things ye cannot be equal in obtaining heavenly things" (D&C 78:6). Two, unity is the foundational principle of celestial law which governs all aspects of a Zion society. The Lord told the Saints on another occasion that if they were not unified, if they were not one in purpose and desire just as he himself is one with his Father, then they (the Saints) were not his (D&C 38:27). Three, the concept of earthly Zion rests on the premise that there is a celestial prototype—"a heavenly society comprised of exalted beings who [live] in the presence of God" (Andrus 26). Zion on earth is to be patterned after that celestial society which thrives in God's literal presence. The fourth notion we derive from this passage follows naturally: the ultimate destiny of a Zion society is to be taken into the presence of the Lord. This seems to be the design and purpose of the real maker and governor of every Zion community, who is God! "And Zion cannot be built up unless it is by the principles of the law of the celestial kingdom; otherwise I cannot receive her unto myself" (D&C 105:5).

This immediately recalls an ancient group of people who became Saints by molding their lives to conform with the principles of Zion and were taken unto the Lord, or translated. We know them as the inhabitants of the city of Enoch, and their achievement is recounted to us in Moses 7:18–21:

And the Lord called his people Zion, because they were of one heart and one mind, and dwelt in righteousness; and there was no poor among them. And Enoch continued his preaching in righteousness unto the people of God. And it came to pass in his days, that he built a city that was called the City of Holiness, even Zion. And it came to pass that Enoch talked with the Lord; and he said unto the Lord: Surely Zion shall dwell in safety forever. But the Lord said unto Enoch: Zion have I blessed, but the residue of the people have I cursed. And it came to pass that the Lord showed unto Enoch all the inhabitants of the earth; and he beheld, and lo, Zion, in process of time, was taken up into heaven. And the Lord said unto Enoch: Behold mine abode forever.

These verses also teach profound truths that add significantly to our understanding of Zion. First, the same principles of purity of heart as well as economic, social, and spiritual unity, which are required by the Lord of the Saints of Zion in the present dispensation, operated anciently among the populace of Enoch's Zion. Second, there is a direct correlation between any society's purity and unity, and God's association with that society. Third, attempts to establish Zion did not begin in Joseph Smith's day, the dispensation of the fulness of times. God has cared about the establishment of Zion throughout the history of our world.

Other Zion Societies

Significant evidence indicates that efforts were put forth to build Zion societies in every gospel dispensation where the fulness of the priesthood operated. President Marion G. Romney taught that "whenever the Lord has had a people who accept and live the gospel, He has established the united order" (92).

Though Enoch's people constitute the best-known example of a Zion society, there were others in ancient times which are just as impressive, and perhaps even more dramatic. Alma teaches that Melchizedek, to whom Abraham submitted himself and paid tithes, was king over the land of Salem (Alma 13:15, 17). Amazingly, all his people were once great sinners being "strong in iniquity and abomination . . . [and] full of all manner of wickedness" (v 17). But because of the efforts of Melchizedek, who preached repentance unto them, they humbled themselves, participated in Melchizedek Priesthood ordinances and received a remission of their sins "that they might enter into the rest of the Lord" (Alma 13:16).

Through the Prophet Joseph Smith we know that the "rest of the Lord" is nothing less than "the fulness of his glory" (D&C 84:24). And also through him we know that Melchizedek succeeded in establishing a Zion society and his people in obtaining heaven while in mortality; they were translated and taken from the earth, as were all people in ancient times who demonstrated supreme faith. From Joseph Smith's inspired translation of Genesis we read:

> Now Melchizedek was a man of faith, who wrought righteousness . . .
> And thus, having been approved of God, he was ordained an high priest after the order of the covenant which God made with Enoch. . . .
> For God having sworn unto Enoch and unto his seed with an oath by himself; that every one being ordained after this order and calling should have power, by faith, to break mountains, to divide the seas . . .
> To put at defiance the armies of nations, to divide the earth, to break every band, to stand in the presence of God . . . and this by the will of the Son of God which was from before the foundation of the world.
> And men having this faith, coming up unto this order of God, were translated and taken up into heaven.
> And now, Melchizedek was a priest of this order; therefore he obtained peace in Salem, and was called the Prince of Peace.
> And his people wrought righteousness, and obtained heaven, and sought for the city of Enoch which God had before taken, having reserved it unto the latter days, or the end of the world. (JST Gen 14:26–27, 30–34)

A careful reading of this passage in conjunction with Alma 13 reveals that the kind of faith which allowed the ancient Saints to arrive at a point whereby they could be translated was a faith rooted in the ordinances of the Melchizedek Priesthood which leads to Jesus Christ. Note again the wording of the Joseph Smith Translation: "everyone being ordained after this order and calling should have faith, to . . . stand in the presence of God . . . and this by the will of the Son of God" (JST Gen 14:30). In this same vein, remember what Alma says about the ordinances practiced among the people of Melchizedek's day:

> Now these ordinances were given after this manner, that thereby the people might look forward on the Son of God, it being a type of his order, or it being his order, and this that they might look forward to him for a remission of their sins, that they might enter into the rest of the Lord. (Alma 13:16)

Thus, another essential component of a Zion society is the operation of the Melchizedek Priesthood.

It seems significant that we possess no record of the establishment of a Zion society among the Israelites living under the Aaronic priesthood-based Mosaic law from the time of Moses down to Jesus Christ. But when the post-resurrection Church became fully functioning in the days of the Apostles, a clear and repeated picture of the social and economic structure of the Church was revealed and it was based on the unmistakable principles of the law of the celestial kingdom or, in other words, a Zion society. In the fourth chapter of Acts, Luke describes the situation this way:

> And the multitude of them that believed were of one heart and of one soul: neither said any of them that ought of the things which he possessed was his own; but they had all things in common. And with great power gave the apostles witness of the resurrection of the Lord Jesus: and great grace was upon them all. Neither was there any among them that lacked: for as many as were possessors of lands or houses sold them, and brought the prices of the things that were sold, And laid them down at the apostles feet: and distribution was made unto every man according as he had need. (vv 32–35)

There is a similarity between this account and the one found in the book of Moses which explicitly describes the establishment of Enoch's Zion. But the Zion community described in Acts was short-lived due to apostasy, as well as basic selfishness and dishonesty. The actions of Ananias and Sapphira (Acts 5:1–11) were most likely included in Luke's record immediately following his description of the early church's Zion-like organization for two reasons: first, to demonstrate the kind of endemic dishonesty which destroyed that Zion society, and, second, to show the special penalty attached to the willful breaking of the covenant of consecration or the order of Zion.

Ananias and Sapphira held back part of that which they had covenanted to consecrate to God. And when they lied about it, they were struck dead. Modern revelation sheds light on this severe punishment for breaking the law of consecration. Speaking of the establishment of Zion in Joseph Smith's day, the Lord said:

> For Zion must increase in beauty, and in holiness. . . .
> Therefore, I give unto you this commandment, that ye bind yourselves by this covenant, and it shall be done according to the laws of the Lord. . . .
> And you are to be equal, or in other words, you are to have equal claims on the properties, . . . every man according to his wants and his needs, inasmuch as his wants are just—

> And all this for the benefit of the church of the living God, that every man may improve upon his talent, that every man may gain other talents, yea, even an hundred fold, to be cast into the Lord's storehouse, to become the common property of the whole church. . . .
>
> And the soul that sins against this covenant, and hardeneth his heart against it, shall be dealt with according to the laws of my church, and shall be delivered over to the buffetings of Satan until the day of redemption. (D&C 82:14–21)

Imitations of Zion

History shows that selfishness, greed, pride, and dishonesty have always been great obstacles in the establishment of any utopian society. However, the existence of these features of our fallen world have also been great motivators among idealists, as well as the oppressed, to establish a better way of life, governed by higher ideals. The "pure in heart" seek not for utopia but for a society founded on celestial principles under the watchful care of God.

Even some groups who did not possess the Melchizedek Priesthood recognized the waywardness of Jerusalem-centered Judaism during the Intertestamental Period. These groups attempted to set up reformed and unified communities, and to enact and live by those same kinds of principles which were established in true Zion societies as revealed in the scriptures.

The Essenes of Qumran were such a sect. They apparently withdrew from what they perceived to be a thoroughly corrupt Judaism of their day and set up a covenant community by the Dead Sea. Their preserved library is known to us as the Dead Sea Scrolls. From the document known variously as the "Manual of Discipline," the "Community Rule," or the "Serek Scroll" (which discusses regulations governing initiation into the sect as well as the community's organization and discipline) we read of their communal ideals, again in language paralleling truths found in the book of Moses, the Doctrine and Covenants, and the Acts of the Apostles.

> Everyone who wishes to join the community must pledge himself to respect God and man; to live according to the communal rule; to seek God . . . to bring into a bond of mutual love all who have declared their willingness to carry out the statutes of God; to join the formal community of God; to walk blamelessly before Him in conformity with all that has been revealed. . . .
>
> All who declare their willingness to serve God's truth must bring all of their mind, all of their strength, and all of their wealth into the community

of God, so that their minds may be purified by the truth of His precepts, their strength controlled by His perfect ways, and their wealth disposed in accordance with His just design. (Gaster 44)

Ultimately the Qumran community was destroyed, but archaeological evidence indicates that it was successful for two centuries.

4 Nephi

Of all the descriptions of Zion found in holy writ, none is as singularly instructive as the one presented in 4 Nephi. It not only teaches us about the social and religious characteristics of Zion in a more detailed way than other descriptions, but also illuminates in unmistakable terms the root causes of the demise of a Zion society.

The Zion society of 4 Nephi was established on the American continent sometime between AD 34 and 36. Discipleship in Christ was *the* foundation of this Zion. All social progress and societal goodness centered in Jesus Christ, whose visit to this continent after his resurrection established an age of unadulterated righteousness lasting about 165 years. Every individual was wholly converted to the Savior—to his ideas and exemplary behavior (4 Nephi 1:2). After repenting, every person was prepared to participate in the life-giving and renewing ordinances available through the Melchizedek Priesthood, especially the Gift of the Holy Ghost (v 1).

A natural by-product of the constant influence and power of the Holy Ghost was the desire of all the people to deal justly and fairly with each other. Therefore, all the people had all things in common and all their acts conformed to the pattern of the Savior's life. In sum, complete conversion to the Lord eliminated contention, produced unselfish self-regulation, and resulted in economic and political equality and freedom.

The scriptural phrase "had all things in common" is undoubtedly used to characterize those who lived the law of consecration (see Acts 4:32; 2:44; 3 Nephi 26:19; 4 Nephi 1:3). As Joseph Smith taught, such a system was *not* a type of Christian communism (*History of the Church* 6:37–38; hereafter *HC*). Every covenant member of this order (all things in common) held some private property and had access to consecrated surpluses according to justified "wants" and "needs" (D&C 82:17–18).

The civil structure described in 4 Nephi displayed a total absence of destructive or divisive elements, including poverty, selfishness, and social Darwinism (survival of the fittest), which resulted in a classlessness that eliminated crime and allowed society's resources to be applied to and focused on urban renewal.

> And the Lord did prosper them exceedingly in the land; yea, insomuch that they did build cities again where there had been cities burned. Yea, even that great city Zarahemla did they cause to be built again. . . . And there were no envyings, nor strifes, nor tumults, nor whoredoms, nor lyings, nor murders, nor any manner of lasciviousness; and surely there could not be a happier people among all the people who had been created by the hand of God. There were no robbers, nor murderers, neither were there Lamanites, nor any manner of -ites; but they were in one, the children of Christ, and heirs to the kingdom of God. (4 Nephi 1:7–8, 16–17)

Only true conversion to Christ and strict adherence to his example and teachings can bring significant and lasting renewal and reconstruction. Only true conversion to Christ can do more than offer mere stop-gap measures to solve problems. President Ezra Taft Benson has said:

> The Lord works from the inside out. The world works from the outside in. The world would take people out of the slums. Christ takes the slums out of people, and then they take themselves out of the slums. The world would mold men by changing their environment. Christ changes men, who then change their environment. The world would shape human behavior, but Christ can change human nature. ("Born of God" 6)

Certainly, the pattern of events described in 4 Nephi bears this out.

One of the attendant developments of socio-economic reform, civic rejuvenation, and urban renewal is the increased health, strength, and vigor of a population. The people of Nephi enjoyed this blessing: "And now, behold, it came to pass that the people of Nephi did wax strong, and did multiply exceedingly fast, and became an exceedingly fair and delightsome people" (4 Nephi 1:10).

In the Christ-centered Zion society of 4 Nephi, the people witnessed a rich and astounding outpouring of miracles, including those which symbolized the mortal Messiah's absolute power over life and death—raising the dead. But, again, indicative of the Christ-centered nature of this religious society, we are told that no miracles were done "save it were in the name of Jesus" (4 Nephi 1:5).

A striking feature of Mormon's description of Zion in 4 Nephi is his emphasis on the total lack of contention in the land, which he mentions in verses 2, 13, 15, and 18. This surely must be due to the complete unity of a civilization in which there were neither Nephites, Lamanites, nor any other -ites, but all were one in Christ (4 Nephi 1:17) because the love of God dwelt in their hearts (v 15). And, like other Zion societies of bygone eras, the people were heirs to the kingdom of God (v 17).

The Zion society described in 4 Nephi was a literal fulfillment of the much repeated prophetic teaching throughout the Book of Mormon that if people would keep God's commandments they would prosper in the land. As Mormon says of the people living during the post-resurrection era of 4 Nephi, "For the Lord did bless them in all their doings" (v 18).

Apostasy

The power and influence of the Savior's literal, physical presence among the Nephites was so strong that they lived the principles of Zion well into the second generation after Christ's visit. But sometime before AD 194 (4 Nephi 1:21) social and religious divisions reappeared in the society and drew away part of the people. Even though it was only a small percentage of the population, its seriousness should not be underestimated; Mormon is clear as to its cause: "The people . . . had *revolted* from the Church and taken upon them the name of Lamanites; therefore there began to be Lamanites again in the land" (4 Nephi 1:20; emphasis added).

This is the classic definition of apostasy from the original Greek term *apostasia*, literally "to stand apart from," "to rebel," or "to revolt." This is the kind of apostasy witnessed in the New Testament many years after the Savior visited his disciples of the early Church in the *Old* World after his resurrection.

The Apostle Paul's Old World prophecy of the Great Apostasy beginning in the middle of the first century AD surely applies to the people of 4 Nephi as Mormon saw them. Paul said: "For I know this, that after my departing shall grievous wolves enter in among you, not sparing the flock. Also of your own selves shall men arise, speaking perverse things, to draw away disciples after them" (Acts 20:29–30).

The motives of these predicted apostates may be associated with the aims and goals of practicing of priestcraft as described in 2 Nephi 26:29: "Priestcrafts are that men preach and set themselves up for a light unto the world, that they may get gain and praise of the world; *but they seek not the welfare of Zion*" (emphasis added). As it was in the Old World so it went in the New World. Priestcraft did reappear:

> Nevertheless, the people did harden their hearts, for they were led by many priests and false prophets to build up many churches, and to do all manner of iniquity. And they did smite upon the people of Jesus; but the people of Jesus did not smite again. And thus they did dwindle in unbelief and wickedness, from year to year, even until two hundred and thirty years had passed away. (4 Nephi 1:34)

Mormon explicitly links apostasy and priestcraft with two other evils profoundly detrimental to the maintenance of a Zion society. These are pride and social stratification, which began to appear in AD 201—less than a decade after the initial cracks in the solidarity of the society were first noted by Mormon. The prosperity of the people of Nephi, owing to their faith in Christ, had produced great wealth among the populace. Unfortunately, this, in turn, led to pride and materialism as the people forgot the source of their strength. The result was that "from that time forth they did have their goods and their substance no more in common among them" (4 Nephi 1:25).

Here the insidious nature of pride is laid bare, and its destructive effects on Zion seen in an unmistakable way. Pride destroys unity and promotes selfishness. As President Benson quoting C. S. Lewis said, "Pride gets no pleasure out of having something, only out of having more of it than the next man" ("Cleansing the Inner Vessel" 7). Pride seeks to create divisions among people purely for the sake of self-interest, so that some may place themselves above others and exploit them. President Benson also stated, "It was essentially the sin of pride that kept us from establishing Zion in the days of the Prophet Joseph Smith. It was the same sin of pride that brought consecration to an end among the Nephites. Pride is the great stumbling block to Zion" ("Beware of Pride" 7). Pride was the cause of social stratification among the people of 4 Nephi. The book of Helaman describes how it came about, which is the same process seen in an earlier period of Nephite history.

> For behold, the Lord had blessed them so long with the riches of the world that they had not been stirred up to anger, to wars, nor to bloodshed; therefore they began to set their hearts upon their riches; yea, they began to seek to get gain that they might be lifted up one above another. (Hel 6:17)

Mormon is also quick to implicate social stratification as a goal of priestcraft as well as a tool of the devil: "And they began to be divided into classes; and they began to build up churches unto themselves *to get gain*, and began to deny the true church of Christ" (4 Nephi 1:26; emphasis added).

Greater and greater dissent from the true church resulted in sacred things (especially the ordinances of salvation) being trifled with (4 Nephi 1:27). By AD 210 this provided Satan with the chance to get greater hold on the hearts of the people (v 28). The true followers of Christ suffered increasing persecution (vv 29–33) because those in open rebellion against God "were taught to hate the children of God" (v 39). The downward slide of this civilization began to pick up momentum. The division of society into classes resulted in irreparable tears in the social fabric. In the 231st year groupings of people began to appear, what Mormon calls the "great division among the people" (v 35). These divisions further fragmented society and accentuated the loss of the celestial condition of unity.

The ultimate result of the rebellion which Satan instigated among the people who once lived in a pure and idyllic society was the formation of those secret combinations which Mormon had noted earlier (Hel 2:13) would prove to be the overthrow and entire destruction of the people of Nephi: "And it came to pass that the wicked part of the people began again to build up the secret oaths and combinations of Gadianton" (4 Nephi 1:42).

Without question Satan was at the very heart of the secret combinations which destroyed once and for all, without hope of recovery, the Zion society of the Nephites. He alone inspires the hearts of wicked men to secretly combine against righteousness (Hel 6:26). And he concocts and administers the oaths and covenants of his kingdom. However, Satan could not have made any inroads without the initial overtures of the people themselves. Joseph Smith taught that "the moment we *revolt* at anything which comes from God, the devil takes power" (*Teachings of the Prophet Joseph Smith* 181; emphasis added; hereafter *TPJS*). The people of 4 Nephi, guilty of this revolt or rebellion, consciously rejected light and truth.

Considering their once blessed condition, and given the greatness of the many witnesses and miracles they enjoyed, the people of
4 Nephi could have remained righteous. Once they revolted, and
Satan took power, the prophetic words of Mormon were fulfilled:

> And thus we can plainly discern, that after a people have been once enlightened
> by the Spirit of God, and have had great knowledge of things pertaining to
> righteousness, and then have fallen away into sin and transgression, they
> become more hardened, and thus their state becomes worse than though they
> had never known these things. (Alma 24:30)

As the 300th year since Christ's birth passed away on the American
continent, Satan's power grew in such strength and came to dominate
the population so completely that "both the people of Nephi and the
Lamanites [became] exceedingly wicked one like unto another"
(4 Nephi 1:45).

Viewing the collapse of this Zion society from a panoramic
perspective, as Mormon was able to do, he shows us that the decline
was progressive. It happened a step at a time, with each successive
step further destroying the purity, unity, and equality of the people.
Over a 100 year period, beginning gradually as a small rebellion
against truth and light around AD 194, the decline of the people
culminated in total wickedness in AD 300. The capstone of this
process was the reappearance of secret combinations administered by
Satan himself. The panoramic perspective of the destruction of Zion
in America validates and demonstrates the great truth declared by the
prophet Nephi at the beginning of the Book of Mormon:

> For behold, at that day shall he rage in the hearts of the children of men, and
> stir them up to anger against that which is good. And others will he pacify, and
> lull them away into carnal security, that they will say: All is well in Zion; yea,
> Zion prospereth, all is well—and thus the devil cheateth their souls, and leadeth
> them away carefully down to hell. (2 Nephi 28:20–21)

Conclusion

The description of Zion in 4 Nephi is the greatest and most
detailed model of those conditions which must exist in order for Zion
to be established. Sadly, it is also the quintessential model which
portrays those events that bring about the dissolution of a Zion society.
But in this there is a great blessing because, as the first Nephi said

long ago, if we liken all scriptures unto ourselves and our circumstances it will be for our profit and learning (1 Nephi 19:23).

In these last days, God cares about and knows the benefits derived from the establishment of Zion. The tenth article of faith reaffirms our belief that Zion will again be built on the American continent. The Prophet Joseph Smith stated that "we ought to have the building up of Zion as our greatest object" (*TPJS* 160). In 1829, before the Church was organized, the Lord gave identical counsel to Joseph Smith, Oliver Cowdery, Hyrum Smith, Joseph Knight, and David Whitmer: "Keep my commandments, and seek to bring forth and establish the cause of Zion" (D&C 6:6; 11:6; 12:6; 14:6).

The scriptures teach that Zion can be built only by following the principles described in 4 Nephi, and by making conscious, correct choices every day. President Spencer W. Kimball said that "creating Zion commences in the heart of each person" (4). He further noted:

> Zion can be built up only among those who are the pure in heart—not a people torn by covetousness or greed, but a pure and selfless people, not a people who are pure in appearance, rather a people who are pure in heart. Zion is to be in the world and not of the world, not dulled by a sense of carnal security, nor paralyzed by materialism. . . . We must sacrifice whatever is required by the Lord. We begin by offering a "broken heart and a contrite spirit." We follow this by giving our best effort in our assigned fields of labor and in our callings. We learn our duty and execute it fully. Finally we consecrate our time, talents, and means as called upon by our file leaders and as prompted by the whisperings of the Spirit. (4–5)

I believe that God has given us 4 Nephi as a blueprint from which to learn how to be a Zion people. If we study its messages carefully, we can avoid the same tragic mistakes its people made.

BIBLIOGRAPHY

Andrus, Hyrum L. *Doctrines of the Kingdom.* Salt Lake City: Bookcraft, 1973.

Benson, Ezra Taft. "Beware of Pride." *Ensign* (May 1989) 19:4–7; also in *Conference Report* (Apr 1989) 3–7.

———. "Born of God." *Ensign* (Nov 1985) 15:5–7; also in *Conference Report* (Oct 1985) 4–6.

———. "Cleansing the Inner Vessel." *Ensign* (May 1986) 16:4–7; also in *Conference Report* (Apr 1986) 3–6.

Gaster, Theodor H. *The Dead Sea Scriptures*. 3rd ed. Garden City, NY: Anchor Books, 1976.

History of the Church. 7 vols. Salt Lake City: Deseret Book, 1978.

Kimball, Spencer W. "Becoming the Pure in Heart." *Ensign* (Mar 1985) 15:3–5.

Romney, Marion G. "The Purpose of Church Welfare Services." *Ensign* (May 1977) 7:92–95; also in *Conference Report* (Apr 1977) 117–21.

Teachings of the Prophet Joseph Smith. Comp. Joseph Fielding Smith. Salt Lake City: Deseret Book, 1970.

Jared and His Brother   23

Thomas R. Valletta

*T*he Book of Mormon chronicle of Jared and his brother is the story of us all in our quest for the eternal land of promise. The first six chapters of Ether typify the "great plan of the Eternal God" (Alma 34:9) for all humankind. Mormon desired to include the Jaredite record in the Book of Mormon because "it gave them much knowledge in which they did rejoice . . . [and] it is expedient that all people should know the things which are written in this account" (Mosiah 28:18–19). Moroni's careful abridgment of Ether's record concerning Jared and his brother is much more than a mere synopsis of dark and dusty history. It is also more than a wonderfully crafted narrative of the travels and travails of one of earth's finest Saints. It is inspired history and record keeping at its best.

The story of Jared and his brother is cut from the same pattern as the accounts of the fall of Adam and Eve and their subsequent search for truth, Noah's escape from a decadent civilization and voyage to the top of Mt. Ararat, the Israelites' exodus from their bondage in Egypt and their eventual crossing of the Jordan into the land of milk and honey, as well as Lehi's deliverance from a dark and dying Jerusalem to a new world of promise. The chronicle of Jared and his brother, like these other accounts, reveals a pattern and type testifying of Jesus Christ and the plan of salvation.

Types Defined

Like the writings of Isaiah, we should study these scriptures diligently, for the things contained therein both "have been and shall be" (3 Nephi 23:1–3). Modern scripture declares that "all things have

Thomas R. Valletta is an institute instructor in Ogden, Utah.

their likeness, and all things are created and made to bear record" of Jesus Christ and the eternal plan of salvation (Moses 6:63). The Book of Mormon emphatically proclaims that "all things which have been given of God from the beginning of the world, unto man, are the typifying of [Jesus Christ]" (2 Nephi 11:4; compare Mosiah 3:15; 13:10, 31; Alma 13:16; 25:15; 33:19; 37:45). Types have been defined as "divinely established models or prerepresentations of corresponding realities" (Eichrodt 225). Grounded in "real people and real events," types "constitute a significant system of intelligible coordinates in the gradual unfolding of God's historical design" (Frye 84; Tate 247). While the events recorded in Ether chapters 1–6 reflect a true and historical account of the Jaredites, their relevance to us may be as a model or pattern of what we must accomplish in the Lord's plan of salvation. Table 1 overviews some of the many possible parallels between the Jaredite exodus and the eternal plan of redemption. A closer examination of the Jaredite experience helps us understand how their story is also our story.

Table 1
The Jaredite Exodus: A Type of the Plan

Exodus of the Jaredites	Eternal Plan of Redemption
The Tower of Babel (Ether 1:33)	Rebellion, A Fallen World, and a Scattering
Jared (To Go Down)	To Go Down Into the Lone and Dreary World
The Brother of Jared	A Deliverer is Prepared
Seeking and Receiving Blessings from God	A New and Everlasting Covenant
Valley of Nimrod and the Wilderness (Ether 2:1–5)	Continually Tested; Land of Rebellion
Directed by God in a Cloud (Ether 2:4–5, 14)	Gift of the Holy Ghost
Crossing Many Waters (Ether 2:6)	Baptism and ordinances

Exodus of the Jaredites	Eternal Plan of Redemption
Brother of Jared Chastened by the Lord (Ether 2:14)	The Lord Chastens Those He Loves
Building the Barges (Ether 2:6, 16)	Building a House of God
Questions of Air and Light (Ether 2:19–23)	Revelation, Agency, and Action
The Shining Stones (Ether 3:1–4; 6:2–3)	The Word and the Light of Christ
Experience on Mt. Shelem (Ether 3)	Experience in the Temple
The Crossing (Ether 6:4–10)	Trials of Life; Putting Off the Natural Man
The Promised Land (Ether 6:11–12; 2:7–11)	Eternal Promised Land

The Tower of Babel

Moroni's record of the Jaredites begins when "Jared came forth with his brother and their families, with some others and their families, from the great tower, at the time the Lord confounded the language of the people, and swore in his wrath that they should be scattered upon all the face of the earth" (Ether 1:33). The tower of Babel, described further in Genesis 11, is considered by many scholars to be a Babylonian temple (Jacobsen 334). This false temple was an attempt by an ambitious and wicked people to imitate true temple worship (Nibley, *Lehi in the Desert/The World of the Jaredites* 154–68; hereafter *Lehi*; Thomas 388–98). In "Babylonian or Akkadian the meaning [of Babel] was 'gate of God'" (Donaldson 60). Traditionally thought to be inspired by Nimrod, whose "name is for the Jews at all times the very symbol of rebellion against God and of usurped authority" (Nibley, *Lehi* 165), the focus of these beguiled followers was to "reach unto heaven . . . [and] make us a name, lest we be scattered abroad upon the face of the whole earth" (Gen 11:4). But what kind of a name might an apostate covet, hoping to avoid being scattered abroad? The biblical meaning of making a name is to give a reputation, fame, or monument (see Gen 12:2). In contrast, the name of Him who would perform the Atonement, which is the reuniting and making whole again of all that was effected by the fall of Adam, is Christ. Centuries later, a prophet-king, speaking from a true temple, declared "that there shall be no other name given nor any other way nor means whereby salvation can come unto the children of men, only in and through the name of Christ, the Lord Omnipotent" (Mosiah 3:17). Elder Dallin H. Oaks, in a general conference address, noted the connection between holy temples and receiving "the name of Jesus Christ." Citing several scriptural examples of the "temple as a house for 'the name' of the Lord God of Israel," Elder Oaks referred to "the inspired dedicatory prayer of the Kirtland Temple, [when] the Prophet Joseph Smith asked the Lord for a blessing upon 'thy people upon whom thy name shall be put in this house' (D&C 109:26)." He concluded the following:

> All of these references to ancient and modern temples as houses for "the name" of the Lord obviously involve something far more significant than a mere inscription of his sacred name on the structure. The scriptures speak of the Lord's putting his name in a temple because he gives authority for his name to be used in the sacred ordinances of that house. That is the meaning of the Prophet's reference to the Lord's putting his name upon his people in that holy house. (Oaks 81)

The rebellion at the tower of Babel was abruptly interrupted when the Lord intervened, driving them out of the land and scattering them abroad (Ether 1:38; Gen 11:9). People were scattered and separated from each other as well as from God (eg, Ether 1:33; Gen 9:19; 49:7; Matt 9:36). Symbolically this is comparable to Lehi's situation in the beginning of his dream of the tree of life. Jared and his brother found themselves in what Lehi described as "a dark and dreary waste," from which the only escape was through an arduous and prayerful journey (see 1 Nephi 8:7–8). The setting for the story of Jared and his brother is "the familiar one of the righteous man who leads his people out of a doomed and wicked world. There is nothing original in that: it is also the story of Noah, Enoch, Abraham, Moses, 'The Church in the Wilderness,' and, for that matter, the restored Church" (Nibley, Lehi 156). Finding ourselves "in a dark and dreary waste," we too must find our way to the light by following Jesus Christ.

Jared and His Brother

Jared, whose name in Hebrew means "to go down," was one of those sent forth when the tower fell. Like Adam and many before and many after, Jared embarked on a new beginning. He was not alone in his journey. Jared had a special though unnamed brother. Although the Prophet Joseph Smith apparently revealed this great prophet's name to be Mahonri Moriancumer, the text of Ether does not record his name. Commentators have suggested many possible reasons for this phenomenon (see Ludlow 310), but it just may be that the book of Ether employs the phrase "the brother of Jared" as a type for Jesus Christ. The exclusion of the name draws attention to the fact that Jared was not left alone, but had a very special brother who intervened in his and his family's behalf. All of us have such a brother in Jesus Christ, whose mission is to give us immortality and help us all gain eternal life (Moses 1:39).

It should not be surprising that the brother of Jared could be a type of Jesus Christ, as all of God's prophets typify Jesus Christ (J. McConkie, *Gospel Symbolism* 146–72). In the case of the brother of Jared, there are many similarities between the recorded facts of his life and events in the life of Jesus Christ. Table 2 summarizes some of the possible comparisons.

Table 2

The Brother of Jared as a Type of Jesus Christ

The Brother of Jared	Jesus Christ
Large and mighty man, highly favored of the Lord (Ether 1:34).	"Jesus increased in wisdom and stature, and in favor with God and man" (Luke 2:52).
Intermediary for his people (Ether 1:34–39).	One mediator between God and men, the man Christ Jesus (1 Tim 2:5).
Commanded to gather his people, flocks, and seeds (Ether 1:40–43).	How often would I have gathered thy children together (Luke 13:34).
Commanded to lead his people in their trek (Ether 2:1–13).	All are commanded to follow Jesus Christ (eg, Matt 4:19; 10:38).

The Brother of Jared	Jesus Christ
Visited by the Lord in a cloud (Ether 2:4–5; 14).	Jesus visited by Father in cloud (Matt 17:5; Mark 9:7; Luke 9:34).
Procured small transparent stones for the Lord to touch for light in the barges (Ether 3:1–4).	Jesus Christ is the light to lead us through darkness (John 8:12; 9:5; 12:46); He is also the stone or rock of Israel (Acts 4:11; 1 Cor 10:4; Hel 5:12).
Had a great vision of Lord on top of an exceedingly high mountain (Ether 3).	Jesus received divine messengers and was transfigured on a high mountain (Matt 17:1–2).
Forbidden to write many of the things which he had seen (Ether 4:1).	Jesus charged his disciples after descending the mount to "tell the vision to no man" (Matt 17:9).

Seeking and Receiving Blessings from God

With the world collapsing around them in apostasy and wickedness, Jared asked his brother to intervene with God, "that he will not confound us that we may not understand our words" (Ether 1:34). As he took on this responsibility, the brother of Jared acted as a mediator between his people and God. Jared also petitioned his brother to "inquire of the Lord whether he will drive us out of the land, and if he will drive us out of the land, cry unto him whither we shall go" (v 37). It was in this latter request that Jared first raised the possibility that "the Lord will carry us forth into a land which is choice above all the earth. . . . And if it so be, let us be faithful unto the Lord, that we may receive it for our inheritance" (v 38). Thus, the Jaredites realized that they must be worthy to receive the blessing they were seeking.

Language and Power

Their request concerning the language was granted. According to Elder Joseph Fielding Smith, "they carried with them the speech of their fathers, the Adamic language, which was powerful even in its written form, so that the things Mahonri [Moriancumer] wrote 'were mighty even unto the overpowering of man to read them.' That was the kind of language Adam had and this was the language with which Enoch was able to accomplish his mighty work" (*The Way to Perfection* 60). There is likely more to the account of the retaining of the original or Adamic language than what initially meets the eye. The book of Moses described the language of Adam as "pure and undefiled" (Moses 6:5–6). It is intimately connected with the "Priesthood, which was in the beginning, [and] shall be in the end of the world also" (v 7; see also Zeph 3:9). As noted earlier, Moroni described the brother of Jared's words in the Adamic language as "mighty even . . . unto the overpowering of man" (Ether 12:24). An example of the relationship between language and power is contained in the book of Moses which describes Enoch's faith as causing him to be feared among men because "so powerful was the *word* of Enoch, and so great was the power of the *language* which God had given him" (Moses 7:13; emphasis added).

Driven Out, But Promised a New Inheritance

Jared's phrase, "drive us out of the land," is like the language used to describe Adam and Eve's being driven from the Garden of Eden (Ether 1:38; Gen 3:24; Moses 4:31), as well as the expression Cain used when he was driven from "the face of the Lord" (Moses 5:39; Gen 4:14). The same words are used when the Israelites are expelled from Egypt (Ex 11:1; 12:31), and when the inhabitants of Canaan are driven out before the children of Israel (33:2; 34:11). The Hebrew word used in these verses is *garash*, which means to "drive out," "cast out," "separate," "divorce" or "expel," sometimes suggesting "forcible or violent expulsion" (Harris 1:173).

God echoed his earlier instructions to Noah and foreshadowed the actions of the Israelites leaving Egypt (Gen 6:19; see also 1 Nephi 8:1; Ex 12:32, 38) when he told the brother of Jared that he and his followers should "go to and gather together thy flocks, both male and female, of every kind; and also of the seed of the earth of every kind" (Ether 1:41). The similarities continued as the brother of Jared was next commanded to lead Jared and their families "down into the valley which is northward" where God would meet them and go before them "into a land which is choice above all the lands of the earth" (v 42). Further, the Lord promised that he would bless them and their seed that they would become "a great nation," and "that there shall be none greater than the nation which I will raise up unto me of thy seed" (Ether 1:43), a promise similar to that made to Abraham and Israel.

The Promises of the Everlasting Covenant

In the opening scenes of the book of Ether, the reader is presented with a people being driven out of a land, but promised that the Adamic language would not be taken from them. In addition, they are promised that they would be led by a prophet under the direction of God to a new inheritance where they and their seed would become a great nation. These promises of God to the Jaredites contain the essential elements of the everlasting covenant detailed later to Father Abraham and to every covenant people. These elements include priesthood, posterity, and a land of inheritance (see Abr 2:11; B. McConkie, *A New Witness* 505). Modern revelation makes it clear that these covenants, often referred to as the Abrahamic covenant, were previously and subsequently made with Adam and the other patriarchs (see Moses 6:65–68; 7:51; 8:2; also see *Old Testament Student Manual* 70–72). This covenant is the new and everlasting covenant that God established in this dispensation (see D&C 49:9; 66:2; 132:2–7). According to Elder Bruce R. McConkie, "the covenant made with the fathers was that their seed after them should receive the same gospel, the same priesthood, the same promise of salvation, that blessed the lives of those with whom the covenant was first made" (*A New Witness* 524).

The Valley of Nimrod

"Jared and his brother, and their families, and also the friends of Jared and his brother and their families went down," as commanded, into the valley called Nimrod, "being called after the mighty hunter" (Ether 2:1). The name "Nimrod" evoked strong feelings among the ancients and was usually associated with "rebellion." It may have carried more meaning than simply a name-title for a valley. Nimrod, who "founded the kingdom of Babel," had "established false priesthood and false kingship in the earth in imitation of God's rule and 'made all men to sin'" (Nibley, *Lehi* 165). He typified Satan. The name of this valley may have been a stark reminder to the Jaredites that they, like all of God's children entering mortality, were strangers and sojourners in a dark and dreary world. Their trek through this valley of Nimrod might well have been a time of testing for them. If so, it can stand as a pattern of a similar temptation and trial the Savior experienced after being in the wilderness following his baptism. The record does not give us much detail concerning this part of their journey, except that it was a time of hard work, gathering and preparation (Ether 2:2–3).

Into the Wilderness

Like the children of Israel departing Egypt, the Jaredites were led "into the wilderness" by the Lord (Ether 2:5; Ex 13:18). In scriptural accounts, the idea of the people of God escaping into the wilderness is a common pattern. Adam and Eve are driven into a world of thorns and thistles (Moses 4:24). The Israelites wandered forty years in the wilderness. Even the Savior preceded his mission by going out into the wilderness to commune with God. Concerning this pattern, Hugh Nibley has observed: "Now the idea that this life is a pilgrimage through the desert did not originate with the Christians or even the Jews: it has been the religious memory of the human race from the earliest dispensations of the Gospel" (*An Approach* 146). Another scholar of antiquity has suggested that, in the ancient view, "The desert is the world one passes through. It is nothing in itself, it is barren and inhospitable. It is not meant for people to remain in. One travels through the wilderness as one travels through time. Just like time, so does the desert lead to a new world, to the promised land" (Weinreb 125).

The Cloud and Many Waters

The Lord did not abandon the Jaredites during their travels. He "did go before them, and did talk with them as he stood in a cloud, and gave directions whither they should travel" (Ether 2:5; compare Ex 13:21–22). As he did with Moses centuries later, "the Lord came down and talked with the brother of Jared; and he was in a cloud, and the brother of Jared saw him not" (Ether 2:4; Ex 19:19). Similar to the Israelites, the Jaredites also had to "cross many waters, being directed continually by the hand of the Lord" (Ether 2:6; compare 2 Sam 22:16–18; Ps 18:15–17). Inasmuch as the Apostle Paul compared the Israelites' crossing the waters and being led by the cloud to baptism and the Holy Ghost, such a comparison might also be made with the Jaredites (see 1 Cor 10:1–4). From the scriptural motifs it seems evident that the Lord often leads his children into the wilderness, but he does not leave them alone. He gives them ordinances, the Gift of the Holy Ghost, and even his own presence.

The Brother of Jared Chastened

When the Jaredites came to the "great sea which divideth the lands," they pitched their tents in a place they named Moriancumer (Ether 2:13). After four years, "the Lord came again in a cloud" and talked with the brother of Jared. The Lord "chastened him because he remembered not to call upon the name of the Lord" (v 14). Many modern readers are puzzled by this apparently ungrateful behavior. One recent commentary notes that "it seems highly unlikely that a man of the spiritual stature of the brother of Jared—one who had received marvelous manifestations and had previously exercised great faith in the Lord—would suddenly cease praying to his Maker." The commentary continues: "It may be that what this verse is saying to us is that Mahonri Moriancumer was chastened by the Lord because he had not fully followed and implemented the counsels of the Lord previously received. It may be that in the relative comfort of the seashore he had allowed his prayers to become less fervent, more casual and routine. He may have been calling upon the Lord in word, but not in faith and deed" (J. McConkie, Millet, and Top 4:269). Whatever the reasons for the Lord's chastening Jared's brother, it is important to remember that other great prophets were also rebuked by the Lord. Moses was reproved for not explicitly following God's instructions in the wilderness of Zin (Num 20:7–11; 27:12–14; Deut 32:51–52). The Apostle Peter received a sharp rebuke for letting his love of the Lord get in his way of comprehending the need for the Atonement (Matt 16:21–23). Even the Prophet Joseph Smith was reprimanded for having "feared man more than God" (D&C 3:7). There is nothing demeaning in being corrected by the Lord, that comes from not humbly receiving the correction. The book of Job reads: "Behold, happy is the man whom God correcteth: therefore despise not thou the chastening of the Almighty" (Job 5:17). The Lord has declared, "as many as I love, I rebuke and chasten: be zealous therefore, and repent" (Rev 3:19). Jared's brother, like the rest of God's prophets, took immediate action to turn away the Lord's wrath (Ether 2:15).

Building the Barges

As soon as the Jaredites were spiritually ready, the Lord commanded them to build barges as they had done before. They immediately "built barges after the manner which they had built, according to the instructions of the Lord" (Ether 2:16). The Jaredites had experience constructing barges earlier, with which they "cross[ed] many waters" (v 6). They had also built these barges "according to the instructions of the Lord." There are only a few examples of the Lord's giving his children intricate instructions for building something, and these are usually associated with temple building (eg, Ex 25; 1 Chron 28; D&C 124). Of course, Noah's ark and Nephi's ship are illustrations of God's giving detailed direction for the building of vessels. According to the Prophet Joseph Smith, "the construction of the first vessel was given to Noah, by revelation. The design of the ark was given by God, 'a pattern of heavenly things'" (*Teachings of the Prophet Joseph Smith* 251; hereafter *TPJS*). Significantly, the barges of the Jaredites were patterned after the ark of Noah (Ether 6:7).

Questions of Air and Light

Jared's brother fulfilled the Lord's instructions strictly and therefore felt the confidence necessary to ask for further light and knowledge concerning the barges: "And behold, O Lord, in them there is no light; whither shall we steer? And also we shall perish, for in them we cannot breathe, save it is the air which is in them; therefore we shall perish" (Ether 2:19). God answered the second question first by telling the brother of Jared how they could "receive air" on their voyage (v 20). Then he responded to the concern about light with a question: "What will ye that I should do that ye may have light in your vessels?" (v 23). Although the Lord willingly provided directions for receiving air, supplying light was a matter wherein he required the brother of Jared to exercise his own "agency, his intelligence, and his faith" (Jackson 250). There is a pattern in these verses worth noting.

God preserves his children "from day to day, by lending [them] breath, that [they] may live and move and do according to [their] own will. . . . And behold, all that he requires of [them] is [that they] keep his commandments" (Mosiah 2:21–22). In other words, God freely grants his children breath and life so that they might exercise their own wills righteously, and thereby grow more like him. This principle is also taught in the revelation concerning Oliver Cowdery given in April, 1829: "Behold, you have not understood; you have supposed that I would give it unto you, when you took no thought save it was to ask me. But, behold, I say unto you, that you must study it out in your mind; then you must ask me if it be right" (D&C 9:7–8). President Harold B. Lee commented on these verses in Ether similarly: "It was as though the Lord were saying to [the brother of Jared], 'Look, I gave you a mind to think with, and I gave you agency to use it. Now you do all you can do to help yourself with this problem; and then, after you've done all you can, I'll step in to help you'" ("How to Receive" 863).

The Molten Stones

Not only did the brother of Jared ponder the problem assigned to him by the Lord, but he also took action based upon his deliberations. He ascended Mount Shelem, "and did molten out of a rock sixteen small stones; and they were white and clear, even as transparent glass" (Ether 3:1). Humbly, he approached God with his solution: "I know, O Lord, that thou hast all power, and can do whatsoever thou wilt for the benefit of man; therefore touch these stones, O Lord, with thy finger, and prepare them that they may shine forth in darkness; and they shall shine forth unto us in the vessels which we have prepared, that we may have light while we shall cross the sea" (Ether 3:4). The text indicates that the Lord, without hesitation, "stretched forth his hand and touched the stones one by one with his finger" (Ether 3:6). Much has been written connecting these stones to ancient traditions of how light was given to Noah's ark, or concerning how the stones were used as oracles of hidden knowledge (eg, Nibley, *An Approach* 337–38; Graves 113). For purposes of this paper it must suffice to state that these stones received their light from Christ and "shine[d] forth in darkness," and provided "light when [the Jaredites were] swallowed up in the depths of the sea" (Ether 2:25; 3:4). In the next chapter, the record identifies Jesus Christ as "the light, and the life, and the truth of the world" (Ether 4:12).

There may also be a comparison between the Jaredite stones and the Liahona, at least as far as types. The Nephite prophet Alma compared the Liahona to the words of Christ. He rhetorically asked: "Is there not a type in this thing [the Liahona]?" Continuing, he declared, "for just as surely as this director did bring our fathers, by following its course, to the promised land, shall the words of Christ, if we follow their course, carry us beyond this vale of sorrow into a far better land of promise" (Alma 37:45). The brother of Jared's shining stones typologically led the Jaredites to the promised land by the power of Christ. By that same power mankind can be led "into a far better land of promise."

Experience on Mt. Shelem

Sacred events transpired when the brother of Jared was on the high mountain calling upon the Lord. Mountains have often been utilized by God and his prophets as actual and symbolic temples where Jehovah has manifest himself, his word, and his will to man (eg, Ex 15:17; Matt 17; Moses 1; 1 Nephi 11:1; J. McConkie and Parry 84). Elder Joseph Fielding Smith has stated: "Of necessity the first sanctified temples were the mountain tops and secluded places in the wilderness. If we are correctly informed, Adam built his altar on a hill above the valley of Adam-ondi-Ahman. At that place the Lord revealed to him the purpose of the fall and the mission of the Savior. . . . It was upon the great mountain Shelem, which was sanctified and made holy, that the brother of Jared was commissioned and received one of the greatest revelations ever given unto man, for he was shown all things from the beginning to the end of time" (*Doctrines of Salvation* 2:232–33).

During his powerfully sacred experience, the brother of Jared was able to penetrate the veil and see "the finger of the Lord" (Ether 3:6). After a brief examination of the brother of Jared's understanding of what was happening to him, the Lord revealed further knowledge to him. Because of the matchless faith and humility of Jared's brother, Jesus Christ "showed himself unto him," and declared, "because thou knowest these things ye are redeemed from the fall; therefore ye are brought back into my presence; therefore I show myself unto you"

(Ether 3:13). Few mortals of record have received this glorious experience.

Then, as if by explanation of the distinctive difference between this revelation and his other appearances to man, Jesus Christ exclaimed: "Behold, I am he who was prepared from the foundation of the world to redeem my people. Behold, I am Jesus Christ. I am the Father and the Son. . . . Never have I showed myself unto man whom I have created, for never has man believed in me as thou hast. . . . Behold, this body, which ye now behold, is the body of my spirit. . . . Even as I appear unto thee to be in the spirit will I appear unto my people in the flesh" (Ether 3:14–18). Moroni intruded into the record at this point with the clarification that he "could not make a full account of these things which are written, therefore it sufficeth me to say that Jesus showed himself unto this man in the spirit, even after the manner and in the likeness of the same body even as he showed himself unto the Nephites" (v 17), adding that Jesus ministered to the brother of Jared "even as he ministered unto the Nephites" (v 18). Elder Bruce R. McConkie explained: "Read in context and in the light of other passages, this means that no prior person had ever had so great faith as Moriancumer and that as a consequence none had gained so comprehensive a revelation of Christ's personality. The veil was completely removed where this Jaredite prophet was concerned; the Lord appeared in a more complete manner and form than ever before had been the case" (*Mormon Doctrine* 464). In other words Jared's brother received the blessing of the Second Comforter, the personal presence and ministration of the Lord God himself (see John 14:18, 21, 23; *TPJS* 149–51; J. McConkie, Millet, and Top 4:274–75).

The perfect knowledge of this man made it so that "he could not be kept from beholding within the veil" (Ether 3:19). Further, "the Lord could not withhold anything from him, for he knew that the Lord could show him all things" (v 26). He was given a vision of "all inhabitants of the earth which had been, and also all that would be . . . even unto the ends of the earth" (v 25). The Lord instructed the brother of Jared to seal these things up to be shown in His own due time (v 27; see also 2 Nephi 27:7, 10).

Like the brother of Jared, Latter-day Saints have available the power, keys, covenants, ordinances, and sanctuaries to receive "the fulness of the priesthood" (see D&C 124:28; *TPJS* 321–24). The

Prophet Joseph Smith taught that "all the prophets that have written, from the days of righteous Abel, down to the last man . . ." have had the goal of gathering the Lord's people (*TPJS* 83). He later added: "Why gather the people together in this place? For the same purpose that Jesus wanted to gather the Jews—to receive the ordinances, the blessings, and glories that God has in store for His Saints" (*TPJS* 312). Like Jesus Christ, Jared's brother ascended a holy mount and received glorious visions and probably his endowments (Ether chapters 2, 3; compare Matt chapter 17). Following the same pattern, Saints of God enter the "mountain of the Lord's house" and have opened to them "all . . . which had been, and also all that would be" (Isa 2:2–3; Ether 3:25). The Prophet Joseph Smith promised that "the least Saint may know all things as fast as he is able to bear them, for the day must come when no man need say to his neighbor, Know ye the Lord; for all shall know Him (who remain) from the least to the greatest. How is this to be done? It is to be done by this sealing power, and the other Comforter spoken of, which will be manifest by revelation" (*TPJS* 149).

The Crossing

Endowed with divine power, the brother of Jared was prepared to lead his people across the seas. They made their temporal affairs ready and "set forth into the sea." The "Lord God caused that there should be a furious wind blow upon the face of the waters, towards the promised land" and "the wind did never cease to blow towards the promised land while they were upon the waters" (Ether 6:4–5, 8). Hugh Nibley has chronicled many "ancient" accounts of tremendous winds during the fall of Babel (*Lehi* 177–78). In the ancient world, wind was often seen as Jehovah's "instrument in overcoming chaos (Gen 1:2; 8:1), and in transporting a prophet (1 Kings 18:12; 2 Kings 2:16; cf. 2:11; Ezek 8:3; 11:1)" (Scott 4:848).

Anciently, water was often symbolic of the primordial chaos, "when darkness was upon the face of the deep" (Gen 1:2; Eliade, *The Myth* 59–60). The act of creation or organization occurred when "the Spirit of God moved upon the deep," and order and life came upon the chaos (Gen 1:2). To pass through the waters symbolized death and renewal. The ordinance of baptism partially draws upon this symbolism. To baptize is to bury the natural man in the dissolutive primordial waters, and then to raise up, by God's Spirit, a new creature. As Paul puts it, "Buried with him in baptism, wherein also ye are risen with him through the faith of the operation of God, who hath raised him from the dead" (Col 2:12; see also Rom 6:4).

In much the same symbolic fashion, to cross the waters or seas is to leave the old decadent world behind to receive the new pristine and promised land. In ancient lore, crossing the great waters evoked images of traveling through time or life and traversing from old to new worlds. Friedrich Weinreb points out that, "The passage through this world is very much like passing through water, hence . . . a passage through time. And lest we should be drowned in water and in time, God gave us the 'teba,' the 'word,' [Ark] which carries us like a ship through the water" (Weinreb 248). Just as the "Flood figures both the descent into the watery depths and baptism," so too would the Jaredite journey into the seas (Eliade, *The Sacred* 134). After all, the Jaredites were "buried in the depths of the sea" but "there was no water that could hurt them, their vessels being tight like unto a dish, and also they were tight like unto the ark of Noah" (Ether 6:6–7). Like Noah, these Jaredites left the old behind, pressing forward to a new land of promise. These historical stories may also typify the fact that "if any man be in Christ, he is a new creature: old things are passed away; behold, all things are become new" (2 Cor 5:17).

The Promised Land

After 344 days on the ocean, "they did land upon the shore of the promised land" (Ether 6:11–12). Having obtained "the land of promise, which was choice above all other lands, which the Lord God had preserved for a righteous people," the Jaredites needed to realize their responsibility to live worthy of such an inheritance (2:7). The Lord had "sworn in his wrath unto the brother of Jared, that whoso should possess this land of promise, from that time henceforth and forever, should serve him, the true and only God, or they should be swept off when the fulness of his wrath should come upon them" (v 8). This divine oath is of such weight that Moroni felt the need to reiterate it: "We can behold the decrees of God concerning this land, that it is a land of promise; and whatsoever nation shall possess it shall serve God, or they shall be swept off when the fulness of his wrath shall come upon them. And the fulness of his wrath cometh upon them when they are ripened in iniquity. . . . Wherefore he that doth possess it shall serve God or shall be swept off; for it is the everlasting decree of God. And it is not until the fulness of iniquity among the children of the land, that they are swept off" (Ether 2:9–10). One additional condition is added by Moroni: "And this cometh *unto you, O ye Gentiles*, that ye may know the decrees of God—that ye may repent, and not continue in your iniquities until the fulness come, that ye may not bring down the fulness of the wrath of God upon you as the inhabitants of the land have hitherto done" (v 11; emphasis added). Modern prophets have echoed these words and stressed their serious-ness to the current inhabitants of this choice land (eg, Smith, *Doc-trines* 3:321–22; Kimball 439–40; and Benson, *Teachings* 580, 596).

The Jaredites immediately acknowledged the hand of the Lord in their great blessings as well as in their future. "When they set their feet upon the shores of the promised land they bowed themselves down upon the face of the land, and did humble themselves before the Lord, and did shed tears of joy before the Lord, because of the multitude of his tender mercies over them" (Ether 6:12).

God's conditional promise of the land of inheritance has an everlasting significance. Although all covenant people have a tempo-ral "promised land" (Lee, "To Know Nothing" 3–4), they also have the assurance of a far better land of promise. As Elder Bruce R. McConkie stated: "Following the millennium plus 'a little season' (D&C 29:22–25), the earth will die, be resurrected, and becoming like a 'sea of glass' (D&C 130:7), attain unto 'its sanctified, immortal, and eternal state' (D&C 77:1–2). Then the poor and the meek—that is, the godfearing and the righteous—shall inherit the earth; it will become an abiding place for the Father and the Son, and celestial beings will possess it forever and ever (D&C 88:14–26, 111)" (*Mormon Doctrine* 211).

Conclusion

This chapter has attempted to examine the typological corre-spondences between the Jaredite exodus and the eternal plan of redemption. Whether we are talking about the exodus of Noah, the Jaredites, the Israelites, or the family of Lehi, the pattern and types seem to testify of Jesus Christ and the plan of salvation, and that plan is taught throughout the scriptures by discourse, testimony, type and/or pattern. Our modern prophets and apostles have similarly stressed the need to teach the "great plan of the Eternal God" (Alma 34:9; see Benson, "The Book of Mormon" 84–85). Elder Boyd K. Packer has said: "The plan is worthy of repetition over and over again. Then the purpose of life, the reality of the Redeemer, and the reason for the commandments will stay with them [the youth]" (2–3).

Like the Jaredites of old, we begin our test of salvation by descending into a fallen world. Like them, we are not alone. Our Father has sent our Elder Brother as our Deliverer and Mediator. There is no way out of this dark and dreary wilderness without Jesus Christ. By living his teachings we can make the trek through the valleys of temptations and travails, to our promised home. We must receive the covenants and ordinances, and by the Gift of the Holy Ghost we can make it to the mountain of the Lord's house and receive further light and knowledge. Thus prepared, we can finish our task of putting off the old natural person and become new creatures in Christ. By feasting on the words of Christ, we will be led on a straight course to eternal bliss.

BIBLIOGRAPHY

Benson, Ezra Taft. "The Book of Mormon and the Doctrine and Covenants." *Ensign* (May 1987) 17:84–85; also in *Conference Report* (April 1987) 3–7.

———. *The Teachings of Ezra Taft Benson*. Salt Lake City: Bookcraft, 1988.

Donaldson, Lee, V. Dan Rogers, and David R. Seely. "I Have A Question: Building the Tower of Babel." *Ensign* (Feb 1994) 24:60.

Eichrodt, Walter. "Is Typological Exegesis An Appropriate Method?" *Essays on Old Testament Hermeneutics*. Trans. James Barr. Ed. Claus Westermann. Atlanta: John Knox, 1963. 224–45.

Eliade, Mircea. *The Myth of the Eternal Return or, Cosmos and History*. Princeton, NJ: Princeton Univ, 1954.

———. *The Sacred & the Profane*. New York: Harcourt Brace Jovanovich, 1959.

Frye, Northrop. *The Great Code, The Bible and Literature*. New York: Harcourt Brace Jovanovich, 1982.

Graves, Robert, and Raphael Patai. *Hebrew Myths*. New York: Greenwich House, 1983.

Harris, R. Laird, Gleason L. Archer, and Bruce K. Waltke. *Theological Wordbook of the Old Testament.* 2 vols. Chicago: Moody Press, 1980. 1:173–74.

Jackson, Kent P., "Christ and the Jaredites." *Studies in Scripture Vol. 8: Alma 30 to Moroni.* Ed. Kent P. Jackson. Salt Lake City: Deseret Book, 1988. 245–58.

Jacobsen, T. "Babel." *The Interpreter's Dictionary of the Bible.* Ed. George A. Buttrick. 4 vols. New York: Abingdon, 1962. 2:334.

Kimball, Spencer W. *The Teachings of Spencer W. Kimball.* Salt Lake City: Book-craft, 1982.

Lee, Harold B. "How to Receive a Blessing From God." *Improvement Era* (Oct 1966) 69:862–63, 896–99.

———. "To Know Nothing Save Jesus Christ and Him Crucified." *Ensign* (Nov 1973) 3:2–4; also in *Conference Report* (Oct 1973) 3–7.

Ludlow, Daniel H. *A Companion to Your Study of the Book of Mormon.* Salt Lake City: Deseret Book, 1976.

McConkie, Bruce R. *Mormon Doctrine.* 2nd ed. Salt Lake City: Bookcraft, 1966.

———. *A New Witness for the Articles of Faith.* Salt Lake City: Deseret Book, 1985.

McConkie, Joseph Fielding. *Gospel Symbolism.* Salt Lake City: Bookcraft, 1985.

———, Robert L. Millet, and Brent L. Top. *Doctrinal Commentary on the Book of Mormon.* 4 vols. Salt Lake City: Bookcraft, 1992.

———, and Donald W. Parry. *A Guide to Scriptural Symbols.* Salt Lake City: Bookcraft, 1990.

Nibley, Hugh. *An Approach to the Book of Mormon.* Vol. 6 of *The Collected Works of Hugh Nibley.* 3rd ed. Salt Lake City: Deseret Book/F.A.R.M.S., 1988.

———. *Lehi in the Desert/The World of the Jaredites/There Were Jaredites.* Vol. 5 of *The Collected Works of Hugh Nibley.* Salt Lake City: Deseret Book/F.A.R.M.S., 1988.

Oaks, Dallin H. "Taking Upon Us the Name of Jesus Christ." *Ensign* (May 1985): 15:80–83; also in *Conference Report* (April 1985) 101–05.

Old Testament Student Manual Genesis–2 Samuel. Salt Lake City, UT: The Church of Jesus Christ of Latter-day Saints, 1980.

Packer, Boyd K. "The Great Plan of Happiness." *Doctrine and Covenants/Church History Symposium Speeches 1993.* Provo, UT: Brigham Young Univ: The Church of Jesus Christ of Latter-day Saints, 1993.

Scott, R. B. "Wind." *The Interpreter's Dictionary of the Bible, R-Z.* Ed. George Arthur Buttrick. 4 vols. New York: Abingdon, 1962.

Smith, Joseph Fielding. *Doctrines of Salvation.* 3 vols. Salt Lake City: Bookcraft, 1954–56.

————. *The Way to Perfection*. Salt Lake City: Deseret Book, 1963.

Teachings of the Prophet Joseph Smith. Comp. Joseph Fielding Smith. Salt Lake City: Deseret Book, 1976.

Tate, George S. "The Typology of the Exodus Pattern in the Book of Mormon." *Literature of Belief*. Ed. Neal E. Lambert. Provo, UT: Brigham Young Univ, Religious Studies Center, 1981. 245–62.

Thomas, Catherine. "The Brother of Jared at the Veil." *Temples of the Ancient World: Sixth Annual F.A.R.M.S. Symposium*. Provo, UT: Brigham Young Univ, F.A.R.M.S., 1993. 388–98.

Weinreb, Friedrich. *Roots of the Bible, An Ancient View for a New Outlook*. Braunton: Merlin, 1986.

Preach the Gospel to Every Creature

24

Bruce A. Van Orden

*I*n this symposium we are discussing the topic "From Zion to Destruction." President Ezra Taft Benson has stated that events in the Book of Mormon symbolize the course events will take in the latter days (4). Surely a mighty destruction will occur to bring an end to the world as we know it. The earth will be cleansed from iniquity and then renewed in its paradisiacal glory. But many of the righteous will be spared of this cleansing as they are caught up to meet the Lord Jesus Christ at his second coming. My purpose is to discuss one significant commandment the Latter-day Saints can keep that will immensely help them survive the prophesied destructions that will come.

I have taken my title from Mormon 9, a most significant treatise in which Moroni called upon people everywhere to repent before "that great day when the earth shall be rolled together as a scroll, and the elements shall melt with fervent heat" (v 2). Moroni emphasized the testimony of the scriptures that the God of Abraham, Isaac, and Jacob is "a God of miracles" (vv 10–11, 15–20). "And the reason why he ceaseth to do miracles among the children of men," Moroni explained, is "that they dwindle in unbelief, and depart from the right way, and know not the God in whom they should trust" (v 20). Current political and social conditions clearly demonstrate the correctness of Moroni's prophecy. Moroni then urged his latter-day readers to believe in Christ and not to doubt him. If a person would exercise this faith, "Whatsoever he shall ask the Father in the name of Christ it shall be granted him; and this promise is unto all, even unto the ends of the earth"

Bruce A. Van Orden is associate professor of Church History and Doctrine at Brigham Young University.

(Mormon 9:21). The implication, as I see it, is that a faithful believer in Christ will recognize and receive mighty miracles from God and will be spared from the terrible destructions that await the wicked (see also v 25). Moroni reiterates this promise twice and extends it "even unto the ends of the earth" (vv 21, 25).

In the midst of his challenge to readers of the Book of Mormon to exercise faith and build trust in Jesus Christ, Moroni cited a statement the Lord made to his disciples when he visited them in the new world. We otherwise do not have this full statement in the Book of Mormon, although the concept of believing and being baptized is in 3 Nephi 11:33–34:

> Go ye into all the world, and preach the gospel to every creature; And he that believeth and is baptized shall be saved, but he that believeth not shall be damned; And these signs shall follow them that believe—in my name shall they cast out devils; they shall speak with new tongues; they shall take up serpents; and if they drink any deadly thing it shall not hurt them; they shall lay hands on the sick and they shall recover. (Mormon 9:22–24)

My interpretation of this quotation, taken in Moroni's context, is that the latter-day readers of the Book of Mormon will reap untold blessings by contributing to the preaching of the gospel to all the world. They will thereby strengthen their faith in their Savior Jesus Christ, they will turn from their sins and unto the God of Mercy, they will witness and be blessed by wondrous miracles in the course of their ministry, and they will abide the day of the Second Coming and be found on the right hand of the Lord Jesus Christ.

We may note that Jesus' statement to his Nephite disciples mirrors almost exactly what he said to his Jerusalem apostles following his resurrection when he met with them in the Upper Room as recorded in Mark 16:15–17. Many biblical scholars, noting that the text of Mark 16:9–20 was not found in the earliest extant manuscripts, have concluded that these verses were added to the text in the second century by an editor named Aristion (or Ariston) and that these passages are therefore not "Markan" (*Interpreter's Bible* 7:915–16). But the Book of Mormon confirms that the Lord indeed taught these principles. It undoubtedly parallels what the Savior taught in the Old World. We also have a briefer account of these teachings the Lord gave to Moroni as he abridged the Jaredite record (Ether 4:18). Thus the Book of Mormon has two witnesses of Jesus' teachings recorded in Mark. This is yet another instance wherein the Book of Mormon text verifies the legitimacy of the biblical text. As an angel testified to Nephi long ago, "These last records [including the Book of Mormon], which thou hast seen among the Gentiles, shall establish the truth of the first [the Holy Bible]" (1 Nephi 13:40; see also D&C 20:11).

The Book of Mormon is replete with teachings on the doctrine of the universal gospel and the command to all faithful disciples to take the gospel to all the world, to every nation, and to every creature.

The Universal Gospel

"Behold, the Lord esteemeth all flesh in one," declared the prophet Nephi (1 Nephi 17:35). This statement confirms the New Testament doctrine revealed to Peter that "God is no respecter of persons: But in every nation he that feareth [the Lord], and worketh righteousness, is accepted with him" (Acts 10:34–35). Peter exclaimed these words after he understood the vision of the sheets he had just been granted. In it he saw a huge sheet let down three separate times from heaven with all manner of beasts and fowls within it (Acts 10:10–17). These creatures represented all humankind, not just the Jews to whom Peter and the apostles had previously taken the gospel.

Nephi recorded in other writings that the gospel of Jesus Christ was meant for all people. For example, he included this teaching of his brother Jacob: "And [the Lord] cometh into the world that he may *save all men* if they will hearken unto his voice; for behold, he suffereth the pains of *all men*, yea, the pains of *every living creature*, both men, women, and children, who *belong to the family of Adam*" (2 Nephi 9:21; emphasis added). This statement certainly appears to be all-inclusive. Naturally, for any of the family of Adam to be saved, they must individually hearken to the voice of the Lord and repent of their sins.

Within his commentary on the prophecies of Isaiah, Nephi asked, "Hath [the Lord] commanded any that they should not partake of his salvation?" He answered, "Nay; but he hath given it free for *all men*; and he hath commanded his people that they should persuade *all men* to repentance," further explaining that "*all men* are privileged the one like unto the other, and *none are forbidden*" (2 Nephi 26:27–28; emphasis added). His conclusion of the matter is that the Lord God does not command men to do evil, but rather to turn unto him. Indeed, "He inviteth them all to come unto him and partake of his goodness; and he denieth none that come unto him, black and white, bond and free, male and female; and he remembereth the heathen; and *all are alike unto God"* (2 Nephi 26:33; emphasis added).

At the millennial day, Nephi testified, the gospel assuredly will be universal: "And the day cometh that the words of the book which were sealed shall be read upon the house tops; and they shall be read by the power of Christ; and all things shall be revealed unto the children of men which ever have been among the children of men, and which ever will be even unto the end of the earth" (2 Nephi 27:11).

Nephi helps us understand that between the beginning of the Restoration in 1830 and the Millennium we must cast off our provincialism and our narrow-minded cultural biases. "Know ye not that there are more nations than one?" he asked (2 Nephi 29:7). I believe this passage has a far broader application than knowing we have the Book of Mormon as a second witness of the Holy Bible. An application for most of us is that the gospel is important not only in the United States of America, but also in all the world. Nephi added the Lord's words: "Know ye not that I, the Lord your God, have created all men, and that I remember those who are upon the isles of the sea, and that I rule in the heavens above and in the earth beneath; and I bring forth my word unto the children of men, yea, even upon all the nations of the earth" (v 7).

Jacob, Nephi's brother and successor as prophet of the Nephites, taught his people that "the one being is as precious in [God's] sight as the other" and that God "created all flesh" (Jacob 2:21). He later included in his writings the invaluable allegory of Zenos, which taught that the Lord of the vineyard would place some of his best fruit in the "nethermost parts of the vineyard" (Jacob 5:13–14, 19, 38–39, 52). That phrase, "the nethermost parts of the vineyard," has come to have great meaning for us and the universal Church as we attempt to preach the gospel to every creature, no matter how difficult the linguistic, religious, and cultural chasms we have to cross to do so.

The prophet Abinadi, citing Isaiah, testified before king Noah and his wicked priests: "The time shall come when all shall see the salvation of the Lord, when every nation, kindred, tongue, and people shall see eye to eye and shall confess before God that his judgments are just" (Mosiah 16:1; compare Isa 52:10).

The great missionary foursome, the sons of Mosiah, were anxious to share the gospel with everyone they could find, even their enemies, the Lamanites. We should have the same desire to share the gospel universally, even with those who may have once been our enemies such as the Iraqies, the Iranians, the Russians, the Chinese, the North Koreans, and the North Vietnamese. At various times we were willing to drop bombs on some of these peoples. Now we must learn to call them our brothers and sisters, and we can use the sons of Mosiah as our model: "Now they were desirous that salvation should be declared to every creature, for they could not bear that any human soul should perish; yea, even the very thoughts that any soul should endure endless torment did cause them to quake and tremble" (Mosiah 28:3).

Alma testified to the people in Ammonihah that the heavenly gospel message was universal: "Yea, and the voice of the Lord, by the mouth of angels, doth declare it unto all nations; yea, doth declare it, that they may have glad tidings of great joy; yea, and he doth sound these glad tidings among all his people, yea, even to them that are scattered abroad upon the face of the earth" (Alma 13:22). A few years later, when Alma and Amulek were preaching throughout all the Nephite cities, Mormon recorded of their labors: "And as many as would hear their words, unto them they did impart the word of God, *without any respect of persons*, continually" (16:14; emphasis added).

From this same Alma we learn the revelation that "The Lord doth grant *unto all nations, of their own nation and tongue*, to teach his word, yea, in wisdom, all that he seeth fit that they should have" (Alma 29:8; emphasis added). In this last gospel dispensation, the dispensation of the fulness of times, the Lord will raise up servants *out of every nation and tongue* to preach the glorious gospel word to their people. That prophecy has already begun to be fulfilled with the hosts of indigenous missionaries of many nations of the earth and with the call of General Authorities out of many different nations.

Toward the end of his life, the prophet Mormon could see that his compilation would play a major role in taking the gospel to the world: "And these things doth the Spirit manifest unto me; therefore I write unto you all. And for this cause I write unto you, that ye may know that ye must all stand before the judgment-seat of Christ, yea, every soul who belongs to the whole human family of Adam. . . . And I would that I could persuade all ye ends of the earth to repent and prepare to stand before the judgment-seat of Christ" (Mormon 3:20–22).

In his farewell statement to those who would read the Book of Mormon, Moroni quoted his father Mormon, writing that "there were divers ways that [God] did manifest things unto the children of men, which were good" (Moroni 7:24). This conclusion corresponds with the First Presidency's 1978 statement:

> The great religious leaders of the world such as Mohammed, Confucius, and the Reformers, as well as philosophers including Socrates, Plato, and others, received a portion of God's light. Moral truths were given to them by God to enlighten whole nations and to bring a higher level of understanding to individuals. . . .
>
> Consistent with these truths, we believe that God has given and will give to all peoples sufficient knowledge to help them on their way to eternal salvation, either in this life or in the life to come. (Palmer v)

Clearly, from these many Book of Mormon prophetic witnesses, we can see that God is no respecter of persons, that all are alike unto him, that he desires that his message spread forth from angels, prophets, and authorized messengers, even including ourselves, to every nation, to every creature. In many instances preparatory voices such as Mohammed and Buddha will set the stage for many of the children of men to receive the fulness of truth from the Lord's authorized messengers. "For verily the voice of the Lord is unto all men," reads the Lord's preface to the Doctrine and Covenants, "and there is none to escape; and there is no eye that shall not see, neither ear that shall not hear, neither heart that shall not be penetrated" (D&C 1:2).

Punishments to Those Who Fight Against Zion

The Book of Mormon also explicitly states that while "the righteous shall not perish . . . the time surely must come that all they who fight against Zion shall be cut off" (1 Nephi 22:19). "For the time soon cometh that the fulness of the wrath of God shall be poured out upon all the children of men; for he will not suffer that the wicked shall destroy the righteous" (v 16).

The adversary, Satan, has a counterfeit plan to thwart the latter-day work of God. Nephi explained from his vision: "And it came to pass that I beheld the church of the Lamb of God, and *its numbers were few*, because of the wickedness and abominations of the whore who sat upon many waters; nevertheless, I beheld that the church of the Lamb, who were the saints of God, were also *upon all the face of the earth*; and their dominions upon the face of the earth were *small*, because of the wickedness of the great whore whom I saw" (1 Nephi 14:12; emphasis added). In his vision Nephi further beheld that Satan's minions gathered "multitudes upon the face of all the earth, among all the nations of the Gentiles, to fight against the Lamb of God" (v 13). Thus we note that unless we join the emerging throng to build the kingdom of God and to take the gospel to all the world, there is a good chance that we will fall prey to the wiles of Satan, who is determined to bring about our destruction. If we righteously participate with the Lord's kingdom, we will be heirs of mighty miracles and promises. Nephi's vision so testifies: "And it came to pass that I, Nephi, beheld the power of the Lamb of God, that it descended upon the saints of the church of the Lamb, and upon the covenant people of the Lord, who were scattered upon all the face of the earth; and they were armed with righteousness and with the power of God in great glory" (v 14). Those who tie in with the evil one, Nephi explained, will lose their reward and be destroyed:

> Wo unto them that turn aside the just for a thing of naught and revile against that which is good, and say that it is of no worth! For the day shall come that the Lord God will speedily visit the inhabitants of the earth; and in that day that they are fully ripe in iniquity they shall perish.But behold, if the inhabitants of the earth shall repent of their wickedness and abominations they shall not be destroyed, saith the Lord of Hosts.But behold, that great and abominable church, the whore of all the earth, must tumble to the earth, and great must be the fall thereof. (2 Nephi 28:16–18)

Alma added a similar witness when he testified to his son Helaman, "Thus saith the Lord God—Cursed shall be the land, yea, this land, unto every nation, kindred, tongue, and people, unto destruction, which do wickedly, when they are fully ripe; and as I have said so shall it be; for this is the cursing and the blessing of God upon the land, for the Lord cannot look upon sin with the least degree of allowance" (Alma 45:16).

Knowledge of a Savior to Spread to Every Nation

We in The Church of Jesus Christ of Latter-day Saints testify that the antidote to Satan's power is the power brought forth by the atoning sacrifice of the Lord Jesus Christ, the most significant part of the merciful plan of the great Creator (see 2 Nephi 9:5; Mosiah 5:15; 26:23; Alma 5:15). Our message must be the fulness of the gospel of Jesus Christ with all its principles and ordinances, particularly the doctrine of the universal atonement and great and last sacrifice of Jesus Christ (see Alma 34:13–14). Therefore, it was only natural that king Benjamin prophesied, "And moreover, I say unto you, that the time shall come when the knowledge of a Savior shall spread throughout every nation, kindred, tongue, and people" (Mosiah 3:20). Having our missionaries merely give an uplifting, ethical message will not do.

In his vision, Nephi beheld that the Book of Mormon would "establish the truth" of the Bible and "make known to all kindreds, tongues, and people, that the Lamb of God is the Son of the Eternal Father, and the Savior of the world, and *that all men must come unto him*, or they cannot be saved. . . . For there is one God and one Shepherd *over all the earth*" (1 Nephi 13:40–41; emphasis added).

Nephi also testified that gathered Israel "shall be brought out of obscurity and out of darkness; and they shall know that the Lord is their Savior and their Redeemer, the Mighty One of Israel" (1 Nephi 22:12). In the same chapter he added, "Behold, all nations, kindreds, tongues, and people shall dwell safely in the Holy One of Israel if it so be that they will repent" (v 28). Yes, the only safety is in the Holy One of Israel. While we believe that many religious leaders outside of Christianity have brought a portion of God's light to hosts of this world's inhabitants (Palmer v), God our Eternal Father requires that all his children come unto his Only Begotten Son Jesus Christ for their salvation. King Benjamin left no room for doubt on this doctrine when he declared, "I say unto you, that there shall be no other name given nor any other way nor means whereby salvation can come unto the children of men, only in and through the name of Christ, the Lord Omnipotent" (Mosiah 3:17; see also 2 Nephi 25:20; 31:21; Mosiah 5:8).

This same Savior, Nephi testified, "doeth not anything save it be for the benefit of the world; for he loveth the world, even that he layeth down his own life that he may draw *all men* unto him" (2 Nephi 26:24; emphasis added). Toward the end of his commentary on Isaiah's prophecies, Nephi added, "And the gospel of Jesus Christ shall be declared among [the Jews]; wherefore, they shall be restored unto the knowledge of their fathers, and also to the knowledge of Jesus Christ, which was had among their fathers" (2 Nephi 30:5). Nephi's greatest emphasis in his concluding testimony was the universal need to believe in Christ. "And now, my beloved brethren, and also Jew, and *all ye ends of the earth*," he urged, "hearken unto these words and believe in Christ; and if ye believe not in these words believe in Christ. And if ye shall believe in Christ ye will believe in these words, for they are the words of Christ" (33:10; emphasis added).

Mormon felt the same compulsion as Nephi to leave his ringing testimony of Christ to all the world:

> And also that ye may believe the gospel of Jesus Christ, which ye shall have among you; and also that the Jews, the covenant people of the Lord, shall have other witness besides him whom they saw and heard, that Jesus, whom they slew, was the very Christ and the very God. And I would that I could *persuade all ye ends of the earth* to repent and prepare to stand before the judgment-seat of Christ. (Mormon 3:21–22; emphasis added)

Latter-day Restoration of the Gospel

Nephi's soul delighted "in proving unto [his] people the truth of the coming of Christ" and "in proving . . . that save Christ should come all men must perish" (2 Nephi 11:4, 6). These were two reasons why he included numerous chapters of Isaiah's prophecies. Among these prophecies were references to the latter-day Restoration that would extend to all the world. "And it shall come to pass in the last days," Isaiah wrote, "when the mountain of the Lord's house shall be established in the top of the mountains, and shall be exalted above the hills, and *all nations shall flow unto it*" (12:2; emphasis added; compare Isa 2:2). Later Isaiah added, "And he will lift up an *ensign to the nations from far*, and will hiss unto them from the *end of the earth*; and behold, they shall come with speed swiftly" (2 Nephi 15:26; emphasis added; compare Isa 5:26).

Later, in commenting on Isaiah's prophecies, Nephi stated that when the Lord performed "a marvelous work" he would remember his covenant to set his hand "the second time to recover my people."

This same prophecy included, "The words of your seed should proceed forth out of my mouth unto your seed; and my words shall hiss forth unto the ends of the earth, for a standard unto my people, which are of the house of Israel" (2 Nephi 29:1–2; see also, 6:14; 21:11; 25:17; Jacob 6:2; and D&C 137:6).

Labor with Love and Diligence

The Book of Mormon enjoins us to labor with our might to bring about this great latter-day work. As he beheld his vision of the latter days, Nephi exclaimed, "And blessed are they who shall seek to bring forth my Zion at that day, for they shall have the gift and the power of the Holy Ghost" (1 Nephi 13:37). This is yet another prophecy that those who take the gospel to all the world will be blessed above measure and will avoid the destructions designed for the wicked.

Zenos' allegory of the olive tree, recorded in Jacob 5, speaks of the latter-day labors of the righteous to the nethermost parts of the vineyard:

> And the Lord of the vineyard said unto them: Go to, and labor in the vineyard, with your might. For behold, this is the *last time that I shall nourish my vineyard*; for the end is nigh at hand, and the season speedily cometh; and if ye labor with your might with me ye shall have joy in the fruit which I shall lay up unto myself against the time which will soon come.
>
> And it came to pass that the servants did go and *labor with their mights*; and the Lord of the vineyard labored also with them; and they did obey the commandments of the Lord of the vineyard in all things. (Jacob 5:71–72; emphasis added)

The Doctrine and Covenants confirms that with the restoration of the gospel in 1830 the Lord was directing his servants to labor in the vineyard for the last time (D&C 33:3; 39:17; 43:28).

Examples of missionary valiance in the book of Alma help us see that laboring with love and diligence is necessary in taking the gospel to every creature. An exulting Ammon delighted that the Lord had made him and his brothers, known collectively as the sons of Mosiah, "instruments in the hands of God to bring about this great work." He added, "Behold, the field was ripe, and blessed are ye, for ye did thrust in the sickle, and did reap with your might, yea, *all the day long did ye labor;* and behold the number of your sheaves!" (Alma 26:3, 5; emphasis added). Later in his discourse, Ammon explained why he and his brothers had undertaken such a dangerous mission to their erstwhile enemies, the Lamanites: "My beloved brethren, we came into the wilderness *not with the intent to destroy our brethren,* but *with the intent that perhaps we might save some few of their souls*" (Alma 26:26; emphasis added). And, as he declared, the missionaries were willing to suffer "all manner of afflictions" so that they "might be the means of saving some soul" (v 30).

Alma the Younger, a close friend of the sons of Mosiah, echoed the same feelings regarding his own missionary labors: "I know that which the Lord hath commanded me, and I glory in it. I do not glory of myself, but I glory in that which the Lord hath commanded me; yea, and *this is my glory, that perhaps I may be an instrument in the hands of God to bring some soul to repentance*; and this is my joy" (Alma 29:9; emphasis added).

When he and the sons of Mosiah conjointly went among the Zoramites to bring them to the fold of Christ, Alma pleaded in prayer, "Behold, O Lord, *their souls are precious*, and many of them are our brethren; therefore, give unto us, O Lord, power and wisdom that we may bring these, our brethren, again unto thee" (Alma 31:35; emphasis added). In our modern day, President Spencer W. Kimball has declared:

> May we emphasize again that numbers are incidental and secondary to our main purpose, which is the same as that of our Heavenly Father—to bring to every soul the gospel which can open the doors to eternal life for man. Our objective is not for power or domain, but totally spiritual. And to every nation and people which opens its borders to the gospel will come unbelievable blessings. ("When the World Will be Converted" 12)

The Scattering and Gathering of Israel

In reality, what we Latter-day Saints are doing with our missionary endeavors is seeking out scattered Israel. A high majority of converts to the Church were members of the House of Israel before they were born (see Deut 32:7–8). When missionaries bring them the restored gospel, they hearken to the same voice and spirit that they obeyed in our premortal existence. When they submit to baptism, they confirm the covenant they made in a previous sphere.

Nephi, interpreting Isaiah chapters 48–49, declared that "the house of Israel, sooner or later, will be *scattered upon all the face of the earth, and also among all nations*" (1 Nephi 22:3; emphasis added). Then, once the scattering among all nations had occurred, and after their previous knowledge of the gospel had been confounded, Nephi explained, "The Lord God will raise up a mighty nation among the Gentiles, yea, even upon the face of this [American] land" (v 7). Then "a marvelous work among the Gentiles" will arise and be "of great worth" unto "all the house of Israel, unto the making known of the covenants of the Father of heaven unto Abraham" (1 Nephi 27:8–9). The Lord will "make bare his arm *in the eyes of all the nations*" and take "his covenants and his gospel unto those who are of the house of Israel" (v 11; emphasis added). All Israel will be "brought out of obscurity and out of darkness" to "know that the Lord is their Savior and Redeemer" (v 12).

Later in his teachings, Nephi made a similar summary of these House of Israel teachings:

> And it shall come to pass that my people, which are of the house of Israel, shall be gathered home unto the lands of their possessions; and *my word also shall be gathered in one*. And I will show unto them that fight against my word and against my people, who are of the house of Israel, that I am God, and that I covenanted with Abraham that *I would remember his seed forever.* (2 Nephi 29:14; emphasis added)

Conclusion

Early in his development as a prophet, Nephi was tutored by an angel and granted many visions of the latter days. "And it came to pass that the angel spake unto me, saying: Look! And I looked and beheld many nations and kingdoms" (1 Nephi 13:1). Yes, we have in our day more than 200 nations and kingdoms in the world, which now has a population exceeding 5.3 billion. Each one of these human beings is a child of the same God. Earlier in this chapter, we noted that Nephi reminded us that "the Lord esteemeth all flesh in one" (17:35). In 1978, the First Presidency declared: "Based upon ancient and modern revelation, The Church of Jesus Christ of Latter-day Saints gladly teaches and declares the Christian doctrine that all men and women are brothers and sisters, not only by blood relationship from common mortal progenitors, but also as literal spirit children of an Eternal Father" (Palmer v). As he arrived at the 1993 Parliament of the World's Religions, Elder Russell M. Nelson of the Council of the Twelve Apostles said the following to the *Church News*:

> We are all together on Planet Earth, and we need to talk to one another, promote understanding, mutual respect and tolerance for each other's viewpoints that are held sacred. We are all sons and daughters of one Eternal Father. We're literally brothers and sisters, so we have much in common. . . . I feel the things that unite us are greater than the things that separate us.[1] (Avant 3)

With these principles in mind, let us take seriously the Lord's charge which is the basis for this presentation: "Go ye into all the world, and preach the gospel to every creature" (Mormon 9:22). By so doing we will increase our faith, we will witness mighty miracles, and we will avoid the damning nature of the destructions that will come upon the earth. The Book of Mormon, the keystone of our religion, obviously is a strong tool in witnessing to us of the importance of this work and in the actual accomplishing of the Lord's command.

In October 1974 President Spencer W. Kimball declared:

> Our goal is nothing less than the penetration of the entire world. Our new office building is a world building with four giant maps, each showing a particular part of the globe. We are not promised that the whole world will believe. Evangelization of the world does not mean that all men will respond, but all men must be given the opportunity to respond as they are confronted with the Christ. (*Teachings* 545)

How can we participate in this enterprise of taking the gospel to every creature? First, we can live righteously under the constant guidance of the Holy Spirit so that, by virtue of our Christlike lifestyles, others will be motivated to turn to the Lord. Second, as President Kimball often urged us, we can pray continually that the Lord will open more doors of nations to the preaching of the gospel. Third, we can prepare our children and grandchildren who are "branches" or extensions of ourselves to go on missions and to be qualified in every necessary way to be superb missionaries. This includes encouraging them to develop their talents, to learn other languages, and to make the most of their educational opportunities. Fourth, we can share the gospel with friends, co-workers, and neigh-

---

[1]   The full text of Elder Nelson's formal talk is printed in Russell M. Nelson, "Combatting Spiritual Drift—Our Global Pandemic." *Ensign* (Nov 1993) 23:102-08.

bors as the Spirit guides us to approach them. Fifth, as our individual finances allow, we can contribute to the ward missionary fund, the general missionary fund, the general Book of Mormon fund, or the Church's humanitarian fund, each of which helps take the gospel to all the world. And, sixth, we can prepare now to go on missions as couples, when our family and financial circumstances are in order.

BIBLIOGRAPHY

Avant, Gerry. "Parliament of the World's Religions: Event is 'Greatest Gathering of Religious Leaders in History.'" *Church News* (11 Sep 1993) 3.

Benson, Ezra Taft. "The Savior's Visit to America." *Ensign* (May 1987) 17:4–7; also in *Conference Report* (Apr 1987) 3–7.

The Interpreter's Bible in Twelve Volumes. New York: Abington Press, 1951.

Kimball, Spencer W. *The Teachings of Spencer W. Kimball*. Ed. Edward L. Kimball. Salt Lake City: Bookcraft, 1982.

———. "When the World Will Be Converted." *Ensign* (Oct 1974) 4:2–14.

Palmer, Spencer J. *The Expanding Church*. Salt Lake City: Deseret Book, 1978.

The Socio-Economics of Zion

25

Warner P. Woodworth

*T*he thrust of this chapter emphasizes the society of 4 Nephi which emerged just after the visitation of Christ to the Nephites. The Savior's teachings in 3 Nephi lay the foundations for what happens next, as he expresses the will of the Father, preaches faith and repentance, establishes his Church (which is to be led by twelve apostles), and shows how righteousness can lead to the good life on earth and eternal life hereafter. A major theme underlying Christ's visit to the Americas is the establishing of Zion. We will explore key scriptural aspects of how God's people "lived after the manner of happiness." Then, after tracing the unfortunate decline of Zion, we will conclude with a discussion of the implications of 4 Nephi for us today.

The Search for Utopia

Throughout history, mankind has sought the "good life," a return to the Garden of Eden or some other definition of utopia which would reduce the pain and pathos of mortal existence and supplant the world with heaven on earth. This utopia has been the dream of philosophers, poets, and writers. Some thinkers have written magnificent treatises on the ideal society including Plato, *Republic*; Thomas Moore, *Utopia*; and the secular humanist, Sir Francis Bacon, *New Atlantis*.

The range of visionary ideals stretches from the Taoists of Asia to Catholic theologians such as St. Augustine, from political strategists like Machiavelli to reformers like Robert Owen. In the United

Warner P. Woodworth is a professor of Organizational Behavior at Brigham Young University.

States, we have witnessed the much-heralded-claim that Wall Street capitalism will save us. Around the globe the false promise that communism would solve the world's problems has likewise been trumpeted.

The truth, however, is that the world's solution to societal stress and strain is stronger on rhetoric than reality. Seeking peace and justice, building a self-sustaining economy, and transforming the human soul are easier to talk about than actually accomplish. A major lesson from 4 Nephi is that without adherence to gospel principles taught by Christ, the true Author of Zion, the search for the good society will ultimately fall short of the ideal.

In fact, efforts of certain extremists may even make things more problematic, exacerbating the travails of mortal life such that participants are actually worse off than before their "utopia" was attempted. The disastrous mass deaths of the followers of Reverend Jim Jones in Guyana in the 1970s and the horrific tragedy of David Koresh's disciples in Waco, Texas, in 1993 are severe reminders. But many other seekers of utopia and dreamers have likewise ended up not creating the good society, but a dystopia instead. The modern literature on utopian visions is plentiful (see Beneri; Elliott; Kumar; Manuel), ranging from high ideals to low-level, anti-utopian notions. Certain contemporary groups currently seek a feminist utopia while some environmentalists pursue an "ecotopia" in nature. Some pursue the good life in rural settings while others attempt to transform the urban center by building brand new communities such as Reston, Virginia—a planned community built in 1962 with an "ideal" layout of homes, industrial center, churches, recreational facilities and a shopping mall.

Many seekers of the good life, regardless of sincere intent and/or noble desires, are tossed to and fro like small boats on a stormy sea. The message of 4 Nephi suggests that utopia ultimately must be grounded in the gospel of Jesus Christ. By so doing, the ultimate good society, Zion, can become a concrete reality, rather than a evasive ideal, and can last for centuries, blessing all who live therein.

The Context

Before 4 Nephi, the Nephite civilization had degenerated to a dangerously low level with great corruption and immorality. Terrible battles occurred between the warriors of Giddianhi and the Nephite army. Hate, greed, and the lust for blood made a "great and terrible . . . appearance" (3 Nephi 4:7). Racism, pride, and the thirst for power were the drivers which overtook peace and led to war and destruction. From within Nephite society itself, secret combinations led to murder, propaganda campaigns, threats and secret tactics—all to get gain. Ravenous ambition, intimidation, and subversion of law and order all combined to bring about the collapse of civilized structures such that the system of government was broken up and "they did separate . . . into tribes, every man according to his family and his kindred and friends" (7:2).

In broad brush strokes, the condition of society in the years preceding the Savior's visit to the Western Hemisphere reveals a tragic picture. The turning of God's once righteous people to evil shows terrible consequences: breaking of covenants, cold hearts, stiffneckedness, excessive wealth and poverty, class distinctions, priestcrafts, envyings and inequality, slothfulness, wars, unwillingness to follow the prophets, lyings and deceivings and so on. The scriptural record documents the symptoms of ancient America's disintegration as follows:

> For there were many merchants in the land, and also many lawyers, and many officers. And the people began to be distinguished by ranks, according to their riches and their chances for learning; yea, some were ignorant because of their poverty, and others did receive great learning because of their riches. Some were lifted up in pride, and others were exceedingly humble . . . and thus there became a great inequality in all the land, insomuch that the church began to be broken up. (3 Nephi 6:11–14)

Conditions made everything ripe for destruction.

Apparently, the only way a major reversal in the degeneration of Nephite civilization could occur was through catastrophic intervention from on high. Thus, God sent mighty earthquakes, tempests, wildfires, and other forms of violent destruction. This physical turbulence served to signify the crucifixion of Jesus in Palestine and also to cleanse all but the more righteous from the Nephite world. Later, after three days of complete darkness, the voice of the Redeemer speaks to the people. He then appears in all his majesty as the resurrected and glorified Savior of all mankind. The remaining chapters of 3 Nephi (11–26) contain the record of Christ's ministry and teachings to the survivors.

He revealed principles and ordinances not only for heavenly exaltation in the next life, but also to help people change from their fallen state here and now. The wicked world of the Nephites underwent a fundamental cleansing and the Church facilitated the process of change, empowering people to function on a higher plane, that of Zion. The good life was not to be discovered through Greek philosophy or mystic poets. Rational thinking alone would not produce utopia.

Rather, true religion was the means that enabled the people to achieve not only a heavenly state after death, but to provide practical solutions to this life's problems as well. President Joseph F. Smith clarified the role of the gospel in Book of Mormon times as well as today, as a practical way of life: "It has always been a cardinal teaching with the Latter-day Saints that a religion that has not the power to save people temporally and make them prosperous and happy here cannot be depended upon to save them spiritually and to exalt them in the life to come" ("The Truth About Mormonism" 242).

Socio-Economic Aspects of Zion Society

Key elements for enhancing our understanding of Zion, as it functioned over a period of two hundred years, are contained in the brief sketch known as 4 Nephi. Additional scripture from earlier sections of the Book of Mormon, as well as the other standard works and teachings of latter-day prophets provide essential details. Critical questions have to do with how the gospel transforms human nature. What individual and collective qualities help to create and maintain the good society? How do religious principles affect social behavior? How can righteous living build economic prosperity, peace, and happiness?

Traditional economists argue that the individual is made up of cold hearted, calculating qualities that only seek efficacy—in short, one is solely interested in maximizing self-interests. However, in the past few years, another theoretical perspective has arisen which suggests that human nature is not necessarily so one-sided. Instead, this theory asserts that human personality is somewhat conflicted, having a dual nature which includes not only the selfish, uncaring side, but also another dimension which has a higher morality, caring, and which possesses social values that are based on love and altruism.

One of the founders of this more comprehensive view is Amitai Etzioni whose classic work on socio-economics declares: "We are now in the middle of a paradigmatic struggle. Challenged is the entrenched utilitarian, rationalistic-individualistic, neo-classical paradigm" (ix), a model which he juxtaposes against this new socio-economic approach. He adds the social dimension to economic behavior which helps explain why and how people may, at times, act in behalf of their neighbors, not just themselves. Etzioni persuasively argues that a more communitarian approach will make for a healthier form of economics and reinforce altruistic tendencies in human nature.

Let us examine some core dimensions of religious practice and socio-economics which 4 Nephi reveals as factors in building a utopian or Zion society. Below are basic elements of such a framework in the Nephite world.

Spiritual Conversion

To begin with, the more righteous who were spared the awful destruction of ancient America looked to God for life. Some of these people were Church members, others were not. They sought righteous principles and practices that would sustain their new lifestyle as they attempted to become true Christians. The membership of the Church enlarged and after a couple of years everyone had been converted to the Church and a critical mass was created. This is important because it is extremely difficult to have a major impact for good in a nation's politics, legal system, enterprise and/or culture if the number of genuine Saints is minuscule. But as growing numbers of people live righteous principles, the ripple effect on a society is leveraged exponentially. In the words of President Ezra Taft Benson, Christ's "gospel is the perfect prescription for all human problems and social ills" (66). As the survivors of the great destruction described in 3 Nephi chapters 8–10 applied the Savior's teachings in their lives, they experienced a "mighty change" in their hearts, having no more desire to do evil, but to do good continually as had groups of earlier Saints who were "spiritually born of God" (Alma 5:12–14). As the vertical relationship between the individual and Heavenly Father takes root, that individual can then begin to build stronger relationships with other human beings, thus strengthening horizontal linkages.

Social Relationships

Rather than the social conflicts which characterized society in 3 Nephi, mutual respect began to govern human interaction in 4 Nephi and the love of God filled people's hearts (4 Nephi 1:15). The emphasis was on serving one another rather than "me vs. thee," and "every one did deal justly one with another" (v 2). These social dimensions required the Saints to reject Korihor's logic centuries earlier which emphasized the "management of the creature; therefore every man prospered according to his genius, and . . . conquered according to his strength; and whatsoever a man did was no crime" (Alma 30:17). Instead of mocking one's brothers and sisters, a sin which seems so widely practiced by most human beings, the Saints of 4 Nephi developed the gift of charity, which is defined by a later prophet as "the pure love of Christ" (Moroni 7:47). Thus, we read in 4 Nephi that people eliminated all disputations and became a genuine community of Saints. "And it came to pass that there was no contention in the land, because of the love of God which did dwell in the hearts of the people" (v 15). Those improved social ties between individuals laid the groundwork for economic linkages and the sharing of material possessions.

All Things Common

Joint sharing of material goods in 4 Nephi was a major characteristic of that Zion society. One's belongings were consecrated to the common stock fund and the needed portion was returned for one's personal and family stewardship. "And they had all things common among them" (4 Nephi 1:3). An overall goal of all true Christians, as Elder Orson Pratt puts it in his great discourse on "The Equality and Oneness of the Saints," is to achieve equality. He declares: "'Be one; and if ye are not one, ye are not mine.'" This is the command of Jesus Christ. . . . In what respects are the Saints required to be one? We answer: They are required to be one in things, temporal and spiritual. . . . The Saints are not only one in doctrine, but they are to be made one in temporal things, without which they cannot be made equal in spiritual things (624–27).

The consecration of real property to the general good of the group has been a distinctive practice among the faithful disciples of

Christ in other generations as well as in the 4 Nephi society. For example, New Testament Saints after the resurrection of Jesus behaved similarly. "And all that believed were together, and had all things common; and sold their possessions and goods, and parted them to all men, as every man had need" (Acts 2:44–45). Unfortunately, the Palestinian attempt to create Zion was short-lived, lasting considerably fewer years than that in the 4 Nephite society. In this latter case, holding all things common led to the removal of class barriers, enabling Book of Mormon Saints to no longer distinguish between economic groups.

No Rich or Poor

According to the conditions in 4 Nephi and later scripture, a feature of God's plan is that the poor are to be exalted and the rich humbled in the end (D&C 104:16–17). In earlier Nephite times, the Zoramites had cast the poor out of the very churches they had earlier helped build "because of the coarseness of their apparel" (Alma 32:2), thus splitting society into *Haves* and *Have Nots*. The later Nephites determined to eliminate social classifications and wealth distinctions altogether so that each person esteemed all others as herself or himself—all grew spiritually and progressed so that the group as a whole was lifted, instead of wealth concentrating in the hands of a few.

Below are several phrases from 4 Nephi which suggest the complete disappearance of traditional class conflicts: "And there were no envyings, nor strifes, nor tumults . . . nor lyings, nor murders, nor any manner of lasciviousness. . . . There were no robbers, nor murderers, neither were there Lamanites, nor any manner of -ites; but they were in one, the children of Christ, and heirs to the kingdom of God" (vv 16–17).

An earlier righteous Nephite leader, king Benjamin, encouraged the *Haves* of his day to "Impart of your substance to the poor, every man according to that which he hath, such as feeding the hungry, clothing the naked, visiting the sick and administering to their relief, both spiritually and temporally, according to their wants" (Mosiah 4:26). Note that the text emphasizes the *wants* of the poor, not what the wealthy think would be appropriate. Nor does it say that the wealthy are to pass judgment as to who is truly worthy of receiving aid (Mosiah 4:26).

Apparently, differentiating by income, lands, flocks and herds, political privileges, race, gender, or any other artificial division is not acceptable to God. Therefore, the community of Saints in 4 Nephi were "not rich and poor, bond and free, but they were all made free, and partakers of the heavenly gift" (1:3). Elimination of castes and social classes reshapes the human heart, and true disciples begin to become humble of heart.

Humility

Just a few decades before the Meridian of Time, the prophet Alma had asked church members of his day: "Behold, are ye stripped of pride? I say unto you, if ye are not ye are not prepared to meet God" (Alma 5:28). He also asked profound and searching questions regarding envy, making a mock of others, and so on. This is a continuous theme running throughout the entire Book of Mormon, even to Moroni, the last prophet who recorded his words on the sacred plates of gold. Moroni's view toward us in the last days is like that of Alma's centuries earlier: "I know that ye do walk in the pride of your hearts; and there are none save a few only who do not lift themselves up" (Mormon 8:36).

But the Saints in 4 Nephi were humble and this facilitated the development of many other aspects of their Zion society. Humility is not only a spiritual phenomenon but it is also an essential building block in creating positive social relationships, interaction in which people esteem others as themselves. Recognizing the thoughts and needs of others to be as legitimate as one's own enables all to recognize their mutual dependence on God above, and that reinforces the ability of people to labor together in reciprocal ways.

Unfortunately, after two centuries, the virtues of humility were no longer universally evident among the Nephite people. The record notes: "And now, in this two hundred and first year there began to be among them those who were lifted up in pride, such as the wearing of costly apparel, and all manner of fine pearls, and of the fine things of the world" (4 Nephi 1:24). Over time, as individuals grew in haughtiness, "They did persecute the true church of Christ, because of their humility" (v 29) and this quality, a necessary condition for

Zion, disappeared from the Nephite nation. The rise in pride is often accompanied by less respect for and adherence to the counsel of those who bear the priesthood, God's authority on earth.

Priesthood Power

In 3 Nephi, Jesus himself established his church, creating organizational relationships and ordaining special witnesses to minister to the membership as a whole. Being led by men who possessed the authority of God allowed the working of miracles through the name of Jesus and the creation and organization of the Saints into a united group of believers. Rather than live the lower-level practices of the law of Moses, the people of 4 Nephi reached to the higher-level gospel of Christ with its emphasis on divine principles and righteous living.

Thus the writings in 4 Nephi depict the labors of missionaries who preached repentance and established congregations of church members. As people believed and repented, they were baptized and given the Gift of the Holy Ghost. Bearers of the priesthood accomplished many miracles, "insomuch that they did heal the sick, and raise the dead, and cause the lame to walk, and the blind to receive their sight, and the deaf to hear" (4 Nephi 1:5). God sanctified their marriages and the people grew in number and quality of life. Attending church meetings in fasting and prayer enabled the new converts to receive the word of God from the Lord's servants with thanksgiving and to be richly edified in spiritual things. Worldly values diminished and the objective of the Saints became focused on living simply and modestly.

Moderate Wealth

Of importance to all communities of Saints is their temporal well being as a group, not individual accumulation and excess. But a primary tool of Satan has always been to dangle the riches of this world before the people of God, tempting them with excessive earthly possessions. To counter this pressure, the Savior during his life on earth taught that "Ye cannot serve God and mammon" (Matt 6:19–21, 24). His counsel is to seek not the things of the Gentiles, but to be true Saints and pursue the things of the kingdom. And when the rich and/or powerful sought his advice on how to qualify for heaven, Jesus often told them they were too materialistic and needed to give their wealth to the poor (see Luke 18:18–25). The Zion Saints of 4 Nephi focused on the things of eternity in contrast to the individuals that the Apostle James condemned in the land of Palestine, those whose "riches [were] corrupted, and . . . [whose] gold and silver [was] cankered" because they hoarded wealth to themselves (James 5:2–3).

As Jacob, son of Lehi, taught the Nephites centuries earlier, material pursuits are appropriate only in order to bless and lift others. He spelled out the proper priorities God's people should have as follows: "But before ye seek for riches, seek ye for the kingdom of God. And after ye have obtained a hope in Christ ye shall obtain riches, if ye seek them; and ye will seek them for the intent to do good" (Jacob 2:18–19). He earlier had quoted Isaiah, counseling true disciples of the Savior as follows: "Wherefore, do not spend money for that which is of no worth, nor your labor for that which cannot satisfy. Hearken diligently unto me, and remember the words which I have spoken; and come unto the Holy One of Israel, and feast upon that which perisheth not, neither can be corrupted, and let your soul delight in fatness" (2 Nephi 9:51; Isa 55:2).

However, as the Zion community of 4 Nephi began to enjoy greater material possessions, even becoming "exceedingly rich" (v 23) as God blessed them, some people began to take pride in their great wealth. The repercussions that followed included a collapse of the practice of consecration, adopting worldly dress styles, hardening of their hearts and a despising of the less fortunate (see vv 24–30). Love of riches also eroded people's productivity, and this led to excess leisure and slothfulness, as depicted below.

Work

The dignity of labor and the importance of a strong work ethic are central economic themes of the Zion society in 4 Nephi. We read of how the people labored and rebuilt their cities which had been decimated by the quakes and fires of the earlier destruction. The result was that many regions were reestablished, homes were constructed, and the people succeeded and became prosperous. This requirement to be productive and hardworking has been stressed among God's people in every age. Witness God's mandate after the first beings were driven from the Garden of Eden: "And unto Adam he said . . . cursed is the ground for thy sake. . . . In the sweat of thy face shalt thou eat bread, till thou return unto the ground" (Gen 3:17–19). So it was down not only through biblical times, but through Book of Mormon history as well. Nephi encouraged his "people to be industrious, and to labor with their hands" (2 Nephi 5:17). Later, that great model of ideal leadership, king Benjamin, worked in the fields himself. "And even I, myself, have labored with mine own hands that I might serve you, and that ye should not be laden with taxes" (Mosiah 2:14).

In our own latter-day dispensation, the Lord has likewise stressed the importance of work. "Thou shalt not be idle; for he that is idle shall not eat the bread nor wear the garments of the laborer" (D&C 42:42). And in this century, the First Presidency of the Church, led by Heber J. Grant declared that idleness should "be done away with, the evils of a dole abolished, and independence, industry, thrift and self-respect be once more established amongst our people. The aim of the Church is to help the people to help themselves. Work is to be re-enthroned as the ruling principle of the lives of our Church membership" (3).

Pure in Heart

The phrase *pure in heart* captures the ultimate definition of Zion: "Therefore, verily, thus saith the Lord, let Zion rejoice, for this is Zion—THE PURE IN HEART" (D&C 97:21). We read in the *Pearl of Great Price* that "The Lord called his people ZION, because they were of one heart and one mind, and dwelt in righteousness; and there was no poor among them" (Moses 7:18). Elder Neal A. Maxwell writes that the Saints in Enoch's Zion were able to "have goods in common because [they] first have Christ in common" (39). This process of practicing love purifies God's children, enabling them to become holy and prepared to enjoy the presence of God. Eventually, experiencing a fulness of the Holy Ghost through becoming pure in heart led to Enoch's and his followers' being translated to another sphere. Thus, "Zion was not, for God received it up into his own bosom; and from thence went forth the saying, ZION IS FLED" (Moses 7:69).

The combined result of all these factors we have reviewed suggests that the people of 4 Nephi had established the essence of the law of consecration, the united order of Zion. Spiritual conversion, humility, priesthood leadership, harmonious human relationships, all things common, social and economic equality, hard work and moderate lifestyles jointly led to a socio-economic paradise. As the sacred record puts it, "Surely there could not be a happier people among all the people who had been created by the hand of God" (4 Nephi 1:16). They lived then, as all true Saints surely must, in a righteous system of consecration and love.

Rise and Decline of Zion

Creating a Zion society can apparently happen through one of several ways. In Enoch's case, an evolutionary process occurred. He was called to prophesy and bear testimony at about age 65 and, in spite of what he perceived as his weaknesses, was endowed with great power from on high during the next 365 years. Gradually the hearts of the people turned to spiritual things and they consecrated everything to the Lord. The city of Zion became a place of holiness in which God himself walked and talked with Enoch and his people. Apparently, after approximately 430 years of Enoch's life, the city and all its inhabitants were translated and lifted beyond this mortal state of existence (see Moses 6:25–33; 7:68–69).

In contrast, the Zion of 4 Nephi was not an evolutionary one that occurred over centuries of prophetic preaching. Instead, it was a sudden occurrence in response to catastrophic destruction and cleansing on the American continent after the death of the mortal Messiah. The great transformation of human hearts began with the ministry of the resurrected Savior himself directly preaching, teaching, and testifying. Within two years, AD 34–36, all the people were converted to Christ, and Zion was established, knit through love into having all things common.

Unfortunately, this Nephite Zion or utopia started to unravel after some 170 years as people first began to feel pride and wear costly clothing, and seek vain pursuits. Individualism infiltrated the sense of community, and soon, having excessive personal property was more important than voluntarily sharing with others. Pride, wealth, and the creation of social classes became like a disease, "Nephititis," or hardening of the heart. After only two centuries, unity among the Saints had diminished considerably (see 4 Nephi 1:35). Disbelief in the teachings of the Savior and the prophets resulted in a dwindling of righteousness and a quantum rise in wickedness. Racism and other social tensions bred stereotyping and hate. Instead of being free and enjoying the blessings of peace, the people saw crime and the works of secret combinations lead to growing manifestations of Satan in the land, and as individuals became more carnal, "the day of grace was passed with them, both temporally and spiritually" (Mormon 2:15).

Implications of 4 Nephi Today

Much of contemporary American society parallels the degeneration of Book of Mormon civilization. Our emphasis is on "dress[ing] for success" and the distinctions of designer clothing have become a major criteria for judging who has worth. Conspicuous consumption of houses, cars, and other "toys" is felt to be essential in keeping up with the Joneses and achieving recognition by the world. Strategists abound in our time to achieve financial rip-offs and commit fraud upon their victims. Salaries, bonuses, and other forms of compensation have created a great chasm among Americans during the past decade. In 1979 the ratio between the highest paid executive and lowest paid employee of a Fortune 500 corporation was 29:1. Currently it is in excess of 150:1 (Bryne & Hawkins 56–64). The average American worker's income in real dollars is 10 percent below what it was in 1983 (Michel and Frankel 12–47). Some 14.5 percent of Americans are officially poor today, a total of 36.9 million people ("America's Poor Showing"). Poverty exacerbates other problems such as rising infant mortality rates, crime, drug usage, illiteracy, and family abuse. Some three million Americans are homeless, and their need for clothes and food donations, temporary shelter and other services is far exceeds that which is being provided. Inner city violence, the breakdown of the family, ethnic discrimination on the job and in the community—all result in growing tensions. Greed and graft at the top of government and business, whether in Washington, DC, or on Wall Street, are symbols of our own national decline.

Still today, however, as in Nephite times, God's purpose is to provide for his Saints, socio-economically as well as spiritually. The mechanism for doing this is the law of consecration, a system of gospel principles and organizational structures which undergirds every genuine Zion society, whether ancient or modern. This law does not merely consist of simple acts of individual charity, but instead it encompasses a whole way of life among God's people.

While many people in today's world currently seek pleasure, wealth, fame and/or power, President David O. McKay declared that, as Latter-day Saints, "We are seeking a social Utopia" (91). This ever-longing dream, which he calls "the quest of the ages" (92) cannot be implemented by reading Plato's *Republic* or Cabet's *Icaria*. Nor is it going to emerge from modern American corporatism or from the socialism of Karl Marx. Rather, the solution to this quest is the establishing of Zion, drawing upon the same principles and practices that were employed in creating socio-economic well-being in the society of 4 Nephi—no contentions, having all things in common, no rich or poor, humility, moderate wealth, priesthood leadership, hard work and purity of heart. President Joseph F. Smith declared that "the Lord has revealed plans for the temporal salvation of the people. . . . If other communities would adopt the plans of consecration . . . poverty and pauperism would be greatly reduced or entirely overcome" (832–33).

Just how the latter-day Zion will be established is not fully clear. Many in the Church anticipate that, like the people of 4 Nephi, having all things common in order to create a Zion society will necessitate another cleansing catastrophe. This view holds that human nature itself preempts the possibility of building a place for the pure in heart without external intervention and destruction of all but the more righteous from on high. Yet an implication of the city of Enoch experience seems to suggest that the outpouring of God's Spirit and the hard work of preaching and prophesying may enable Zion to evolve over time. Surrounded by monstrous evil and works of darkness, Enoch testified and his people repented and were converted. In the decades that followed, Zion was fully established, although Enoch's people were still surrounded by evil that was afraid to challenge or even approach Zion.

In our own dispensation it seems we have a concrete opportunity to labor for the establishment of a modern era of Zion. This does not necessarily mean we should merely wait until, in today's vernacular, we can "leap tall buildings in a single bound." Rather, we can climb upward toward Zion, one step at a time. On 6 April 1994, the Church will have been on the earth for 164 years. While some individuals might argue that we are a long way from the Zion societies of old, compared to the 365 years it took Enoch, we may be well on our way toward that goal. My feeling is that it is up to us whether we simply wait for destroying angels to cleanse the earth, or roll up our sleeves and get to work ourselves, here and now.

The counsel of modern prophets that we labor to create a heaven on earth is not only relevant to the world at large, but a mandate to the Saints in particular. As President Lorenzo Snow put it, Zion will be established through a socio-economic system known as the united order: "The purpose of the Order is to make the members of the Church equal and united in all things; . . . to banish pride, poverty, and iniquity and to introduce a condition of things that will prepare the pure in heart for the advent of the world's Redeemer" (259).

These are the lessons from 4 Nephi and what occurred in ancient times. The Book of Mormon reveals the crux of what we need to do currently to truly become a Zion people today. The Lord now requires of us the transformation of our lives and the creation of a genuine community of Saints. To do so will only be possible through the concentration of our moral and economic energy, and the consecration of all we have and are, to the building of the kingdom of God on earth. From Enoch to the Saints in the book of Acts, from Alma to the era of 4 Nephi, this constant theme runs throughout sacred scripture. The same is true of latter-day prophets as well. President Ezra Taft Benson has declared this doctrine in unmistakable fashion: "We must not lose sight of the fact that all that we are doing now is but a prelude to the establishment of the united order, and living the law of consecration. The individual Saints must understand this" (123).

BIBLIOGRAPHY

"America's Poor Showing." *Newsweek*. (18 Oct 1993) 44.

Beneri, Marie. *Journey Through Utopia*. New York: Books for Libraries Press, 1969.

Benson, Ezra Taft. *The Teachings of Ezra Taft Benson*. Salt Lake City: Bookcraft, 1988.

Byrne, John A., Dean Faust and Lois Therrien. "Executive Pay." *Business Week* (30 March 1992) 52–58. See also Byrne, John A., Lori Bongiorno, and Ronald Grover. "That Eye-Popping Executive Pay: Is Anybody Worth This Much?" *Business Week* (25 Apr 1994) 52–58.

Elliott, Robert C. *The Shape of Utopia: Studies in a Literary Genre*. Chicago: Univ of Chicago, 1970.

Etzioni, Amitai. *The Moral Dimension: Toward a New Economics*. New York: Free Press, 1988.

Grant, Heber J. "Message of the First Presidency to the Church." (October Conference 1936) as cited in *Messages of the First Presidency*. James R. Clark, ed. 6 vols. Salt Lake City: Bookcraft, 1975. 6:19.

Kumar, Krishan. *Utopia and Anti-Utopia in Modern Times*. Oxford: Basil Blackwood, 1987.

Manuel, Frank E., ed. *Utopias and Utopian Thought*. New York: Beacon Press, 1965.

Maxwell, Neal A. *Of One Heart: The Glory of the City of Enoch*. Salt Lake City: Deseret Book, 1979.

McKay, David O. *Gospel Ideals*. Salt Lake City: Improvement Era, 1953.

Michel, Lawrence and David Frankel. *State of Working America*. Armonk, NY: Sharpe, 1991.

Pratt, Orson. *Masterful Discourses and Writings of Orson Pratt*. Comp. N. B. Lundwall. Salt Lake City: Bookcraft, 1962.

Smith, Joseph F. "The Message of the Latter-day Saints on Relief for the Poor." *Improvement Era* (Aug 1907) 10:831–33.

———. "The Truth About Mormonism." *Out West* (1905) 23:242.

Snow, Lorenzo. "'Mormonism,' By Its Head." *Land of Sunshine* (Oct 1901) 15:259.

Subject Index

A

Abortion, 140
Abrahamic covenant, 228
Accountability, 5-6, 16, (199-212), 213
Adam and Eve, 34
Adamic language, 308-10
Adam-ondi-Ahman, 195, 232, 315
Agency, 140-42
Angels
    appearances of, 45, 63
Anger, 170-73, 269
Apostasy, 6, 40, 192, 293, 297-99
Apostles, 123-25
    as judges, 199-204
    latter days, 209-11
    who they are, 208-09
Atonement, the, 2-3, 5-6, 8-10, 21-23, 86, 212, 264, 271, 279-80, 312, 330

B

Babylon, 187, 196
Baptism, 3, 91, 265, 270
    little children, 1, 5-10, 12, 16, 236
Bible
    accuracy of, 2
Book of Mormon, 78, 129-30, 133, 141, 205, 210, 217, 221, 238, 277, 279
    antidote to materialism, 101
    church under condemnation, 102
    sealed portion, 26-28
    verifies Bible, 324-25, 330
    witness of Christ, 285
Book of Mormon, Covenant of, 69-79
    plates as witnesses, 74
    plates of Ether, Mormon, and

Nephi parallels, 74-79
Brother of Jared, 19-23, 148, 241-42
    as mediator, 308
    built barges, 313
    calling and election, 24, 28, 38, 316-17
    chastened, 312-13
    faith, hope, and charity of, 81-84, 88-89, 91-92
    given great promises, 309-10
    knew the Godhead, 32-33
    knowledge of God, 35-38
    molten stones, 20, 313-15
    one of greatest prophets, 19
    powerful language, 308-10
    recorded vision, 27-28
    sanctification of, 37-38
    saw all things, 26-27
    saw Jesus Christ, 23-24, 315-16
    travels of, 309-19
    type of Christ, 307-08, (307-20)

C

Calling and election, 24, 28, 38-39, 41-43, 66, 88, 163-64, 229, 316-17
Capt. Moroni, 107, 236
Celestial, 224, 230, 274
Celestial earth, 219-21, 226-27, 230, 233, 319
Celestial law, 222, 290
Charity, 65, 86-92, 101-02, 122, 177, 181, 254-55, 263-75, 285, 342, 350
    covers sins, 268-69
    overcomes anger, 269-70
    through repentance, 270-71
Chastening, 312
Children, Little, 260-61
    baptism of, 1, 5-10, 12, 16, 236
    cannot sin, 7, 12-14

M

Man
  carnal nature of, 4, 21-23
  in likeness of Christ, 23-25, 28
Martyr, 64, 98, 129
Materialism
  leads to destruction, 95, 98-103
Melchizedek, 220-21, 232, 291-92
Mentally handicapped, 12
Millennium, 13, 180, 218-20, 222,
    224, 227, 231, 233, 326
Miracles, 345
Missionary work, 141, 213, 237,
    258
  blessings of, 324
  Israel, house of, 333-34
  labor with love, 332-33
  teach of Jesus Christ, 330-31
  to all people, 325-28, 332-35
Mohonri Moriancumr
  See Brother of Jared
Mormon, 117-30, 157-58
  a great genius, 105-09
  a witness and judge, 203-04,
    206-08
  as father, 126-28
  as a general, 106-09, 120-23
  as an apostle, 123-25
  as prophet, 125-26, 236
  faith, hope and charity of, 81-82,
    87, 92
  final testimony, 331
  like Capt. Moroni, 107
  literary style of, 106, 118-19,
    121
  saw the Savior, 105, 120
  writer and abridger, 117-19, 130
Mormon, Like Ether, 153-65
  calling and election, 163-64
  differences, 153-55
  final witnesses, 155-56
  finished record, 162-63
  foreordained, 156-58
  record keepers, 158-59
  warning voice, 159-60
  witnessed destruction, 160-62
Mormon, Like Joseph Smith, 61-67,

  128-29
  at judgment bar, 67
  calling and election, 66
  charismatic leader, 64-65
  charity, 65
  foreordained, 66
  good boy, 62
  led army, 64-65
  lifelong service, 66
  martyr, 64
  noble heritage, 62
  received plates, 64
  saw angels, 63
  saw Jesus Christ, 63
  seen by ancestor, 62
Moroni, 235-49
  abridged book of Ether, 241
  appeared to Joseph Smith, 208,
    247-48
  at judgment bar, 241, 285
  buried plates, 247-48
  calling and election, 88
  closing testimony, 112-15,
    277-88
  death of, 248
  dedicated temple sites, 243-44
  faith, hope and charity of, 83-86,
    88, 92
  feels weak in writing, 109-111
  last Nephite, 109-110
  leader in church, 236-37
  maps of travels, 244-46
  military career, 109, 237
  prophecies of, 239-41
  prophet, 248
  saw latter-days, 133, 152
  traveled the country, 243-47
  witness and judge, 206-08
  writing style, 109-14
  wrote on plates, 238-41
  wrote sealed portion
    of plates, 241-43
Moroni, Capt, 107, 236
Mothers, 14-16
Mountains, 315-17, 331
  as place of inspiration, 20-21
Mysteries of God, 31-32, 36, 40-42

Scripture Index

OLD TESTAMENT

NEW TESTAMENT

BOOK OF MORMON

Ether

DOCTRINE AND COVENANTS

PEARL OF GREAT PRICE